SAMUEL BECKETT: THE CRITICAL HERITAGE

THE CRITICAL HERITAGE SERIES

GENERAL EDITOR: B. C. SOUTHAM, M.A., B.LITT. (OXON.)
Formerly Department of English, Westfield College, University of London

For a list of books in the series see the back end paper

SAMUEL BECKETT

THE CRITICAL HERITAGE

Edited by
LAWRENCE GRAVER
Professor of English, Williams College, Massachusetts

and

RAYMOND FEDERMAN
Professor of English, State University of New York at Buffalo

ROUTLEDGE & KEGAN PAUL
LONDON, HENLEY AND BOSTON

First published in 1979
by Routledge & Kegan Paul Ltd
39 Store Street,
London WC1E 7DD,
Broadway House,
Newtown Road,
Henley-on-Thames,
Oxon RG9 1EN and
9 Park Street,
Boston, Mass. 02108, USA
Printed in Great Britain by
Redwood Burn Ltd, Trowbridge and Esher

British Library Cataloguing in Publication Data

Samuel Beckett, the critical heritage. - (Critical
heritage series).
1. Beckett, Samuel - Criticism and interpretation -
Addresses, essays, lectures
I. Graver, Lawrence II. Federman, Raymond
III. Series
828'.9'1209   PR6003.E282Z/   78-40719

ISBN 0 7100 8948 1

General Editor's Preface

The reception given to a writer by his contemporaries and near-contemporaries is evidence of considerable value to the student of literature. On one side we learn a great deal about the state of criticism at large and in particular about the development of critical attitudes towards a single writer; at the same time, through private comments in letters, journals or marginalia, we gain an insight upon the tastes and literary thought of individual readers of the period. Evidence of this kind helps us to understand the writer's historical situation, the nature of his immediate reading-public, and his response to these pressures.

The separate volumes in the *Critical Heritage Series* present a record of this early criticism. Clearly, for many of the highly productive and lengthily reviewed nineteenth- and twentieth-century writers, there exists an enormous body of material; and in these cases the volume editors have made a selection of the most important views, significant for their intrinsic critical worth or for their representative quality—perhaps even registering incomprehension!

For earlier writers, notably pre-eighteenth century, the materials are much scarcer and the historical period has been extended, sometimes far beyond the writer's lifetime, in order to show the inception and growth of critical views which were initially slow to appear.

In each volume the documents are headed by an Introduction, discussing the material assembled and relating the early stages of the author's reception to what we have come to identify as the critical tradition. The volumes will make available much material which would otherwise be difficult of access and it is hoped that the modern reader will be thereby helped towards an informed understanding of the ways in which literature has been read and judged.

B.C.S.

Contents

'How It Is' (1961)

'Happy Days' (1961)

'Poems in English' (1961)

'Play' (1964)

'Film' (1964)

'Imagination Dead Imagine' (1965)

'No's Knife' (1967)

Beckett Awarded Nobel Prize for Literature (1969)

'Mercier and Camier' (1970)

'The Lost Ones' (1971)

'Not I' (1972)

CONTENTS

Encounters With Beckett (1975)

'That Time' and 'Footfalls' (1976)

'For to End Yet Again' (1976)

'Ghost Trio' and '. . . but the clouds . . .' (1977)

'Collected Poems in English and French' (1977)

x

Acknowledgments

For permission to reprint acknowledgment is due to: Mme
Geneviève Bonnefoi; Georges Borchardt, Inc.; James Brown
Associates, Inc.; Professor Ruby Cohn; Professor Donald
Davie; Professor Tom F. Driver; 'Esprit' © 1951, 1963;
'Express' © 1955, 1961, 1963; 'French Review'; David
Higham Associates Ltd for Dylan Thomas's review of
'Murphy'; 'Hudson Review' for Northrop Frye's review of
'The Trilogy'; Professor Hugh Kenner; Professor Frank
Kermode and the editors of 'Encounter'; Professor David
Lodge; Professor Jean-Jacques Mayoux; M. Maurice Nadeau;
'New Statesman' for reviews by Vivian Mercier, V.S.
Pritchett, Donald Davie and Benedict Nightingale; 'New
Yorker' for Edith Oliver's review of 'Not I' © 1972 The
New Yorker Magazine Inc.; 'Nouvelles littéraires' © 1955,
1957, 1969; The Observer Ltd; 'Quinzaine littéraire' ©
1969, 1971; Random House and André Deutsch Ltd for John
Updike's How 'How It Is' Was; Reuters Agency; Professor
Christopher Ricks; 'San Quentin News'; Mr Alan Schneider;
Mr Richard Seaver; 'Spectator'; The Times Newspapers
Ltd; Brooks Atkinson's review of 'Endgame' © 1958 by the
New York Times Company, reprinted by permission.   Eric
Bentley's review of 'Waiting for Godot' reprinted from
'What Is Theatre?' © 1956 by Eric Bentley, reprinted by
permission of Atheneum Publishers, New York.   Maurice
Blanchot's review of 'The Unnamable,' 'Nouvelle Revue
Française,' October 1953 © Editions Gallimard, 1959.
Robert Brustein's reviews of 'Krapp's Last Tape,' 'Happy
Days' and 'Play' reprinted by permission of 'New Repub-
lic' © 1960, 1961, 1964 by the New Republic Inc.
Raymond Federman's review of 'Film' © 1966 by the Regents
of the University of California, reprinted from 'Film
Quarterly,' volume 20, no. 2, pp. 46-51 by permission of
the Regents.   Lawrence Graver's Guides to the Ruins © 1975
by 'Partisan Review' Inc. Israel Shenker's Moody Man of

Letters © 1956 by the New York Times Company, reprinted by permission. Unsigned reviews of 'Proust,' 'More Pricks Than Kicks,' 'Murphy,' 'Waiting for Godot,' 'All That Fall,' 'How It Is,' 'Imagination Dead Imagine' and 'The Lost Ones' reproduced from the 'Times Literary Supplement' by permission. Richard Coe's review of 'Collected Poems in English and French' reproduced from the 'Times Literary Supplement' by permission. E.M. Cioran's 'Encounters with Beckett' © 1976 by 'Partisan Review' Inc. Irving Wardle's review of 'Play,' 'Footfalls,' and 'That Time' and Michael Ratcliffe's review of 'Ghost Trio' and '...but the clouds...' © 1976, 1977 by the 'Times.' 'Listener' review of 'Play,' 'That Time,' and 'Footfalls' © John Elsom, 1976.

For the translations prepared especially for this volume we are grateful to Jean M. Sommermeyer, Françoise Longhurst, Larysa Mykyta and Mark Schumacher; for the use of translations originally published elsewhere we wish to thank Ruby Cohn, Richard Howard and Christopher Waters.

Librarians at the State University of New York at Buffalo and at Williams College, Massachusetts, were exceptionally helpful in locating inaccessible materials. We would like particularly to thank Sarah C. McFarland and Lee Dalzell. We also appreciate the assistance of Judith Raab, who helped read proofs and prepare the index.

It has proved difficult in certain cases to locate the proprietors of copyright material. However all possible care has been taken to trace ownership of the selections and to make full acknowledgment for their use.

Chronological Table

1906	Samuel Barclay Beckett born on Good Friday, 13 April, at Foxrock, south of Dublin, the second son of William and Mary Roe Beckett.
1920-3	Educated at Portora Royal School, Enniskillin.
1923-7	Reads French and Italian at Trinity College, Dublin. Spends summer vacation of 1926 in France, summer vacation of 1927 in Italy. Earns BA degree in December, 1927.
1928	French tutor at Campbell College, Belfast. October - Arrives in Paris to teach in exchange program at the École Normale Supérieure. Gradually becomes involved in the literary life of Paris; meets James Joyce and editors and writers in the 'transition' circle. Does research on René Descartes.
1929	Essay called Dante...Bruno.Vico..Joyce appears in the anthology 'Our Exagmination Round His Factification for Incamination of Work in Progress,' in May, and in the June issue of 'transition.' Assumption, a 1,500-word short story, also appears in in the June 'transition.' Submits 'Whoroscope' (a monologue spoken by Descartes) in Nancy Cunard's poetry competition and wins the £10 prize.
1930	For Future Reference, a 74-line poem, appears in the June 'transition.' August - 'Whoroscope' published by the Hours Press, Paris. September - Appointed as Assistant in French at Trinity College, Dublin.
1931	19 February - 'Le Kid,' a parody of Corneille, presented at the Peacock Theatre, Dublin, as one of three foreign plays staged by the Dublin University Modern Languages Society.

5 March - 'Proust' published in London.

May - Translation of Joyce's Anna Livia Plurabelle (in collaboration with Alfred Péron and others) appears in the 'Nouvelle Revue francaise.'

Publishes four poems in 'The European Caravan: an Anthology of the New Spirit in Literature.'

October - Alba, a poem, appears in 'Dublin Magazine.'

December - Awarded MA degree from Trinity College, Dublin. Soon afterwards resigns his lectureship and travels in Germany.

1932   Lives for brief periods in Kassel, Paris, London and Dublin.

Works on first novel, 'Dream of Fair to Middling Women' (unfinished and unpublished). Two extracts, Sedendo et Quiescendo and Text, are published in 'transition' (March) and the 'New Review' (April).

Dante and the Lobster, short story, published in the December issue of 'This Quarter.'

1933   Lives in Dublin and works on the stories that will make up 'More Pricks Than Kicks.'

May - His cousin Peggy Sinclair dies at Wildungen.

26 June - William Beckett dies in Dublin. His son eventually receives an annuity of £200 a year.

December - Makes plans to move from Dublin to London.

1934   Lives in London and tries unsuccessfully to support himself as a literary journalist.

May - 'More Pricks Than Kicks' published in London by Chatto & Windus.

A Case in a Thousand, a short story, and a pseudonymous article on 'Recent Irish Poetry' (signed Andrew Bellis), published in the August issue of the 'Bookman.'

Christmas issue of the 'Bookman' has three reviews by Beckett on Pound, Dante and O'Casey.

1935   Writing 'Murphy' in London.

September - Hears Jung lecture at the Tavistock Clinic.

November - 'Echo's Bones,' a cycle of thirteen poems, published by Europa Press, Paris.

1936   Returns to Dublin and finishes 'Murphy.'

Review of novel by Jack Yeats appears in the July number of 'Dublin Magazine.'

October issue of 'Dublin Magazine' features Cascando, a poem.

At the end of the year travels in Germany.

1937   Travels in Germany; returns to Dublin in the spring; moves to Paris in October.

Works on a play about Samuel Johnson and Mrs Thrale.

November - Testifies in Dublin at libel trial of
Oliver St John Gogarty.
December - Routledge accepts manuscript of 'Murphy'
after it had been rejected by forty-two publishers.
Beckett begins writing the poems in French that
eventually appear as a twelve-poem cycle in 1946.

1938   7 January - Stabbed on the street by a Parisian pimp
named Prudent. A pesser-by, Suzanne Deschevaux-
Dumesnil, a piano student, helps Beckett to recover.
They live together and marry in 1961.
7 March - 'Murphy' published in London.
Ooftish, a poem, appears in the tenth anniversary
issue of 'transition' (April-May).
April - moves to apartment at 6 rue des Favorites,
Paris.
Begins work on French translation of 'Murphy.'
September - Writes the essay Les Deux Besoins.

1939   Working on the French translation of 'Murphy.'
When Germans invade Poland in September, Beckett is
visiting his mother in Dublin. He returns to Paris.

1940   By the end of October 1940 he is involved with a
Resistance group gathering information about German
troop movements.

1941   James Joyce dies in Zürich.

1942   In August the Resistance group is betrayed to the
Gestapo. Beckett and Suzanne hide in Paris and
then flee to the south. By the end of the year they
reach Roussillon, a village in the Vaucluse.

1943   Remains in Roussillon for the next two years, and
during this period writes 'Watt.'

1945   Awarded the Croix de Guerre for work in the Resis-
tance movement.
April - Leaves Roussillon, travels to London and then
to Dublin.
Tries unsuccessfully to publish 'Watt.'
June - Dieppe, a poem translated from the French,
is published in the 'Irish Times.'
Learns of the death of Alfred Péron.
August - Review of Thomas McGreevy's book on Jack
Yeats appears in the 'Irish Times.'
August through October - Works as interpreter and
storekeeper at the Irish Red Cross Hospital at
Saint-Lô.
October - Back in Paris.
Essay entitled La Peinture des Van Velde; ou: le
monde et le pantalon appears in 'Cahiers d'Art.'
Beckett begins writing fiction in French.

1946   June - Sain-Lô, a poem, appears in the 'Irish Times.'

July - Suite, early version of La Fin, first pub-
lished French fiction, appears in 'Temps modernes.'
Between July and December writes 'Mercier et Camier,'
 L'Expulsé, 'Premier Amour,' and 'Le Calmant.'
November - Twelve poems appear in 'Temps modernes.'
December - L'Expulsé published in 'Fontaine.'

1947 May - 'Murphy' in Beckett's French translation is
published in Paris.
During the year he writes 'Eleuthéria' and 'Molloy,'
both in French. 'Eleuthéria,' his first completed
play, has not been published.
By winter he is working on 'Malone meurt.'

1948 Finishes 'Malone meurt' in May.
Trois poèmes published in June 'transition.'
October - Begins writing 'En attendant Godot.'

1949 Finishes 'En attendant Godot' in late January.
Begins writing 'L'Innomable' at the end of March.
Three Dialogues appear in the December 'transition.'

1950 Finished 'L'Innomable' at the end of January.
25 August - Mary Roe Beckett dies.
15 November - Contract signed with Jérôme Lindon of
Éditions de Minuit to publish 'Molloy,' 'Malone
meurt,' and 'L'Innomable.'
Accepts UNESCO commission to translate anthology
of Mexican poetry. The volume is published in 1958.

1951 10 March - 'Molloy' published in Paris.
8 October - 'Malone meurt' published in Paris.

1952 17 October - 'En attendant Godot' published in Paris.

1953 5 January - World premier of 'En attendant Godot'
at the Théâtre de Babylone, Paris.
18 July - 'L'Innomable' published in Paris.
August - 'Watt,' in English, published in Paris.

1954 'Waiting for Godot,' translated by Beckett, is
published by Grove Press in New York.

1955 March - 'Molloy,' translated by Patrick Bowles and
Beckett, published by Olympia Press, Paris, and
later in the year by Grove Press in New York.
Beckett working on 'Fin de Partie' at Ussy.
Begins a novel in English; the result in the fragment later to be published as 'From an Abandoned
Work.'
3 August - first British performance of 'Waiting
for Godot' at the Arts Theatre Club, London.
18 November - 'Nouvelles et Textes pour rien'
published in Paris.

1956 3 January - 'Waiting for Godot' performed for first
time in USA at Coconut Grove Playhouse, Miami Beach.
10 February - 'Waiting for Godot' published in London.
19 April - 'Waiting for Godot' performed in New York.

'Malone Dies,' Beckett's translation of 'Malone meurt,' published in New York.

7 June - From an Abandoned Work printed in 'Trinity News,' a Dublin weekly.

21 June - Beckett finishes 'Fin de partie.'

September - Works on 'All that Fall,' a play for radio suggested by the BBC.

1957   13 January - 'All that Fall' broadcast by the BBC.

1 February - 'Fin de Partie' published in Paris (with 'Acte sans paroles I').

3 April - World première of 'Fin de partie,' in French, at the Royal Court Theatre, London.

26 April - First French production of 'Fin de partie' at Studio des Champs-Élysées, Paris.

August - 'All That Fall' published in London.

October - 'Tous ceux qui tombent,' translation by Robert Pinget and Beckett of 'All That Fall,' published in Paris.

1958   28 January - 'Endgame,' Beckett's translation of 'Fin de partie,' performed for the first time in the USA and in English at the Cherry Lane Theatre, New York.

7 March - 'Malone Dies' published in London.

28 April - 'Endgame' published in London.

Summer - 'Krapp's Last Tape' published in 'Evergreen Review.'

28 October - World première of 'Krapp's Last Tape' and first British performance in English of 'Endgame' at the Royal Court Theatre, London.

'Endgame' and 'The Unnamable,' Beckett's translation of 'L'Innommable,' published in New York.

1959   24 June - 'Embers' broadcast by the BBC.

26 June - 'Gedichte,' a collection of Beckett's poems in the original English and French, with German translations, published in Wiesbaden.

Beckett receives an honorary degree from Trinity College, Dublin.

October - 'Molloy, Malone Dies and The Unnamable: a Trilogy' published in one volume by Olympia Press, Paris, and Grove Press, New York.

December - 'Krapp's Last Tape' and 'Embers' published in London.

1960   'La Dernière Bande,' translation of 'Krapp's Last Tape' by Pierre Leyris and Beckett, published in Paris.

14 January - 'Krapp's Last Tape' performed for the first time in the USA at the Provincetown Playhouse, New York.

25 January - 'Act Without Words II' first
performed at the Institute of Contemporary Arts,
London.
22 March - First performance of 'La Dernière
Bande' at Théâtre Récamier, Paris.
31 March - 'The Trilogy' published in London.
'Krapp's Last Tape and Other Dramatic Pieces'
published in New York.

1961   9 January - 'Comment c'est' published in Paris.
August - 'Poems in English' published in London.
17 September - World première of 'Happy Days' at
Cherry Lane Theatre, New York. Later published
by Grove Press.
Beckett shares International Publishers' Prize
with Jorge Luis Borges.

1962   1 November - British première of 'Happy Days,'
Royal Court Theatre, London.
13 November - First broadcast of 'Words and
Music' by the BBC.

1963   Beckett's translation of 'Happy Days' ('Oh les
beaux jours') is published in Paris.
May - Works on the scenario for 'Film.'
14 June - World première of 'Play' in German
translation at Ulm-Donau.
'Poems in English' published in New York.
28 September - 'Oh les beaux jours' first performed at International Festival of Prose Drama,
Venice (Teatro del Ridotto), with Madeleine
Renaud and Jean-Louis Barrault.
13 October - 'Cascando,' written in French,
first performed on ORTF-France Culture.

1964   4 January - 'Play' performed for the first time
in English at Cherry Lane Theatre, New York.
7 April - First performance of 'Play' in Great
Britain at National Theatre, London.
'Comédie,' Beckett's translation of 'Play,'
published in Paris.
'How It Is,' Beckett's translation of 'Comment
c'est,' published in New York and London.
11 June - 'Comédie' first performed in Paris at
Pavillon de Marsan.
July - Working on 'Film' in New York.
'Play' published in London (includes 'Words and
Music' and 'Cascando').
6 October - 'Cascando' broadcast by the BBC.
30 December - Revival of 'Waiting for Godot' at
Royal Court Theatre, London, directed by Anthony
Page, with the assistance of Beckett.

1965   4 September - 'Film' shown at the Venice Film
Festival.

'Come and Go' performed in German at the
Schiller Theatre, Berlin.
October - 'Imagination morte imaginez' published
in Paris.
November - 'Imagination Dead Imagine' published
in London.

1966   19 February - 'Assez' published in Paris.
28 February - 'Va-et-Vient,' Beckett's translation of 'Come and Go,' performed at Odéon-Théâtre,
Paris.
8 March - BBC broadcast: 'Poems by Samuel Beckett.'
4 July - 'Eh Joe' performed on BBC television.
30 October - 'Bing' published in Paris.

1967   'Têtes-mortes' published in Paris.   (Includes
D'un ouvrage abandonné,' 'Assez,' 'Imagination
morte imaginez,' and 'Bing.'
'Eh Joe and Other Writings' published in London
(includes 'Act Without Words II' and 'Film.')
'Stories and Texts for Nothing' published by
Grove Press in New York.
'Come and Go' published in London.
'No's Knife: Collected Shorter Prose 1947-1966'
published in London.
25 September - Beckett directs 'Endgame' at
Schiller Theatre in Berlin.

1968   28 February - 'Come and Go' performed for the
first time in English at Peacock Theatre, Dublin.
1 March - 'Poèmes,' collected French poetry,
published in Paris.
'L'Issue,' a prose text, published in Paris.
'Cascando and Other Short Dramatic Pieces'
published in New York.
'Watt,' translated into French by Ludovic and
Agnès Janvier in collaboration with Beckett,
published in Paris.

1969   'Sans' published in Paris.
23 October - Beckett awarded the Nobel Prize for
Literature. His editor, Jérôme Lindon, later
accepts the prize in Stockholm.

1970   'Lessness,' Beckett's translation of 'Sans,'
published in London.
'Mercier et Camier' published in Paris.
'Collected Works' published by Grove Press in
New York.
'Premier Amour' published in Paris.

1971   'Le Dépeupleur' published in Paris.
August-September - Directs 'Glükliche Tage'
('Happy Days') at Schiller Theatre.

1972　　　'The Lost Ones,' Beckett's translation of 'Le
Dépeupleur,' published in London and New York.
22 November - World première of 'Not I' at
Lincoln Center, New York.

1973　　　16 January - First British performance of 'Not I'
at Royal Court Theatre, London; Beckett assists
Anthony Page with direction. 'Not I' published
in London.
'First Love,' Beckett's translation of 'Premier
Amour,' published in London.
'Breath and Other Shorts' published in London.

1974　　　'Mercier and Camier,' in Beckett's English
translation, published in London and New York.
'First Love and Other Shorts' published in New
York (includes From an Abandoned Work, 'Enough,'
'Imagination Dead Imagine,' 'Ping,' 'Not I' and
'Breath.')

1975　　　Directs 'Waiting for Godot' at Schiller Theatre,
West Berlin.
'Pas Moi,' with Madeleine Renaud, performed at
Petit Théâtre d'Orsay, Paris.

1976　　　May and June - 'That Time' and 'Footfalls' per-
formed at the Beckett 70th Birthday Season,
Royal Court, London.
'Pour finir encore et autres foirades' published
in Paris.
'For to End Yet Again' published in London (the
American edition, ordered differently, and
titled 'Fizzles,' is published in New York).
'Ends and Odds' published in London and New
York.
8 December - American premiere of 'That Time'
and 'Footfalls,' directed by Alan Schneider,
Arena Stage, Washington, DC.

1977　　　17 April - 'Ghost Trio' and '... but the
clouds ...' performed on BBC television.
'Collected Poems in English and French' published
in London.
'Drunken Boat,' translation of Rimbaud's 'Le
Bateau ivre,' published in Reading, England.

Introduction

Samuel Beckett's writing has always posed stubborn problems for literary critics and historians. His astonishing
inventiveness and the bizarre nature of his inventions;
the mingling of anguish and elegance - talking of first
and last things through the masks of clownish vagabonds -
have made his work uncommonly difficult to describe and
evaluate; and his movements through countries, languages
and genres make a brief, comprehensive account of his
career almost impossible to compose.

When he first began to write in English, Beckett
published poetry, criticism, short stories and a novel.
'Whoroscope' (1930) and the collection of poems 'Echo's
Bones' (1935) were generally unnoticed, but 'Proust'
(1931), 'More Pricks Than Kicks' (1934) and 'Murphy'
(1938) were reviewed by well-known (or about to be well-
known) critics and poets. As if to predict the future,
young Beckett's odd and refractory talent aroused contradictory responses, praise and blame coming from unexpected
sources. In an essay devoted almost entirely to 'Remembrance of Things Past', the popular Desmond MacCarthy
spoke of Beckett's eccentric, often obscure commentary as
'admirable ... one of the best ... on Proust' ('Sunday
Times,' 24 May 1931); and the 'Times Literary Supplement'
saw 'a great deal of subtle analysis packed into 72 pages'
(No. 1). Bonamy Dobrée, however, in a generally sympathetic notice, complained of jargon, prolixity and excessive
cleverness, traits that led the poet F.S. Flint to retreat
behind an impatient confession of incomprehension (Nos 2
and 3).

Despite the strictures, Beckett could easily have found
encouragement in these responses to 'Proust,' but he had
little interest in analyzing the writing of others and was

never again to publish an extended work of criticism. Most
of his creative energies in the early 1930s went into an
unfinished novel called 'Dream of Fair to Middling Women'
and into the ten connected stories that make up 'More
Pricks Than Kicks.' About this beginner's book critical
opinion was understandably divided. Peter Quennell dismissed it as pastiche, annoyingly derivative of Joyce
('New Statesman,' 26 May 1934, 802). Arthur Calder-
Marshall glimpsed Ronald Firbank rather than Joyce behind
Beckett's strutting prose, yet he felt the Irishman
'capable of coming into the open as a humourist, instead
of retiring as he too often does into the allusive shelter
of the "really cultivated man"' ('Spectator,' 1 June 1934,
863). In the 'Observer' (10 June 1934, 6), Gerald Gould
insisted that Beckett was not imitative of 'Mr. Joyce or
anybody else'; and he spoke of Beckett's 'dry, harsh manner
not untouched by beauty, though betrayed by an artificial
whimsicality and unnecessary obscurity.' Similarly, the
'Times Literary Supplement' critic (No. 5) saw a fresh
though uncertain talent in this 'very uneven book,' and
made apt comments about the 'curious blend of colloquialism, coarseness and sophistication' so distinctive of
Beckett's early comic style.

Edwin Muir's contention (No. 4) that in Beckett 'everything depends on style' was repeated in different forms by
several early reviewers. Given the extravagant, often
esoteric qualities of Beckett's language, it is not surprising that few readers could perceive serious emotions
and ideas behind the chilly glitter of his university wit.
Nor were they likely to recognize that in Belacqua, Beckett
was experimenting with a new kind of anti-hero: a randy,
quizzical, physically collapsing, 'sovereign booby,' ever
in search of the means to 'consecrate his life to stasis.'
With his obsessive system-making, crack-brained notions of
perfection and 'strong weakness for oxymoron,' Belacqua was
the first of many figures destined to perform in Beckett's
'tragi-comedy of the solipsism that will not capitulate.'
Little of this, however, could be seen through the ornate
screen of language in 1934.

When 'Murphy' appeared four years later, there was
still talk of the quirky blend of bar-room humor, social
satire and philosophical speculation. Frank Swinnerton
found the first hundred pages 'almost intolerable in their
jocose exhibitionism,' though he confessed that 'some of
the later pages - particularly the account of the asylum -
have an amusingness that is quite genuine and equal to
about half of the author's estimate of their brilliance'
('Observer,' 20 March 1938, 6). Edwin Muir properly located a major part of the novel's interest in the picture of

Murphy's mind, but he was uneasy about the absence of plot,
character and any 'perceptible aim.' After speaking of
'laboured' fantasy, he ended with a carefully hedged bet:
'...if this book does not completely bore or exasperate
the reader, it will probably give him more than ordinary ·
amusement' ('Listener,' 16 March 1938, 597).

The critic for the 'Times Literary Supplement' (No. 6)
showed greater responsiveness, praising Beckett for creating his 'own world, an elaborate parody of the world we
know, but oddly real.' Yet he too found parts of the
novel tedious and felt at times 'that the talent and knowledge it reveals deserve a theme of more depth and substance.' Writing in the 'New English Weekly,' the twenty-
four-year-old Dylan Thomas recognized that 'Murphy' had a
theme of depth and substance: 'the study of a complex and
oddly tragic character who cannot reconcile the unreality
of the seen world with the reality of the unseen' (No. 7).
Although Thomas's statement was cribbed almost word for
word from the dust-jacket, he did perceive Beckett's originality and general intention. Anxious, however, to
match the author's verbal high jinks with his own, Thomas
built an elaborate and unconvincing argument to show where
the book went wrong, ending with a witless dismissal of
Beckett's humor as 'Freudian blarney: Sodom and Begorrah.'

The only reviewer who greeted 'Murphy' with the kind of
enthusiasm it was later to generate in other readers was
Kate O'Brien. In the 'Spectator' (No. 8) the Irish novelist and playwright managed in less than five hundred words
to convey both her pleasure and a reliable sense of the
novel's peculiar distinction. Refusing to be bothered by
Beckett's occasionally opaque scholasticism, O'Brien was
delighted by the rare mixture of impudence, lyricism,
crazy learning, and serious intellectual speculation. This
'book in a hundred thousand' - this 'glorious, wild story
starred all over with a milky way of sceptic truth' - was
a novel she would read 'again and again before I die.'

Although 'Murphy' was by no means a popular success, it
did become something of a cult book. In the years following publication, a legend persisted that the novel was a
failure and the bulk of the unsold edition of 1,500 copies
were destroyed by the blitz. However, Norman Franklin of
Routledge insists there is no truth to the story. Sales
were satisfactory if not brilliant: 568 copies in the first
year; 50 in each of the next three; and the remaining
copies sold as a cheap edition in 1942. Among the novel's
admirers were James Joyce and the young Iris Murdoch.
Joyce was said to have been able to recite from memory the
description of the disposal of Murphy's ashes amidst the
detritus of a London pub; while Murdoch was so absorbed by

Beckett's philosophical comedy on the nature of contin-
gency and desire that she placed it among Jake Donaghue's
few choice possessions in 'Under the Net.' Joyce was also
given to fooling with Beckett's name in 'Finnegans Wake':
'You is feeling like you was lost in the bush, boy? You
says: It is a puling sample jungle of woods. You most
shouts out: *Bethicket* me for a stump of a beech if I have
the poultriest notions what the farest he all means.'

Between the spring of 1938 and the winter of 1950-1,
Beckett published two reviews, two stories, two essays on
painting, the Three Dialogues, sixteen poems and a translation of 'Murphy.' Of 3,000 copies of the French 'Murphy'
only ninety-five were sold and there seem to have been no
reviews. To follow Beckett's reputation in print during
those years would be a barren gesture: for most readers who
knew his name, he was a once promising novelist now silent
- as Joyce put it, 'bethicketed, lost in the bush.'
Silent in public, however, Beckett was immensely productive
in private. Between 1942 and 1944, he wrote 'Watt' in
English; from 1945 to 1952 he wrote 'La Fin,' 'Mercier et
Camier,' 'L'Expulsé,' 'Premier Amour,' 'Le Calmant,' 'Éleu-
théria,' 'Molloy,' 'Malone meurt,' 'En attendant Godot,'
'L'Innommable' and 'Textes pour rien.' When the last five
of these works were published, performed and translated in
the early 1950s, Beckett gradually became one of the most
famous and controversial writers in the world.

II

To move from the last lines of Kate O'Brien's response to
'Murphy' (No. 8) to the opening paragraphs of Maurice
Nadeau's review of 'Molloy' (No. 9) is a startling experi-
ence. O'Brien is praising a richly gifted beginner;
Nadeau is talking about the accomplishments of a master.
And yet, looking back at some of the earliest pieces on
'Molloy,' one is struck by how difficult a novel it must
have been in 1951. Beckett once said that he often thanked
heaven at not being a critic about to write a book on
Beckett; similarly, it must have been an ambiguous gift to
have been given an early review copy of 'Molloy.'
Although the critics struggled manfully, scoring occasional hits and testifying to Beckett's dark power to disturb,
'Molloy' looks proudly unassimilable, beyond the reach of
anyone trying to give an adequate account of its range and
originality.

Most formidable about 'Molloy' was its grotesque mixture of elements rarely found together in the same narrative. The tale is murky, baffling, circular,

contradictory, full of offensive details, furious violence
and sardonic, terrifying insights into the meaninglessness
of human life. The speakers, moreover, talk in voices
never before heard in literature. Sometimes detached,
matter-of-fact, naive, even amiable, Molloy is at another
moment sweaty with anguish and the sophisticated disillusionment of 2,000 years of European history. Suffering a torment 'with no limits to its stations and no hope
of crucifixion,' he has a matchless - sometimes graceful,
sometimes lunatic - faculty for analyzing his own desolation and for finding infinite, often comic ways to bear it.
A poet of rich and expansive gifts, he can - in one mood -
celebrate his bicycle with an ode beginning, 'I shall not
call you bike, you were green, like so many of your generation'; and in another, mourn his barren testicles as
'decaying circus clowns.' Rhapsodist and elegist, he also
has his epic moments, as in the heroic, 'inordinately
formal' attempt to order his sixteen sucking-stones. In
Wallace Stevens's phrase, he is 'prince of the proverbs of
pure poverty,' and his acidulous reflections have a pithi-
ness that is unforgettable. Who but Molloy - explaining
how 'all things run together in the body's long madness'
- can make us share his fascination and fright at 'contemplating this extraordinary body both at rest and in
motion'? Inspired in his fantastic scheme for communicat-
ing with his mother, effervescent in his description of
Lousse's parrot, brutal in his anger and atavistic fury,
awesome in his indomitability - he is one of the most
fully drawn and original of literary creations.

Moran, of course, is very different. Smug, methodical,
sanctimonious, with an intelligence 'a little short of
average,' he is by his own admission, 'cold as crystal and
free from spurious depths.' At the beginning of his adventure, he is very much a creature of his garden, keys
and bourgeois conventions, but sent in search of Molloy,
he encounters ancient night, breaks down and is stripped
of that which 'has always protected me from all I was
always condemned to be.' He is forced in his suffering
to recognize those parts of Molloy - the harsh primitivism
and disillusioned sensitivity - that have been hidden
elements in his own nature.

Of the early reviews of 'Molloy,' Maurice Nadeau's -
though fragmentary and at times misleading - was one of
the most perceptive (No. 9). Nadeau was especially ad-
roit at describing the unsettling effects of Beckett's
structural and stylistic subversions: how the events seem
to have little meaning and manage to suggest 'all meanings'; and how the circular, obscure narrative and the
ironical, insistently negative language both tease and

undermine our efforts to read the tale symbolically. Several of his phrases nicely caught essential Beckettian paradoxes: 'champion of the Nothing exalted to the height of the Whole.' He was also one of the first to argue that Beckett is better served by analysis than interpretation and to suspect that in fundamental ways he may not be well served by either (a suspicion that has haunted other critics). Like many early reviewers, Nadeau was dubious about the worth of summarizing the novel's plot, did so nevertheless, and in vital details got it wrong. (He thought, for example, that Molloy narrates his journey while it is taking place rather than afterwards while in his mother's room, an oversight that destroys several important structural ironies.) Despite the errors and a certain evasive rhetoric, Nadeau was the first critic to communicate the force and strangeness of one of Beckett's greatest novels.

The three pieces by Georges Bataille, Jean Pouillon and Bernard Pingaud (Nos 10, 11, 12) illustrate some of the extremes of emphasis and judgment in the immediate French reactions to the publication of 'Molloy.' For Bataille, Beckett had created a monstrous myth 'arising from the slumber of reason,' an epic about the essence of being - anguish, fathomless misery - and the language or silence we use to express it. In his abstract, solemn meditation, he says nothing about the novel's humor, but admits that this 'sordid wonder' has such 'unquenchable verve that we read it with no less impatient interest than a thrilling adventure novel.' Like Bataille, Bernard Pingaud also saw 'Molloy' as a 'monstrous and disturbing myth, mysterious in its origins,' and found its picture of degradation 'deeply credible' and 'not without seduction.' Pingaud, however, was so preoccupied with the pernicious possibilities of Beckett's narrative (a threat to rationality and decorum, a 'stone fallen from the sky'), that he was insensitive to much of the novel's art and variety. If Bataille and Pingaud stressed the fantastic, abnormal elements in the twin narratives of 'Molloy,' Jean Pouillon insisted that the novel's truths were more homely, more obviously related to the way we all behave in our ordinary lives, and he saw a certain joyful, perhaps even mischievous quality in Molloy's refusal to live life seriously, to 'play the game.'

The difference between these reviews (and the many others that appeared in the months following publication) justify the remarks made by Maurice Nadeau in the summer of 1951:

'Molloy' has been hailed both as an 'event' and a *ne*

plus ultra of literature. It has been heaped with
praise and learned comment, and such diverse meanings
have been attributed to it that the more people talk
about it the more obscure it seems. One person sees it
as a masterpiece of humor, another as an epic of disaster. To some it is silence translated into words, to
others no more than a literary exposition of complexes
belonging more properly to psychoanalysis. In fact,
everyone sees in it what he wants to see, which is
proof at once of the book's richness and of its ambiguity. ('Mercure de France,' August 1951)

And proof too, perhaps, of some familiar lessons about the
limits of criticism.

The publication of 'Malone Dies' in October 1951 added
to Beckett's reputation as an enigmatic writer of great
originality and power. Maurice Nadeau's brief review in
'Mercure de France' (No. 15) skillfully summarizes an
argument that was already becoming familiar: Beckett's
ruling passion was 'to hunt down an inner being ... which
escapes all attempts at definition. Nothing is certain
apart from that inaccessible reality which the narrator's
voice alone ultimately expresses. However metaphysics
here is very concrete and explosive, even merry.' Concluding that 'Malone Dies' (and a new work soon to be published - 'L'Innommable') will have taken this obsessive
exploration about as far as it could go, Nadeau wondered
(as many later critics were to do) if there was anything
left for Beckett but silence.

At a time when Nadeau was speculating about the ex-
haustion of Beckett's unique yet claustrophobic area of
concern, other writers were publishing essays to introduce the novels to a wider audience. The first of many
such surveys was Richard Seaver's Samuel Beckett: an
Introduction (No. 16), a useful sketch of Beckett's place
among French and English writers in 1952 on the eve of
'Godot.' Although Seaver's essay was by design elementary and provisional, it did point to some of the subjects
that would later dominate critical discussion of Beckett's
achievement - the links to Kafka and Joyce, the role of a
writer in exile, the switch from English to French, the
increasing subjectivity, and the resistance of his work to
conventional modes of analysis.

III

On 5 January 1953 modern literature and Beckett's life
were changed in ways that no one could conceivably have

predicted. Under the direction of Roger Blin, 'Waiting
for Godot' opened in Paris at the Théâtre de Babylone to a
reception that was later repeated in nearly identical
forms throughout the world: boredom, incomprehension,
irritation, occasional ridicule from one part of the audience; exhilaration and passionate advocacy from another.
In the first review to appear in print, Sylvain Zegel (No.
17) got the proportions right and proved to be an excellent
prophet. Realizing that some people were frustrated by a
play in which nothing seemed to happen, he nevertheless
argued that they were blind to Beckett's magic and that
'Waiting for Godot' would be spoken of for a long time.
Insisting that Beckett deserved comparison with the greatest writers of the European theatre, Zegel ended with a
concise, sensible answer to what would soon be the most
notorious question in modern drama:

> Who is Godot? [The two vagabonds] don't know. And in
> any case, this myth hasn't the same form, the same
> qualities, for each of them. It might be happiness,
> eternal life, the ideal and unattainable quest of all
> men - which they wait for and which gives them strength
> to live on.

Zegel's excitement was shared by Jacques Lemarchand (No.
18) and by several well-known writers. In the weeks that
followed, Jean Anouilh compared the première of 'Godot'
to the opening of Pirandello's 'Six Characters' in 1923
and coined the image that has since become the most frequently quoted description of the play: a 'music-hall
sketch of Pascal's "Pensées" as played by the Fratellini
clowns' (No. 19). Armand Salacrou confessed that 'we
were waiting for this play of our time, with its new tone,
its simple and modest language, and its closed circular
plot from which no exit is possible' ('Arts-Spectacles,'
27 January 1953, 1). Jacques Audiberti insisted that symbolism might be optional but applause obligatory ('Arts-
Spectacles,' 16 January 1953, 3); and Alain Robbe-Grillet
wrote a passionate, admiring essay in 'Critique.'
    The Continental success was repeated in London when
'Waiting for Godot' opened at the Arts Theatre Club on 3
August 1955. Among the most influential notices were
those by Harold Hobson (No. 20) and Kenneth Tynan (No.
21) which captured the excitement and perplexity of sympathetic viewers first encountering a baffling new work.
Both critics began defensively, as if in deference to
hard-dying Anglo-Saxon attitudes. Beckett's play may seem
drab and undramatic; it violates conventional expectations
and seems to offer little to stir the senses or to engage

the understanding. Look past custom, however, and you
will find a work of splendid originality and loveliness,
a masterpiece that annexed previously unclaimed territory
for the theatre. 'It is validly new,' Tynan said, 'and
hence I declare myself, as the Spanish would say,
godotista.'

These ardent responses and others like them guaranteed
a modest commercial success for the Arts Theatre Club
experiment; and five weeks later, after revisions to calm
the Lord Chamberlain, the production moved to the Criterion Theatre. An uneasy reviewer for the daily 'Times'
admitted that Beckett's 'sophisticated fantasy' appeared
'to hold last night's audience; and in the attentive
silence one could almost hear the seeds of a cult growing.'

The cult, of course, was not without its debunkers.
Some disgruntled members of the audience simply walked out;
others (like the visiting American journalist Marya
Mannes) spoke of the play as 'typical of the self-delusion
of which certain intellectuals are capable, embracing
obscurity, pretense, ugliness, and negation as protective
coloring for their own confusions.' Terence Rattigan
invented an imaginary Aunt Edna, a cagy, unpredictable
representative of middle-brow theatre-goers, with whom to
chat about the pleasures but inflated reputation of
Beckett's first play. 'Waiting for Godot' had become
quite literally the talk of the town and soon afterwards
of the country. In February 1956, the published text was
the subject of a long article, They Also Serve, in the
'Times Literary Supplement' (No. 22), that set off one of
the liveliest literary controversies in years. Earlier
critics had tended to treat 'Godot' as ritual rather than
argument and implied that although the play certainly contained ideas no one idea was likely to contain the play.
In his bold, ingenious and almost certainly reductive
argument, the 'TLS' critic (later identified as G.S.
Fraser) claimed that there *was* one shaping idea: Didi and
Gogo stood for the contemplative life and Beckett, offering religious consolation, had written a modern morality
play on permanent Christian themes.

The letters inspired by Fraser's article (and by Ronald
Gray's on the same subject in the 'Listener,' 7 February
1957) testified to the remarkable impact of Beckett's play
and helped to establish the lines of future contention
about how it should be perceived. Some viewers saw Christ,
some Marx, some Sartre as the guiding spirit of Beckett's
insinuating parable; others argued that 'Godot' was not to
be read as an allegory, but as a ritualized expression of
basic human concerns - a play in which variations of feeling and mood - rhythmical rather than cognitive

progressions - were paramount. Years later, Beckett gave
support to those in the second camp: '...the early success
of "Waiting for Godot" was based on a fundamental misunderstanding, critics and public alike insisted on interpret-
ing in allegorical or symbolic terms a play which was
striving all the time to avoid definition.' Years later,
in conversation, Beckett asked Raymond Federman: 'When
are they going to stop making me mean more than I say?'

No matter how Beckett intended to avoid definition, the
history of early performances suggests that 'Godot' had
qualities destined to keep many people from taking him at
his word. In the USA, for instance, the play was given
four productions that added to its reputation as something
of a theatrical Rorschach test, a work that meant wildly
different things to different audiences. In Miami Beach,
advertised as the 'laugh hit of two continents,' it infur-
iated vacationers looking for easy diversion. 'Sand-
bagged by an allegory' said the Miami 'Herald': and taxi-
drivers quickly identified the Coconut Grove Playhouse as
a spot to pick up early fares - after the first act of
'Godot.'

Following the fiasco in Miami, performances scheduled
for Washington, Boston, Philadelphia and New York were
cancelled and the original cast disbanded. Plans for a
New York production were revived, however, with a different director and four new actors. After opening at the
John Golden Theatre in April 1956, 'Godot' received as
many different notices as there were critics to respond to
it. Brooks Atkinson's 'New York Times' review (20 April)
was breezy, generally positive, evasive and misleading.
'Don't expect this column to explain "Waiting for
Godot".... It is a mystery wrapped in an enigma.'
Admitting Beckett's strange power to convey 'melancholy
truths,' Atkinson called the play 'an allegory written in
a heartless modern tone,' and thought it perfectly natural
for audiences to 'rummage through ... in search of a meaning.' His own hasty effort revealed that Godot most
likely stood for God and that Beckett, though, puzzling,
'is no charlatan.' Exasperated theater-goers might 'rail
at the play but they cannot ignore it.' Walter Kerr in
the 'Herald Tribune' (29 April) called the work 'a cerebral tennis match' that 'can be read variously and furiously as Christian, existentialistic or merely stoic
allegory,' and gave most credit for the pleasures of the
evening to the antics of Bert Lahr. In the widely read
'Saturday Review' (5 May), Henry Hewes was more confident
about how Beckett's 'guessing game' was to be taken:

[The vagabonds] are waiting for a mysterious Mr. Godot

(God) who has promised to meet them there. Along comes
a well-dressed European landowner named Pozzo
(Capitalist-Aristocrat) followed by a wretched, exhausted slave named Lucky (Labor-Proletariat).... After
this pair depart, one of Godot's two sons shows up to
inform Vladimir, whom he calls Mr. Albert - (Schweit-
zer?), that Mr. Godot won't come this evening but will
surely come tomorrow.

Hewes ended with praise for the director's ability to keep
'the vitality-level high on stage,' but observed that keeping it high in the audience was another matter: 'There Mr.
Beckett's skeletal synthesis of postwar European despair
engenders less dramatic excitement than it provokes post-
theater discussion.'
    Mistaken about Beckett's intention, Hewes was right
about the discussion 'Godot' would inevitably stir. Playgoers huddled in groups, attended symposia and bought
copies of the paperback recently issued by Grove Press.
Two especially revealing encounters were recorded by Eric
Bentley (No. 23) and Norman Mailer ('Village Voice,' 7
May 1956, reprinted in 'Advertisements for Myself,' 1959).
Bentley provided an analysis of the play in the broad context of American cultural life; Mailer offered an idiosyncratic yet stimulating confession and an attack on
the snobbery of sex-starved New York intellectuals.
Although Mailer's personal interpretation will eventually
be of greater use to his biographer than to an historian
of Beckett's literary reputation, it again reveals the
intensity with which first viewers were engaged by Godot.'
    Two other American performances of 1957 contributed to
the legend developing around the play. In response to the
interest stimulated by the first New York performance,
'Godot' was revived with an all-Negro cast in January; and
some months later, the Actors Workshop staged their version in San Francisco. Soon afterwards, the California
company was invited to perform to an audience of 1,400
convicts at San Quentin prison. Blacks and convicts -
connoisseurs of waiting - had eloquent and much-publicized
reactions to Beckett's play (No. 24).
    Since the middle of the 1950s, 'Waiting for Godot' had
been one of the most influential and widely discussed
works of modern literature. The original French performances numbered 400; the British 257; and hundreds of other
productions have been staged around the world. Few serious playwrights have remained uninfluenced by Beckett's
genius for talking about sacred and profane things in a
relevant modern idiom. William Saroyan once said that
'Godot' would 'make it easier for me and everyone else to

write freely in the theatre'; and it is difficult to think
of an important dramatist writing in the 1960s whose work
did not (for good or ill) reveal some evidence of its
author having been captivated by Beckett. Writers as different as Fernando Arrabal, Tom Stoppard, Edward Albee,
David Storey and Harold Pinter were - to borrow Martin
Esslin's phrase - children of 'Godot.' Pinter has always
been passionate about his admiration for Beckett. He
wrote to a friend in 1954:

> The farther he goes the more good it does me. I don't
> want philosophies, tracts, dogmas, creeds, ways out,
> truths, answers, *nothing from the bargain basement.*
> He is the most courageous, remorseless writer going and
> the more he grinds my nose in the shit the more I am
> grateful to him. He's not fucking me about, he's not
> leading me up any garden, he's not slipping me any wink,
> he's not flogging me a remedy or a path or a revelation
> or a basinful of breadcrumbs, he's not selling me any-
> thing I don't want to buy, he doesn't give a bollock
> whether I buy or not, *he hasn't got his hand over his
> heart.* Well, I'll buy his goods, hook, line and sinker,
> because he leaves no stone unturned and no maggot
> lonely. He brings forth a body of beauty. His work is
> beautiful.

In the late 1960s, Pinter habitually sent each of his new
plays in manuscript to Beckett before anyone else was
allowed to see it. 'He writes the most succinct observations,' Pinter said ('New York Times,' 18 November 1971).
     As one further index of the success of 'Godot,' Grove
Press announced in March 1975 that the American paperback
edition had sold more than one million copies and was
still selling at the rate of 2,500 a week.

IV

In 1953, however, Beckett was still very much an Irishman
writing in French whose earlier accomplishments were forgotten, minimized, or seen simply as preparations for the
major work in his adopted language. More than a hundred
reviews and essays had already been devoted to 'Molloy,'
'Malone meurt' and 'En attendant Godot,' and many of the
issues raised by those radical experiments in fiction and
drama, and by Beckett's frightening vision of the world,
were regularly discussed in French periodicals. Very
little of this was known to English and American readers
and what was known was often inchoate and distorted.

Three reviews published within a few weeks of each other illustrate the differences between French and English perceptions of Beckett's work at this period.

Maurice Blanchot's response to 'The Unnamable' (No. 26) represents early French criticism at its best. Having assimilated Beckett's other work and the arguments swirling about it, Blanchot described with great skill the intolerable pressure of contradictory compulsions that had by this time become a signature of Beckett's style. ('...in my life, since we must call it so, there are three things, the inability to speak, the inability to be silent, and solitude.') Recognizing that 'The Unnamable' was a book of unendurable and yet mysteriously endured torment, Blanchot refused to domesticate it, to treat it (as critics sometimes did) as a manageable work of art. He admitted that Beckett was a hero for having gone down into the depths of consciousness where fictions may fail but misery and incomprehension still exist; yet he would not conceal his uncertainty about the nature, implications and value of the exploration.

Next to Blanchot's gift for conveying the unruliness and danger of Beckett's fanatic experiments in fiction – the way 'The Unnamable' is at once a break-through and a dead-end, an exorcism and a new curse – the pieces by Seaver and Hartley on 'Watt' (Nos 27, 28) were rather tame. In their praiseworthy effort to bring Beckett's work to a larger public, both reviewers assumed a chatty, familiar air, underplaying the savagery and dismay that make the comedy of 'Watt' so chilling. Seaver wittily remarked on the profit Beckett's characters sometimes gain from lying down (alive to inner voices, neglected sounds) without letting on that Watt is driven mad by the voices he is eventually forced to accommodate. Hartley's essay – the fullest account of Beckett's work yet to have appeared in England – fairly described the disintegration and ambiguity at the heart of every novel. But almost as if the nihilistic implications of his own summaries were too grim, Hartley ended by pointing to Beckett's hopefulness: 'Who knows? Godot may come after all.'

By the end of 1953, 'Godot' had arrived in Paris; Beckett was recognized as an important figure in French literature; and interest in his work was beginning to quicken elsewhere. He himself, however, had never sought fame and it was of no help in dealing with one of the most painful crises of his writing life. As he told Israel Shenker two years later (No. 33):

I wrote all my work very fast – between 1946 and 1950. Since then I haven't written anything. Or at least

nothing that has seemed to me valid. The French work
brought me to the point where I felt I was saying the
same thing over and over again. For some authors
writing gets easier the more they write. For me it
gets more and more difficult. For me the area of possibilities gets smaller and smaller.... In the last
book - 'L'Innommable' - there's complete disintegration. No 'I,' no 'have,' no 'being.' No nominative,
no accusative, no verb. There's no way to go on.

Beckett's way of 'going on' in 1953-4 was characteristic:
he tried unsuccessfully to sustain a novel in English
('From an Abandoned Work'), translated 'En attendant
Godot,' and worked with Patrick Bowles on an English version of 'Molloy.' Meanwhile his name was occasionally
mentioned in British and American periodicals and by
writers and editors on both sides of the Atlantic. Surveying the contemporary French theatre for the 'Listener'
(28 January 1954, 174-6), Pierre Schneider called 'En
attendant Godot' 'the most important dramatic work of the
past few seasons'; and an anonymous writer for the 'Times
Literary Supplement' (27 May 1955) named Beckett as the
most significant of expatriate authors in Paris. The
first general account of his work to appear in the USA
was Niall Montgomery's No Symbols Where None Intended
('New World Writing,' April 1954, 324-37). Although Montgomery's swaggering style tended to trivialize his subject, the essay did bring Beckett's work to the attention
of thousands of new readers in one of the most respected
literary magazines of its day. The survey was accompanied
by the first nine pages of the Bowles-Beckett translation
of 'Molloy,' other extracts of which (particularly the
sucking stones episode) were attracting attention in
'Merlin' and the 'Paris Review.' The same period saw the
first American scholarly essay on Beckett (Edith Kern's
Drama Stripped for Inaction, 'French Review,' 1954-5, 41-
7); two of Vivian Mercier's perceptive early pieces ('New
Republic,' 19 September 1955, 20-1; and 'Hudson Review,'
winter 1955, 620-4); and French reactions to Beckett's
crisis volume 'Nouvelles et textes pour rien' (Nos 31, 32).
   By 1957 the English-speaking countries had begun to
catch up with the French. Godot had entered the realm of
contemporary mythology (in cartoons, editorials and graf-
fiti); and translations of 'Molloy' and 'Malone Dies' had
been reviewed in England by Vivian Mercier (No. 13) and
Philip Toynbee (No. 14), and in the USA by Herbert Gold
('Nation,' 10 November 1956, 397-9) and Horace Gregory
('Commonweal,' 26 October 1956). And yet the title of
Madeleine Chapsal's article in 'L'Express' (8 February

1957) - Un Célèbre inconnu - had an obvious pertinence and
truth. Beckett was becoming internationally famous but the
ambiguities of his work, the controversies that surrounded
it, and his extreme personal reticence gave his name a significant aura of mystery. Having previously refused to be
interviewed, Beckett relented once in the spring of 1956.
The intensity of public interest and hunger for words in
the author's own voice can be measured by the fact that
every one of the remarks by Beckett reported by Israel
Shenker (No. 33) has been quoted hundreds of times in articles and books around the world.

1957 brought an important article by Jean-Jacques Mayoux
('Études Anglaises,' October-December 1957, 350-66); a poem
by Donald Davie; scores of essays and reviews; and two
masterpieces by Beckett: 'All That Fall' and 'Fin de
partie.' The Davie poem, Samuel Beckett's Dublin, is one
of the first important tributes from another creative
writer and skillfully sums up an essential Beckettian paradox in its final stages:

> When it is cold it stinks, and not till then
> Can it be fragrant. On canal and street,
> Colder and colder, Murphy to Molloy,
> The weather hardens round the Idiot Boy,
> The gleeful hero of the long retreat.
>
> When he is cold he stinks, but not before,
> This living corpse. The existential weather
> Smells out in these abortive minims, men
> Who barely living therefore altogether
> Live till they die; and sweetly smell till then.

V

Even as Beckett's work was being welcomed with increasing
hospitality in England, critics were of very different
minds about where to locate its distinction. Reviewing
'All That Fall' a week after the BBC broadcast, Richard
Robinson ('Sunday Times,' 20 January 1957, 12) called the
play remarkable, praised its strong dialogue and emotional
power, but complained that Beckett,

> like all allegorists, has dwelt first and longest upon
> the universal significance ... and only secondarily
> upon the creatures who are to express it. His charac-
> ters are not at all the mere symbols of the medieval
> allegorist, they are flesh and blood - but the flesh and
> blood has been grafted to them, they did not grow it of
> themselves.

For the 'Times Literary Supplement' critic (No. 34)
exactly the opposite was the case. 'All That Fall' gained
its phenomenal power from being set in a 'recognizable
though stylized ... rural Ireland of perhaps thirty or
forty years ago,' and not 'among allegorical dustbins.'
He especially admired the rhetorical exuberance, wild
laughter that had 'the effect of comic blasphemy,' compassion that broke through nihilism, and a richness of implication that allowed each auditor to interpret the catastrophe according to his own sense of evil. Donald Davie,
though, deplored the particularity of setting, the fascination with blasphemy ('which most non-Irish readers will
find childish and trivial'), and the 'tediously insoluble
whodunnit' quality of the climax, with 'ambiguities flying
off in all directions...' (No. 35). Despite his severe
objections and a parochialism that in 1958 could claim
Beckett had never before been seen as a comic writer, Davie
offered several brilliant observations about Beckett's use
of parody and his distrust of the language he so match-
lessly manipulated.

The differences of opinion about 'Endgame' were even
more extreme. Although Beckett was one of the most eminent
writers in France, the management that had originally promised to stage 'Fin de partie' in late 1956 reneged and
Roger Blin (already in rehearsal) accepted an invitation
to hold the première at the Royal Court on 3 April 1957.
Since the engagement was brief and the language French,
there were not many early reviews. Among those that did
appear, however, three of the most prominent divided along
lines that had become predictable. Harold Hobson (No. 36)
and Kenneth Tynan (No. 37) again devoted their Sunday
columns to Beckett, but this time disagreed strongly about
his achievement. Hobson argued that 'Fin de partie,' despite its desolation, was 'a magnificent theatrical experience,' evoking a 'sombre and paradoxical joy.' Tynan,
on the other hand, found the agony skull-cracking and
looked in vain for the satire, savage parody and glimmers
of hopefulness that he thought existed in the printed
text.

If Hobson spoke for those who saw nobility and variousness in Beckett's harrowing vision and Tynan for those who
found it unbearably stifling, J.C. Trewin expressed
another common viewpoint. Covering the play for the
'Illustrated London News' (20 April 1957, 652), he confessed to having been hardly able to fix his attention on
this 'apparent mixture of repetitive repartee, chess symbolism and dustbins'; and to have relieved his boredom by
spinning couplets: 'Clov and Hamm and Nagg and Nell/Lead
us steadily to Hell/Life is fleeting; none can check it/

Hear at once the worst with Beckett.' Then, in the familiar Philistine tone of fatigued contempt for the vagaries of the avant-garde, Trewin concluded:

> Undeniably, these plays will be analysed to shreds.
> That is what happened to the worthier 'Waiting for
> Godot'. The libretti of the Savoy operas might help.
> Did not Lady Blanche, who lectures on Abstract Philo-
> sophy, propose to consider at length how 'the Is and
> Might be stand compared with the inevitable Must'?
> I am sure in the words of another opera, that Mr.
> Beckett is 'very singularly deep'; we have not seen the
> last of those dustbins.

Beckett later expressed disappointment with the London audience and felt the play worked more forcefully in Paris. As he told Alan Schneider: 'The creation at the Royal Court was rather grim, like playing to mahogany, or rather teak. In the little Studio des Champs-Élysées the hooks went in.' The French critics, though, were no more agreed about the meaning and merit of what they saw than the English. Like Tynan, Marc Bernard (No. 38) lamented the loss of the vitality he admired in 'Godot,' offered an allegorical reading (Hamm = Intellectual; Clov = Common Man) and ended by rejecting the play as product of a particularly nasty form of masochism. Jacques Lemarchand, however, saw universality and greatness in Beckett's vision of the terrible comedy 'that the end of everything arouses in man'; and he provided the most reliable early account of the play's sumptuous destitution (No. 39). For the philosopher Gabriel Marcel, 'Fin de partie' meant boredom, claustrophobia, and one of the most painful evenings he had ever spent in the theatre ('Nouvelles littéraires,' 20 June 1957). In a characteristically derisive review, Jean-Jacques Gautier called the play 'ugly, foul, unwholesome, vacant, wretched, infantile' ('Figaro,' 3 May 1957); and his contempt prompted the director of the Studio des Champs-Élysées to write asking if perhaps the ugliness was in the eyes of the beholder. A week later Alain Spiraux reported in 'Combat' that 'Fin de partie' (as could have been expected) had aroused some of the wildest controversy of the theatrical season (10 May 1957).

Despite these mixed notices, the oddities of script and staging and the growing curiosity about Beckett brought 'Endgame' international notoriety. Within days after the London production, articles appeared in Germany, Switzerland and Scandinavia; and 'Life' magazine in New York ran a picture story about this weird 'blend of acid hokum and dank despair' attracting so much attention in Europe.

Like several other middle-brow periodicals, 'Life' sensed
that Beckett was 'news' but with predictable coarseness
patronized him as a quaint, eccentric old nay-sayer: 'an
inveterate apostle of hopelessness, author Beckett finds
no answer to the riddle of human existence. But like the
image of his people in the ash can, the way he delivers
his melancholy message is too compelling to dismiss.'

When 'Endgame' opened in New York on 28 January 1958,
critics again split on the issues of pessimism and obscurity. Walter Kerr spoke of those already 'familiar problems' of Beckett's plays: 'an aura of smugness that always
hovers around a private language, the defiant treadmill of
directionless conversation, the knowledge that the author
is deliberately playing blindman's buff, the emotional
aridity of a world without a face' ('Herald Tribune,' 29
January 1958). Brooks Atkinson (No. 40) was not sure if
Beckett's insistent negations were 'acceptable or rational,' but he did admit the production had 'a continuous
tension and pressure' and his uneasy praise was influential enough to secure the production a modest success (see
Alan Schneider's memoir, No. 41). The closing note on the
first critical reception of 'Endgame' in the USA was
sounded by 'Theatre Arts' in April. As they customarily
did, the editors printed a 'critical box score' following
their own harsh notice of the play: 'two of the six reviewers were generally favorable and there were three
fairly negative votes.' 'Extraordinary,' as Molloy once
said, 'how mathematics help you to know yourself.'

When 'Endgame' finally reached London in an English
version (along with the world première of 'Krapp's Last
Tape') resistance in some quarters had hardened and the
production ran for only thirty-eight performances.
Kenneth Tynan's review (No. 42) had some outrageously apt
one-line jokes ('Themes, Madam? Nay, it is, I know not
themes') and communicated the inverted forms of truth
about Beckett's genius that good parody can often embody.
But Tynan's cleverness could not conceal the fact that
the two plays he ridiculed had not yet been intelligently
perceived and would, when they were, enter into the repertoire of dramatic masterpieces. The widely-read reviews by
T.C. Worsley ('New Statesman,' 8 November 1958, 630) and
Alan O'Brien ('Spectator,' 7 November 1958, 609) were mix-
tures of intensity and ignorance that had little more than
stridancy to recommend them. Worsley renewed the attack
on Beckett as an obscurantist locked in the cage of his
own neurosis. 'Endgame,' he said, 'tells us a good deal
about Mr. Beckett's solitary despairs, if you are interested in them. But who is?' Dismissing 'Krapp's Last
Tape' as 'a crazy monologue' that would have been 'yawned

off stage' if it weren't for the acting of Patrick Magee,
Worsley expressed final relief at being able to move away
from 'these inverted explorations of the seamier side of
Mr. Beckett's nasty unconscious' to write about a revival
of Gerhart Hauptmann. For O'Brien, the two plays were in-
sufferable 'exercises in peevish despair'; and Beckett -
'terrified that he is swimming up too far towards the surface of comprehensibility' - was 'a literary suicide desperate to die alone.'

While Beckett's work was arousing uncomprehending
irritation and anger, it was also winning admirers among
theatre-goers, readers and critics who were responding
with greater subtlety. Experience, of course, helped
some; one idiosyncratic work illuminated another; a knowledge of 'Malone Dies' (a novel about histrionics and
story-telling, among other things) helped clarify 'Endgame' (a play on the same subjects). Although a record of
first reactions to Beckett sometimes looks as much like an
epistemological nightmare as his novels and plays, criticism was a collaborative and progressive effort. Having
read Beckett's four major novels and three great plays,
critics began to see the magnitude and originality of his
achievement. Essays with titles like Beckett Country were
followed by Beckett's World and Beckett's Universe, and it
was generally acknowledged that - like Balzac, Dickens,
Faulkner, and Joyce - Beckett had created a distinctive
environment with its own unexpected amplitude and surprising coherences. A reviewer for the 'Times Literary
Supplement' (28 March 1958, 168) provided a most helpful
account of how the fiction should be read, and argued that
those grotesque stories 'exorcise and console, for the
ludicrous horror of old objects and futile actions is
brought into the light and undergoes a poetic transformation in the hands of one of the greatest prose-writers of
the century.'

A few months later, K.W. Gransden, in a piece called
The Dustman Cometh ('Encounter,' July 1958, 84-6), summarized the landscape and inhabitants of Beckett's 'world
without end at the end of the world, a world always on the
point of ending yet never quite able to bring itself to
end.' He then offered a concise portrait of the Beckett
hero: that decrepit, irascible, meticulous, horribly
funny, lyrical, holy beggar with his axioms and reveries,
his endless vicissitudes and his limitless gift for talking about dissolution and not dying.

> This view of the fag-end of human effort, the prolonged
> soliloquy at the cemetery gate, is Beckett's contribu-
> tion to contemporary literature. 'It must be nearly

finished': the last articulate mumble of man marooned
in the moments between 'Time, Gentlemen, Please', and
closing time. The trouble is, the next bloody awful
day they open again. The end is what never ends.
There is no doubt that Beckett refashions this medieval
view of mortality in terms of modern spiritual decline
with astonishing force and power.

At the same time in the USA, Granville Hicks praised
'The Trilogy' in 'Saturday Review' (4 October 1958, 14);
Stephen Spender wrote about 'The Unnamable' for the 'New
York Times Book Review' (12 October 1958, 5); and Hugh
Kenner published the first of the essays that would cul-
minate three years later in his important book ('National
Review,' 11 October 1958, 248-9; and 'Spectrum,' winter
1958, 8-24). In 1959, Ruby Cohn wrote the first doctoral
dissertation and edited the first journal devoted entirely
to Beckett's work. The dissertation was later published
as 'Samuel Beckett: The Comic Gamut'; the journal 'Perspective' (published by Washington University, St Louis)
printed influential essays by Kenner, Jean-Jacques Mayoux,
Edith Kern, Samuel Mintz and Jacqueline Hofer.

VI

In many respects 1960 marked a turning-point for Beckett's
reputation in England and the USA. The New York production of 'Krapp's Last Tape' was warmly received, most notably by Robert Brustein (No. 43); and the publication of
'Molloy,' 'Malone Dies' and 'The Unnamable' in one volume
brought substantial retrospective essays by three prominent modern critics: V.S. Pritchett (No. 44), Frank Kermode
(No. 45), and Northrop Frye (No. 46). Valuable as single
statements, these essays also demonstrated the challenges
Beckett's work offered to three very different critical
perspectives.
    Pritchett's Beckett is a manic monologist speaking from
the depths of Irish rage and European disillusionment.
His themes are old age, flight, decrepitude, and the need-
ful, hopeless search for self; his manner mocking and ear-
nest, innocent and sly, vindictive and forgiving, lyrical
and indecent, frenzied and serene. His true ancestor was
Sterne not Joyce, and like the author of 'Tristram Shandy,'
he is a wayward comic genius soliloquizing about some of
our deepest, most vexing concerns. Kermode's Beckett is a
more poised, speculative figure, grounded in Bergson and
intuitionist esthetics of the 1920s, obsessed with the
deadening effects of Habit, the 'inaccessibility of value'

and the 'expiatory nature of human life.' From this vant-
age point, Beckett's career is seen as a lifelong effort to
undermine language and meaning in the hope of breaking
through to some unconscious, pre-verbal, bed-rock source of
being. According to Kermode, the experiment works in the
plays and in 'Molloy' because the pessimism has 'rotted
down into images,' the subman 'has acquired the color of
myth,' and the 'banalities of Habit fall into the rhythms
of poetry.' But in the last two-thirds of 'The Trilogy,'
Beckett has gone past the point of diminishing returns and
his exploration is barren and almost impossible to read.
However one responds, Kermode's essay is the strongest,
best-argued expression of a point of view frequently heard
in the years that followed. Useful, too, is his effort to
begin making reasoned evaluative distinctions among Beckett's work - a task that had hardly begun in 1960.

Predictably enough, Northrop Frye's Beckett is the maker
of a myth with profound psychological, social and religious
implications - the myth of the quest for a discrete, continuous ego. According to Frye, Murphy had sought a self-
contained egocentric consciousness but was defeated by
weakness (a desire to communicate with others); the characters in 'The Trilogy' progressively find that such a notion
is unreal, an illusion. Eventually Malone accepts the fact
that there is no escape from fiction, no true self, but
only a choice of rhetorical masks, and the Unnamable re-
solves to 'find in art the secret of identity, the paradise
that has been lost.' Frye's intricate argument is often
brilliant, but by locating the figure so insistently in one
part of the carpet and ignoring many other designs, he at
times makes Beckett's work seem like a myth boldly created
by Northrop Frye.

Criticism of Beckett's work in the early 1960s was becoming better informed and more serviceable but hardly more
consonant. The novels and plays seemed to be as problem-
atical and elusive as the essence of being for which Beckett was searching all his life; and the critical inquiry
appeared at times to resemble the words and images that ran
riot in Malone's head: 'pursuing, flying, clashing, merg-
ing, endlessly.' Some observers responded by quoting
Molloy ('the truth is I don't know much'; 'something has
gone wrong with the silence'); others Malone ('what
tedium!'); and others the Unnamable ('some of this rubbish
has come in handy on occasions.... Next instalment, quick
.... Dear incomprehension, it's thanks to you, I'll be
myself, in the end...').

Reviews of the two important works appearing in 1961 -
'Comment c'est' and 'Happy Days' - illustrate some of the
issues about which critics were continuing to disagree.

Maurice Nadeau (No. 49), Raymond Federman (No. 50), and
Jean-Jacques Mayoux (No. 51) expressed surprise that Beckett could still ruthlessly pursue his reductive experiments and manage (in the mud and without punctuation) to
find mysterious links with the living. Did so extreme an
innovation as 'Comment c'est' remain in the realm of literature? Was Beckett's tormented yet meticulous evocation
of indeterminacy likely to disarm judgment and 'annihilate
all desire to comment'? Nadeau nervously said Yes to the
first question and Perhaps to the second. Federman and
Mayoux said Yes to one, No to the other. Federman argued
here (and later in 'Journey to Chaos') that simplicity,
economy and strange absorbing power make 'Comment c'est' a
triumph of art over dark reality. Mayoux, opening with a
wonderfully apt quotation from Melville, expounded Beckett's 'principle of parsimony' and tried to show in detail
how he remained 'an artist, in spite of himself.' In his
characteristically ingenious and suggestive essay, Hugh
Kenner (No. 52) was less apologetic. Coming at 'Comment
c'est' by way of Newton, Wordsworth and Beckett's other
books, he found 'a beautifully and tightly wrought structure,' an 'absolute sureness of design,' and a richness of
thematic implication that made the novel one of Beckett's
greatest achievements.

Three years later, when 'Comment c'est' became 'How It
Is,' Beckett's anguish and obscurity again evoked diverse
reactions. Although the 'Times Literary Supplement' (No.
53) found great poetic energy in his de-creation, most
other readers were more negative, inventing - like the
author - an unusually large number of different ways to
say No. In an amusing parody, How 'How It Is' Was, John
Updike (No. 54) attacked the novel as inert - 'hermetic
avantgardism unviolated by the outerworld.' Praising
Beckett's integrity and dedication, the novelist B.S.
Johnson none the less also saw the exploration headed up
a cul-de-sac where the light and color of the earlier fiction were shut out ('Spectator,' 26 June 1964, 858). What
Johnson saw as a cul-de-sac was for Denis Donoghue that
'modish place called the End of the Line,' and he dismissed the novel as arbitrary and in paradoxical ways 'too
easy' ('Guardian,' 1 May 1964, 11). Referring to the publisher's assertion that Beckett had broken through to a
new plane,' V.S. Pritchett concluded: 'he has indeed. It
is uninhabited' ('New Statesman,' 1 May 1964, 683).
Another disaffected admirer, John Simon, argued that 'murmurs, cries of pain, ghastly laughter' are indeed significant, but should be encountered 'in the form which
achieves greatest scope with the least sacrifice of coherence. Instead of sinking in the morass of "How It Is,"

one should re-read "Molloy"' ('Book Week,' 8 March 1964,
8). R.H. Glauber rejected Beckett's work for a different
reason - because it makes 'the life and death of our Lord
just one more of the legends man has used to delude himself - and not a very effective one at that...' ('Christian Century,' 8 April 1964, 461). One of the few reviewers unable to form a judgment was Gene Baro, who called
Beckett's vision 'important,' insisted 'a vision cannot be
proved,' and left each reader 'to decide for himself how
far it convinces' ('New York Times Book Review,' 22 March
1964, 5). In the most discerning of what might be called
the 'agnostic' reviews, Frank Kermode brought the entire
Beckett *oeuvre* to play in an effort to make some sense of
a novel that refuses 'to employ the ordinary referential
qualities of language, and frustrates ordinary expectations as to the relation between a fiction and real life.'
At the close of his long essay, Kermode summarized the
problem that other sympathetic but skeptical critics had
expressed in less helpful ways:

> It is nevertheless true that the more accustomed we be-
> come to his formal ambiguity, the more outrageously he
> can test us with inexplicitness, with apparently closed
> systems of meaning. 'How It Is' differs from the
> earlier work not in its mode of operation, but princi-
> pally in that it can assume greater knowledge of the
> Beckett world. Such assumptions have often and legiti-
> mately been made by major artists, though we should not
> forget that this is not a certain indication of great-
> ness. Prolonged attention given (from whatever mot-
> ives) to a minor but complex author may allow him to
> make them. But who can be sure which is which. It is
> a perennial problem for critics of avant-garde art, and
> Beckett raises it in a very acute form. ('New York
> Review of Books,' 19 March 1964, 9-11)

That Beckett continued to raise this and many other
problems can be demonstrated by the reception of 'Happy
Days.' For weeks before the New York opening the play had
generated the now familiar buzz of incredulous gossip.
Beckett was up to one of his stunts again: a drama for two
characters in which an endlessly talking heroine remains
buried in a mound of scorched grass. On the eve of the
première, Herbert Mitgang wrote a 'New York Times' article
surveying Beckett's bizarre theatrical career, describing
rehearsals and quoting comments by Alan Schneider, labeled
the 'thinking man's filter for the far-out Beckett cate-
chism.' Something of the same evasive jauntiness was expressed two days later by reviewers for the popular daily

papers: Happy Days Aren't, said the 'Journal American';
Just a Rocky Gabfest - 'New York Mirror.' Reproaching
Beckett for wallowing in his own despair and fashioning
snob symbols for jaded intellectuals, 'Time' concluded:
'with "Happy Days," he has reached the point where less is
least.'

Even the more hospitable and perceptive reviewers were
in varying degrees resistant to the harshness of Beckett's
vision and the austerity of his dramatic presentation.
Writing twice in the 'New York Times' (18 September and 1
October 1961), Harold Taubman felt that the heroine's
sorrow and the author's compassion gave this 'grim threnody' a beauty that would haunt the inner ear long after
the monologue ended; but he could not help being repelled
by the weariness and pessimism of Beckett's philosophy of
life. Edith Oliver ('New Yorker,' 30 September 1961, 119)
confessed to a long-standing belief that Beckett was 'a
murky, self-important bore'; yet on the evidence of 'Happy
Days,' she decided that he 'is not a bore and may be
important.' Winnie's monologue - the 'longest and most
complex part ever written for a woman' - was 'funny,
pathetic, frightened, callous, bawdy, charming,' and there
was enough 'in this examination of the ins and outs of the
mind and heart to more than hold anyone for an evening.'

Both Robert Brustein (No. 55) and John Simon ('Hudson
Review,' winter 1961-2) celebrated Beckett's power and
originality, yet raised doubts about the price he had paid
for his unremitting effort to see 'how much the theatre can
do without and still be theatre.' Claiming that Beckett
had used these stripped materials to more brilliant advantage elsewhere, Brustein titled his piece An Evening of
Déjà Vu. Simon was more positive:

> Beckett the acrobat has hung on to his dramatic thread
> first by his feet, than by one hand, next by his teeth,
> and now he proceeds to take out his dentures in mid-air.
> Needless to say, he is performing without a net. And
> there are moments, indeed minutes, when the play lapses
> into _longeurs_, when the existential _ennui_ becomes plain
> old-fashioned boredom. All the same, the play is full
> of that Beckettian strategy which presents the most
> innocuous trifles of human existence dripping with
> blood and bile, and the most unspeakable horrors rak-
> ishly attired and merrily winking. The heroine who
> keeps blithering about the great mercies of existence
> as she is pressed deeper and deeper into the sod is an
> egregiously valid theatrical metaphor - particularly as
> portrayed by Ruth White, whose performance is formid-
> able in its broad outlines, and irrefutable in the
> accuracy of its deadly details.

When 'Happy Days' was first performed in London (1 November 1962), there were differences of opinion about every
aspect of the text and production. 'The Times' critic
argued that Beckett's play should be most fruitfully
approached as 'an elaborate structure of internal harmonies, with recurring clichés twisted into bitter truths.'
Key phrases, he said, chimed 'ironically through the
development as in a passacaglia' (a seventeenth-century
musical form consisting of continuous variations on a
ground bass in slow triple meter). If properly performed,
'Happy Days' might have as 'fiercely moving' an effect as
that other 'one-character masterpiece' 'Krapp's Last
Tape.' However, 'The Times' reviewer expressed disappointment with Brenda Bruce's inability to handle Beckett's
poetic style: 'her eyes, one feels, have never looked on
[such an] ashen landscape. And why on earth does she play
the part in a Scottish accent?'

Admiring Miss Bruce, Philip Hope-Wallace ('Guardian,'
2 November 1962, 7) was a good deal less fond of Beckett's
text:

years after 'Godot' it seems remarkably matter of fact,
without power to shock or greatly to surprise. I think
that is ultimately the proper criticism: I am hooked
but I am not surprised, delighted, or feel in anyway
entranced. 'Endgame' and 'Krapp's Last Tape' - both
leave their mark, but the message is slight and faintly
debilitating. But one might say as much of a Chopin
nocturne.

For Kenneth Tynan ('Observer,' 4 November 1952, 29) 'Happy
Days' was 'a dramatic metaphor extended beyond its capacity' - too long and full of infertile pauses; but,
admitting Beckett's strange, insinuating power, he urged
his readers to buy tickets for the play. Bamber Gascoigne
('Spectator,' 9 November 1962, 715) found 'Happy Days'
untheatrical, the language much thinner than ever before
in Beckett, and the playwright a victim of 'sentimental
resignation.' In spite of gallant work by Brenda Bruce, he
confessed to having been 'grievously bored.' Eric Keown
('Punch,' 7 November 1962, 698) applauded both the text and
the actress: '"Happy Days" is an original and moving essay
on human loneliness.... Miss Bruce cannot be over-
praised....' In a long, respectful essay for 'New Statesman' (9 November 1962, 679), Roger Gellert commended the
indomitability of Beckett and Miss Bruce, but concluded:
'Beckett's world is Beckett's only ... [his] clowning
from a position of sincere agony, must be respected, but
should not be wallowed in. He is a superb writer, but he

is not a sage and he is less and less a playwright.'

The most abusive review of 'Happy Days' appeared in the
'Labour Weekly Tribune' (16 November 1962, 11) and set off
a brief controversy that again illustrated Beckett's
power to provoke and disturb. For Iain Shaw, Beckett had
nothing to say that had not been said before; his message
was 'as limited as a child banging his head against a wall';
and with a swiftly diminishing talent, he was trying to
pass off as philosophy 'a collection of not very funny
sick jokes.' 'Happy Days,' Shaw insisted, 'must surely be
the greatest bore ever to be presented as a public entertainment since they abandoned six-day cycle racing at
Wembley.' The next week's 'Tribune' carried a response
from the novelist and essayist Clancy Sigal, who - after
calling Shaw 'an ass braying sullenly at himself in a
mirror' - worried that such 'miserably sneering' reporting
could damage the 'Tribune's' claim 'to speak for an optimistic and open-lunged Left.' One correspondent backed
Sigal by cancelling his subscription; another supported
Shaw by dismissing Beckett's work as the product of bourgeois sickness and decay.

The last important episode in the first chapter of the
critical fortunes of 'Happy Days' was the appearance of
Nigel Dennis's No View from the Toolshed in 'Encounter'
(No. 56). Dennis's funny attack on the solemnity of the
Royal Court production is extreme and often misfires, but
it is memorably shrewd about the nature of Beckett's comic
genius.

With 'Happy Days' - as with other Beckett works - the
future brought more critical accord. After Madeleine
Renaud's brilliant success with 'Oh les beaux jours' in
Paris, London and New York, the play has been revived many
times to great critical acclaim. At a New York opening
in 1968, Clive Barnes expressed a sentiment that was
already becoming commonplace:

Beckett's plays age magnificently. I remember when I
first saw 'Waiting for Godot.' I was amused by the wit,
impaled by the poetry, and bewildered by the message.
But later productions made everything obscurely clear..
.... About 'Happy Days' I feel the same. At first I
thought it was a slight work - a metaphor of death
overextended to the breaking point - yet now in this
production my doubts dissipate. ('New York Times,' 14
October 1968, 54)

Writing about the Lincoln Center Beckett Festival performance in November 1972, Barnes sounded like an ancient
critic comparing acresses in 'Phaedra':

I remember Madeleine Renaud, the first Winnie [sic],
Brenda Bruce, its first English-speaking interpreter
[sic], and while missing Ruth White [in actuality the
first Winnie in any language], I recall Sada Thompson,
the second American Winnie, Jessica Tandy, the present
Winnie, has a special shrill-voiced gentility.

In 1971, Beckett himself directed Eva Katherina Schultz at
the Schiller Theatre in Berlin; and in March 1975 Peggy
Ashcroft triumphed at the Old Vic in what was by then considered one of the greatest and most challenging roles in
the dramatic repertoire.

VII

After 1961 four developments dominate the history of
Beckett's reputation: the increased interest in his earlier novels and plays; the unparalleled proliferation of
books and essays devoted to his writings; the continued
controversy about the new work he was producing; and the
final institutionalization of his status as a major writer
by the award of the Nobel Prize.

In the early 1960s reprints, revivals, translations,
recordings, radio and television programs, operas, and
anthologies of Beckett's work multiplied rapidly all over
the world. If the original editions of 'Molloy' and
'Malone Dies' numbered about 3,000, a popular reprint
might now begin at 20,000 or 25,000. At new productions
of 'Godot,' of 'Endgame,' of 'Krapp's Last Tape,' critics
and audiences customarily echoed Penelope Gilliatt's
remark of 1965: 'the only puzzling thing about "Godot"
now is not the play, but the way we took it....' Time
caught up with Beckett's eccentric genius and he himself
had helped create the taste by which his own best work
was welcomed and better understood.

Another source of assistance came from the universi-
ties where Beckett's books were frequently taught and
were the subject of hundreds of essays and monographs.
The custom of teaching and of writing books about living
authors is, of course, a relatively recent phenomenon;
but even so it is unlikely that any writer (perhaps not
even Sartre, Eliot, or Faulkner) has ever been so exhaustively studied while he was still alive. The irony that
Beckett - poet of incomprehension, enemy of systems -
should be so systematically studied has been remarked many
times. The simplest way to illustrate the nature, the
magnitude and the international flavor of the response to
Beckett's work is to list some (by no means all) of the

books published year by year between 1958 and 1973 (the history of this part of Beckett's reputation will be written elsewhere).

1958 - Niklaus Gessner, 'Die Unzülanglichkeit der
        Sprache (Zurich)
1959 - Luís Carlos Maciel, 'Samuel Beckett e a solidão
        humana (Rio Grande de Sol)
1960 - H. Delye, 'Samuel Beckett ou la philosophie de
        l'absurde' (Aix-en-Provence)
1961 - Hugh Kenner, 'Samuel Beckett' (New York)
1962 - Juan José López Ibor, 'El lenguaje subterraneo'
        (Madrid)
1962 - Ruby Cohn, 'Samuel Beckett: the Comic Gamut'
        (New Brunswick)
1963 - André Marissel, 'Samuel Beckett' (Paris)
1964 - Richard Coe, 'Samuel Beckett' (Edinburgh)
1964 - John Fletcher, 'The Novels of Samuel Beckett'
        (London)
1965 - Raymond Federman, 'Journey to Chaos' (Berkeley)
1966 - Ludovic Janvier, 'Pour Samuel Beckett' (Paris)
1966 - Pierre Mélèse, 'Samuel Beckett' (Paris)
1967 - Renato Oliva, 'Samuel Beckett: Prima del Sil-
        enzio (Milan)
1967 - Aldo Tagliaferri, 'Beckett e' l'iperdetermin-
        azione letteraria' (Milan)
1968 - Georg Hensel, 'Samuel Beckett' (Hanover)
1969 - Olga Bernal, 'Langage et fiction' (Paris)
1970 - Fernand Ponce, 'Samuel Beckett' (Madrid)
1970 - Lawrence Harvey, 'Samuel Beckett: Poet and
        Critic' (Princeton)
1970 - Eugene Webb, 'Samuel Beckett' (Seattle)
1970 - Manfred Smuda, 'Becketts Prosa als Metasprache'
        (Munich)
1970 - Melvin Friedman, 'Samuel Beckett Now' (Chicago)
1971 - David Hesla, 'The Shape of Chaos' (Minneapolis)
1972 - Brian Finney, 'Since How It Is' (London)
1973 - Ruby Cohn, 'Back to Beckett' (Princeton)
1973 - Hugh Kenner, 'A Reader's Guide to Samuel Beckett'
        (New York)
1973 - A. Alvarez, 'Samuel Beckett' (New York)
1973 - H. Porter Abbott, 'The Fiction of Samuel Beckett'
        (Berkeley)

The most complete biographical studies of the first four decades of Beckett's critical reputation are 'Samuel Beckett: His Works and His Crticis', by Raymond Federman and John Fletcher (Berkeley, 1970) and the volume in the Calepins series, 'Samuel Beckett,' edited by R.J. Davis,

J.R. Bryer, M.J. Friedman and P.C. Hoy (Paris, 1972).

As the critical industry was expanding its empire,
Beckett was dissolving his own. Each new experiment in
drama or fiction was an indeflectible, admittedly hopeless
effort to explore essence within an increasingly narrow
range - not only the essence of being but of the fictional
forms in which being was customarily expressed. What used
to be a short story was now a 'prose text'; a miniature
for the stage would be called 'Play,' or dramaticule
('Come and Go,' 'Breath'); a fifteen-minute invention for
cinema, 'Film.' In each form, form was suspect, the
artist's tools inadequate, the exploration agonizing,
futile and necessary. 'What do you do,' Beckett once
asked, 'when "I can't" meets "I must"'; and he compared
himself to a man 'on his knees, head against the wall -
more like a cliff - with someone saying "go on" - Well,
the wall will have to move a little, that's all.'

Sometimes the wall moved an inch or two; twice - with
'The Lost Ones' and 'Not I' - it moved further than anyone
would have dreamed possible. The more persistent Beckett's search for new shapes to distill his ever-
diminishing vision, the more often critics tried to find
metaphors of their own to make vivid the extremity of his
abnegation. For one 'Times Literary Supplement' reviewer
(16 May 1968), Beckett was an equilibrist who would 'climb
an unsupported ladder and sit nonchalantly on the top rung
while all the lower rungs, and finally one pole, fell away
beneath him.' Then having discarded nearly everything, he
begins to whittle at his last support. To another critic
for the same journal (No. 71), he was a celestial clerk
annotating the insanities of life in a cypher appropriate
to that life. Matthew Hodgart compared him to an early
Christian stylite living unsheltered at the top of a lofty
pillar ('New York Review of Books,' 7 December 1967). For
Robert Martin Adams, he was at one moment the great
'hunger-artist of the modern imagination, a virtuoso performer in the lean art of doing without'; and at another,
an Antaeus of literature, the mythical giant who - whenever he was thrown - arose stronger than before from contact with his mother Earth ('New York Review of Books,'
25 September 1969).

At the same time, however, there was considerable disagreement about the value of Beckett's heroic but ruthlessly minimal art. The questions - How much can he do
without? How far can he go? 'Fin de Beckett'? - received
answers depending very much on a critic's tolerance for
experiment and on his earlier attitudes toward Beckett's
work. One reviewer felt that 'instead of suggesting the
emptiness at the centre of existence,' a Beckett fragment

begins 'to smell of the operating theatre, of a willed and
contrived sterility. But Beckett has so often found ways
out of apparent cul-de-sacs that one hesitates to suppose
that this time he has not only courted failure but achieved
it' ('Times Literary Supplement,' 11 December 1970).
Another critic went even further to argue that Beckett
'seems to require the pressure of an impossible demand.
bafflement is part of his vision of how things are, part
of his method as a writer, and, perhaps, his necessary
spur' ('Times Literary Supplement,' 16 May 1968).

The responses to 'Play' in New York and London illustrate the range of reactions to Beckett's desperately inspired inventiveness. Most admiring was Robert Brustein
(No. 59) who skillfully caught the aural and visual intentions of the work by calling it 'a litany of adultery ...
a hellish triptich in a bourgeois inferno.' Of all the
early reviewers, only Brustein fully understood the vital
function of Beckett's capricious, diabolical inquisitor -
the spotlight. Howard Taubman had a few good words for
the electrician ('the busiest person in this performance'),
but not for Beckett. In his view, 'Play' was 'an intellectual stunt,' perversely titled because it clearly bore so
little resemblance to a work for the stage ('New York
Times,' 6 January 1964).

The basic form of Taubman's dismissal was repeated many
times after 'Play' opened in London. David Pryce-Jones
('Spectator,' 17 April 1964, 516) insisted that no one
could call Beckett's work imaginative or poetic: 'it bears
about the same relation to the human endeavour as sky-
writing in an aeroplace does to literature.... The only
artist at work [is] Anthony Ferris operating the spotlight.' In 'Punch' (15 April 1964, 575) Basil Boothroyd
allowed that the cast 'dignified this brain-swill with
performances of unquestioning dedication and efficiency,
and the man on the spotlight was pretty good too.'
Bamber Gascoigne ('Observer,' 12 April 1964, 24) suggested
that the actors might in fact be replaced by a cattle
auctioneer whose rapid and rhythmic elocution could serve
the audience just as nicely, and he managed to be offensive as well as opaque:

Beckett's career as a dramatist seems to present the
strange picture of a man stifling the goose because he
is so offended by the charms of the golden egg - the
goose being his own rich talent to create words and
characters which are warm, hilarious, sad and robust.
With his latest work ... he has the fertile beast
safely trussed to the tip of his long neck. All that
is needed now is one sharp tap on the head and the

struggle will be over.... It is usual after each
Beckett play to say that this time he can really go no
further. But there is still plenty to be done away
with.... The end, of course, is Beckett himself in a
sealed box - fitting enough - since three of his five
stage plays deal with old age and the approach of
death - but there is a limit to the extent to which
symbolism should be allowed to influence life.

There were, however, several London notices which were
more discerning of Beckett's intentions and sympathetic to
his narrow but remarkable achievement. 'The Times' critic
(8 April 1964) recognized the complex analogy with music
and the fact that the first section of 'Play' presents
themes which are powerfully developed in the movement that
follows. He understood, too, that 'play' referred not only
to the form but to the subject matter: the sardonic treatment of adultery as 'just play.' Harold Hobson also pointed out that the formal use of the *da capo* repetition made
everything that at first seemed vague become sharp and
clear: 'the incidents stand out; only the emotions - the
sadness, the compassion, and the pain - are still beyond
computation' ('Sunday Times,' 12 April 1964). Surprisingly, J.C. Trewin - customarily hostile to Beckett -
called 'Play' an oddly haunting theatrical exercise,' but
could not help reminding the director, George Devine, that
by calling Beckett 'a profound and brilliant poet of the
theatre,' he was seriously 'over-playing his hand.'
  Mixed reactions to what soon became known as 'the residual Beckett' continued throughout the 1960s (Beckett
explained the phrase in response to a question about his
late prose texts and drama: 'They are residual (1) Sever-
ally, even when that does not appear of which each is all
that remains and (2) In relation to whole body of previous
work.') Even such sympathetic critics as Christopher
Ricks thought it possible to 'find his lifelong and total
consistency not only massively impressive but also blood-
chilling.' To critics who praised Beckett for destroying
not only the novel and the play but the sentence, Ricks
responded: 'but in destroying the sentence, Beckett seems
to me to have destroyed the extraordinary rhythms and
cadences of his style.... We may be impressed by the
severity and dedication ... but it is indisputable that
Beckett pays a price for his singlemindedness' ('New
Statesman,' 14 February 1964, 255).
  Reviewing 'No's Knife' in 1967 (No. 62), Ricks called
the final stages of Beckett's career 'heroic and dispirit-
ing,' accepted the progression as open-eyed and inevitable,
and turned (as many admirers did) to take what pleasures

he could from those last steely miniatures. For Ricks,
the pleasures offered by Beckett had always been ice-cold
yet exhilarating. Writing of the horrors of growing old,
the desire for oblivion, the fear of immortality, and the
terror of giving up consciousness, Beckett in his major
work created unforgettable myths about human beings and
the inquisitorial God they had so 'cruelly imagined.' If
not the old richness, the minor works could still display
Beckett's characteristic vehemence and vigilance, and show
how good he was 'at falling in slow motion.' Ricks continued to be one of the most knowing and laudatory of
Beckett's English critics; for additional examples see his
reviews of 'The Lost Ones' in the 'New York Review of
Books,' 14 December 1972, 42-4; of 'First Love' and 'Not I'
in the 'Sunday Times,' 15 July 1973, 39; and of 'Mercier
and Camier' (No. 68).

VIII

Although Beckett's artistic explorations after 1964 seemed
increasingly compacted and austere ('work in regress' he
once called it), his reputation during this period can only
be described as expanding endlessly. The award of the
Nobel Prize in October 1969 (No. 64) confirmed a widely
held belief that he was the most influential, perhaps the
greatest writer of his generation, and his novels and
plays continued to attract larger and more appreciative
audiences. The public response to the award of the prize
tells us a good deal about Beckett's reputation at the end
of the 1960s. Most newspapers and magazines greeted the
announcement with acclaim and obvious satisfaction: 'Le
Nobel à l'Ecrivain du Silence,' said 'L'Express' and 'Le
Monde' headed its front-page story: 'Le maître du texte
pour rien.' 'Godot has Arrived' declared 'The Times' of
London, and 'Life' announced, with characteristic flip-
pancy, 'From Ashcans, a Nobel Prize.' Long, admiring
essays appeared in publications all over Europe and the
USA (No. 65), and W.L. Webb, literary editor of the
'Guardian,' expressed a sentiment shared by many:

> The only surprising thing about Samuel Beckett's Nobel
> Prize is that it did not come sooner. For most of the
> 'sixties, while people like Steinbeck and Sholokhov
> were being bidden to Stockholm, he has been acknowled-
> ged by critics of quite different schools as a writer
> of classic weight and stature whose plays and novels
> can't be bypassed by anyone who cares about these
> things and who wants to understand what has been

happening to our civilization in the last thirty years. If he had been left to wait much longer, it would have been not just surprising but scandalous. (24 October 1969, 11)

Even those critics who were skeptical about the ultimate significance of Beckett's achievement agreed that he had undeniably earned the acclamation. Philip French's extended remarks in the 'New Statesman' (31 October 1969) are worth quoting because they can stand as representative of the reserved, qualified respect of a section of the literary community:

Beckett has of course been an obvious candidate for several years, though not in my view as the uniquely deserving recipient that several commentators have suggested. Graham Greene, Jorge Luis Borges, W.H. Auden and Robert Lowell, for instance, seem equally worthy, and frankly, I prefer them all to Beckett, towards whom my attitude is somewhat ambivalent. The work I really enjoy mostly dates from before the mid-fifties: the early novels, some poems, 'Waiting for Godot'. The uncompromisingly bleak view of life is there, but together with a vividness of language, a sense of the complexity of life and a bitter humour that makes him one of the greatest comic writers of the day, an aspect of his art almost entirely ignored by dedicated exponents of his Weltanschauung. I find too little of these qualities in the writing of the past 10 years, and while I admire him for the way he's undeviatingly ploughed his lonely furrow, ever deeper and narrower, finding increasingly precise forms for his austere vision, his recent work engages me scarcely at all. Furthermore, the numerous enthusiastic explications I've read have done little to change my opinion. Driven into the corner by Beckett devotees, I'm forced to say that minimal art usually excites only minimal interest in me or to declare naively that life just isn't like that. But what I really mean is that Beckett has moved into an abstract world of unchallengeable assertion. A writer with whom he might be compared is Conrad, whose view of the human condition was not one whit less pessimistic or stoical, but who always recognized, formally and psychologically, the complexities of individual experience and the possibility of alternative interpretations. I don't find this in the later Beckett. Nonetheless he remains a formidable, courageous figure, with whose work anyone else writing today must come to terms.

French's remarks - though they would be forcefully chal-
lenged by Beckett's admirers - are a reasonable summary of
the opinions of many people in the late 1960s. If a writer
as fiercely pessimistic and as formally uncompromising as
Beckett did not elicit such responses, one could suspect a
conspiracy of silence.

After 1969, however, the coarseness of much early criticism was less often exhibited and Beckett's writing was
customarily treated with respect. The old hostility was
likely to give way to passive misunderstanding or to rejection on the grounds of taste and temperament; admiration could sometimes result in solemnity, fanciful mis-
reading, praise for the wrong reasons, or simple-minded,
unquestioning acceptance; but criticism was generally more
alive to the nature and implications of Beckett's achievement. Among his best commentators even work admitted to
be minor was often discussed with a sensitivity to intention and an alertness to detail that could only have been
earned by a major writer (see Raymond Federman on 'Film'
(No. 60) and David Lodge on 'Ping' (No. 63)).

And yet the critical response to one important work
that appeared after the Nobel Prize suggested some of the
ways in which encountering Beckett would continue to be a
disturbing, unforgettable experience. When 'Not I' was
first performed at the Lincoln Center Beckett Festival on
22 November 1972, there was much that the New York audience could find familiar. The image of the raw, ever-
jabbering Mouth and her cloaked and hooded Auditor were
reminiscent of other Beckett diminishments: dustbins
housing parents, urns encasing adulterers, earth devouring Winnie. The narrator - a voice-tormented voice confessional and evasive - revealed long cultivated obsessions: the simultaneously expressed desire to achieve self-
knowledge and to avoid it; and an anguish obscurely related to a lifelong absence of love. Some people who had
read 'The Unnamable' might have recalled Beckett's promise
of twenty years earlier to 'carry if necessary this process of compression to the point of abandoning all other
postulates.... Evoke at painful junctures, when discouragement threatens to raise its head, the image of a vast
cretinous mouth, red, blubber and slobbering, in solitary
confinement, extruding indefatigably, with a noise of wet
kisses and washing in a tub, the words that obstruct it.'

When the first reviews appeared, however, it was clear
that the critics were emotionally overwhelmed by Beckett's
work, but not at all sure about the nature of its distinction. Writing in the 'New York Times' (23 November 1972,
49), Clive Barnes announced that Beckett's new play 'lasts
about 15 minutes and a lifetime,' and spent his entirely

affirmative review describing the effects of having been
assaulted by a verbal barrage - 'words, words, more words
per minute than Hamlet ever nightmared on - or James Joyce,
wandering as lonely as a Dublin crowd, ever drank.'
According to Barnes, though, the words meant little, only
the impact mattered. There was, however, a generalized
implication: the play was 'a squalid night-time cry against
the monstrous regiment of death ... the title is totally
explicit. The title is going to die - but Not I.'
  In the 'New Republic' (16 December 1972, 24), Stanley
Kauffmann compared the play to a piece of music and an
abstract painting: 'the tormented tone, the mysterious picture, these are what the play is "about", I think.... Out
of it all [Beckett] has fashioned a brief sharp visible
cry of loss.' Kauffmann offered the further view

> not provable as Beckett's intent but still one for
> which I'm grateful to him, that the blackness is the
> inside of the mind, the voice is that of 'she' herself,
> which 'she cannot' stop, and the hooded figure is a
> testament of failed control. A Freudian might call it
> a portrait of a wounded id and an impotent ego.

For Edith Oliver (No. 73), 'Not I' was 'an aural mosaic of
words' and 'about as densely packed as any 15 minutes I
can remember.' Admitting that the play has a 'stunning
impact upon the audience,' she argued that it was (and
should remain) shadowy and elusive. She did, however, try
to sketch the 'story' that emerged fitfully from the con-
vulsive monologue, and (as often happened in first reviews of Beckett) she got some of the facts wrong. She
thought, for instance, that the April morning on which the
old woman was mysteriously coerced into frenzied speech
was a sexual episode; and she confessed to being in the
dark about the title (unlike Clive Barnes who called the
title explicit and then mistook what it meant). Even when
the monologue is properly spoken very fast, it should at
least be clear that the speaker is the old woman being described, hiding from self-perception by refusing to say I.
  The only important New York critic who wrote unfavor-
ably about 'Not I' was John Simon ('Hudson Review,' Spring
1973, 185-6). After praising the Festival production of
'Happy Days,' Simon complained that far too much had been
discarded in the new piece:

> such minimalism is not, I believe, to be countenanced
> from anyone, not even from Beckett. Up to a point,
> Less may indeed be More; but beyond that point, Less is
> Nothing. It is all very well for Beckett to return the

drama to the Aeschylean essentials, but further back
than Aeschylus no one can go: the terrain there is not
merely uncharted it is no longer terrain.

And Simon concluded by quoting Eugene Ionesco's remarks to
Claude Bonnefoy:

Beckett's plays seem to be moving toward gimmickry.
It's as if now he were making concessions to *his* audience, the audience he formed.... He's no longer trying
to say what he has to say, but to find gimmicks that
will leave the audience gasping.... It's a permanent
succession of daredevil feats.

In defense of some of the New York reviewers, one
should grant that Mouth's monologue is extraordinarily
difficult to grasp on first hearing, and that Beckett himself told Jessica Tandy: 'I am not unduly concerned with
intelligibility. I hope the piece may work on the nerves
of the audience, not its intellect.' Yet - in responding
to Beckett's work, and to most other great writers' - the
nerves and the intellect best work together; and when 'Not
I' opened in London in January 1973, the strongest reviews were generally more precise about what Beckett's
words actually meant.
     Calling the play 'a small masterpiece' and 'the most
shattering theatre event of the entire London season,'
Robert Brustein ('Observer,' 21 January 1973) recognized
that the speaker was engaged in a 'denial of subjective
identity' in an effort to 'palliate the pain'; and he
accurately placed her in that Beckettian purgatory where
'blighted souls are doomed to re-enact their suffering,
half-conscious that this suffering has no end.' Most
other critics joined Brustein in testifying to the play's
terrifying evocation of psychological distress; the fullest, most helpful account being Benedict Nightingale's review in the 'New Statesman' (No. 74).
     The only extended negative commentary appeared in
'Encounter' (April 1973, 38-9). John Weightman compared
the experience of seeing 'Not I' to

finding oneself in a mental home and hearing a voice
raised in a wild rhythmical rant in the next room,
where some poor creature has lost the centre of her
being; poignant enough, while it lasts, but not a variegated aesthetic speech, like Winnie's monologue in
'Happy Days'.

Some months later, reviewing the printed text for the

'Sunday Times' (15 July 1973, 39), Christopher Ricks found
the speech variegated enough:

> 'Not I,' in its grinding of self deception against self-
> incrimination, in its profound bitterness at parent-
> hood, and in its merciless conception of destiny and of
> expiation, is a miniature 'Oedipus Rex.' The idea will
> not seem far-fetched to anyone who remembers how often
> Oedipus has haunted Beckett's writings. The theatrical
> experience was unforgettable, the preposterous horror
> of that lit-up socket pulsating like a psychedelic
> polyp.

IX

Perhaps the simplest, most concise way to describe Beckett's reputation in the first half of the 1970s is to say
that he continued to be a controversial classic. Having
spoken powerfully of dominant modern concerns in forms
that revolutionized fiction and the theatre, he was widely
recognized as one of the major European writers of the
century. For a generation that had long been 'thinking of
the unthinkable,' he created mysterious parables and
commanding myths about the old age of the human race: the
absence of God, of coherent systems, of physical suffic-
iency, of self-knowledge, and of a trustworthy language to
describe the supports and faculties people felt they no
longer had. What were left, of course, were physical
objects (hats, tapes, urns, stones, pencils, bicycles,
painkillers); the body collapsing endlessly into decrepitude and death; consciousness as goad, treasure house,
delirium; a heightened apprehension of vacancy; and words
as the suspect but necessary way to speak about the unspeakable. The roar inside Beckett's skull - expressed
with an amazing stylistic variety, demented humor and
philosophical suggestiveness - became for many people a
sombre music suited to their perceptions of mid-twentieth-
century life.
    But not for everyone. What was a Modernist symphony
for some listeners became 'Last Post' or 'Taps' for
others. Many people found Beckett's unremitting pessimism too constrictive, false to life's variousness - his
perturbation a neurosis not a vision. If he were a saint,
he belonged in the desert not amidst a congregation.
Others simply found his work too difficult or boring,
without the sensuous surface and range of thought and
feeling they expected in great art. His extraordinary
fame seemed to some a distressing symptom of a dying

culture, and his writings unlikely to hold the imagination
of the future.

Although the future can be left to come to its own
terms with Beckett, the arguments started during his own
lifetime are certain to continue. How should he best be
read: as myth-maker, comedian, parablist, philosopher, God-
hater, demystifier, stoic wit - if all of these, in what
proportions? Early Beckett, or late, and where does one
draw the line? What kind of man is that fanatic explorer
who changed the shape of the novel and the theatre? How
does he relate to the major cultural movements of his
time? Where are his deepest roots: in Dante, Descartes,
Dublin? Shakespeare, Paris, Swift, Joyce? his relationship
with his mother, with his own unconscious? Questions that
kept the past busy are likely to preoccupy the future.

'Proust'
(1931)

[Written in English; published by Chatto & Windus, London]

---

1. UNSIGNED REVIEW, 'TIMES LITERARY SUPPLEMENT'

2 April 1931, 274

Mr. Beckett's analysis of Proust is largely an analysis of
the nature and effect in Proust's work of 'that double-
headed monster of damnation and salvation - Time', with
its attributes 'Memory and Habit'. He skilfully summarizes
the Proustian distinction between 'involuntary memory' -
'this accidental and fugitive salvation in the midst of
life' - and 'voluntary memory', which he calls, typically,
'an application of a concordance to the Old Testament of
the individual', and proceeds to examine the fortuitous
occurrences of involuntary remembrance throughout Proust's
work, from the incident of the tea-steeped madeleine to
the final revelation beginning in the courtyard of the
Princesse de Guermantes. It is impossible here to do more
than sketch the main outline of Mr. Beckett's book; he
contrives to pack a great deal of subtle analysis into
seventy-two pages. His prose is compact, full of energy
and rich in valuable metaphors, such as this: 'The individual is the seat of a constant process of decantation,
decantation from the vessel containing the fluid of future
time, sluggish, pale and monochrome, to the vessel containing the fluid of past time, agitated and multicoloured
by the phenomena of its hours.'

2.   BONAMY DOBRÉE IN 'SPECTATOR'

18 April 1931, 641-2

Bonamy Dobrée (1891-1974), critic and professor of literature. Among his many books are 'The Lamp and the Lute' (1929), 'Modern Prose Style' (1934) and 'The Early 18th Century' (volume VII in the Oxford History of English Literature, 1959).

Mr. Beckett's little book on 'Proust' is a spirited piece of writing; but it is a good deal too 'clever,' and disfigured with pseudo-scientific jargon and philosophic snippets. For him Proust is an *auto-symbolist*. He deals with only one or two aspects ('read Blickpunkt for this miserable word'), says some good things, and is interesting on the Proustian time-concept. He does not tell us so much about Proust as Mr. Wilson does,(1) who would disagree with him when he says that Proust was in no way concerned with morals: for he is not so much concerned to probe the truth about Proust as to write sparklingly about him. Mr. Beckett obtrudes himself a little too much, and indulges in too many digressions. Still, for all its faults, it is an agreeable and stimulating pamphlet, if only because Mr. Beckett is obviously so hugely enjoying himself.

Note

1   The earlier part of Dobrée's review dealt with Edmund Wilson's 'Axel's Castle.' (Eds)

3.   F.S. FLINT IN 'CRITERION'

July 1931, 792

F.S. Flint (1855-1960), British poet, essayist, translator and civil servant. His principal works, 'In the Net of the Stars' (1909), 'Cadences' (1915) and 'Otherworld'

(1915), are important in the history of the Imagist movement.

If we could understand this essay, we might be able to
praise it. 'Exemption from intrinsic flux in a given
object,' writes Mr. Beckett, 'does not change the fact
that it is the correlative of a subject that does not
enjoy such immunity. The observer infects the observed
with his own mobility.'

'More Pricks than Kicks'
(1934)

[Written in English; published by Chatto & Windus, London.]

---

4. EDWIN MUIR IN 'LISTENER'

4 July 1934, 42

Edwin Muir (1887-1959), Scottish-born English poet, critic, and - with his wife Willa - translator of Kafka. His books include 'The Structure of the Novel' (1928), 'Essays on Literature and Society' (1949), 'Collected Poems' (1952) and 'An Autobiography' (1954).

'More Pricks than Kicks' is a book very difficult to de-scribe. It consists of a number of what may be called short stories about Belacqua, a young Dublin man. The incidents themselves do not matter much, though one of them concerns Belacqua's death. The point of the story is in the style of presentation, which is witty, extravagant and excessive. Mr. Beckett makes a great deal of every-thing; that is his art. Sometimes it degenerates into excellent blarney, but at its best it has an ingenuity and freedom of movement which is purely delightful. The author has been influenced by Mr. James Joyce, but the spirit in which he writes is rather that of Sterne, and he reduces everything, or raises it, as the case may be, to intellectual fantasy. He has the particularity of both writers; the toasting of a slice of bread, or the purchase and cooking of a lobster, can become matters of

intellectual interest and importance to him. He gives
again, like Sterne and Mr. Joyce, an intrinsic substance
and style to his dialogue; and although he does not nearly
come up to them, he does give us the feeling that his dialogue could go on for ever, and thus calls up a prospect
of endless diversion. The whole book is somewhat like
extremely good and calculated and quite impossible talk;
it wanders round the subject and delights us with its
wanderings. These divagations are in reality an exploration of a subtle and entertaining mind which is carried
out with great wit, and is very much worth following.

5.   UNSIGNED REVIEW, 'TIMES LITERARY SUPPLEMENT'

26 July 1934, 526

This odd book ... consists of nine episodes in the career
of a Dublin youth called Belacqua (the tenth episode is
devoted to his widow). In them we learn something of his
friends, his love affairs, his diversions, his abortive
attempt at suicide and his marriages. Belacqua is a queer
creature, a very ineffectual dilettante, much given to
introspection and constantly involved in clownish misfortunes. The humour which Mr. Beckett extracts from the
trivial and vulgar incidents which make up his career is
largely achieved by bringing to bear on them an elaborate
technique of analysis. Belacqua's preparations to eat a
cheese sandwich, well 'fomented' with mustard and salt,
occupy an important place in the first episode, which is
one of the best. This may indicate the perspective in
which Belacqua's affairs are viewed. An implicit effect
of satire is obtained by embellishing the commonplace with
a wealth of observation and sometimes erudition, alternat-
ed with sudden brusqueness. Belacqua is more of a theme
than a character, an opportunity for the exercise of a
picturesque prose style. Sometimes Mr. Beckett allows his
prose to run away with him. In a few of the episodes,
such as A Wet Night and Draff, the triviality of theme
is not redeemed by its treatment but aggravated by verbal
affectation. Part of Draff is transcribed from an earlier
prose piece of Mr. Beckett's which appeared in 'Transition' and showed strongly the influence of Mr. Joyce's
latest work - a dangerous model. There is still more than
the setting of 'Dubliners' to remind us of this writer,

but a comparison between the piece in 'Transition' and
the present book shows how much Mr. Beckett's work has
gained from discipline of his verbal gusto.

It is still a very uneven book; but there is a definite,
fresh talent at work in it, though it is a talent not yet
quite sure of itself. The chapter or episode which describes Belacqua in hospital, waiting for the doctors to
give him 'a new lease of apathy,' is perfect in its way,
and there are few pages not enlivened by Mr. Beckett's
gift for apt extravagance. His humour, with its curious
blend of colloquialism, coarseness and sophistication, is
unlikely to appeal to a large audience. His book sometimes invites us to compare Mr. Beckett with one of his
characters, an author, who thought out a very pretty joke
but could find no one subtle enough to appreciate it:
'The only thing he did not like about it was its slight
recondity.... Well, he must just put it into his book.'

'Murphy'
(1938)

[Written in English; published by Routledge, London.]

6. UNSIGNED REVIEW, 'TIMES LITERARY SUPPLEMENT'

12 March 1938, 172

It is difficult to give an adequate impression of this
book by summarizing its plot or events. One might explain
that its hero, Murphy, is an unemployed Irishman in London,
who lives on the difference between the cost of his lodgings and the amount he claims for them from his guardian;
that his mistress, Celia, is a prostitute who does her
best to make him look for work; that his Dublin friend,
Neary, loves a girl who loves Murphy, and they spend most
of the book looking for him; and that finally, but too
late, they track him to an asylum, where he has found a
congenial job as attendant. One might suggest Murphy's
attitude towards life by citing his admiration of the
lunatics whom he has to attend,

> his loathing of the text-book attitude towards them,
> the complacent scientific conceptualism that made con-
> tact with outer reality the index of mental well-
> being.... All this was duly revolting to Murphy, whose
> experience as a physical and rational being obliged him
> to call sanctuary what the psychiatrists called exile
> and to think of the patients not as banished from a
> system of benefits but as escaped from a colossal
> fiasco.

A synopsis of this kind, however, will not suggest the curious flavour of the book except perhaps to those who have read Mr. Beckett's earlier work, 'More Pricks than Kicks.' It is the author's method which is important, and though it is a method as old as Rabelais, Mr. Beckett's use of it is peculiarly his own. Erudition, violent wit and a large vocabulary are brought to his analysis of Murphy, and what his hero lacks in zest or liveliness is fully supplied by the manner in which his disposition is studied. The book creates its own world, an elaborate parody of the world we know, yet oddly real; it is a bur-lesque of a sophisticated kind, relying more on verbal dex-terity than on situation for its comic effects. This dex-terity is not quite enough to sustain one's interest from first to last; the book has its tedious moments, and one feels at times that the talent and knowledge it reveals deserve a theme of more depth and substance. It is, none the less, a very unusual and spirited performance.

7.   DYLAN THOMAS IN 'NEW ENGLISH WEEKLY'

17 March 1938, 454-5

Dylan Thomas (1914-53), Welsh poet and story writer. His 'Eighteen Poems' (1934) won him fame, and his subsequent volumes, 'The Map of Love' (1939), 'Deaths and Entrances' (1946), 'In Country Sleep' (1952), 'Under Milk Wood' (1954) and 'Adventures in the Skin Trade' (1955), estab-lished him as one of the major figures of contemporary literature. He was twenty-four when the following review appeared.

It is easy, flippant, and correct to say that Mr. Samuel Beckett - whose first, very imitative novel, 'More Pricks than Kicks,' I remember more by Joyce than chance - has not yet thrown off the influence of those writers who have made 'Transition' their permanent resting-place. But Mr. Beckett, who is a great legpuller and an enemy of obvious-ness, would hate to be reviewed by the cash-register system that deals in the currency of petty facts and penny praises, so if I do not straight-forwardly praise his new book 'Murphy,' for its obvious qualities - of energy,

hilarity, irony, and comic invention - then it is his
fault: he should never try to sell his bluffs over the
double counter. I must say that 'Murphy' is difficult,
serious, and wrong.

It is difficult because it is written in a style that
attempts to make up for its general verbosity by the difficulty of the words and phrases it uses for the sake of
particular economy, and because the story never quite
knows whether it is being told objectively from the inside
of its characters or subjectively from the outside. It is
serious because it is, mainly, the study of a complex and
oddly tragic character who cannot reconcile the unreality
of the seen world with the reality of the unseen, and who,
through scorn and neglect of 'normal' society, drifts into
the society of the certified abnormal in his search for 'a
little world.' Murphy is the individual ostrich in the
mass-produced desert.

I call the book wrong for many reasons. It is not
rightly what it should be, that is what Mr. Beckett intended it to be: a story about the conflict between the inside
and the outsides of certain curious people. It fails in
its purpose because the minds and the bodies of these
characters are almost utterly without relations to each
other. The Dublin Professor, whose mental adventures and
adventurous conversations are loud and lively and boister-
ous, is a slap-stick, a stuffed guy, when he moves; his
mind is Mr. Beckett's mind, and is full of surprises, but
his figure is that of the taped and typed 'eccentric
professor' of music-hall and cartoon. The Dublin tart
talks furiously and excessively, with a vocabulary like a
drunken don's; the street bookie can speak like this in a
pub, 'The syndrome known as life is too diffuse to admit
of palliation. For every symptom that is eased, another
is made worse. The horse leech's daughter is a closed
system. Her quantum of wantum cannot vary;' but tart and
bookie are no more than walking, gesticulating brains, and
the story fails because no-one can care at all what happens to their bodies. And much of the book is loosely
written; 'The imperturbable negligence of Providence to
provide money goaded them to such transports as West
Brompton had not known since the Earl's Court Exhibition,'
for instance.

The story begins in London, and progresses through a
conventional Dublin, where every tart is a crank and every
pub-bore a self-starter, to a series of obscure events in
lunatic-asylums and lodging-houses that might have been
created by P.G. Wodehouse, Dickens, and Eugene Jolas
working in bewildered collaboration. Mr. Beckett supposes
that he writes about the lowest strata of society, about

the dispossessed and the regardless-of-possession, but he
takes a most romantic view of it; he looks generously at
the dregs, and makes every dirty, empty tankard wink at
the brim; romantically he searches in the gutter for splen-
dour and, in every fool and villain he finds, substitutes
the gunpowder brain for the heart of gold.

And, lastly, Mr. Beckett's humour, for the book is
packed with it even in the most serious sections and the
most pathological discussions. Sometimes the humour is
like that of an Irish comic journalist forced to write in
an advanced Paris-American quarterly, sometimes like that
of an old-fashioned music-hall character-comedian attempting to alter his act for a pornographers' club. And
always it is Freudian blarney: Sodom and Begorrah.

8. KATE O'BRIEN IN 'SPECTATOR'

25 March 1938, 546

Kate O'Brien (1897-1974), Irish playwright and novelist.
Her play, 'Distinguished Villa,' was produced in 1926 and
her first novel, 'Without My Cloak,' won both the Haw-
thornden and the John Tait Black Prizes in 1931. Among
her later works are 'That Lady' (1946) and 'Teresa of
Avila' (1951).

Ireland, Russia, England and India attempt our entertainment in this week's list, and five novels more sharply
differentiated from each other it would be hard to
find.(1) All are definitely readable, informed with
intelligence and feeling, and presented efficiently, but
whereas honours, first, second or third, may clearly be
awarded to the three foreign entrants, the home country,
though presenting two of the five competitors, can only
be given a couple of passes this time.

'Murphy', at least for this humble examiner, sweeps all
before him. Rarely, indeed, have I been so entertained
by a book, so tempted to superlatives and perhaps hyper-
boles of praise. It truly is magnificent and a treasure -
if you like it. Quite useless to you, quite idiotic, if
you don't. It is a sweeping, bold record of an adventure
in the soul; it is erudite, allusive, brilliant, impudent

and rude. Rabelais, Sterne and Joyce - the last above
all - stir in its echoes, but Mr. Beckett, though moved
again and again to a bright, clear lyricism - as for the
kite-flying of Mr. Kelly in the park, or always for Celia,
lovely, classic figure - is not like Joyce evocative of
tragedy or of hell. He is a magnificently learned sceptic,
a joker overloaded with the scholarship of great jokes.
There are two ways for the man in the street to read him -
the one, which has been mine at first reading, is to sweep
along, acknowledging points lost by lack of reference in
oneself, but seeing even in darkness the skirts of his
tantalising innuendo, and taking the whole contentedly, as
a great draught of brilliant, idiosyncratic commentary, a
most witty, wild and individualistic refreshment. If he
takes it so, with modesty and without a fuss, the sympathetic reader will be amply rewarded by the gusts of his
own laughter, by the rich peace of his response to Murphy's
flight from the macrocosm into the microcosm of himself
and his own truth, and by the glorious fun of his world's
pursuit of him - Neary, Wylie, Miss Counihan - never has
there been a more amusing presentation in fiction than
Miss Counihan - and the sweet, classic Celia. There is no
plot, as novel-readers mean plot, but there is a glorious,
wild story, and it is starred all over with a milky way of
sceptic truths. And read once simply and sportingly as it
flies, this book is then to be read again, very slowly,
with as many pauses as may be to pursue the allusions and
decorations which may have had to be guessed at in first
flight. There is no more to be said. One can only hope -
being eager for the gladdening, quickening and general
toning up of readers' wits - that a very great number of
people will have the luck and the wit to fall upon
'Murphy' and digest it. For the right readers it is a book
in a hundred thousand. My own great pleasure in it is not
least in the certainty that I shall read it again and again
before I die.

Note

1   The other books reviewed were 'The Mountain and the
    Stars' by Valentin Tikhanov, 'The Time of Wild Roses'
    by Doreen Wallace, 'The Larches' by John Hampson and
    L.A. Pavey, and 'Kanthapura' by Raja Rao. (Eds)

'Molloy'
(1951)

[Written in French; published by Éditions de Minuit, Paris; translated into English by Patrick Bowles and Beckett; published by Olympia Press, Paris, 1955, and Grove Press, New York, 1955.]

---

9. MAURICE NADEAU IN 'COMBAT'

12 April 1951

Maurice Nadeau (b. 1911), French critic and editor, is known as a discoverer of new talent. He was one of the first to write about Samuel Beckett in France, and has reviewed most of his novels. He is the author of numerous books, among these, 'Littérature présente' (1952), 'Le Roman Français depuis la guerre' (1963) and 'Histoire du Surréalisme' (1964).

> And truly it matters little what I say, this or that or any other thing. Saying is inventing. Wrong, very rightly wrong. You invent nothing, you think you are inventing, you think you are escaping, and all you do is stammer out your lesson, the remnants of a pensum one day got by heart and long forgotten, life without tears, as it is wept. To hell with it anyway.

This disillusioned and strong statement is the best definition of the intentions and style of an author who will very probably be heard about in the coming months: the

Irishman Samuel Beckett, who has however a well-deserved
reputation of being difficult, obscure, disconcerting.

He was born in Dublin in 1906. He was James Joyce's
friend and favorite disciple. He is mostly known as a
translator, even though his translations are not well-
known (but famous ones, to which he has not put his name,
such as that of Anna Livia Plurabelle, are attributed to
him). Settled in France since 1938, he has rewritten in
our language and published in 1947, his first work,
'Murphy,' which went unnoticed, although, the same year, a
short story which he gave to 'Fontaine,' L'Expulsé (The
Expelled), earned him a reputation. 'Molloy' was written
directly in French. With remarkable boldness, the Éditions
de Minuit are undertaking the publication of his complete
works.

It is through The Expelled that one should approach
Beckett, never clearer nor more disturbing than in that
piece. It is the story, told in the first person, of a
man who has been brutally thrown out of his home by an
irascible landlord. He gets himself taken on an aimless
ride throughout the city by a cabman, with whom he develops
a fellowship, and who finally gives him shelter, for the
night, in his shed. At dawn he runs away and starts wandering again, going east 'the quicker to come into the
light.' This adventure, told with zest, and full of a
somewhat Kafkaesque brand of humor, either has little
meaning or includes all meanings, although in this case
our flight toward symbolic areas is hampered by this
apparently insignificant final remark: 'I don't know why I
told this story. I could just as well have told another.
Perhaps some other time I'll be able to tell another.
Living souls, you will see how alike they are.' Indeed
'Murphy' which, this time, has the size of a novel, is
also the story of a quest. Of a double quest, the object
of which disappears, as one seems to get closer to it; and
leaving us similarly in doubt as to the author's intentions. On the one hand a young man, Murphy, whose well-
established aim is to spend his life doing nothing and who,
in order to escape temptations, has had himself tied to a
rocking-chair where he indulges in the most extravagant
daydreams, finds himself obliged to seek a position in
order to deserve the hand of a prostitute of whom he has
become enamoured. On the other hand, at least three
characters, not including his peculiar fiancée, intend to
lay hands upon him: a passionate and sentimental virgin,
herself courted and hard pressed by Murphy's two friends:
Neary and Wylie.

Such a plot resembles Schnitzler's 'La Ronde' or René
Clair's 'Million' but in a more complex form, each

character following his own, mysterious way, which inevitably loses itself in the labyrinth of the ways followed by
the others. In the end, we are in an impenetrable network
of comical or odd situations which the characters themselves, all their efforts notwithstanding, are unable to
disentangle, and of course everybody is frustrated. Murphy
kills himself after finding his peace of mind among the
insane, where he had obtained employment, and leaves
behind some odd provisions in his will. He asks that his
ashes be dropped in 'the necessary house' of a famous
theatre in Dublin during the performance of a piece and
that the flush should be pulled and 'repaired if necessary
for that purpose.' They suffer a hardly less enviable
fate: wrapped up, they are thrown at a customer's face in
a pub where one of the characters has ended up and got
drunk. They are swept up the next morning 'with the sand,
the beer, the butts, the glass, the matches, the spit, the
vomit.'

This sacrilegious outcome gives an idea of the tone of
the work, in which humor, cerebral subtlety and ironic
complexity hardly manage to disguise tragedy. Not only, it
goes without saying, is man for Beckett alone thrown into
a meaningless world, but in addition, there is not one of
his attempts, not one of his thoughts, not one of his
feelings which is not based on illusion or mistake. No
sooner is a plan conceived than it is corrupted at the
start and turns into its opposite. Betrayed by life,
others, our own body, our most personal thoughts, our most
passionate feelings, we wander aimlessly in the night and
are condemned to wander there, without any hint of greatness to redeem this wretched situation. In a formula which
defies decency, and of which my pen refuses to spell out
all the terms, Beckett writes, this time in 'Molloy,' that
we are in the muck and we never do anything but change
muck, where we flutter like a butterfly. In the forest of
obscure symbols through which the author takes us, here is
at least a clear path.

Murphy tried to escape from the world, his body, his
mind. Did he kill himself because he managed to do so, or
on the contrary because he failed? One does not know.
Still one would not understand anything in the next work,
'Molloy,' were one to neglect the strange geography which
Murphy maps out of his mind, into which he at first hoped
to retire. The first zone is that of the 'light' where 'a
radiant abstract of the dog's life' takes shape; the second
one is that of the 'half-light,' a zone of 'esthetic pleasure' where 'a system which has no other mode in which to
be out of joint and therefore does not need to be put
right' is created; the third, toward which he aims, is that

of 'the dark,' 'a flux of forms, a perpetual coming
together and falling asunder of forms, nothing but forms
becoming and crumbling into the fragments of a new becoming, without love or hate or any intelligible principle of change. Here he was not free, but a mote in the
dark of absolute freedom, a missile without provenance or
target, caught up in a tumult of non-Newtonian motion.'
In 'Molloy' it is this zone of the dark which the hero and
his creator are exploring.

An obscure work therefore, a second, a third reading of
which makes the meanings that one wanted to see it assume
even more improbable. Product of an insane or inspired
mind (one dares not say), it is a monument which is destroyed as it is built under our eyes and which finally
vanishes into dust or smoke. Defiance here is all-
embracing and dynamic. It even extends to the language
which, to use a fashionable verb, dissolves into nothingness (annihilates itself) as soon as it is established,
erases instantly its faintest traces. Where other novelists lightheartedly write: 'It rains'; Beckett writes:
'It rains. No, it does not rain.' Every one of his
assertions is thus coupled with a contradictory, no less
strong and no less credible assertion, so that in the end
one is no longer even in the realm of the ridiculous where
for instance The Expelled or 'Murphy' were set, but in a
vacuum marked with a plus sign. Beckett settles us in the
world of the Nothing where some nothings which are men
move about for nothing. The absurdity of the world and
the meaninglessness of our condition are conveyed in an
absurd and deliberately insignificant fashion: never did
anybody dare so openly to insult everything which man
holds as certain, up to and including this language which
he could at least lean upon to scream his doubt and despair. For the author, it is too much even to talk and
to try, using that swing of words denied as soon as
uttered to elucidate something. No human sound can express 'these wastes where true light never was, nor any
upright thing, nor any true foundation, but only these
leaning things, forever lapsing and crumbling away, beneath a sky without memory of morning or hope of night.'

It is therefore rather unimportant to relate the thread
of a story, or rather of two stories without obvious links
between them, in which all the events are controversial,
the characters are not sure of being alive and deny their
own words. Besides, these curiously parallel stories do
not lead anywhere.

In the first one, Molloy is speaking. He has lost his
memory, one of his legs and soon both are paralyzed; he
wants to go to see his mother, although we see him at her

bedside, and he does not know himself whether she is alive or dead. In order to cover the few hundred yards which separate him from her, he gets on his bicycle, leaves and will never arrive. We see him at the police station where his contempt for traffic rules has brought him, at a widow's whose dog he has run over and who has taken him in; in the depth of the country, miles from the town; in a forest where, starving, having lost his bicycle and no longer able to walk, he drags himself deliberately in circles on his stomach and elbows. Through pure chance, he reaches the edge of the forest, but only to let himself drop into a ditch. We will hear no more about him.

The second story is told by one Jacques Moran, whom a mysterious messenger orders to find Molloy. How and to what end? Moran does not know. He sets off with his young son in the direction of the same city and finds himself, too, struck with paralysis in one leg. He sends his son to get him a bicycle, murders somebody he happens to meet, sets off again on the carrier of the bicycle which, one morning, disappears together with the son. The messenger then orders him to go back home, where he eventually returns, months later, after the worse sufferings. If he failed in his mission, at least he got back to port. But only to find his home deserted, and after having himself gone down all the degrees which lead to inhumanity. On the way, he has unlearnt the language of men and, formerly a good Catholic, he now no longer believes in anything. 'I have been a man long enough,' he says cryptically, 'I shall not put up with it any more, I shall not try any more.' Does this mean that he has found elsewhere a kind of wisdom or truth? Nothing is less sure. He still expresses himself like Molloy and like Beckett: 'It is midnight. The rain is beating on the windows. It was not midnight. It was not raining.'

After that, should one attempt to draw a conclusion? Were we presumptuous enough to believe that our summaries allow us to do so, Samuel Beckett's smallest sentence, his very special approach and his agonizing, unrelenting quest should certainly prevent us from so doing. In whichever way one seeks to define the border case he represents in today's literature, one can only betray him, and even more seriously by interpretation than by analysis. Ironic genius, subtle charmer, humorist besides which the most famous black humorists pale, champion of the Nothing exalted to the height of the Whole, and conversely, giant conqueror of an elusive reality, he took us along with him into his forest. We too will only come out of it on our elbows and our knees. It will take years.

[Translated by Françoise Longhurst]

10. GEORGES BATAILLE IN 'CRITIQUE'

15 May 1951, 387-96

Georges Bataille (1897-1962), French novelist, essayist,
founder of the famed review 'Critique,' was the author of
several novels, 'Madame Edwarda' (1956), 'Le Bleu du ciel'
(1957), 'Ma Mère' (1963), and many other books of essays,
'L'Expérience intérieure' (1943), 'Sur Nietzsche' (1945),
'La Littérature et le mal' (1957), 'Les Larmes d'Eros'
(1961). He was among the first to recognize Samuel
Beckett's talent in France.

What the author of 'Molloy' has to tell us is, if you
please, the most unabashedly unbearable story in the
world: nothing in it but an exorbitant imagination; the
whole thing is fantastic, extravagant, sordid to be sure,
but of a wonderful sordidness; to be more precise,
'Molloy' is a sordid wonder. No other story could be so
necessary and so convincing at the same time; what
'Molloy' reveals is not simply reality but reality in its
pure state: the most meagre and inevitable of realities,
that fundamental reality continually soliciting us but
from which a certain terror always pulls us back, the
reality we refuse to face and into which we must ceaselessly struggle not to sink, known to us only in the
elusive form of anguish.

If I were indifferent to cold, hunger, and the myriad
difficulties that overwhelm a man when he abandons himself to nature, rain, and the earth, to the immense quick-
sand of the world and of things, I myself would be the
character Molloy. I can say something more about him, and
that is that both you and I have met him: seized by a terrified longing, we have encountered him on street corners,
an anonymous figure composed of the inevitable beauty of
rags, a vacant and indifferent expression, and an ancient
accumulation of filth; he was *being*, *defenseless* at last,
an enterprise, as we all are, that had ended in shipwreck.

There is in this reality, the essence or residue of
being, something so *universal*, these complete *vagabonds* we
occasionally encounter but immediately *lose* have something
so essentially indistinct about them, that we cannot
imagine anything more anonymous. So much so that this
name *vagabond* I have just written down misrepresents them.

But that of *wretch*, which has perhaps the advantage over
the other of an even greater indeterminacy, is equally a
misrepresentation. What we have here is so assuredly the
essence of being (but this expression alone, 'essence of
being,' could not determine the *thing*) that we need not
hesitate: to *this*, we cannot give a name, it is indistinct, necessary, and elusive, quite simply, it is *silence*.
This thing we name through sheer impotence *vagabond* or
wretch, which is actually *unnamable* (but then we find ourselves entangled in another word, *unnamable*), is no less
mute than death. Thus we know in advance that the attempt
to speak to this phantom haunting the streets in broad
daylight is futile. Even if we knew something about the
precise circumstances and conditions of his life (?) and
his wretchedness, we would have made no headway: this man,
or rather this being whose speech, sustaining him, might
have made him human - whatever speech subsists or rather
exhausts itself in him no longer sustains him, and similarly, speech no longer reaches him. Any conversation we
might have with him would be only a phantom, an appearance of conversation. It would delude us, referring us to
some appearance of humanity, to something other than this
absence of humanity heralded by the derelict dragging himself through the streets, who fascinates us.(1)

We should make this essential point clear: there is no
reason to think that Samuel Beckett meant to describe this
'essence of being' or this 'absence of humanity' I have
been speaking of. It even seems to me unlikely that he
intended Molloy to be a typical vagabond (or whatever
unnamable thing this name indicates), in the same way that
Molière intended Harpagon to be a typical miser, Alceste
a typical misanthrope. To tell the truth, we hardly know
anything about the intentions of Molloy's creator, and on
the whole, what we do know about him amounts to nothing.
Born in 1906, Irish, he was a friend of Joyce, and has
even remained his disciple to some extent. His friend-
ships - or his relations - place him, it seems, in the
milieu Joyce was familiar with in France. Before the war
he wrote a novel in English, but at the same time published his own French translation, and, being bilingual,
he seems to have a decided preference for French. The
obvious influence of Joyce on Beckett, however, is far
from being the key to the latter. At most the two writers
show a similar interest in the chaotic possibilities given
in the free - nevertheless controlled and composed, yet
violent - play of language. And certainly this sort of
confidence, with one eye open perhaps but apparently un-
seeing, in the creative violence of language locates precisely the abyss that separates Beckett from Molière.

But after all, would not this abyss be similar to the one
that separates the misanthrope or the miser from the
absence of humanity and the *amorphous* personality of
Molloy? Only an unrestrained flow of language would have
the power to achieve this absence (this lack of restraint,
this flow would themselves be equivalent to a negation, to
the absence of that 'discourse' that gives to the figures
of miser and misanthrope the completed *form* without which
we would be unable to imagine them). And conversely, it
may be that the freedom of a writer who no longer reduces
writing to a means of expressing his meaning, who consents to respond to possibilities present, though chaotic-
ally mingled, in those deep currents that flow through the
oceanic agitation of words, results of its own accord,
yielding to the weight of destiny, in the *amorphous* figure
of *absence*.

'All I know,' says Molloy (or the author), 'is what the
words know, and the dead things, and that makes a handsome
little sum, with a beginning, a middle and an end as in
the well-built phrase and the long sonata of the dead.
And truly it little matters what I say, this or that or
any other thing. Saying is inventing. Wrong, very
rightly wrong. You invent nothing, you think you are
inventing, you think you are escaping, and all you do is
stammer out your lesson, the remnants of a pensum one day
got by heart and long forgotten, life without tears, as it
is wept.' This is not a school's manifesto, not a manifesto at all but one expression, among others, of movements that go beyond any school and that want literature,
finally, to make language into a façade, eroded by the
wind and full of holes, that would possess the authority
of ruins.

Thus, without, or because of, and even for lack of
having intended to do so, literature as inevitably as
death - compelled by the imperative necessity characteristic of every road that leads to a summit and that no
longer allows any room for choice - leads to the fathomless misery of 'Molloy.' This irresistible movement seems
to follow the most arbitrary of whims, yet it is governed
by the weight of fatality. Language is what determines
this regulated world, whose significations provide the
foundation for our cultures, our activities and our relations, but it does so in so far as it is reduced to a
means of these cultures, activities and relations; freed
from these servitudes, it is nothing more than a deserted
castle whose gaping cracks let in the wind and rain: it is
no longer the signifying word, but the defenseless expression death wears as a disguise.

A disguise nevertheless. Death itself would be that

final silence that has never been attenuated by its imit-
ations. Literature, on the other hand, lines up a torrent
of incongruous words next to silence. Though it allegedly
conveys the same meaning as death, this silence is only a
parody of the latter. Nor is it, moreover, genuine language: it is even possible that *literature* may have the
same fundamental meaning as silence, but it recoils before
the final step that silence would be. Likewise this Molloy, who is its incarnation, is not precisely a dead man.
The profound apathy of death, its indifference to every
possible thing, is apparent in him, but this apathy would
encounter in death itself its own limit. The interminable
meandering in the forest of this death's equivalent on
crutches is, nevertheless, different from death in one
respect: that out of habit, or for the sake of persevering
more diligently in death and in the amorphous negation of
life - in the same way that literature is in the end silence in its negation of meaningful language, but remains
what it is, literature - the *death* of Molloy is *in* this
death-obsessed life, in which not even the desire to for-
sake it is permitted.

'But did it make such a difference after all, as far as
the pain was concerned,' says Molloy (disturbed though not
distressed by an aggravation of his infirmities), 'whether
my leg was free to rest or whether it had to work? I
think not. For the suffering of the leg at rest was constant and monotonous. Whereas the leg condemned to the
increase of pain inflicted by work knew the decrease of
pain dispensed by work suspended, the space of an instant.
But I am human, I fancy, and my progress suffered, from
this state of affairs, and from the slow and painful progress it had always been, whatever may have been said to
the contrary, was changed, saving your presence, to a
veritable calvary, with no limit to its stations and no
hope of crucifixion, though I say it myself, and no Simon,
and reduced me to frequent halts. Yes, my progress reduced me to stopping more and more often, it was the only
way to progress, to stop. And though it is no part of my
tottering intentions to treat here in full, as they deserve, these brief moments of the immemorial expiation, I
shall nevertheless deal with them briefly, out of the
goodness of my heart, so that my story, so clear till now,
may not end in darkness, the darkness of these towering
forests, these giant fronds, where I hobble, listen, fall,
rise, listen and hobble on, wondering sometimes, need I
say, if I shall ever see again the hated light, at least
unloved, stretched palely between the last boles, and my
mother, to settle with her, and if I would not do better,
at least just as well, to hang myself from a bough, with

a liane. For frankly light meant nothing to me now, and
my mother could scarcely be waiting for me still, after so
long. And my leg, my legs. But the thought of suicide
had little hold on me, I don't know why, I thought I did,
but I see I don't....'

It goes without saying that so faithful an attachment
to life can only be unreasonable; indeed it is pointless
to mention that the object of this fidelity is really
death: this would only mean something if death - or existence in death - or death in existence - meant anything;
now the only meaning in all this lies in the fact that
nonsense in its own way makes sense, a parody of meaning,
perhaps, but finally a distinct meaning, which is to obscure within us the world of significations. Such in fact
is the blind purpose of this brisk narrative, borne at
length by such an unquenchable verve that we read it with
no less impatient interest than a thrilling adventure
novel.

Lasciate ogni speranza voi qu'entrate.... [Abandon all
hope, ye that enter....]

Such could well be the epigraph for this absolutely
striking book, whose exclamation, uninterrupted by paragraphs, explores with unflinching irony the extreme possibilities of indifference and misery. An isolated passage gives only a lifeless, feeble impression of this vast
journey, which the narrative paradoxically arranges into
an immense, shattering epic, borne along in an irresistible, inhuman onrush (as a matter of fact it is difficult
to take Molloy at his word when he chances to call himself
human, for in the depths of misery, he monstrously allows
himself the incongruity, obscenity and moral indifference
that all of *humanity*, anxious and afflicted with
scruples, would deny themselves). *Abandon all hope...*,
frankly speaking, is accurate only in one sense, and the
violence of irony imposes itself almost as soon as these
funereal words are pronounced. For at the very moment
when he is limping along, brutalized by the police, mol-
ested, Molloy notes its precise limit: 'While still putting my best foot foremost,' he says in his naïveté, 'I
gave myself up to that golden moment, as if I had been
someone else. It was the hour of rest, the forenoon's
toil ended, the afternoon's to come. The wisest perhaps,
lying in the squares or sitting on their doorsteps, were
savouring its languid ending, forgetful of recent cares,
indifferent to those at hand. ...Was there one among them
to put himself in my place, to feel how removed I was then
from him I seemed to be, and in that remove what strain,
as of hawsers about to snap? It's possible. Yes, I was

straining towards those spurious deeps, their lying promise of gravity and peace, from all my old poisons I
struggled towards them, safely bound. Under the blue sky,
under the watchful gaze. Forgetful of my mother, set free
from the act, merged in this alien hour, saying, Respite,
respite.' Strictly speaking it would have been more effective to let this aspect remain implicit: I do not mean
to say that the book would have definitely gained by this,
but there are one or two brilliant phrases here that are
out of tune. The reader's own subtlety of perception
could have come to his assistance: that subtlety would
have responded to the failure inherent in all of literature, which only with difficulty and in a burst of brutal
naïveté overcomes the movement that draws it towards confusion. In part this passage is flawed, out of place,
but it provides us with the key to the narrative, in which
the tension that rivets us to depression never lets up.
Certainly, here all reasonable _hopes_ and plans are engulf-
ed in indifference. But perhaps it is to be assumed that,
in the moment given here, within the limits of this present time, there is nothing that matters, nothing that
could matter. Nothing, not even a persistent feeling of
inferiority, not even a destiny linking the hero to an
expiation of his sins, which could in no way abase or humi-
liate him: it pursues its course doggedly, without anxiety, in an obstinate silence: 'But perhaps I was mistaken,
perhaps I would have been better advised to stay in the
forest, perhaps I could have stayed there, without remorse, without the painful impression of committing a
fault, almost a sin. For I have greatly sinned, at all
times, greatly sinned against my prompters. And if I cannot decently be proud of this I see no reason either to be
sorry. But imperatives are a little different, and I have
always been inclined to submit to them, I don't know why.
For they never led me anywhere, but tore me from places
where, if all was not well, all was no worse than anywhere
else, and then went silent, leaving me stranded. So I
knew my imperatives well, and yet I submitted to them. It
had become a habit. It is true they nearly all bore on
the same question, that of my relations with my mother,
and on the importance of bringing as soon as possible some
light to bear on these and even on the kind of light that
should be brought to bear and the most effective means of
doing so. Yes, these imperatives were quite explicit and
even detailed until, having set me in motion at last, they
began to falter, then went silent, leaving me there like a
fool who neither knows where he is going nor why he is
going there.' In the end this expiation, to which Molloy
is submissive, requires him to leave the forest as quickly

as possible. Although it eludes him every time he becomes aware of it, it imposes itself upon him with such
convincing force that in his bewilderment there is nothing
he will not do to obey it. No longer able to walk, he
continues his journey crawling like a slug: 'Flat on my
belly, using my crutches like grapnels, I plunged them
ahead of me into the undergrowth, and when I felt they had
a hold, I pulled myself forward, with an effort of the
wrists. For my wrists were still quite strong, fortunately, in spite of my decrepitude, though all swollen and
racked by a kind of chronic arthritis probably. That then
briefly is how I went about it. The advantage of this
mode of locomotion compared to others, I mean those I have
tried, is this, that when you want to rest you stop and
rest, without further ado. For standing there is no rest,
nor sitting either. And there are men who move about
sitting, and even kneeling, hauling themselves to right
and left, forward and backward, with the help of hooks.
But he who moves in this way, crawling on his belly, like
a reptile, no sooner comes to rest than he begins to rest,
and even the very movement is a kind of rest, compared to
other movements, I mean those that have worn me out. And
in this way I moved onward in the forest, slowly, but with
a certain regularity, and I covered my fifteen paces, day
in, day out, without killing myself. And I even crawled
on my back, plunging my crutches blindly behind me into
the thickets, and with the black boughs for sky to my closing eyes. I was on my way to mother. And from time to
time I said, Mother, to encourage me I suppose. I kept
losing my hat, the lace had broken long ago, until in a
fit of temper I banged it down on my skull with such violence that I couldn't get it off again. And if I had met
any lady friends, if I had had any lady friends, I would
have been powerless to salute them correctly.'

But, you may say, this sordid extravagance is of little
importance, these immense phantasmagorias bore us, they
leave us strictly cold. This is possible. But there is a
primary reason why this absence of interest is not necessarily justifiable: the power and passion of the author
force us to become brutally convinced of the contrary.
This frantic progress toward ruin that animates the book,
which, being the author's attack on the reader, is such
that not for an instant is the latter given the leisure to
withdraw into indifference - could it have been produced
if so persuasive a conviction did not originate in some
powerful motive?
    As I have said, we have no right to assume that the
author began with a detailed plan in mind. Doubtless the

birth we should attribute to 'Molloy' is not that of a
scholarly composition, but rather the only one that would
be suitable to the elusive reality I have been speaking
of, that of a myth - monstrous, and arising from the slumber of reason. There are two analogous truths that can
only take shape in us in the form of a myth, these being
death and that 'absence of humanity' that is death's
living semblance. Such absences of reality may not indeed
be present in the clear-cut distinctions of discourse, but
we may be sure that neither death nor inhumanity, both
non-existing, can be considered irrelevant to the existence that we are, of which they are the boundary, the
backdrop, and the ultimate truth. Death is not simply
that sort of concealed base on which anguish rests: the
void into which misery plunges everything, if the latter
absorbs us completely and we decompose, is none other than
death, object of that horror whose positive aspect is full
humanity. Thus this horrible figure painfully swinging
along on his crutches is the truth that afflicts us and
that follows us no less faithfully than our own shadows:
it is fear of this very figure that governs our human gestures, our erect postures and our clear phrases. And,
conversely, this figure is in some way the inevitable
grave that in the end will draw this parade of humanity
into itself to be buried: it is oblivion, impotence....
It is not unhappiness, at the end of its strength, that
succumbs to misfortune, but rather indifference, in which
a man forgets even his own name, perfect indifference to
the most loathsome misery. 'Yes, there were times when I
forgot not only who I was, but that I was, forgot to
be.' Thus Molloy's thought, or absence of thought,
evaporates.... And yet this is a bit of chicanery.
Molloy or rather the author is *writing:* he is writing and
what he writes is that the will to write is slipping away
from him.... Never mind that he tells us 'I have always
behaved like a pig.' There is not a single human prohi-
bition that has not been swallowed up in an indifference
that would like to be definitive and is not, but even
being limited to a limping, imperfect indifference, how
can one after all not be indifferent? If the author goes
back on his decision to 'behave like a pig,' admits that
he has been lying and ends his book with these words:
'Then I went back into the house and wrote, It is midnight. The rain is beating on the windows. It was not
midnight. It was not raining.' - it is simply because he
is not Molloy: Molloy would in fact admit *nothing,* because he would write *nothing.*

An author writing while consumed with indifference to what

he writes might seem to be acting out a charade; yet is
not the mind that discovers this pretence also engaged in
pretenses - every bit as fallacious, but with the naïveté
of unawareness? The truth, stripped of pretenses, is not
to be so easily attained, for before we can attain it we
must not only renounce our own pretenses, but forget
everything, no longer know anything, be Molloy: an impotent idiot, 'not knowing what [he] was going to do until it
was done.' All we can do is to set out ourselves in
search of Molloy, as does the Jacques Moran of the second
part of the book. This character, non-existing as it
were, whose dutiful nature and selfish widower's idiosyn-
cracies have something hopeless about them, is the hero of
the second part, in which Molloy has disappeared but Moran
is sent out to look for him. As though the overwhelming
figure of the first part had not sufficiently represented
the silence of this world, the impotent search of the
second seems to correspond to the need to deliver the universe wholly over to absence, since Molloy is more precisely not to be found than present. But Moran in search
of the inaccessible Molloy, slowly stripped of everything,
becoming more and more infirm, little by little will be
reduced in turn to the same repulsive ambulation as Molloy
in the forest.

Thus *literature* necessarily gnaws away at existence and
the world, reducing to *nothing* (but this *nothing* is
horror) these steps by which we go along confidently from
one result to another, from one success to another. This
does not exhaust the possibilities available in literature. And it is certain that the use of words for other
than utilitarian ends leads in the opposite direction into
the domain of rapture, defiance, and gratuitous audacity.
But these two realms - horror and rapture - are closer to
one another than we have supposed. Would the joys of
poetry be accessible to someone who turns away from
horror, and would authentic despair be any different from
the 'golden moment' Molloy experiences at the hands of the
police?

[Translated by Jean M. Sommermeyer]

Note

1 I recall having had at an early age a long conversation
   with a *vagabond*. It lasted the better part of a night
   I spent waiting for a train in a small station. He, of
   course, was not waiting for any train; he had simply
   taken shelter in the waiting-room, and he left me

towards morning to go to make some coffee over a camp-
fire. He was not precisely the sort of being I am
speaking of; he was even talkative, more so than I was,
perhaps. He seemed satisfied with his life, and being
an old man, amused himself by expressing his happiness
to the adolescent I was, listening to him with admiration. Yet the memory he left with me, and the amazed
terror it still arouses in me, continue to remind me of
the silence of animals. (This encounter impressed me
so deeply that soon afterwards I began to write a novel
in which a man who has met him in the countryside kills
him, perhaps in hopes of gaining access to the animal-
ity of his victim.) On another occasion, while driving
with friends, we found in broad daylight, in a forest,
a man alongside the road stretched out on the grass
and, so to speak, in the water, in a pouring rain. He
was not asleep, perhaps he was ill; he did not respond
to our questions. We offered to drive him to a hospital: I seem to recall that he still did not answer,
or that if he bothered to respond, it was with a vague
grunt of refusal.

11.   JEAN POUILLON IN 'TEMPS MODERNES'

July 1951, 184-6

Jean Pouillon (b. 1921), French critic, was a regular
contributor to Jean-Paul Sartre's review, 'Temps
modernes.' He is the author of 'Le Temps et la littérature.'

If one finds this book strange, one has to judge it a
failure, because its aim is: evidence. For my part I did
not understand the critics' surprise - whether laudatory
or disparaging. This book reads like the novel it is; it
tells a story which *per se* is not so mysterious, and the
style is perfectly adapted to the author's purpose. But
maybe this is the real reason for surprise. Here indeed
we have a novel of the 'absurd,' to use a word which has
become convenient, which is presented like an ordinary
novel. Beckett does not respect the rules of the game!
Absurdity with him seems peaceful, even joyful or maybe

mischievous, and Molloy, this tramp, is of a far more
sedate disposition than many of our friends.   If he does
have disturbing and fascinating attributes, they can only
be seen properly if one first admits his clear vision of
things: absurdity is not mysterious at all, it is, as
Sartre wrote about 'L'Etranger,' 'nothing less than the
relationship of man to the world.' Already Camus had
presented his stranger like a man among others, living
everybody's life, while illusions and bad faith were on
the side of his judges and more generally of so-called
normal men, who are thus only because of this very will to
deceive themselves, to deny that the absurd is reality
itself.   But under the seeming objectivity of 'L'Etranger,'
an expedient was hidden.   Camus showed us his hero in such
a light that we could at the same time sympathize with him
and maintain our usual attitude of mind.   Hence the classical form of the tale, which was to make all the more
obvious the character's strangeness; things and behaviors
were shown to us as they always are, they were described
with a cautious realism, only their meaning was lacking
and it is this lack which was to generate the feeling of
the absurd.   The trouble is that the method, once revealed, greatly devalued the vision of the world which was
offered us.   If the absurd is such only in relation to a
norm which one has to deny for it to appear, one might say
that its very presence destroys the norm, but it also destroys itself: it then becomes only a word, hiding perhaps
an unavowed and therefore somewhat ridiculous nostalgia
for the disputed order, and defining the original situation of man to whom no values are given because it is he
who must establish them.   The absurd can even become the
sign of an obscure belief in order: everything will be
deemed void of meaning if it is assumed that meaning MUST
be GIVEN, if it is not understood that meaninglessness is
the first condition of meaning, if one still aspires, even
without admitting it to oneself, to a perfectly full meaning, excluding any meaninglessness.
     In other words, the absurd should not be separated from
the normal, or opposed to it like reality to illusion,
because in this logical game the terms are exchanged and
one does not really know who benefits by it.   One should
on the contrary recognize the lack of meaning in meaning
itself as an essential component.   This is what 'Molloy'
invites us to do.   Once again I do not see this tale as
devoid of meaning: one cannot possibly blame somebody who
wanted to be a tramp, to wander without any definite aim.
Anyway to say this - without any definite aim - is going
too far.   Molloy's wanderings correspond to certain preoccupations, even though he does not take much trouble to

make them fit together. But do we behave so differently?
The inconsistency of his plans becomes obvious more
quickly than ours, that is all; but it does not make any
difference to the final inconsistency of our intentions,
nor to the fact that he too looks for something. Similarly in the second part, one may wonder at the fact that
the man who in the end kills Molloy does not really ask
himself the questions which we would ask ourselves in his
place about his mission; he does ask himself questions,
however, only they are not the same ones. Moreover our
surprise stems mainly from the fact that he quickly
accepts the lack of answer, but the difference with us is
only one of degree: maybe we are only a little more skillful in covering up our ignorance, in extending our knowledge somewhat. In any case it is not really cleverness
which is involved. The truth is that Molloy puts little
persistency into what he does, little of that touching
and ridiculous obstinacy which makes us stick to our
goals for so long and so totally that we exhaust ourselves
in the process. He tries to find his mother, but if he
does not find her, well, so much the worse. He does not
give up his plan, but that plan remains up in the air,
vague, waiting for its author's good will. Usually we
rush headlong into our undertakings, they gain clarity,
precision, they get organized and constitute our world,
they are what exist, not us. It is true that we would not
exist without that impetus. But is it necessary that we
should absorb ourselves in it to that extent? Molloy
stays in-between. He sketches out behavior patterns, but
quickly drops them. One feels that he is looking for a
proper dividing line between himself and them. Whether
we are reduced to ourselves, a pure conscience, or to
what we accomplish: in either case it is our death if in
fact we are both. What could be truer? Molloy preserves
both meaning and lack of meaning. He sketches out the
first just enough so that it is, not enough for it to
hide its opposite, its twin, its non-meaning.

In short, this book is not a novel, it offers a morality, the most classical one, that of an absolute, almost
scientific conscience:

To be literally incapable of motion at last, that must
be something! My mind swoons when I think of it. And
mute into the bargain! And perhaps as deaf as a post!
And who knows as blind as a bat! And as likely as not
your memory a blank! And just enough brain intact to
allow you to exalt! And to dread death like a regener-
ation.

In 'Homo Ludens,' culture is said to be acted.
Beckett confirms this thesis, but in a negative way: his
'hero' is a man who refuses to play, he is the 'game
wrecker' that Huizinga talks about, the one who laughs
about the players' seriousness. In Molloy's opinion, one
should do no more than see, although without imagining
that one then sees something. It is certainly not an
ideal, it is only a makeshift: it would be even more
absurd to take the trouble to give a meaning to what does
not need any. Does not need: to be or not to be? The
question is not answered. We only have a choice between
torpor and silliness. It is understandable that this book
should have disconcerted people who are lucky enough to
feel neither foolish nor dazed.

[Translated by Françoise Longhurst]

12.   BERNARD PINGAUD IN 'ESPRIT'

September 1951, 423-5

Bernard Pingaud (b. 1923), French novelist, critic, editor, published several novels and critical studies of
contemporary writers. He devoted a number of articles to
the works of Samuel Beckett.

It is conceivable that, when he wrote 'Molloy,' Mr Samuel
Beckett intended, as some authoritative critics believe,
to enrich the literature of the novel with an 'important'
work; by this I mean a work which, overflowing the narrow
frame of the novel, would constitute a kind of 'Epitome'
- a Summa -, as Joyce's 'Ulysses' or, more recently,
Malcolm Lowry's 'Under the Volcano' were and intended to
be 'Summae.' I do not think that such was his purpose.
Rather than an Epitome, 'Molloy' appears like a monstrous
and disturbing myth, mysterious in its origins, whose
power over the imagination and whose gratuitousness the
author seems to have been well aware of. The book's
success is easy to understand: this excessively human and,
despite its arbitrariness, so deeply credible picture of
degradation is not without seduction. We live in a time
of despair, where wrecks are everywhere, and Molloy is a

wreck, hardly a man, an absence of a man. He is what
would appear in man if all his human, logical, rational,
polished and decent attributes were erased at a stroke.
And we have learned only too cruelly, for the last ten
years, where some lyrical apologies of the unconscious
and the irrational could lead, not to feel a joy mixed
with bitterness in reading such a lucid description of
what each of us might be, of what each of us is when he
gives in to the blind and heavy inertia of existence.
Molloy entering a town whose name he has forgotten,
searching for his mother whom he makes no serious en-
deavor to join, Molloy unable to speak, to think, Molloy
who does not know what he is, who hardly knows that he
is, Molloy eternal wanderer, solid ghost which the world
gradually whittles down, takes apart, and who finishes his
life exhausted, invalid, crawling in a dark and spongy
forest, we all know him, we have all met him at some time
in our life. Like him we have aspired to the deadly silence of decay, dreamt of a mute acquiescence to the non-
existence of things, of a desolate quietness; like him too
we have known those 'golden moments' when one fancies
'being another,' we have sunk in the present instant, at
last forgetful of time and transfigured.

But this cruel testimony on mankind's condition is
also, and perhaps primarily, a game, with all that implies
of ambiguity and unconscious seriousness. Nothing is less
deliberate, less composed than Mr Beckett's story. One
would search it in vain for winks to the reader, meaningful words cleverly hidden in the undergrowth of the sentences, by which the author lets us know the breadth of
his design. It looks as if Mr Beckett has no other intention but that of not having any, of letting himself be led
by a capricious, agitated language, in the same way as
Molloy lets himself be carried by life. Hence these meanders, these gaps in a narrative which denies itself as it
goes along, this impression of fog, which at times gets
thicker and at times clears away, revealing for a moment a
possible meaning which is quickly covered up again by the
night of meaninglessness.

One could rightly say that not to have any design is
still to have one. It might even be the most ambitious
one for a writer. It is trying to express in words the
tangled chaos upon which all the plans we make, all the
attitudes we take are recorded, thereby sketching an
appearance of order and reason in a world which has none.
Mr Beckett is undoubtedly obsessed by the idea of death
and nothingness; and if we think that this book is a
healthy one, it is precisely because death and nothingness are not disguised in it. The author does not make

them say what they do not mean; he does not elicit from
them an obscure and scholarly philosophy of the non-
knowledge, of darkness. However, like in any literature
of destruction, something positive is there, latent, the
miracle to which writers always refer. Mr Beckett cannot
help our seeing in our mind the 'other life,' which, using
different means, Mr Dormandi gave us a glimpse of in 'La
Vie des autres.' But perhaps more lucid than this author,
he always keeps some distance between himself and his
hero. One has the feeling that he is playing with Molloy;
and if he sometimes has fun in placing two contradictory
remarks in the same sentence, or two conflicting thoughts,
it may not be just to give us artificially an image of
meaninglessness. It is also to remove Molloy, to destroy
him, to destroy his own book, which in a way is only a
pirouette; as in all serious works - which are such by
nature and not because they were deliberately conceived
as such - irony alleviates what might be heavy and final
in the narrative. Of particular significance in this respect is the second part of the novel, where we learn how
a man called Moran was sent looking for Molloy, left
dying in the forest, and what happened to his search.
This story begins in a very savory Kafka-like manner.
Moran is presented to us as an 'agent' in the service of
a mysterious Youdi, who gives him orders through a 'messenger' called Gaber. One might think, reading these
pages, that suddenly Mr Beckett took his book seriously.
But Moran's preparations for his departure, the odd
worries which delay him, his contentions with the maid,
with the local priest from whom he asks communion, with
his son who has indigestion at the time of departure, the
character's naive self-infatuation and nonentity, the
ridiculous importance which he gives to the most trivial
details, everything indicates that this is a 'satire,'
a very spirited one indeed. Once Moran gets going, the
tone changes. Off on his search for Molloy, the seeker
falls victim to the same fate as the latter. He becomes,
so to speak, the Molloy that he will not manage to find,
he wanders, like him, in the country, indulges in the same
poor jokes, and falls prey to the same disabilities.
Abandoned by his son in the heart of the forest, he is a
dying man when Gaber reappears and tells him to go home,
without having completed his mission. Molloy will remain
beyond reach and Moran, unrecognizable, will get back to
his house and garden, also unrecognizable and deserted
by their usual inhabitants. It is then that he will hear
a voice which will enjoin him to narrate his adventure.
Moran will go on living, as Molloy probably lives on,
crawling in the forest; an absent life, eaten by contempt,

a desolate life, which may be - such is the hypothesis proposed at the end of the book - the free life. Because 'this would keep hope alive, would it not, hellish hope. Whereas to see yourself doing the same thing endlessly over and over again fills you with satisfaction.'

Although this second volet of the diptych contains some good pieces, entertainingly humorous, it seems to me on the whole less successful than the first. I cannot help seeing in it an exercise in composition, undoubtedly skillful - interest never fails - but in fact too skillful and irritating by its gratuitousness.

It is actually very difficult to pass any judgment on this book, which one does not immediately feel like weakening by a contrary opinion. 'Molloy' is a rickety house, open to all winds. Some will settle in it, find in it the refuge they always dreamt of, and will make this book their Bible. Others will go through it in disgust or contempt and will not even enter. This is probably just what Mr Beckett wanted. If additional proof was needed, one could find it in the style he uses, which is carefully negligent and always disconcerting; at times icy, lacking ornaments, without even that refined ornament, the deliberate lack of ornaments; a style which does not leave any memory of elegance in the ear, unlike Kafka's or Camus'. Mr Beckett has attained the enviable achievement of speaking without saying anything, while knowing perfectly well that to say nothing is to mean a great deal. Whatever one understands, did he really want it to be understood? Or are we making a drastic mistake in trying to interpret this monstrous tale, which is like a stone fallen from the sky? Who can find his way in the play of mirrors in which a literature that has reached such a degree of refinement indulges in?

[Translated by Françoise Longhurst]

13.   VIVIAN MERCIER IN 'NEW STATESMAN'

3 December 1955, 754

Vivian Mercier (b. 1919) is Professor of Literature at the University of California, Santa Barbara. Author of 'The Irish Comic Tradition' (1962) and 'The New Novel from Queneau to Pinget' (1971), he also wrote several of the most appreciative and perceptive early reviews in English of Beckett's work. His 'Beckett/Beckett' appeared in 1977.

Irish - and even Anglo-Irish - boys do not take kindly to cricket as a rule, but Samuel Beckett was captain of cricket at the Irish public school where Oscar Wilde learnt his first Greek. The urge to excel at the subtle game of the foreigner has led Beckett very far since then - to Paris, in fact, where the game may be roughly described as existentialism.

In assimilating French language and culture Beckett has not himself become assimilated - an extraordinary achievement for an Anglo-Irishman. The typical Anglo-Irish boy learns that he is not quite Irish almost before he can talk; later he learns that he is far from being English either. The pressure on him to become either wholly English (Beckett's cricketing phase) or wholly Irish (Synge's Aran Islands pilgrimages) may erase segments of his individuality for good and all. Yeats and Wilde were preoccupied with the idea of preserving one's individuality behind a mask, but realised the danger - and the fascination - of becoming what the mask pretends to be. Shaw, I sometimes think, became the prisoner of *his* mask, whiskers and all.

More typical, though - *experto crede* - is the Anglo-Irishman who becomes exactly what others want him to be: Burke, 'who to Party gave up what was meant for Mankind'; Goldsmith, whose classically urbane English style belied the wildly romantic bog-trotter underneath; Charles Lever, who, like so many careerists after him, deliberately catered to the nineteenth-century English burgess's yearning for his own anti-self, the stage Irishman.

'Who am I?' is the question that every Anglo-Irishman has to answer, even if it takes him a life-time, as it did Yeats. In 'Waiting for Godot' Beckett departed from the narrow logic of his development as a writer to ask the fashionable question 'Where are we?' - to which the play's title no doubt gives the answer. In his five novels, however (two in English, three in French), he has explored, without any of the autobiographical reference supplied by Shaw, Yeats or Wilde, the nature of the self and the means by which a self is found, preserved, and annihilated. The protagonist of 'Murphy' struggles to maintain his uniqueness against the parasitism of those who lack a self, while 'Watt' is essentially a study of a man who may be said to have no self at all. 'Malone meurt,' the second of the French novels, shows us a man clinging to his

selfhood, almost involuntarily, in the face of death;
'L'Innommable,' the third, a fantastic *tour de force,* is
the interior monologue of one who refuses to be born or to
admit that his self already exists.

The 'Godot' fan who wishes to know more of Beckett may
as well start with 'Molloy,' the first of the French
novels, though I'd prefer him to begin with the original
English of 'Murphy' if it were in print. He will recognize the Beckett world right away, for the protagonists of
the novels, besides being congenitally ugly and unemploy-
able, have usually grown old, crippled and weak in the
sphincters as well. They masturbate, but without pleasure. Almost to a man, they wear bowler hats, with or
without brims, which they often do not take off even to
sleep. Their pockets contain pebbles, broken pipes, anything that has no cash value. Their memories are, merci-
fully, bad.

'Molloy' is divided into two first-person narratives -
the first Molloy's, the second that of Jacques Moran,
agent. Molloy, an elderly cripple, is writing his story
in a room which he believes to have been his mother's
though he does not know how he got there. Once a week a
man brings him money and takes away what he has written.
Most of his narrative - so rambling as better to deserve
the name of interior monologue - tells of a journey in
search of his mother, during which he grows progressively
more crippled, until he is dragging himself along the
ground through a forest, with the help of his crutches, at
the rate of fifteen paces a day. Among the episodes preceding this final phase are a love passage and a fight so
abject that only a Beckett could imagine them. At last
Molloy makes his way out of the forest and hears a voice
say, 'Don't fret Molloy, we're coming.' His narrative
ends with the words 'I longed to go back into the forest.
Oh not a real longing. Molloy could stay, where he happened to be.'

Moran's narrative adheres much more closely to chronological order. It begins with the Sunday when a messenger
named Gaber brought Moran instructions from Youdi, their
employer, to go and find Molloy. Moran was then a tyran-
nically orderly man, a widower who nagged his only son
'for his own good,' an excessively scrupulous and yet
hypocritical Catholic. Moran never did find Molloy nor
succeed in remembering what he was to do if he found him,
but after reaching the Molloy country he was ordered by
Youdi (via Gaber) to return home at once. By then his son
had robbed him and run away, he himself had killed a man,
and he had inexplicably become a cripple like Molloy. It
took him months to get home, propping himself on his

umbrella; in the meanwhile his house and all his possessions had gone to rack and ruin.   But he feels happy and
free as never before:

> I am clearing out.   Perhaps I shall meet Molloy.   My
> knee is no better.   It is no worse either.   I have
> crutches now.   I shall go faster, all will go faster.
> They will be happy days.   I shall learn.   All there was
> to sell I have sold.   But I had heavy debts.   I have
> been a man long enough, I shall not put up with it any
> more, I shall not try any more.

In these two narratives we can study the problem of
selfhood from an almost clinical viewpoint.   But it is
tempting to go farther - acting on a hint dropped by
Thomas Hogan in a brilliant article ('Irish Writing,' No.
26, March 1954) - and read them also as an allegory of the
Ego and the Id.   Molloy, like the Id, has no sense of
time, no unified will, nothing but instinctual drives.
'Contradictory impulses,' in Freud's words, 'exist side by
side without neutralising each other or drawing apart....'
Moran, on the other hand, is hounded by the super-ego and
chock-full of anxiety and guilt.   Read this way, the book
changes very little in total effect, for when Moran comes
to identify himself more and more with Molloy and decides
that he has been a man long enough, selfhood as we know it
is being annihilated, even if we do not choose to describe
the process in terms of the Ego's being reabsorbed by the
Id.   Every reader must decide for himself whether the last
state of Moran is worse than the first.

14.   PHILIP TOYNBEE IN 'OBSERVER'

18 December 1955, 11

Philip Toynbee (b. 1916), novelist, poet and travel writer,
is also a regular reviewer for the 'Observer.'   Among his
many books are 'Savage Days' (1937), 'The Garden to the
Sea' (1953) and 'Views from the Lake' (1968).

This is a novel by the Irish-Parisian author of 'Waiting
for Godot,' and it has been translated from his adopted

French into his native English. An unusual book was to be
expected, and these expectations are fulfilled.

Mr. Beckett belongs to the dwindling phalanx of the
European *avant-garde*, and his reputation is very high
along the Boulevard Saint-Germain. Yet he is by no means
a solitary or original figure, for his play and his novels
follow the current Paris fashion without demur. He is the
end-product of a fictional tradition which has flowed from
Kafka through Sartre, Camus, and Genet, and of a tradition
in French nihilistic writing which goes back to Jarry, to
Lautréamont, to Sade. What he has done is to carry his
despair and disgust to ultimate limits of expression -
indeed beyond them.

'Molloy' resembles 'Waiting for Godot' so closely that
we may reasonably suspect Mr. Beckett of being a self-
plagiarist. It is difficult, granted his attitude to life,
to see how he could be anything else. Molloy himself is a
very old, very crippled, very dirty and very scatological
tramp - a Wandering Jew combined with a Tom o' Bedlam.
During the first part of the book he seems to be dragging
himself about in a formalised Ireland, philosophising,
tumbling into one ignominy after another, suffering without protest and inflicting suffering without remorse. He
is distinguished from the tramps of 'Godot' only by the
fact that he is going nowhere instead of waiting for
nobody.

The second part of the book introduces us to the equivalent of 'Godot's' Pozzo, a figure ('man' is not the word
for anything in Mr. Beckett's pages) of helpless brutality,
enslaved by his role as a petty tyrant. This figure,
Moran, appears to be the agent of a mysterious power
(straight out of Kafka, this) and he is deputed by unknown
authority to set out from his home in search of Molloy.
He leaves with his schoolboy son, who plays the role of
Pozzo's harnessed slave, and after quickly disintegrating
on the road into a condition closely similar to Molloy's,
Moran returns home without having succeeded in his quest.

The 'philosophy' of the book is summed up in these words
of Molloy's: -

'Oh, I know, even when you mention only a few of the
things there are, you do not get done either, I know, I
know. But it's a change of muck. And if all muck is the
same muck that doesn't matter, it's good to have a change
of muck, to move from one heap to another, a little further on, from time to time, fluttering, you might say,
like a butterfly, if you were ephemeral.'

Now, even in the most foolish literary circles a book
like this one would not have been admired without any

cause at all. Mr. Beckett is a very clever writer and
often a very funny one (though 'Molloy' lacks the brilliant and saving humour of 'Godot'). He is skilful and
authoritative and we may feel quite sure that whatever he
does is what he meant to do. There is not even any falsity in this novel beyond the gigantic falsity of its
whole conception and existence. Above all, of its existence. For surely the whole point of the thesis that life
is horrible and meaningless and nothing else must be that
there is no more than this to be said about it. It is not
a theme which is capable of any development, for the act
of developing it immediately provides a qualification to
the thesis. Mr. Beckett tries to get over this difficulty
by presenting Molloy at the beginning as some kind of
prisoner to whom blank sheets of paper are periodically
brought from outside with instructions to fill them in as
he chooses: -

'They are marked with signs I don't understand. Anyway
I don't read them. When I've done nothing he gives me
nothing, he scolds me. Yet I don't work for money. For
what then? I don't know'.

And the other obvious problem, the problem of why
Molloy does not kill himself, is dealt with by precisely
the same sleight of hand: -

'But the thought of suicide had little hold on me, I
don't know why, I thought I did, but I see I don't'.

By continuing to live and, still more, by continuing to
write, the author refutes his own message. And it is no
use saying, in such a case, that we must not confuse the
creator with his creature and so on. This book is a serious statement of a personal attitude or it is nothing. I
am inclined to think that it is nothing.

That 'Molloy' is almost unendurably boring to read would
not be denied, I imagine, by its keenest admirers. They
could not very well deny it, since the boredom of it, the
laboured circumstantiality, the giving of equal weight to
every detail, is quite clearly a deliberate element of the
author's technique.

As for the excrement, the blasphemy, the cruelty, the
reiterated indifferentism, it seems to me that this is an
attitude to life which cries out for at least some hint of
an opposing one. The danger of this kind of easy extrem-
ism is the danger of sentimentality; and this is avoided
in this book only by the admirable dexterity of Mr. Beckett's language. When Shakespeare wrote of life that

> it is a tale
Told by an idiot, full of sound and fury,
Signifying nothing

he was saying the same thing as Mr. Beckett. But he was
saying it in a context which showed that this was only a
single and contradicted aspect of the truth. It is not
this simple message which we receive from 'Macbeth' any
more than it is a simple message of good cheer which we
receive from 'The Tempest.' Sentimentality creeps in
when hope is provided without the corrective of despair,
or despair without the corrective of hope. Mr. Beckett
fails as a serious novelist because he has involved himself in a false emotional simplification.

'Malone Dies'
(1951)

[Written in French; published as 'Malone meurt' by
Éditions de Minuit, Paris; translated into English by
Beckett; published by Grove Press, New York, 1956, and
John Calder, London, 1958.]

15. MAURICE NADEAU IN 'MERCURE DE FRANCE'

March 1952, 503-4

A new work by the author of 'Molloy.' The narrator,
Malone, who says that he imagined the characters of
Beckett's previous works, and often confuses his own story
with theirs, is going to die. Before his end, he wants to
tell himself stories and make an inventory of his 'possessions,' in order to pass the time as best as he can. He
lies motionless on a miserable bed, in a cell bathed day
and night in the same grey light, not really knowing where
he is nor who he is. His memories are evanescent, perhaps
imaginary. He fails to create stories which 'hold together,' confusing the characters and the adventures which
happen to them. Is he talking about himself, or are they
just creations of his mind? He dies without having managed to elucidate anything: his past life, his present
illness, the places where he lived, the people he met. He
was searching for something, but what? Everything,
including himself, disappears in an indistinct mist beyond
time and space. Even the reality of his approaching death
is not certain.
    Even more rigorously than in 'Molloy,' Samuel Beckett
tries in 'Malone Dies' to hunt down an inner being

(principle of life?) which escapes all attempts at definition. Nothing is certain apart from that inaccessible
reality which the narrator's voice alone ultimately expresses. However metaphysics here is very concrete and
explosive, even merry. It proclaims the nothingness of
life, the nothingness of man; it moves in an absolute
nihilism. 'Molloy' gave the impression that it was impossible to go further in the conquest of Nothingness.
'Malone Dies' pushes back the boundaries of the undertaking which is pursued in another work still to be published. After which, it is difficult to imagine that
there could be anything left for Beckett but silence.

[Translated by Françoise Longhurst]

'Samuel Beckett: an Introduction' (1952)

16. RICHARD SEAVER IN 'MERLIN'

Autumn 1952, 73-9

Richard Seaver (b. 1926), editor and critic, wrote several essays introducing Beckett's French work to English and American readers in the early 1950s. He also collaborated with Beckett on the translations of The Expelled, The Calmative, and The End. His anthology of Beckett's writings, 'I Can't Go On, I'll Go On,' appeared in 1977.

Samuel Beckett, an Irish writer long established in France, has recently published two novels which, although they defy all commentary, merit the attention of anyone interested in this century's literature.

The position of Mr. Beckett is quite unique. He has, since his association with James Joyce in the late twenties and early thirties been recognized as an astute critic. In 1929 he contributed an excellent critical article to Shakespeare and Co.'s collective commentary on Joyce, 'Our Exagmination Round His Factification for Incamination of Work in Progress.' It was he who in 1930 undertook the first trial translation of Anna Livia Plurabelle into French. That translation presaged one of the directions Mr. Beckett's work was later to take. For it is a noteworthy fact that he undertook the translation from English, his first language, into French, his second. Some twenty years later, Mr. Beckett was to publish a startling novel, written not in English, but directly in his adapted language.

The example of a language-switch leads one inevitably

to think of Joseph Conrad. Both writers chose finally to
write in tongues not theirs by birth. But there the
similarity ends, for, whereas Conrad ultimately gained, in
the sense that he forsook a minor for what is generally
considered a major language, Mr. Beckett has, in a numeri-
cal sense at least, lost in choosing to write in French.

No one is questioning the unquestionable merits of
French as a language, nor trying to hold a brief for English as in any way the superior of the two languages. It
is nevertheless a *fait accompli* that Mr. Beckett has become a French writer, as much as Conrad or Henry James or
Mr. T.S. Eliot have become English writers, and his work
will ultimately be judged as a part of twentieth century
French literature.

One could speculate further on the reasons for Mr.
Beckett's decision to write in French, but it would be
pointless to do so. It is sufficient to notice that he
is undoubtedly a more adaptable, and perhaps a more honest
person than most of his colleagues-in-exile; he is a prime
example of that literary phenomenon which began some time
during the last century and continues today, the writer in
exile.

A writer divorced from his society places himself in a
precarious position. An artist, a musician, can work under
whatever sky, but a novelist, one of whose sources of
material is the society into which he was born, risks, in
turning his back on that society, cutting himself off both
from that source of material and from his rightful literary heritage. Moreover, by prolonged contact with a foreign environment, he risks losing his mastery of idiom,
unless, as is the instance of James Joyce, he is strong
enough to take his country with him, or, as in the instance of Beckett, he is adaptable enough to assume the
obligations of his new environment.

Whether Mr. Beckett consciously felt all this is a moot
point. As late as 1938 he was still an Irish writer working in English. 'Murphy,' his second novel, was published
in that year. With 'More Pricks Than Kicks,' his first
novel, published four years earlier, it will doubtless
remain his sole contribution to English literature.

It is unfortunate that no English edition of either
'More Pricks Than Kicks' or 'Murphy' is available, and we
can judge the latter work only from the French translation
which was published in 1947.(1) Both books passed almost
without notice. The only commentary I have ever found
which makes mention of them is Mr. W.Y. Tindall's remark,
in 'Forces in Modern British Literature,' '"More Pricks
Than Kicks" and "Murphy," by Samuel Beckett, the best of
Joyce's followers, are precious, elegant and absurd.'

'Murphy' is at times precious, for it is not a fully
mature work. Mr. Beckett's erudition sometimes clutters
the novel like unnecessary though colorful and often
humorous bric-a-brac. It is 'absurd' only in the sense
that M. Albert Camus' 'l'Étranger' or 'Le Malentendu' are
absurd, that is, to use the Sartrean term, 'nothing less
than the relationship of man to the world.'

Already in 'Murphy' there are clear indications of
Beckett's future development. The novel is set in the
everyday surroundings of London and Dublin, with only
minor deformations. Murphy is a comparatively young man
- as in all Mr. Beckett's novels, the protagonist's age is
not specified - whose desire for 'repose' places him *a
priori* at odds with the human condition. The symbol of
that repose is his *berceuse,* his rocking chair, to which
he attaches himself 'by seven scarfs.' He is seated, nude,
because 'c'était seulement le corps apaisé qu'il pouvait
commencer à vivre dans son esprit... Et le genre de vie
qu'il menait dans son esprit lui faisait plaisir, un tel
plaisir que c'était presque une absence de douleur.'(2)

Murphy has lived in this manner 'for months, perhaps
for years,' but even relative repose is difficult to
attain, and once arrived at, almost impossible to hold on
to: the building in which Murphy lives has been condemned
by the authorities and he must find new lodgings; the girl
he loves, the ex-prostitute Celia, threatens to leave him
unless he hunts for work, and so the precarious tranquillity is upset.

Murphy, who lives by an astrological system in which he
has complete faith, realizes that 'en gagnant sa vie il
perdrait ce qui la constituait.'(3) Nevertheless, spurred
on by Celia, he relinquishes his rocker, and after a
series of perfunctory attempts, at last secures work as a
male nurse in an insane asylum. In finding work he has
earned the right to Celia's love, but he has also lost his
repose. Influenced by the environment of the asylum, he
commits suicide. Those of his acquaintances who throughout the book have been hunting for him - Miss Counihan,
who thinks she loves Murphy, Neary, who thinks he loves
Miss Counihan, etc. - arrive only in time to discover
Murphy's at last 'peaceful body.'

A long short-story, L'Expulsé, published before but
obviously written after the French translation of
'Murphy,' links 'Murphy' to his third novel 'Molloy.'
L'Expulsé tells of a man, more world-weary than Murphy,
who is ejected from his lodgings for an unexplained and
no doubt unexplainable reason. It is obvious that he must
find another room. He rents a horse-drawn cab, whose
obliging chauffeur, after fruitless efforts to find his

homeless client a room, offers him the hospitality of his
own apartment. L'Expulsé accepts, but prefers to sleep in
the stable where the cabman keeps his horse. At dawn he
abandons the stable for the street. And the story ends:
'Je ne sais pas pourquoi j'ai raconté cette histoire.
J'aurais pu tout aussi bien en raconter une autre. Peut-
être qu'une autre fois je pourrais en raconter une autre.
Ames vives, vous verrez que cela se ressemble.'(4)

Mr. Beckett's next novel is one of those 'other
stories' he might just as well have told. Molloy, an old
man with one stiff leg and the other stiffening, sets out
to find his dying mother, who lives somewhere in a city
called X. From as far back as he can remember - Molloy's
memory is as imprecise as the city he is searching for is
vague - he has been going towards his mother in order to
establish their relationship on a less unsettled basis.
'Et quand j'étais chez elle, et j'y suis souvent arrivé,
je la quittais sans avoir rien fait. Et quand je n'y
étais plus, j'étais à nouveau en route vers elle, espérant
faire mieux la prochaine fois. Et quand j'avais l'air d'y
renoncer et de m'occuper d'autre chose ou de ne plus
m'occuper de rien, en réalité je ne faisais que fourbir
mes plans et chercher le chemin de la maison.'(5)

Molloy's wanderings take him first to a city, which may
or may not be the city X, then to the country, then into
a forest. There, no longer able to walk, even with the
aid of his crutches, he lies down and begins to crawl,
serpent-like, progressing 'fifteen paces a day without
exerting (himself) to the limit.' Finally, completely
exhausted, he falls into a ditch at the edge of the
forest.

The second half of the book is a story parallel to
Molloy's, which begins at the end and ends at the beginning. Jacques Moran, who leads a tidy life tending his
bees and his chickens, receives an order from the messenger Gaber, sent by the invisible Youdi, to go to find
Molloy. In company with his son, Moran sets out, knowing
that the mission is futile, and that it will lead to the
ruin of both himself and his son. Later, having failed to
find Molloy, having lost his son somewhere along the way,
Moran receives the order from Youdi to return home. He
obeys and arrives to find his hives dry, his chickens
dead, his house abandoned.

This second part of 'Molloy,' which begins: 'Il est
minuit. La pluie fouette les vitres. Je suis calme.
Tout dort... Mon rapport sera long. Je ne l'achèverai
peut-être pas', concludes: 'Alors je rentrai dans la maison et j'écrivis. Il est minuit. La pluie fouette les
vitres. Il n'était pas minuit. Il ne pleuvait pas.'(6).

Already, in 'Molloy,' the 'story' has been relegated to
a place of secondary importance. It has become almost
gratuitous. In 'Malone,' whose very name implies solitude, the telling of stories is avowedly a way of killing
time, of filling the silence with something less monotonous than silence. 'Je serai quand même bientôt tout à
fait mort enfin,' are Malone's first words. 'Peut-être
le mois prochain. Ce serait alors le mois d'avril ou de
mai... Je mourrais aujourd'hui même, si je voulais, rien
qu'en poussant un peu, si je pouvais vouloir, si je pouvais pousser.'(7)

Beyond desire, beyond hope, beyond illusion, pretension, hypocrisy, suspended in the vacuum between the end
of life and the beginning of death, the only real repose
possible, Malone is left with the absorbing problem of
how to spend his remaining time. 'Je crois', he says,
'que je pourrai me raconter quatre histoires, chacune sur
un thème différent. Une sur un homme, une autre sur une
femme, une troisième sur une chose quelconque et une
enfin sur un animal, un oiseau peut-être... Peut-être que
je mettrai l'homme et la femme dans la même, il y a si peu
de différence entre un homme et une femme, je veux dire
entre les miens.'(8)

If by chance he should finish 'too soon', then he'll
talk about his possessions. 'It will be a sort of inventory.' The possessions include the stub of a pencil, an
almost filled notebook, one yellow shoe, a long stick that
he uses to push his chamber pot to the door and to draw
his food, left from time to time by an anonymous hand,
from the door to the bed.

Malone's stories, which are abandoned, resumed, and
abandoned again, become more and more disjointed as they
progress. Sapo, the sixteen year old boy, is subsequently
transformed into MacMann, who crosses endless plains, beneath a driving rain, and finally lies down, Molloy-like,
until he almost dissolves into the mud itself. He finishes in an insane asylum, grows older, weaker, until his
condition approaches that of Malone, his creator.

Mr. Beckett's first play, 'En attendant Godot,' is as
yet unpublished, but extracts from it recently transcribed for the French Radio reveal that same illogical
profundity, that same dark, terrible humor which charac-
terize 'Molloy' and 'Malone.'

Two *clochards,* who have long tramped the world together,
meet in front of a tree set in an uncertain countryside.
While waiting for their friend, Godot, whom they only
vaguely remember, they pass the time conversing endlessly
and pointlessly. They are interrupted by the nobleman of
the neighborhood, in front of whose tree they have chanced

to wander. The nobleman is leading a man, Lucky, on a
leash. It is Lucky's duty to 'perform' whenever his
master so indicates by cracking his whip. To perform,
Lucky stands upright, doffs his hat and recites, at an
incredible pace, a tirade in which the worst blasphemies
and the purest poetry intermingle at random. Lucky continues until his master, at first distracted but then
bored, cracks his whip a second time, the signal for Lucky
to don his hat again and stem the flow. 'It helps kill
time,' Lucky's master says resignedly.

In the end, a little boy arrives to announce that Mr.
Godot will not come tonight, but that he will in all
probability come tomorrow. The two tramps decide that,
since the reason for their vigil no longer exists, or is
at least postponed, they may as well lie down and go to
sleep.

The progression from 'Murphy' through 'Molloy,' to
'Malone' is evident. The movement is away from the world
of the body towards the world of the mind. Murphy moves
past the still recognizable landmarks of Hyde Park, Marble
Arch, and West Brompton. Molloy's city has become anonymous; Malone's is no more than a cry beyond his window, a
light in the window across the street.

Murphy's external universe still has substance, his
friends, names, Molloy's contact with the world of blood
and flesh and identity cards still exists. He is aware of
his own body, if only of its infirmities. He, like
L'Expulsé, is still plagued by the police. Malone's
external universe is reduced to his four walls and to that
hand which reaches through the door to draw forth the
filled chamber-pot.

As space has dissolved, so has time. Murphy, despite
lapses, lends an ear to the tower chimes in order to reach
Celia and home in time for supper. Molloy, if beyond
hours, still moves through sunlight into shadow and back
to sunlight again. In Malone's room, day and night have
withered to a constant, though slightly changing tone of
gray.

The movement, then, is away from external precision towards the increasing autonomy of consciousness. And
within the borders of that pure consciousness there are
three divisions, as Murphy gives them, 'clarté, pénombre
et noir,' (brightness, semidarkness and darkness). Beckett's characters move progressively away from *clarté* towards the *noir*, which is made up of 'neither elements nor
states, but only of forms which come into being and slide
away into the dust of a new becoming, without love or hate
or any principle of conceivable change.'

It is unfortunate for Mr. Beckett's literary reputation
that his name is invariably linked with that of James
Joyce, and that very often he is dismissed as merely
another of the master's too numerous disciples. Joyce
undoubtedly had a profound influence on his younger com-
patriot, but Mr. Beckett's work is completely personal,
in line with certain tendencies of contemporary literature
and yet very new and different. 'Murphy' and 'Molloy'
inevitably recall Kafka, but neither is imitation Kafka.
They likewise have an affinity with M. Camus's 'L'Etranger'
and with M. Henri Michaux's 'Plume.' But if one desired
to delve deeper, it would be possible to return to Xavier
de Maistre's 'Voyage autour de ma Chambre' - compare, for
example, Mr. Beckett's theory of the division of mind and
body, in 'Murphy,' with de Maistre's theory of 'l'âme et
la bête' - or even further to Laurence Sterne's 'Tristam
Shandy.'

Whether Mr. Beckett was influenced by any or all of
these writers, whether he borrowed from them, seems quite
secondary. For as Mr. Eliot once remarked, the mature
artist steals, the immature artist imitates. And Mr.
Beckett's work is not imitation.

The inevitable question remains to be asked, What does
Mr. Beckett's work mean? The meaning, if there must be
one, is perhaps latent in the lack of meaning. 'Nothing
is more real than nothing,' says Malone. What is significant is insignificant; what is insigificant, significant,
and therefore insignificant, and so on around the circle.
Murphy's arrangement for eating his assorted crackers,
Molloy's sucking stones, Malone's pencil stub are as
important as another man's car or twenty room mansion; no
more so perhaps, but certainly no less.

Mr. Beckett builds, because building is a part of living, as destruction is a part of living. Building or destroying, 'cela n'a pas d'importance,' 'I am what I do,'
says Celia. 'No,' says Murphy, 'you do what you are. You
do a fraction of what you are... "Can't go, Mama." That
kind of doing. Inevitable and stinking.'

And as he builds, so Mr. Beckett destroys. His characters are never certain of their facts. The city across
the plain from Molloy's ditch might be *his* city, 'although
nothing let (him) suppose it was his.' 'It is raining,'
says Jacques Moran. 'It is not raining.' The paralyzed,
bed-ridden Malone is almost certain that it is the month
of April or May, 'a thousand little symptoms tell him so.'
But it is possible that he is mistaken, and that the Feast
Day of Saint John or even the 14th of July, 'anniversary
of liberty', are already past. At the end of 'Malone,'
Lemuel, the guardian of the asylum, takes a group of

inmates on a picnic, and proceeds to murder them by split-
ting their skulls with an axe. So Mr. Beckett (Samuel-
Lemuel?) destroys his characters, his created world,
bringing again to nothing what was nothing.

Is it possible for Mr. Beckett to progress further
without succumbing to the complete incoherence of inarticulate sound, to the silence of nothingness where mud and
Molloy, where object and being are not only contiguous,
but one? Mr. Beckett's next book, announced for publication early this winter, will have to reply. Perhaps the
name is significant. It is called 'L'Innommable.'

Notes

1 In preparing his original essay, Mr Seaver used the
   French translation of 'Murphy' and provided his own
   versions of the then untranslated 'Molloy' and 'Malone
   Dies.' For historical interest, we have left the original versions of Beckett's French and Mr Seaver's
   English. (Eds)
2 'only when his body was pacified could he begin to live
   in his mind...And the kind of life he led in his mind
   gave him pleasure, such a pleasure that it was almost
   an absence of pain'.
3 'that in earning his living he would lose that which
   constitutes his life.'
4 'I don't know why I told that story. I could just as
   well have told another. Perhaps another time I shall
   tell another. Lively souls, you will see how much
   they resemble one another.'
5 'And when I was with her, and I often arrived there, I
   left her without having done anything. And when I was
   no longer there, I was again on my way towards her,
   hoping to do better the next time. And when I appeared
   to give up the project, and to busy myself with something else or no longer to busy myself with anything, I
   was, in reality, polishing my plans and hunting for the
   road to her house'.
6 'It is midnight. Rain lashes the windows. I am calm.
   Everything is asleep... My report will be long. Perhaps I shall never finish it.'...
       'Then I came back into the house and wrote. It is
   midnight. Rain lashes the windows. It was not midnight. It was not raining.'
7 'All the same I shall soon be completely dead at last.
   Perhaps next month. That would make it the month of
   April or May... I could die today this very day, if I
   wished, merely by pushing a little, if I could wish, if
   I could push.'

8   'I think that I'll be able to tell myself four stories,
    each on a different theme. One about a man, one about
    a woman, one about any old thing, and one about an
    animal, perhaps a bird. Maybe I'll put the man and the
    woman together, there is so little difference between a
    man and a woman, I mean between mine.'

'Waiting for Godot'
(1952-3)

[Written in French as 'En attendant Godot'; first performed at Théâtre de Babylone, Paris, 5 January 1953;
first performed London, Arts Theatre Club, 3 August 1955;
first American performance, Coconut Grove Playhouse,
Miami, Florida, 3 January 1956; published by Éditions de
Minuit, Paris, 17 October 1952; translated into English by
Beckett; published by Grove Press, New York, September
1954, and by Faber & Faber, London, February 1956.]

---

17. SYLVAIN ZEGEL IN 'LIBÉRATION'

7 January 1953

Sylvain Zegel is a little-known French critic who wrote
the perceptive first review of 'En attendant Godot' soon
after its première in Paris.

Theater-lovers rarely have the pleasure of discovering a
new author worthy of the name; an author who can give his
dialogue true poetic force, who can animate his characters
so vividly that the audience identifies with them, suffering and laughing with them; who, having meditated, does
not amuse himself with mere word-juggling; who deserves
comparison with the greatest. When this occurs, it is an
event which will be spoken of for a long time, and will be
remembered years later. In my opinion, Samuel Beckett's
first play 'Waiting for Godot,' at the Théâtre de Babylone, will be spoken of for a long time.

Perhaps a few grumblers complained that it is 'a play in which nothing happens,' because they didn't find the more or less conventional plot used by innumerable authors from Aristophanes and Plautus on; or because, on leaving the theater, they couldn't summarize the play, or explain why they had laughed with embarrassed laughter.

They heard people using everyday words, and they did not feel that by an inexplicable miracle - which is called art - the words suddenly acquired a new value. They saw people being happy and suffering, and they did not understand that they were watching their own lives. But when the curtain fell, and they heard the enthusiasm of the audience, they understood at least this much: Paris had just recognized in Samuel Beckett one of today's best playwrights.

It is hard not to be amazed that this is the first play of a writer who has achieved critical acclaim for his novels 'Molloy' and 'Malone Dies,' since he has mastered all the exigencies of the stage. Each word acts as the author wishes, touching us or making us laugh.

These two tramps, who represent all humanity, utter remarks that any one of us might utter. These two men are feeble and energetic, cowardly and courageous; they bicker, amuse themselves, are bored, speak to each other without understanding. They do all this to keep busy. To pass time. To live or to give themselves the illusion that they are living. They are certain of only one thing: they are waiting for Godot. Who is Godot? They don't know. And in any case, this myth hasn't the same form the same qualities, for each of them. It might be happiness, eternal life, the ideal and unattainable quest of all men - which they wait for and which gives them the strength to live on...

[Translated by Ruby Cohn]

18.   JACQUES LEMARCHAND IN 'FIGARO LITTÉRAIRE'

17 January 1953, 10

Jacques Lemarchand (1908-74), influential French critic and journalist, wrote a regular drama column for 'Figaro littéraire.' He reviewed most of Beckett's plays when they were first performed in Paris.

I do not quite know how to begin describing this play by
Samuel Beckett, 'Waiting for Godot' (directed by Roger
Blin, now playing at the Théâtre de Babylone). I have
seen this play and seen it again, I have read and reread
it: it still has the power to move me. I should like to
communicate this feeling, to make it contagious. At the
same time I am faced with the difficulty of fulfilling the
primary duty of the critic, which, as everyone knows, is
to explain and narrate a play to people who have neither
seen it nor read it. I have experienced this difficulty
several times before; the sensation is infinitely agreeable. One feels it each time one is called upon to describe a work that is beautiful, but of an unusual beauty;
new, but genuinely new; traditional, but of eminent tradition; clever, but with a cleverness the most clever
professors are unable to teach; and finally, intelligent,
but with that clear intelligence that is non-negotiable in
the schools.

In addition, 'Waiting for Godot' is a resolutely comic
play, its comedy borrowed from the most direct of all
forms of humor, the circus.

Two men, two vagabonds, stand on a road, beneath a tree
ravaged by winter, in a barren, desolate place. They are
waiting for Godot. When Godot comes, everything will be
better, and their meeting with Godot is set for today,
under this tree. To pass the time they talk, they talk
about Godot, whom they really do not know much about.
Along the road a strange team passes by, composed of the
rich Pozzo, holding the reins of his valet Lucky. Before
the eyes of the vagabonds, to whom he has taken a sudden
liking, Pozzo puts the well-trained Lucky through his
paces. Lucky walks, dances and thinks on command. They
go on their way and we all settle down to wait for Godot,
when a little boy arrives, saying he has been sent by
Godot: Godot is busy today, sends his apologies and will
come tomorrow.

In the second act, on the same spot, beneath that tree
from which they occasionally feel like hanging themselves,
now, it seems, sprouting a few leaves, the vagabonds are
still there. They are waiting for Godot. And Pozzo reappears. And so does the little boy, and, as in a nightmare, everything begins all over again, waiting, hope and
disappointment.

I would not say that this analysis falsifies the play:
it is a pure and simple suppression of the play. I would
be extremely sorry if anyone should say to himself after
reading it, 'I see what it's about....' For 'Waiting for
Godot' is something entirely different from the bare outline I have sketched here. The extraordinary success of

Samuel Beckett is primarily due to the artistry with
which he gives life and presence to this waiting - we
know very well what it represents. We do it too, we par-
ticipate in it completely. But Beckett is not a heavy-
handed manipulator of symbols of the sort we are used to:
we do not see him coming, and when we see where he means
to lead us it is too late, we are caught.

'Waiting for Godot' is a profoundly original work:
because of this it will necessarily be a disconcerting
one. Either it will charm the public or arouse contempt,
even fury. As for myself, I found in it - but successfully worked out, masterfully accomplished - all those
singular, sometimes awkward but always moving innovations
that I have hailed after random evenings in works of unknown writers, young writers - I have in mind the works of
Eugene Ionesco, of 'Capitaine Bada' by Jean Vauthier, and
of the first plays by Adamov as well. What these works
tried to express, to make us understand, I see much more
clearly in 'Waiting for Godot.' I understood very well
just how such attempts as these could irritate certain
spectators - at the same time knowing very well that this
irritation was unjust, and that it would disappear if they
took the trouble to listen attentively. I would find it
much more difficult to understand, I admit, if Beckett's
play should provoke in them the same reactions of with-
drawal and flight. It marks the true path of an entire
movement in theatre that is still in an experimental
phase.

I stated above that 'Waiting for Godot' is also a funny
play - sometimes very funny. The second night I was there,
the laughter was natural and unforced; and I believe that
in spite of this the emotional power of so many of the
scenes in this play, which resembles so little of what is
familiar to us, was in no way diminished.

As I mentioned above, 'Waiting for Godot' is directed
by Roger Blin. For several years Blin has been providing
us with excellent performances, though far too rare. I do
not think he has ever brought off anything so perfectly as
his staging of Beckett's play. To attain such simplicity,
such clarity and expressive power, one must possess that
sincere intelligence and generosity without which talent
and experience are of little use. The role of the rich
Pozzo is played by Blin: he has made of it an unforgettable composition in buffoonery.

Pierre Latour and Lucien Raimbourg play the pair of
vagabonds. I know Pierre Latour quite well; his cool
humor and sensitivity please me infinitely; but I did not
know Lucien Raimbourg: an actor whose lack of affectation
and comic force are surprising. I am told he used to play

in music halls; it does not surprise me. One senses in
his acting the rigor and awareness of a man who has worked
before a public infinitely more demanding than the theater
audience. Along with them, Jean Martin as Lucky, the
valet-automaton, gives a remarkable recital of the parodic,
baroque monologue of 'man thinking'; and young Serge
Lecointe is a charming Godot's messenger.

Whatever may be the fate of 'Waiting for Godot,'
Mr J.-M. Serreau deserves our thanks for having welcomed
it to this theater.

[Translated by Jean M. Sommermeyer]

19.   JEAN ANOUILH IN 'ARTS SPECTACLES'

27 February-5 March 1953, 1

Jean Anouilh (b. 1910), the internationally known French
playwright, is the author of 'Antigone' (1944), 'Waltz of
the Toreadors' (1952), 'Poor Bitos' (1958), 'The Lark'
(1953) and many other works. He has been a great admirer
of Beckett's theater.

'Nothing happens, nobody comes, nobody goes, it's awful,'
This line, spoken by one of the characters in the play,
provides its best summary. 'Godot' is a masterpiece that
will cause despair for men in general and for playwrights
in particular. I think that the opening night at the
Théâtre de Babylone is as important as the opening of
Pirandello in Paris in 1923, presented by Pitoeff.

One can only raise one's hat - a bowler to be sure, as
in the play - and pray to heaven for a little talent.
The greatness, the artful playing, a style - we are
'somewhere' in the theater. The music-hall sketch of
Pascal's 'Pensées' as played by the Fratellini clowns.

[Translated by Ruby Cohn]

20   HAROLD HOBSON IN 'SUNDAY TIMES'

7 August 1955, 11

Harold Hobson (b. 1904). Drama critic of the 'Sunday
Times' 1947-76. His enthusiastic reviews of the early
plays helped establish Beckett's reputation as a major
contemporary playwright.

The objections to Mr. Samuel Beckett's play as a theatrical entertainment are many and obvious. Anyone keen-
sighted enough to see a church at noonday can perceive
what they are. 'Waiting for Godot' has nothing at all to
seduce the senses. Its drab, bare scene is dominated by a
withered tree and a garbage can, and for a large part of
the evening this lugubrious setting, which makes the worst
of both town and country, is inhabited only by a couple of
tramps, verminous, decayed, their hats broken and their
clothes soiled, with sweaty feet, inconstant bladders, and
boils on the backside.
     This is not all. In the course of the play, nothing
happens. Such dramatic progress as there is, is not towards a climax, but towards a perpetual postponement.
Vladimir and Estragon are waiting for Godot, but this
gentleman's appearance (*if* he is a gentleman, and not
something of another species) is not prepared with any
recognisable theatrical tension, for the audience knows
well enough from the beginning that Godot will never come.
The dialogue is studded with words that have no meaning
for normal ears; repeatedly the play announces that it has
come to a stop, and will have to start again; never does
it reconcile itself with reason.
     It is hardly surprising that, English audiences notori-
ously disliking anything not immediately understandable,
certain early lines in the play, such as 'I have had
better entertainment elsewhere,' were received on the
first night with ironical laughter; or that when one of
the characters yawned, the yawn was echoed and amplified
by a humorist in the stalls. Yet at the end the play was
warmly applauded. There were even a few calls for
'Author!' But these were rather shame-faced cries, as if
those who uttered them doubted whether it were seemly to
make too much noise whilst turning their coats.

Strange as the play is, and curious as are its processes

of thought, it has a meaning; and this meaning is untrue.
To attempt to put this meaning into a paragraph is like
trying to catch Leviathan in a butterfly net, but nevertheless the effort must be made.   The upshot of 'Waiting
for Godot' is that the two tramps are always waiting for
the future, their ruinous consolation being that there is
always tomorrow; they never realise that today is today.
In this, says Mr. Beckett, they are like humanity, which
dawdles and drivels away its life, postponing action,
eschewing enjoyment, waiting only for some far-off, divine
event, the millenium, the Day of Judgment.

Mr. Beckett has, of course, got it all wrong.   Humanity
worries very little over the Day of Judgment.   It is far
too busy hire-purchasing television sets, popping into
three-star restaurants, planting itself vineyards, building helicopters.   But he has got it wrong in a tremendous
way.   And this is what matters.   There is no need at all
for a dramatist to philosophise rightly; he can leave that
to the philosophers.   But it is essential that if he
philosophises wrongly, he should do so with swagger.   Mr.
Beckett has any amount of swagger.   A dusty, coarse,
irreverent, pessimistic, violent swagger?   Possibly.   But
the genuine thing, the real McCoy.

Vladimir and Estragon have each a kind of universality.
They wear their rags with a difference.   Vladimir is
eternally hopeful; if Godot does not come this evening,
then he will certainly arrive tomorrow, or at the very
latest the day after.   Estragon, much troubled by his
boots, is less confident.   He thinks the game is not worth
playing, and is ready to hang himself.   Or so he says.
But he does nothing.   Like Vladimir, he only talks.   They
both idly spin away the great top of their life in the
vain expectation that some master whip will one day give
it eternal vitality.   Meanwhile their conversation often
has the simplicity, in this case the delusive simplicity,
of music-hall cross-talk, now and again pierced with a
shaft that seems for a second or so to touch the edge of
truth's garment.   It is bewildering.   It is exasperating.
It is insidiously exciting.

Then there is Pozzo, the big, brutal bully, and the terrible, white-faced gibbering slave he leads about on the
end of a rope.   These are exasperating, too, but they
have astonishing moments of theatrical effectiveness.   The
long speech into which the silent Lucky breaks, crammed
with the unintelligible, with vain repetitions, with the
lumber of ill-assorted learning, the pitiful heritage of
the ages, the fruits of civilisation squashed down and
rotten, is horrifyingly delivered by Mr. Timothy Bateson.

Equally startling and impressive is Mr. Peter Bull's
sudden expression of Pozzo's anguish, when he cries out
that one is born, and one eats, and then one dies, and
that is all. This Bull's bellow, if I may call it so,
troubles the memory like the swan-song of humanity. Mr.
Paul Daneman and Mr. Peter Woodthorpe play the tramps
without faltering, and the last scene in which a little
boy is involved, has a haunting and inexplicable beauty.
Over the whole play lies a great and sad compassion.

Go and see 'Waiting for Godot.' At the worst you will
discover a curiosity, a four-leaved clover, a black tulip;
at the best, something that will securely lodge in a
corner of your mind for as long as you live.

21.   KENNETH TYNAN IN 'OBSERVER'

7 August 1955, 11

Kenneth Tynan (b. 1927), former drama critic and literary
consultant and manager of the National Theatre. During
the 1950s, he was one of the most influential drama critics in England. His books include 'Curtains' (1961),
'Tynan Right and Left' (1967), and 'The Sound of Two Hands
Clapping' (1976).

A special virtue attaches to plays which remind the drama
of how much it can do without and still exist. By all the
known criteria, Samuel Beckett's 'Waiting for Godot' is a
dramatic vacuum. Pity the critic who seeks a chink in its
armour, for it is all chink. It has no plot, no climax,
no *dénouement*; no beginning, no middle, and no end.
Unavoidably, it has a situation, and it might be accused
of having suspense, since it deals with the impatience of
two tramps, waiting beneath a tree for a cryptic Mr. Godot
to keep his appointment with them; but the situation is
never developed, and a glance at the programme shows that
Mr. Godot is not going to arrive. 'Waiting for Godot'
frankly jettisons everything by which we recognise theatre. It arrives at the custom-house, as it were, with no
luggage, no passport, and nothing to declare; yet it gets
through, as might a pilgrim from Mars. It does this, I
believe, by appealing to a definition of drama much more

fundamental than any in the books.   A play, it asserts and proves, is basically a means of spending two hours in the dark without being bored.

Its author is an Irishman living in France, a fact which should prepare us for the extra, oddly serious joke he now plays on us.   Passing the time in the dark, he suggests, is not only what drama is about but also what life is about.   Existence depends on those metaphysical Micawbers who will go on waiting, against all rational argument, for something which may one day turn up to explain the purpose of living.   Twenty years ago Mr. Odets had us waiting for Lefty, the social messiah; less naively, Mr. Beckett bids us wait for Godot, the spiritual signpost.   His two tramps pass the time of day just as we the audience, are passing the time of night.   Were we not in the theatre, we should, like them, be clowning and quarrelling, aimlessly bickering and aimlessly making up - all, as one of them says, 'to give us the impression that we exist.'

Mr. Beckett's tramps do not often talk like that.   For the most part they converse in the double-talk of vaudeville: one of them has the ragged aplomb of Buster Keaton, while the other is Chaplin at his airiest and fairiest. Their exchanges are like those conversations at the next table which one can almost but not quite decipher - human speech half-heard and reproduced with all its *non-sequiturs* absurdly intact.   From time to time other characters intrude.   Fat Pozzo, Humpty Dumpty with a whip in his fist, puffs into sight with Lucky, his dumb slave. They are clearly going somewhere in a hurry: perhaps they know where Godot is?   But the interview subsides into Lewis-Carrollian inanity.   All that emerges is that the master needs the slave as much as the slave needs the master; it gives both a sense of spurious purpose; and one thinks of Laurel and Hardy, the ideal casting in these roles.   Commanded to think, Lucky stammers out a ghostly, ghastly, interminable tirade, compounded of cliché and gibberish, whose general tenor is that, in spite of material progress and 'all kinds of tennis,' man spiritually dwindles.   The style hereabouts reminds us forcibly that Mr. Beckett once worked for James Joyce.   In the next act Pozzo and Lucky return, this time moving, just as purposefully, in the opposite direction.   The tramps decide to stay where they are.   A child arrives, presenting Mr. Godot's compliments and regretting that he is unable to meet them today.   It is the same message as yesterday; all the same, they wait.   The hero of 'Crime and Punishment' reflects that if a condemned man 'had to remain standing on a square yard of space all his life, a thousand years,

eternity, it were better to live so than to die at once...
Man is a vile creature! and vile is he who calls him vile
for that!' Something of this crossed my mind as the curtain fell on Mr. Beckett's tatterdemalion stoics.

The play sees the human condition in terms of baggy
pants and red noses. Hastily labelling their disquiet
disgust, many of the first-night audience found it pretentious. But what, exactly, are its pretensions? To state
that mankind is waiting for a sign that is late in coming
is a platitude which none but an illiterate would interpret as making claims to profundity. What vexed the
play's enemies was, I suspect, the opposite: it was not
pretentious enough to enable them to deride it. I care
little for its enormous success in Europe over the past
three years, but much for the way in which it pricked and
stimulated my own nervous system. It summoned the music-
hall and the parable to present a view of life which ban-
ished the sentimentality of the music-hall and the parable's fulsome uplift. It forced me to re-examine the
rules which have hitherto governed the drama; and, having
done so, to pronounce them not elastic enough. It is
validly new, and hence I declare myself, as the Spanish
would say, *godotista*.

Peter Hall directs the play with a marvellous ear for
its elusive rhythms, and Peter Woodthorpe and Paul Daneman give the tramps a compassionate lunacy which only professional clowns could excel. Physically, Peter Bull is
Pozzo to the life; vocally, he overplays his hand.
Timothy Bateson's Lucky is anguish made comic, a remarkable achievement, and perfectly in keeping with the spirit
of the play.

22. G.S. FRASER IN 'TIMES LITERARY SUPPLEMENT'

10 February 1956, 84

G.S. Fraser (b. 1915), poet, translator, editor and
critic, is the author of 'The Modern Writer and His World'
(1964) and other books. Since 1959, he has been on the
English faculty at the University of Leicester. His
review of 'Waiting for Godot' provoked a lengthy and spirited correspondence in the 'Times Literary Supplement.'

No new play on the London stage has had a more unexpected
and exciting success in recent years than Mr. Samuel
Beckett's 'Waiting for Godot.' Audiences and critics
have, in this country, immediately apprehended its appeal,
but there has been no serious attempt to define its theme.
Any discussion about what 'Waiting for Godot' 'means' soon
loses itself in a tangle of cross-purposes. Nor do Mr.
Beckett's novels, such as 'Molloy' and 'Watt,' throw much
light on the appeal of the play. In one sense, indeed,
they do not share that appeal. In his narrative prose,
Mr. Beckett presents the paradoxical picture of a man of
very great talent, and possibly even of genius, using all
his gifts with enormous skill for the purpose of reducing
his readers to a state of tired disgust and exasperated
boredom.   But 'Waiting for Godot' is not, except to the
most squeamishly fastidious of playgoers, in the least
disgusting. It is anything but boring, it instead extracts from the *idea* of boredom the most genuine pathos
and enchanting comedy. Again, the message of Mr. Beckett
as a novelist is perhaps a message of blank despair. The
message of 'Waiting for Godot' is perhaps something nearer
a message of religious consolation. Audiences do not
leave the theatre, after seeing his play, feeling that
life has been deprived of meaning. They feel rather that
a new light has been cast on life's meaning, at several
deep levels.
   What sort of light, however? That is what so far
eluded critics of the play as performed. Mr. Beckett is
rumoured to have instructed his English producer not, by
any manner of means, to tell the actors what the theme of
the play was. Yet unless Mr. Beckett whispered his central secret in the producer's ear, the warning was probably unnecessary. The elusiveness of the core has,
indeed, led some critics to contend that there is no core;
that the whole startling effect of the play on the stage
depended on excellent production and acting and on Mr.
Beckett's own mastery of the mechanics of stagecraft. The
play, on this theory, would resemble the machine recently
invented by an ingenious Californian, which works perfectly, with the minimum of friction, but does no 'work,'
performs no function. Or, to put this with more dignity,
the theory might be that Mr. Beckett in 'Waiting for
Godot' dramatizes the notion of emptiness. This, or something like this, was the reaction of the French dramatist
Jean Anouilh to the first performance of 'En Attendant
Godot' in Paris. 'Nothing happens. Nobody comes, nobody
goes, it's awful! But,' M. Anouilh added, 'I think the
evening at the Babylone is as important as the première
of Pirandello, put on in Paris by Pitoeff in 1923.' And

from what we know of Mr. Beckett's other work, we might
assume that to dramatize emptiness, to have his much ado
literally about nothing, may have been his conscious intention. Yet, with a play even more than a poem, we have
to consider not the author's conscious intention - not
what the author, in a conversation, might say he believed
about 'life' - but the whole complex significance, the
valid levels of meaning, of a coherent structure. What
'Waiting for Godot' essentially is is a prolonged and sustained metaphor about the nature of human life. It is a
metaphor also which makes a particular appeal to the mood
of liberal uncertainty which is the prevailing mood of
modern Western Europe; and which makes (to judge by the
play's failure in Miami) much less appeal to the strenuous
and pragmatic temper of the contemporary American mind.
It is also a play by an Irishman, by a friend and disciple
of James Joyce; a play, therefore, by a man whose imagination (in the sense in which Mr. Eliot used this phrase of
Joyce himself) is orthodox. In other words, we should
consider where Mr. Beckett springs from and what he is
reacting against in his roots. Even at his most nihilistic he will come under Mr. Eliot's category of the Christian blasphemer.

The fundamental imagery of 'Waiting for Godot' is
Christian; for, at the depth of experience into which Mr.
Beckett is probing, there is no other source of imagery
for him to draw on. His heroes are two tramps, who have
come from nowhere in particular and have nowhere in particular to go. Their life is a state of apparently
fruitless expectation. They receive messages, through a
little boy, from the local landowner, Godot, who is always
going to come in person to-morrow, but never does come.
Their attitude towards Godot is one partly of hope, partly
of fear. The orthodoxy of this symbolism, from a Christian point of view, is obvious. The tramps with their
rags and their misery, represent the fallen state of man.
The squalor of their surroundings, their lack of a 'stake
in the world,' represents the idea that here in this world
we can build no abiding city. The ambiguity of their
attitude towards Godot, their mingled hope and fear, the
doubtful tone of the boy's messages, represents the state
of tension and uncertainty in which the average Christian
must live in this world, avoiding presumption, and also
avoiding despair. Yet the two tramps, Didi and Gogo, as
they call each other, represent something far higher than
the other two characters in the play, the masterful and
ridiculous Pozzo and his terrifying slave, Lucky. Didi
and Gogo stand for the contemplative life. Pozzo and
Lucky stand for the life of practical action taken,

mistakenly, as an end in itself. Pozzo's blindness and
Lucky's dumbness in the second act rub this point in. The
so-called practical man, the man of action, has to be set
on his feet and put on his way by the contemplative man.
He depends - as becomes clear, in the first act, from
Pozzo's genuine though absurd gratitude for the chance of
a little conversation - on the contemplative man for such
moments of insight, of spiritual communication, as occur
in his life. The mere and pure man of action, the comic
caricature of the Nietzschean superman, Pozzo, is like an
actor who does not properly exist without his audience;
but his audience are also, in a sense, his judges.
Pozzo and Lucky, in fact, have the same sort of function
in 'Waiting for Godot' as Vanity Fair in 'The Pilgrim's
Progress.' But they are, as it were, a perambulating
Vanity Fair; Didi and Gogo are static pilgrims. It is
worth noting, also, that Didi and Gogo are bound to each
other by something that it is not absurd to call charity.
They treat each other with consideration and compunction
(their odd relationship, always tugging away from each
other, but always drawn together again, is among other
things an emblem of marriage). Pozzo and Lucky are drawn
together by hate and fear. Their lot is increasing
misery; but if Didi and Gogo are not obviously any better
off at the end of the play than they were at the beginning, neither are they obviously any worse off. Their
state remains one of expectation.

'Waiting for Godot' - one might sum up these remarks -
is thus a modern morality play, on permanent Christian
themes. But, even if the Christian basis of the structure
were not obvious, Mr. Beckett is constantly underlining it
for us in the incidental symbolism and the dialogue. The
first piece of serious dialogue in the play, the first
statement, as it were, of a theme, is about the 'two
thieves, crucified at the same time as our Saviour.'

> VLADIMIR: And yet...(*pause*)...how is it - this is not
> boring you I hope - how is that of the four evangelists
> only one speaks of a thief being saved? The four of
> them were there - or thereabouts, and only one speaks
> of a thief being saved. (*Pause.*) Come on Gogo, return
> the ball, can't you, once in a way?
> ESTRAGON: (*with exaggerated enthusiasm*). I find this
> really most extraordinarily interesting.

The discussion goes on to canvas the melancholy possibility that perhaps both thieves were damned. And the effect
of the dialogue on the stage is, momentarily, to make us
identify the glib Didi and the resentful and inarticulate

Gogo with the two thieves, and to see, in each of them, an overmastering concern with the other's salvation. There is also towards the end of the first act a discussion about whether their human affection for each other may have stood in the way of that salvation:

> ESTRAGON: Wait! (*He moves away from Vladimir.*) I wonder if we wouldn't have been better off alone, each one for himself. (*He crosses the stage and sits down on the mound.*) We weren't made for the same road.
> VLADIMIR: (*without anger*). It's not certain.
> ESTRAGON: No, nothing is certain.

The tree on the stage, though it is a willow, obviously stands both for the Tree of the Knowledge of Good and Evil (and, when it puts on green leaves, for the Tree of Life) and for the Cross. When Didi and Gogo are frightened in the second act, the best thing they can think of doing is to shelter under its base. But it gives no concealment, and it is perhaps partly from God's wrath that they are hiding; for it is also the Tree of Judas, on which they are recurrently tempted to hang themselves.

Here, in fact, we have the subtle novelty, the differentiating quality, of 'Waiting for Godot,' when we compare it with 'Everyman' or with 'The Pilgrim's Progress.' Didi and Gogo do not complete their pilgrimage nor are we meant to be clear that they will complete it successfully. The angel who appears to them at the end of the first act is an ambiguous angel: the angel who keeps the goats, not the angel who keeps the sheep. And Godot - one remembers that God chastises those whom he loves, while hardening the hearts of impenitent sinners by allowing them a term of apparent impunity - does not beat him but beats his brother who keeps the sheep:

> VLADIMIR: Whom does he beat?
> BOY: He beats my brother, sir.
> VLADIMIR: Ah, you have a brother?
> BOY: Yes, sir.
> VLADIMIR: What does he do?
> BOY: He minds the sheep, sir.
> VLADIMIR: And why doesn't he beat you?
> BOY: I don't know, sir.
> VLADIMIR: He must be fond of you.
> BOY: I don't know, sir.

Are Didi and Gogo in the end to be among the goats? The boy who appears as a messenger at the end of the second act looks like the same boy, but is not, or at least does

not recognize them. He may be, this time, the angel who
keeps the sheep. That Godot himself stands for an anthropomorphic image of God is obvious. That is why Vladimir -
if he had a blonde or a black beard he might be more
reassuringly man or devil - is so alarmed in the second
act when he hears that Godot, Ancient of Days, has a white
beard.

> VLADIMIR (softly): Has he a beard, Mr. Godot?
> BOY: Yes, sir.
> VLADIMIR: Fair or ...(*he hesitates*) ... or black?
> BOY: I think it's white, sir.
> > *Silence.*
> VLADIMIR: Christ have mercy on us!

The peculiar bitter ambiguity of the use of the Christian
material is most obvious, perhaps, in the dialogue about
Gogo's boots towards the end of the first act:

> VLADIMIR: But you can't go barefoot!
> ESTRAGON: Christ did.
> VLADIMIR: Christ! What's Christ got to do with it?
> You're not going to compare yourself with Christ!
> ESTRAGON: All my life I've compared myself to him.
> VLADIMIR: But where he was it was warm, it was dry!
> ESTRAGON: Yes. And they crucified quick.

One main function of Pozzo and Lucky in the play is to
present, and to be the occasion of the dismissal of what
might be called 'alternative philosophies.' Pozzo, in the
first act, is a man of power, who eloquently - too consciously eloquently, as he knows - expounds Nietzschean
pessimism:

> But - (*hand raised in admonition*) - but - behind this
> veil of gentleness and peace (*he raises his eyes to the
> sky, the others imitate him, except Lucky*) night is
> charging (*vibrantly*) and will burst upon us (*he snaps
> his fingers*) pop! like that! (*his inspiration leaves
> him*) just when we least expect it. (*Silence. Gloomy.*)
> That's how it is on this bitch of an earth.

Like an actor, he asks for applause:

> ESTRAGON: Oh, tray bong, tray tray tray bong.
> POZZO: (*fervently*) Bless you, gentlemen, bless you!
>   (*Pause.*) I have such need of encouragement! (*Pause.*)
>   I weakened a little towards the end, you didn't
>   notice?

VLADIMIR: Oh, perhaps just a teeny weeny little bit.

In the second act, in his far more genuinely desperate
state, his pessimistic eloquence is less obviously
'theatrical':

> (*Calmer*). They give birth astride of a grave, the
> light gleams an instant, then it's night once more.
> (*He jerks the rope.*) On!

There is an echo in the rhythm and idiom of the first sentence, there, of Synge. And since it is the only overtly
'poetical' sentence which Mr. Beckett allows himself in
this play, and since he is the most calculatingly skilful
of writers, one may take it that the echo is meant as a
criticism of Pozzo - a criticism of romantic stylized
pessimism. If the Nietzschean attitude is dismissed in
Pozzo, it is harder to suggest just what is dismissed in
Lucky. He is the proletarian, who used to be the peasant.
He used to dance 'the farandole, the fling, the brawl, the
jig, the fandango, and even the hornpipe.' Now all he can
dance are a few awkward steps of a dance called 'the Net.'
But in Lucky's long speech - the most terrifyingly effective single sustained episode in the play - he stands for a
contemporary reality, composite, perhaps, but when presented to us immediately recognizable. He stands for half-
baked knowledge, undigested knowledge, the plain man's
naive belief in a Goddess called Science, his muddled
appeals to unreal authorities:

> ... but not so fast for reasons unknown that as result
> of the public works of Puncher and Wattman it is estab-
> lished beyond all doubt that in view of the labours of
> Popov and Belcher left unfinished for reasons unknown
> of Testew and Cunard left unfinished it is established
> what many deny that man in Possy of Testew and Cunard
> that man in Essy that man in short that man in brief
> in spite of the progress of alimentation and defecation
> wastes and pines wastes and pines and concurrently
> simultaneously what is more for reasons unknown in
> spite of the strides of physical culture the practice
> of sports such as tennis football running cycling
> swimming flying floating....

And so on to the length of almost two complete pages!
Lucky's speech is the great bravura piece of writing in
the play. Mr. Beckett has never been more brilliantly
unreadable; not only Didi, Gogo, and Pozzo but the audience want to scream. What is dismissed in Lucky's speech

is perhaps Liberalism, Progress, Popular Education, what
Thomas Love Peacock used to call, sardonically, 'the March
of Mind.' The Nietzschean and the Liberal hypothesis being
put out of court, the christian hypothesis is left holding
the stage. It is at least a more comprehensive and profound hypothesis, whatever Mr. Beckett may personally think
of it; and the total effect of his play, therefore - since
most of us, in the ordinary affairs of the world, have more
of Pozzo or Lucky in us, than of Didi or Gogo - is not to
lower but unexpectedly to raise our idea of our human dignity. Questioning and expectation do give life dignity,
even though expectations are never satisfied, and even
though the most fundamentally important questions can
expect, perhaps, at the most an implicit answer.

23.   ERIC BENTLEY IN 'NEW REPUBLIC'

14 May 1956, 20-1

Eric Bentley (b. 1916), playwright, editor, translator,
drama critic and former professor of literature. From
1952 to 1956 he was the influential drama critic of the
'New Republic,' and from 1953 to 1969, Professor of
Dramatic Literature at Columbia University. His best-
known books on theatre are 'The Playwright as Thinker
(1946), 'Bernard Shaw' (1947), 'What is Theatre' (1956),
and 'Theatre of War' (1972).

The minute a statement was released to the press that
Beckett's 'Waiting for Godot' was not for casual theatre-
goers but for intellectuals, I could have written Walter
Kerr's review for him. And I felt myself being jockeyed
into writing a defense of the play as if by its success or
failure civilization would stand or fall. Such is criticism.

Or is it? Besides the intellectual anti-intellectualism of a Walter Kerr, two other attitudes, both of them
less objectionable, have defined themselves in modern
America: one is non-intellectual pro-intellectualism and
the other is non-intellectual anti-intellectualism. Both
these attitudes were represented in the newspaper reviews
of 'Waiting for Godot,' and obviously the production

benefited as much from the first as it suffered from the second. Both groups of critics found the writing beyond them. The first was prepared to be respectful toward what was not fully understood. The second joined Mr. Kerr in finding something of a scandal in the very existence of difficulty. And there emerged, in his review and theirs, one of the big ideas of the century:

> Thinking is a simple, elementary process. 'Godot' is merely a stunt...
>> - John Chapman, 'The Daily News'

> The author was once secretary to that master of obfuscation, James Joyce. Beckett appears to have absorbed some of his employer's ability to make the simple complex...
>> - Robert Coleman, 'The Daily Mirror'

> ...the rhythms of an artist [Bert Lahr] with an eye to God's own truth. All of them, I think, are the rhythms of musical comedy, or revue, of tanbark entertainment - and they suggest that Mr. Lahr has, all along in his own lowbrow career, been in touch with what goes on in the minds and hearts of the folk out front. I wish that Mr. Beckett were as intimately in touch with the texture of things.
>> - Walter Kerr, 'New York Herald Tribune'(1)

The superior insight of genius is unnecessary. All we need, to take upon us the non-mystery of things, is constant communion with the man of non-distinction.

Speaking of obfuscation, what could obfuscate our experience of Beckett's play more than the cloud of conflict between highbrow and lowbrow, highbrow and highbrow, lowbrow and lowbrow? This conflict is, of course, anterior to the play. The play itself presents a problem for our audiences too, and that is the problem of nausea as a playwright's conscious attitude to life.

Though it is permissible to be nauseated by existence, and even to say so, it seems doubtful whether one should expect to be paid for saying so, at any rate by a crowd of people in search of an amusing evening. Yet, since the humor which provides amusement is precisely, as Nietzsche observed, a victory over nausea, it would be hard to stage the victory without at least suggesting the identity and character of the foe. It has taken Krafft-Ebing and Freud to force a general admission of the importance of nausea even, say, in the work of Swift, where it is most prominent.

American optimism drives American nausea a little more
deeply underground: that is the difference between America
and Europe. For, if the conscious 'thought' of 'serious'
literature and drama becomes more insistently 'positive,'
a nation's humor, arising from the depths of discomfort,
repression, and guilt, will become more and more destructive. Even now, if there is nothing quite so happy-drunk
as American confidence, there is also nothing quite so
blackly despondent as American cynicism, the 'hardboiled-
ness' of the 'tough guy.' But the ranks of the community
close in order to hide the fact. Hence the great loathing
and fear of any more conscious type of pessimism, such as
that which flows in a steady stream from France. For
Broadway use, the professional pessimism of Anouilh is
made over into professional idealism.

Samuel Beckett's point of view seems pretty close to
that of Anouilh or Sartre. 'Waiting for Godot' is, so to
speak, a play that one of them ought to have written. It
is the quintessence of 'existentialism' in the popular,
and most relevant, sense of the term - a philosophy which
underscores the incomprehensibility, and therefore the
meaninglessness, of the universe, the nausea which man
feels upon being confronted with the fact of existence,
the praiseworthiness of the acts of defiance man may perform - acts which are taken, on faith, as self-justifying,
while, rationally speaking, they have no justification because they have no possibility of success.

Like many modern plays, 'Waiting for Godot' is undramatic but highly theatrical. Essential to drama, surely, is
not merely situation but situation in movement, even in
beautifully shaped movement. A *curve* is the most natural
symbol for a dramatic action, while, as Aristotle said,
beginning, middle, and end are three of its necessary
features. Deliberately anti-dramatic, Beckett's play has
a shape of a non-dramatic sort; two strips of action are
laid side by side like railway tracks. These strips are
One Day and the Following Day in the lives of a couple of
bums. There *cannot* be any drama because the author's conclusion is that the two days are the same. That there are
also things that change is indicated by a play-within-
this-play which also has two parts. The first time that
the characters of the inner play come on they are a brutal
Master and his pitiful Man; the second time they are both
equally pitiful because the Master has gone blind.

What has brought the play before audiences in so many
countries - aside from snobberies and phony publicity - is
its theatricality. Highbrow writers have been enthusiastic about clowns and vaudeville for decades, but this
impresses me as the first time that anything has

successfully been done about the matter. Mr. Kerr gave
Bert Lahr all the credit for a traditional yet rich
characterization, which, however, had been skillfully
put together by Mr. Beckett. The author, to recapitulate,
has not only been able to define the 'existentialist'
point of view more sharply than those who are more fam-
ously associated with it, he has also found for its expression a vehicle of a sort that people have been recom-
mending without following their own recommendation.

It is, therefore, an important play. Whether it is
more important than these two achievements suggest is the
question. To me, the play did not come over with the
force of revelation, nor with that of sheer greatness.
Mr. Beckett's voice is interesting, but one does not quite
find it individual, because it does not quite seem new.
One is surely not exploiting an external fact unfairly in
saying that Mr. Beckett is excessively - if quite inevitably - over-influenced by Joyce. If Russian literature is
cut from Gogol's 'Overcoat,' Irish literature is cut from
those coats of many colors, 'Ulysses' and 'Finnegans
Wake.'

I do not think the play is obscure except as any rich
piece of writing is obscure. No doubt there are meanings
that will disengage themselves in time as one lives with
such a work, yet enough is clear from the first not only
to arouse interest but to communicate a sense of a unified
and intelligible image of life. I take it that Beckett
belongs to that extensive group of modern writers who have
had a religious upbringing, retain religious impulses and
longings, but have lost all religious belief. I should
differentiate him from, say, Sartre, in that he does not
write from the standpoint of atheism but, theologically
speaking, from that of skepticism. People who have seen
'Godot' are able to suggest this or that solution -
Christian, anti-Christian, etc. - precisely because Beckett has left the door open for them to do so. They are
wrong only if they intimate that the author himself passed
through the door and closed it behind him. Rough words
have been spoken about the allegedly excessive symbolism
of the play. This is unjust. Beckett's finest achievement is to have made the chief relationships, which are
many, so concrete that abstract interpretations are
wholly relegated to the theater lobby. He gives us, not
tenets, but alternatives seen as human relationships
(between bum and bum, master and man); also as ordinary
human attitudes to God, Nature, and Death on the one hand,
and, on the other, to the 'trivialties,' such as clothes,
defecation, smells....

The New York production is so good that I can dispose

of the only serious shortcomings in a few lines. The
lighting is of that 'modern' sort which is now old-
fashioned and was always awful: you don't see the actors'
faces properly, and every time an actor moves he is either
moving into much less light or much more. One of the
actors seems miscast. This is Kurt Kasznar as Pozzo, the
Master, who gave us a playful stage villain instead of a
stomach-turning real one; Mr. Kasznar was so brilliant as
the Director in 'Six Characters' that he has been lured
into repeating part of the characterization in a very different role.

On the first night, Alvin Epstein as Lucky, the Man,
threw away the content of the most effective speech in the
play, into which Beckett seems to have poured all his
training in Catholic philosophy. At the second performance, which I also attended, the fault had largely been
corrected, without detriment to the pantomime, which is
Mr. Epstein's specialty. E.G. Marshall, as one of the
bums, was overshadowed by his partner. His acting seemed
to me defensive - and therefore, as things work out on the
stage, a little self-destructive. The part was under-
acted - sometimes almost to the point of inaudibility.
Long speeches were attacked diffidently with the usual
result: that they constantly seemed to be over before they
were, and one thought: Heavens, is he starting up again?
Yet all this is by no means as disastrous as spelling it
out makes it sound. In any part, Mr. Marshall is interesting.

Estragon, the less philosophical bum, the *dummer August*
of this particular circus, is played by Bert Lahr. If to
Mr. Kerr this fact just means the saving of a highbrow
play by a lowbrow actor, it is just as fair to look upon
it as the perfect execution by a lowbrow actor of a highbrow writer's intentions. If the perfection of it is
bound to hurt the less perfect impersonations by contrast,
it has the merit of enabling us to visualize a perfect
production of the play as a whole and even, by extension,
a perfect play of this type perfectly produced.

We sentimentalize vaudeville now, and overrate it; go
back to the reports of William Archer and Bernard Shaw,
and you'll find it was usually atrocious. I shall not
insult Mr. Lahr by giving the credit for his work to an
institution that did not in fact have very high standards.
That he acquired certain habits is all to the good though
there are plenty of actors with those habits who would
have failed in 'Godot.' The triumph here is partly due to
his bringing to the script a respect which has not been
shared by all the commentators on it. One does see the
advantage of his training, for, while Mr. Marshall has to

create a clown and constantly work at it, Mr. Lahr did his
creating in that line so long ago that he settles and
relaxes into a clown personality as others do into a
smoking jacket and carpet slippers. He reminds me strongly of Menasha Skulnik in 'The Flowering Peach.' On both
occasions, literature and popular comedianship met. But
it was a matter of marriage, not lifesaving. Both actors
showed respect for the words they spoke, while the words,
gratefully, but with a proper pride, gave something to the
actor that made him larger and richer than he had been,
perhaps ever, before.

Herbert Berghof directed. I have less reverence for
this play than he, and would have lopped off the last bit
of the first act. I would also have been tempted to make
cuts at several points where the dialogue stumbles. (The
rhythm is very firm for longish stretches but will from
time to time just go to pieces.) But reverence toward a
script is a good fault, and, on Broadway, an unusual,
almost exemplary, one.

Though many directors have their characteristic tricks,
or their famous and much-publicized manner, very few give
to their shows the imprint of an individual human being.
This imprint Mr. Berghof - in the quietest way in the
world - imparts. In a brief commentary, one has to point
to particular touches - such as the delicate way one bum
takes the other's thumb out of his mouth while he sleeps,
or the soft and stealthy way in which Mr. Lahr would curl
up and go to sleep, or the confident way in which one
actor or the other would undertake moves which the realistic directors don't use (such as walking in a circle).
But Mr. Berghof's personality - gentle, sensitive, youth-
ful, fanciful - is not found only in the 'blocking' and
stage business; it is far more subtly interfused and, with
the co-operation of the actors, gives the evening its
special aroma and dignity.

A remark - perhaps irrelevant - about the title.
'Godot' is the person you are waiting for who, presumably,
will set things to rights when he arrives. I assume that
Mr. Beckett made up the French word from the English one,
God. But, as someone will no doubt inform 'The Times
Literary Supplement,' there is a once well-known play of
Balzac's in which we spend the whole evening waiting for a
character called Godeau, who has still not come on stage
when his arrival is announced just before the final cur-
tain falls.

Postscript 1967

My 'New Republic' review of eleven years ago records my
first impressions of 'Godot.' 'No doubt,' I wrote, 'there
are meanings that will disengage themselves in time, as
one lives with such a work. And, in fact, with time I
ceased to believe that the play was 'undramatic' and only
'theatrical,' and I set down my later belief - that 'Godot'
is truly dramatic - in my book 'The Life of the Drama'
(New York: Atheneum, 1964, pp. 99-101 and 348-351). My
early reading of Beckett missed out an essential element
both dramatic and moral. I might even blame the error, in
part, on Beckett himself, in that his English title does
not translate the much more apt French one: 'En attendant
Godot,' which means '*while* waiting for Godot.' The subject
is not that of pure waiting. It is: what happens in certain human beings *while* waiting. Estragon and Vladimir
do not only wait. *In* waiting they show, ultimately, human
dignity: *they* have kept their appointment, even if Godot
has not. A lot of comment on Beckett goes wrong in taking
for granted a pessimism more absolute than 'Godot' em-
bodies, in other words in taking for granted that Godot
will not come. This philosophical mistake produces a mistake in dramatic criticism, for to remove the element of
uncertainty and suspense is to remove an essential tension - in fact the essential drama.
    So much for the insufficiency of my earlier comments on
the play. As for its historic destiny, it is summed up in
Polish critic Jan Kott's answer to a questioner who asked:
'What is the place of Bertolt Brecht in your [i.e., the
Polish] theater?' He said: 'We do him when we want Fantasy. When we want Realism, we do "Waiting for Godot."'
This remark might also bring to mind the comment of the
English poet and critic, Al Alvarez: 'The real destructive
nihilism acted out in the [extermination] camps was expressed artistically only in works like Beckett's 'Endgame' or 'Waiting for Godot,' in which the naked unaccom-
modated man is reduced to the role of helpless, hopeless,
impotent comic, who talks and talks and talks in order to
postpone for a while the silence of his own desolation.'
It is the historic destiny of 'Waiting for Godot' to represent the 'waiting' of the prisoners of Auschwitz and
Buchenwald, as also the prisoners behind the walls and
barbed wire of Walter Ulbricht, as also the prisoners
behind the spiritual walls and barbed wire of totalitarian
society generally, as also the prisoners behind the spiritual walls and barbed wire of societies nearer home. I
would add to Alvarez's observation that, in this waiting,
there is not only an adjustment to desolation, there is a

rebuff to desolation. Even the Auschwitz prisoners hoped,
however improbably, to get out: it is not certain that
Godot *won't* come. And what Beckett's work ultimately em-
bodies is this hope. Which again might be contained
within the definition of what Kott playfully calls Realism. For, whether they should or not, people do continue
to hope for Godot's arrival.

Note

1 Mr Kerr had also written: '"Waiting for Godot" is not
   a real carrot; it is a patiently painted, painstakingly
   formed plastic job for the intellectual fruit-bowl ...
   the play, asking for a thousand readings, has none of
   its own to give. It is, in the last analysis, a veil
   rather than a revelation. It wears a mask rather than
   a face.' (Eds)

24. C.B. IN 'SAN QUENTIN NEWS'

28 November 1957, 1, 3

Godot was a world play; a theme emboldening every element
of individual and group personality. It was an expression, symbolic in order to avoid all personal error, by an
author who expected each member of his audience to draw
his own conclusions, make his own errors. It asked nothing in point, it forced no dramatized moral on the viewer,
it held out no specific hope.
    The dramatis personae were five. Robert Symonds and
Eugene Roche played the tramps Didi and Gogo: indigent,
half-conscious, groping spirits. They were the protagonists, if indeed there were any such. Joseph Miksak and
Jules Irving were two mimes, or muses, called Pozzo and
Lucky. Young Anthony Miksak appeared as a small oracle.
Within these five players was entwined the most provo-
catively negative synthesis of the mechanics of human
culture that it has been our pleasure to enjoy for a long
time.
    If you will allow an explanation, see this play with
us as the vast world housed right inside your own mind.
See the tramps as a continually ambivalent humanity, Didi
more outgoing, Gogo more withdrawn; both, as one, living

on the periphery, nihilistic and morose. Together,
possessing the sum of all human attributes. See Master
Pozzo as the compelling spirit, the drive which makes the
world go round, whose psychic armature may occasionally
turn the shaft straight in our collective backs. Study
the numen he controls, which carries his whip and throne
and does all the work. Watch it cower humbly when its
spur attracts the limelight, disinterestedly put on its
thinking hat and review the sweeping scene with gutty
poetry - until roughly subdued by a two-man humanity made
of the common audience, Gogo and Didi.

Let this same Lucky, the caricature of intellect with
his white clown face, pound home fruitless insight into
the ductile, malleable, impressionable force which may
create, but never command the respect of the promoter-
master. Lucky may devise and do the work, but Pozzo will
organize. Then, for a moment, imagine that these are just
two people coming to more and more unequal odds. Project
yourself onto the stage. And endure - for just one night
away? Add the coup-de-grace of a young immemorial child-
conscience which prods the mighty midgets of mankind,
Gogo and Didi, into waiting for something more, tomorrow
night. Keep them waiting. Even though they cannot help
it.

Let one night pass, as they reckon time in make-
believe, and find all the characters in the same place.
Feel the almost limbo-like tenuity of existence broaden,
approach a climax - just a step away - a climax which
almost, but never quite arrives. Listen to the quick re-
surgences of hope and faith (that Godot WILL come); and
watch them finalize into precursors of doubt, depression
and death. Always in the background lurking the sign of
the fast way out, the Judas-tree to hang on - if there
were just a little rope!

Now let us be carried back into the action, let the
mimers reappear. Enter Pozzo and Lucky. But a little
more slowly, for the whip of cultural libido has been
blinded! Hear Pozzo's cries for help, for mercy. Feel
pity for a beaten Fury, and hold out your hand - but wait!
Should we forget what we've learned in waiting and watching? What's it worth? If we help him, then what? Let us
ponder and discuss: weigh the pros and cons. And then,
overcome with 'spiritual' effulgence, help this flailing
vital force in its sightless death throes. Yet in our
selfless charity we overlook the obvious. Even blind, he
is stronger than we! We fall. But resiliently. We are
pulled down by the dying only to become renewed, and in
turn set death on its feet again.

Now look closely at Lucky. He is dissembling. It only

seems he's more tired. He is the same. For thought
exists without physical bound; it cannot tire, for that
which motivates thought is perfect in itself. Naively,
uncomprehendingly, the clown is whipped back into shape.

Then the old roles assume, and pandering our own new
intimacies with this maimed but hard-core essence, we try
to outdo his servant clown with the thinking hat. And
this clown of social conscience never fights back. Never
this spirit alone. Finally, both master and harlequin
leave the stage. Only humanity remains, with diseased
body and tired feet.

We're still waiting for Godot, and shall continue to
wait. When the scenery gets too drab and the action too
slow, we'll call each other names and swear to part forever - but then, there's no place to go!

The play's the thing. This one was effective.

25. PIERRE MARCABRU IN 'ARTS-SPECTACLES'

10-16 May 1961, 14

Pierre Marcabru is a drama critic and journalist who
writes regularly for French newspapers.

(Eight years ago, Roger Blin presented Samuel Beckett's
'Waiting for Godot' at the Théâtre de Babylone. Five
years ago, the play was restaged at the Théâtre Hébertot.
Today it is playing at the Théâtre de France.)

From avant-garde playhouse to bourgeois playhouse, then
from bourgeois playhouse to official playhouse, the road
is well-known. It is the road followed by texts that
become aware of their respectability, texts that become
established without cries and without pain.

This sort of accepted security, coming about naturally
and without the slightest effort, draws some of the teeth
out of dangerous plays. One reaches the harbor, develops
a paunch, the face grows heavier, the features thicken,
one becomes hefty. Then one gets out of breath. It is
the time of peaceful success.

But one must still believe in peaceful success and know
its resources. It no longer improvises, it organizes,
slowly. Nothing led us to suppose that Beckett was

capable of such setting-up exercises. And yet 'Waiting for Godot' has become an easy-going play, a contented play. That which was formerly astonishing, and that to the point of scandal, is now no more than a game whose rules are completely unmysterious. And it is this absence of mystery, this clarity, that destroys anxiety. We are left with malaise.

The stage of the Théâtre de France, too wide and too deep, does not leave much of a chance to two clown-like, metaphysical tramps. They have to inhabit that plateau, traverse all its paths; in short, occupy it. It is the director's task to set up the scheme of this occupation. Roger Blin, a man of small stages, does not seem to have discovered the necessary perambulations. The play slackens. Once it was a clenched fist, today it is an open hand.

The actors, Raimbourg and Bierry, who were the original players, have a certain tendency to force their stage business, to give the audience time to wait for Godot. This is done with infinite talent, and Raimbourg's comic sense and cunning are admirable, but one senses at times the desire to reassure the audience, to distract them from the essential point, the human malediction that triumphs over all.

This malediction and anguish have been called Pascalian. Since the symbolic dimension gave a sly eloquence to these clowns' entrances, some have wished to add a little noble brilliance to despair. Hence a fine determination to discover here something other than a rigid and hostile pessimism, a terror of being that slowly turns to disgust.

And yet, what prevails is a physical, and not a metaphysical, horror of the human condition. Everything is carnally experienced. And we have here a little summary of the decomposition of bodies. As for the all too obvious symbols, they are only decoys. It is at the level of writing that everything is played out.

It is not Pascal at all, but rather Joyce who holds the reins. The freedom of language, its disorder, its calculated follies, and this prodigious equilibrium of words are all derived from Joyce. The battering ram of writing, used to force open the gates of a melancholy philosophy. What is striking, what remains to us are the harmony of rejoinders, the carefully prepared falls, the daring acrobatics: the exercises of language.

And this language is a language of the theatre. With all that implies of guile, pretense, false windows and false doors. It is a duel: the author on one side, the public on the other. Suddenly one perceives that Beckett, like Roussin, like Achard, can be cautious, knows every ruse, and does not push violence to the point of blindness.

This is where our disappointment begins, this is where the play breaks down. *Do you want to play with me?* follows the same path. And it is not just because they are playing here at death instead of at love that everything is thrown into confusion. The moment the audience flags, they smile, they encourage us, they make accomplices out of us. One has to join the dance. Beckett is holding out his hand. And sometimes he holds it out with a little too much complacency.

All this construction was not done hastily. This requires that. Everything is in its place. One retort calls for another retort. They are measured and weighed, placed there where they will be most efficacious. Impulse is stifled, calculation is king. Not a word comes freely. This is theater marked out with a compass and built with a plumb line. One discovers in it an architect's inventions, symmetries, cornerstones, an entire work of precision with points of equilibrium, delicate adjustments, balanced tensions.

Eight years ago all this was not as perceptible. Construction was effaced by surprise. Surprise is dead, what remains is a somewhat too methodical arrangement. We are surrounded by curt, dry, yet cajoling speeches, we are familiar with their tics and grimaces, and especially with the inevitable conclusions. Even Jean Martin, who bustles about like a sorrowful ape, no longer moves us. We see too clearly just how much the actor is responsible for, and the very quality of the performance, its perfection, exposes its method. It lacks thunder and lightning. The unexpected, the unsuspectible. That abyss which is called theater.

Only the stomach is affected. And this is the great power of 'Waiting for Godot': nausea rises, malaise remains. This malaise, as in all of Beckett's plays, is due to a sort of passion for the morbid, for decay, for the ruin of flesh and brains. A disgust fascinated by anything decomposing on its feet. The mannerisms of a gourmet presented with gamy meat. A sort of genius at inhaling the smell of gangrene. Odors and pus.

Thus we arrive at a theater of dying, but a stagy kind of dying, where nothing exists any more but the obscene twitches of an interminable death, theater of a twilight slowly eaten away by time, that will not survive this expiring society, to which it holds up the last mirror. With Beckett, theater is already in its grave. It is about time to lay a stone on top of it.

[Translated by Jean M. Sommermeyer]

'The Unnamable'
(1953)

[Written in French; published by Éditions de Minuit, Paris, as 'L'Innommable'; translated in English by Beckett; published by Grove Press, New York, 1958.]

26. MAURICE BLANCHOT IN 'NOUVELLE REVUE FRANÇAISE'

October 1953, 678-86

Maurice Blanchot (b. 1907), French novelist and critic, has published several novels, the best known, 'Thomas L'Obscur' (1941); but he is particularly influential for such critical works as 'La Part du feu' (1949), 'L'Espace littéraire' (1955), 'Le Livre à venir' (1959), 'L'Entretien infini' (1969).

Who is doing the talking in Samuel Beckett's novels, who is this tireless 'I' constantly repeating what seems to be always the same thing? What is he trying to say? What is the author looking for - who must be somewhere in the books? What are we looking for - who read them? Or is he merely going round in circles, obscurely revolving, carried along by the momentum of a wandering voice, lacking not so much sense as center, producing an utterance without proper beginning or end, yet greedy, exacting, a language that will never stop, that finds it intolerable to stop, for then would come the moment of the terrible discovery: when the talking stops, there is still talking; when the language pauses, it perseveres; there is

no silence, for within that voice the silence eternally
speaks.

An experiment without results, yet continuing with
increasing purity from book to book by rejecting the very
resources, meager as they are, that might permit it to
continue.

It is this treadmill movement that strikes us first.
This is not someone writing for beauty's sake (honorable
though that pleasure may be), not someone driven by the
noble compulsion many feel entitled to call inspiration
(expressing what is new and important out of duty or
desire to steal a march on the unknown). Well, why *is* he
writing then? Because he is trying to escape the treadmill by convincing himself that he is still its master,
that, at the moment he raises his voice, he might stop
talking. But is he talking? What is this void that
becomes the voice of the man disappearing into it? Where
has he fallen? 'Where now? Who now? When now?'

He is struggling - that is apparent; sometimes he
struggles secretly, as if he were concealing something
from us, and from himself too, cunningly at first, then
with that deeper cunning which reveals its own hand. The
first stratagem is to interpose between himself and language certain masks, certain faces: 'Molloy' is a book in
which characters still appear, where what is said
attempts to assume the reassuring form of a story, and of
course it is not a successful story, not only because of
what it has to tell, which is infinitely wretched, but
because it does not succeed in telling it, because it will
not and cannot tell it. We are convinced that this wanderer who already lacks the means to wander (but at least
he still has legs, though they function badly - he even
has a bicycle), who eternally circles around a goal that
is obscure, concealed, avowed, concealed again, a goal
that has something to do with his dead mother who is still
dying, something that cannot be grasped, something that,
precisely because he has achieved it the moment the book
begins ('I am in my mother's room. It's I who live there
now.'), obliges him to wander ceaselessly around it, in
the empty strangeness of what is hidden and disinclined
to be revealed - we are convinced that this vagabond is
subject to a still deeper error and that his halting,
jerky movements occur in a space which is the space of
impersonal obsession, the obsession that eternally leads
him on; but no matter how ragged our sense of him, Molloy
nevertheless does not relinquish himself, remains a name,
a site within bounds that guard against a more disturbing
danger. There is certainly a troublesome principle of
disintegration in the story of 'Molloy', a principle not

confined to the instability of the wanderer, but further
requiring that Molloy be mirrored, doubled, that he
become *another*, the detective Moran, who pursues Molloy
without ever catching him and who in that pursuit sets out
(he too) on the path of endless error, a path such that
anyone who takes it cannot remain himself, but slowly
falls to pieces. Moran, without knowing it, becomes
Molloy, that is, becomes an entirely different character,
a metamorphosis which undermines the security of the narrative element and simultaneously introduces an allegorical sense, perhaps a disappointing one, for we do not feel
it is adequate to the depths concealed here.

'Malone Dies' evidently goes further still: here the
vagabond is nothing more than a *moribund*, and the space
accessible to him no longer offers the resources of a
city with its thousand streets, nor the open air with its
horizon of forests and sea which 'Molloy' still conceded
us; it is nothing more than the room, the bed, the stick
with which the dying man pulls things toward him and
pushes them away, thereby enlarging the circle of his immobility, and above all the pencil that further enlarges
it into the infinite space of words and stories. Malone,
like Molloy, is a name and a face, and also a series of
narratives, but these narratives are not self-sufficient,
are not told to win the reader's belief; on the contrary,
their artifice is immediately exposed - the stories are
invented. Malone tells himself: 'This time I know where I
am going ... it is a game. I am going to play ... I think
I shall be able to tell myself four stories, each one on a
different theme.' With what purpose? To fill the void
into which Malone feels he is falling; to silence that
empty time (which will become the infinite time of death),
and the only way to silence it is to say something at any
cost, to tell a story. Hence the narrative element is
nothing more than a means of public fraud and constitutes
a grating compromise that overbalances the book, a conflict of artifices that spoils the experiment, for the
stories remain stories to an excessive degree: their brilliance, their skillful irony, everything that gives them
form and interest also detaches them from Malone, the
dying man, detaches them from the time of his death in
order to reinstate the customary narrative time in which
we do not believe and which, here, means nothing to us,
for we are expecting something much more important.

It is true that in 'The Unnamable' the stories are
still trying to survive: the moribund Malone had a bed, a
room - Mahood is only a human scrap kept in a jar fest-
ooned with Chinese lanterns; and there is also Worm, the
unborn, whose existence is nothing but the oppression of

his impotence to exist. Several other familiar faces
pass, phantoms without substance, empty images mechanically revolving around an empty center occupied by a nameless *I*. But now everything has changed, and the experiment, resumed from book to book, achieves its real profundity. There is no longer any question of characters
under the reassuring protection of a personal name, no
longer any question of a narrative, even in the formless
present of an interior monologue; what was narrative has
become conflict, what assumed a face, even a face in fragments, is now discountenanced. Who is doing the talking
here? Who is this *I* condemned to speak without respite,
the being who says: 'I am obliged to speak. I shall never
be silent. Never.' By a reassuring convention, we answer
it: it is Samuel Beckett. Thereby we seem to draw closer
to what is of concern in a situation that is not fictional,
that refers to the real torment of a real existence. The
word experiment is another name for what has actually been
experienced - and here too we try to recover the security
of a name, to situate the book's 'content' at the stable
level of a person, at a personal level, where everything
that happens happens with the guarantee of a consciousness, in a world that spares us the worst degradation,
that of losing the power to say *I*. But 'The Unnamable' is
precisely an experiment conducted, an experience lived
under the threat of the impersonal, the approach of a
neutral voice that is raised of its own accord, that
penetrates the man who hears it, that is without intimacy,
that excludes all intimacy, that cannot be made to stop,
that is the incessant, *the interminable*.

Who is doing the talking here then? We might try to
say it was the 'author' if this name did not evoke capacity and control, but in any case the man who writes is
already no longer Samuel Beckett but the necessity which
has displaced him, dispossessed and disseized him, which
has surrendered him to whatever is outside himself, which
has made him a nameless being, The Unnamable, a being
without being, who can neither live nor die, neither begin
nor leave off, the empty site in which an empty voice is
raised without effect, masked for better or worse by a
porous and agonizing *I*.

It is this metamorphosis that betrays its symptoms
here, and it is deep within its process that a verbal
survival, an obscure, tenacious relic persists in its
immobile vagabondage, continues to struggle with a per-
severance that does not even signify a form of power,
merely the curse of not being able to stop talking.

Perhaps there is something admirable about a book
which deliberately deprives itself of all resources, which

accepts starting at the very point from which there can be
no continuation, yet which obstinately proceeds without
sophistry and without subterfuge for 179 pages, exhibiting
the same jerky movement, the same tireless, stationary
tread.   But this is still the point of view of the *external* reader, contemplating what he regards as only a tour
de force.   There is nothing admirable in inescapable torment when you are its victim, nothing admirable in being
condemned to a treadmill that not even death can free you
from, for in order to get on that treadmill in the first
place, you must already have abandoned life.   Esthetic
sentiments are not called for here.   Perhaps we are not
dealing with a book at all, but with something more than
a book; perhaps we are approaching that movement from
which all books derive, that point of origin where, doubtless, the work is lost, the point which always ruins the
work, the point of perpetual unworkableness with which the
work must maintain an increasingly *initial* relation or
risk becoming nothing at all.   One might say that The
Unnamable is condemned to exhausting the infinite.   'I
have nothing to do, that is to say, nothing in particular.
I have to speak, whatever that means.   Having nothing to
say, no words but the words of others, I have to speak.
No one compels me to, there is no one, it's an accident, a
fact.   Nothing can ever exempt me from it, there is
nothing, nothing to discover, nothing to recover, nothing
that can lessen what remains to say, I have the ocean to
drink, so there is the ocean then.'

   It is this approach to *origin* which makes the experience of the work still more dangerous, dangerous for the
man who bears it, dangerous for the work itself.   But it
is also this approach which assures the experiment its
authenticity, which alone makes of art an essential re-
search, and it is by having rendered this approach evident in the nakedest, most abrupt manner that 'The Unnamable' has more importance for literature than most
'successful' works in its canon.   Try listening to 'this
voice that speaks, knowing that it lies, indifferent to
what it says, too old perhaps and too humiliated ever to
be able to say at last the words that might make it stop.'
And try descending into that neutral region where the self
surrenders in order to speak, henceforth subject to
words, fallen into the absence of time where it must die
an endless death: '... the words are everywhere, inside
me, well well, a minute ago I ha no thickness, I hear
them, no need to hear them, no need of a head, impossible
to stop them, impossible to stop, I'm in words, made of
words, others' words, what others, the place too, the air,
the walls, the floor, the ceiling, all words, the whole

world is here with me, I'm the air, the walls, the walled-
in one, everything yields, opens, ebbs, flows, like
flakes, I'm all these flakes, meeting, mingling, falling
asunder, wherever I go I find me, leave me, go toward me,
come from me, nothing ever but me, a particle of me, re-
trieved, lost, gone astray, I'm all these words, all these
strangers, this dust of words, with no ground for their
settling, no sky for their dispersing, coming together to
say, fleeing one another to say, that I am they, all of
them, those that merge, those that part, those that never
meet, and nothing else, yes something else, that I'm quite
different, a quite different thing, a wordless thing in an
empty place, a hard shut dry cold black place where nothing stirs, nothing speaks, and that I listen, and that I
seek, like a caged beast born of caged beasts born of
caged beasts born of caged beasts ...'

[Translated by Richard Howard]

'Watt'
(1953)

[Written in English; published by Olympia Press, Paris; translated into French by Ludovic and Agnès Janvier in collaboration with Beckett; published by Éditions de Minuit, Paris, 1968.]

27. RICHARD SEAVER IN 'NIMBUS'

Autumn 1953, 61-2

It is difficult to imagine anyone reacting passively to Beckett's work. In France, where he enjoys a reputation as one of the most important of post-war literary figures, his admirers are fervent, his detractors intransigent.

Despite the ambiguous and often puzzling nature of his work, he has received the almost unanimous approval of the French critics, whose judgment is based upon the trilogy, 'Molloy,' 'Malone meurt' and 'l'Innommable,' and the play, presented last winter, 'En Attendant Godot,' all of which were written directly in French.

'Collection Merlin,' a young Paris publishing venture devoted to publishing, in English, little known or neglected authors, has just made available the last work Beckett composed in English before turning - in desperation, it would seem, of ever interesting an English-speaking audience - to French as a literary medium.

Watt, like all Beckett's heroes, is a personage more acted upon than acting, who drifts through a curious, dreamlike world which, we suspect, he accepts either because he understands nothing whatsoever about it, or because his comprehension is such that he realises the

primary exigency to be the unquestioned acceptance of
whatever forces may buffet him about.
'"A milder, more inoffensive creature (than Watt) does
not exist," said Mr. Nixon. "He would literally turn the
other cheek, I honestly believe, if he had the energy."'
Watt, like other Beckett personages, has an undeniably
pure, almost Christlike quality about him. But his
martyrdom is unconscious, taken to be the way of the
world, the *status quo*. His purity, lacking the energy to
inflame, is inoffensive. A strange sort of purity indeed,
the inert purity of objects. It is doubtless significant
that Watt, when first encountered, is referred to in the
neuter: seen, but dimly to be sure, through the eyes of
other characters, he is barely distinguishable from the
objects he evokes.

He first appears, having been tossed from a tramway at
dusk, a 'motionless ... solitary figure lit less and less
by the receding lights, until it was scarcely to be distinguished from the dim wall behind it. Tetty was not
sure whether it was a man or a woman. Mr. Hackett was not
sure that it was not a parcel, a carpet for example, or a
roll of tarpaulin, wrapped up in dark paper and tied about
the middle with a cord.'

Rising, Watt proceeds to the railway station, is
knocked down by a milkcan porter, gets up, takes a train,
alights, goes to the house of Mr. Knott, where he is to
work as the ground floor retainer, replacing one Arsene,
who had previously replaced one Vincent. In time –
Watt's deducing mind leads him to believe the period a
year – and after a series of often intriguing experiences
and observations, he replaces Erskine as the second floor
retainer, whose departure is compensated by the arrival of
a new ground floor man, Arthur. After another lapse of
time, logically a second year, and another series of experiences and observations, Watt comes downstairs one
morning to find a new retainer seated in the kitchen. It
is the signal for Watt's departure. 'As Watt came, so he
went, in the night, that covers all things with its cloak,
especially when the weather is cloudy.'

Acceptance, inertness, both are an integral part of the
Beckett scheme. Not once, but several times Watt falls, or
is knocked down. So be it. Better to rejoice in the recli-
ning position than bewail the accident, lose one's temper,
join the jostling, maddening crowd. Prone, there is profit
to be gleaned, neglected sounds and inner voices to be listened to. 'Under the neck and under the distant palms he
felt the cool damp grasses of the ditch's edge. As so he
rested for a little time, listening to the little night-
sounds in the hedge behind him, in the hedge outside him,

hearing them with pleasure, and other distant night-sounds
too, such as dogs make, on bright nights, at the ends of
their chains, and bats, with their little wings, and the
heavy daybirds changing to a more comfortable position, and
the leaves that are never still, until they lie rotting in
a wintry heap, and the breath that is never quiet.'

The various characters who people Watt's world have no
more apparent *rapport* or contact with him than do the
people whom, in the course of the day, we pass on the
street. Of Mr. Knott himself we have a dozen, if not two
dozen descriptions, all different, either because Mr.
Knott is forever changing, or because Watt, in changing,
sees him each day differently, or because Watt's memory is
extremely poor, or perhaps because of all three.
'... the few glimpses caught of Mr. Knott, by Watt, were
not clearly caught, but as it were in a glass, not a
looking-glass, a plain glass, an eastern window at morning, a western window at evening. Add to this that the
figure of which Watt sometimes caught a glimpse, in the
vestibule, in the garden, was seldom the same figure, from
one glance to the next, but so various, as far as Watt
could make out, in its corpulence, complexion, height and
even hair, and of course in its way of moving and of not
moving, that Watt would never have supposed it was the
same, if he had not known that it was Mr. Knott.'

One may find 'Watt' either completely disjointed, or a
carefully conceived whole, utterly boring or completely
captivating. One may judge it devoid of meaning, or profoundly significant, ludicrously droll, or even tragic.
It is quite possible that one may have no patience with
this author, whose apparent caprices often result in passages of incredibly repetitious lengths, whose every positive statement is so carefully qualified as to reduce to
nothing what has been advanced. Should Watt dare an un-
qualified judgment ('Mr. Knott was a good master'), it is
impossible that this should stand as such, without the
addition: 'in a way,' and the concluding destructive process: 'Watt had no direct dealings with Mr. Knott, at this
period. Not that Watt was ever to have any direct dealings with Mr. Knott, for he was not. But he thought, at
this period, that the time would come when he would have
direct dealings with Mr. Knott....'

Like 'Molloy' and 'Malone meurt,' 'Watt' will probably
either be placed carefully on the shelf reserved for those
books to be read and re-read, or tossed angrily into the
wastepaper basket. Which one does is perhaps less a
judgment of the author than of oneself.

28. ANTHONY HARTLEY IN 'SPECTATOR'

23 October 1953, 458-9

Anthony Hartley has worked as diplomatic correspondent and
leader writer on papers such as the 'Spectator,' the
'Guardian' and 'The Economist,' and was until recently
editor of 'Interplay Magazine' in New York. His publications include 'A State of England' (Hutchinson, 1963) and
'Mallarmé' (Penguin, 1966) and he has also compiled the
'Penguin Book of Nineteenth Century French Verse' (1957)
and the 'Penguin Book of Twentieth Century French Verse'
(1959).

Samuel Beckett is not yet well-known in this country.
Some notice was taken of his play 'En attendant Godot'
which was the dark horse of the last Paris season, but his
three novels in French remain unread and undiscussed.
This is the more curious in that his first publications
were in English. For Mr. Beckett is an Irishman: he was
born in Dublin in 1906, but soon trod the well-worn road
to Paris, becoming Reader in English at the Ecole Normale.
His first two novels, 'More Pricks than Kicks' and
'Murphy' were published in London in 1934 and 1938,
attracting little attention at the time. They were much
influenced by Joyce - Mr. Beckett was a contributor to
Shakespeare and Co.'s collective commentary and the first
French translator of 'Anna Livia Plurabelle' - and
'Murphy,' at any rate, is full of cranky, difficult
talent. Both these works are at present unobtainable and
should be reprinted. They were to be followed by a third
English novel, 'Watt,' which has only just been published,
but which precedes the French novels in order of writing.
Since 'Watt' Mr. Beckett has produced four major works in
his adopted language: 'Molloy' (1951), 'Malone meurt'
(1951), 'L'Innommable' (1953) and 'En attendant Godot'
(1953).
   Some of the elements of the Beckett universe are
already present in 'Murphy.' The hero is pressed by his
mistress Celia to get a job, but he does not want to work.
By nature Murphy is a contemplative, and throughout the
book he increasingly loses touch with the world outside
himself. At last, he gets a post in Dr. Killiecrankie's
lunatic asylum, but is soon killed by an escape of gas.
His death is the consequence, perhaps the condition, of

his passing into a kind of Nirvana. He is the first of a
long line of solitaries, and with 'Watt' the sense of
ambiguity and isolation is accentuated. Watt sets out to
take up some ill-defined position in the house of Mr.
Knott. He is to replace a departing servant and will be
replaced in his turn. When the time comes he leaves the
place without ever having spoken to Mr. Knott and disappears from human ken on the local railway station. In
this novel all attempt at a rational superstructure is
abandoned. Since in Mr. Knott's house there is no reason
for doing one thing rather than another, every alternative
has to be put: 'Here he moved to and fro, from the door to
the window, from the window to the door, from the window
to the door, from the door to the window: from the fire to
the bed, from the bed to the fire....' This passage continues with various permutations of door, window, bed and
fire for a whole page, and the frequent occurrence of
catalogues of possibilities, explains why 'Watt' is hard
reading. It is the least successful of Mr. Beckett's
novels.

The French works contain less to torture the reader.
'Molloy' is divided into two parts. In the first Molloy,
an old tramp, is trying to reach his mother - with a good
deal of difficulty, as he has to go on crutches. At last
he falls into a ditch, where he lies with the obscure
feeling that someone is coming to help him. In the second
part Jacques Moran and his son set out to find Molloy on
the orders of Moran's employer Youdi. Moran, however,
does not succeed in his search. His own leg becomes stiff,
he cannot move, he kills an inoffensive stranger, his son
deserts him and he struggles home to find his house
empty, his bees and his hens dead. His quest has ruined
him, but given him new understanding. 'Malone meurt' is
still simpler. Malone, paralysed and dying in bed in some
sort of institute, amuses himself by making up stories.
His hero, a young man called Saposcat, changes his name to
Macmann and ends up in a lunatic asylum. On a patients'
outing Lemuel, the keeper, kills the two sailors managing
the boat. The story ends presumably as Malone dies:
voilà jamais ... voilà voilà ... plus rien.(1) 'L'Innommable,' Mr. Beckett's latest book, provides even less of
the usual ingredients of a novel. The narrator (*je*) is
somewhere in the dark. He suffers from other conscious-
nesses who speak with his voice, but he must keep on
speaking in spite of the intrusions of Mahood or Worm. He
feels dimly that this is due to someone he calls 'the
master.' In the end he has to accept the situation: *Là ou
je suis, je ne sais pas, je ne saurai jamais, dans le
silence on ne sait pas, il faut continuer, je vais*

continuer.(2)   The same thing is true of the two tramps
who are the principal characters in 'En attendant Godot.'
They are waiting for a M. Godot to come and employ them,
but he does not come. They have to go on waiting,
diverted from time to time by the antics of Pozzo, a local
squire, and his man-dog Lucky. They cannot even hang
themselves. They too must continue.

What does it all mean? What is the key to this strange
world? The critic must attempt an answer, even if it
entails sticking his neck out. After all, it is the business of critics to stick their necks out. And he need not
despair: certain common features emerge. In fact, all Mr.
Beckett's solitaries - Malone, Watt, Murphy and the rest -
have an unmistakable family likeness. Their abjection is
complete and is symbolised in their physical condition:
Malone is paralysed, Molloy has a game leg. Mahood is a
mere trunk in a barrel. A free use is also made of scatological imagery to express human degeneration. In places
Mr. Beckett recalls Swift, though Swift's insane savagery
is lacking. To the physical abjection corresponds mental
disintegration: from Watt onwards there is a progressive
disorganisation. These misty figures become increasingly
unconscious of time, place and the external world,
increasingly absorbed in their own consciousness, but
increasingly incapable of controlling it till the hero -
if hero is the right word - of 'L'Innommable' is reduced
to a disembodied voice, invaded and usurped upon by other
voices. The only character who is given to normal rational
processes is Jacques Moran, and the pathos of the second
part of 'Molloy' is essentially Moran's reduction to the
same state as Molloy himself - stiff leg and all. Yet it
is only when he has reached rockbottom that he can hear
and understand the voice that speaks to him. There is
something singularly moving in his renunciation of his
previous beliefs: Et je ne saurais faire à mes abeilles le
tort que j'avais fait à mon Dieu, à qui on m'avait appris
à prêter mes colères, mes craintes et désirs, et jusqu'à
mon corps.(3) Mr. Beckett has his moments of poetry.
Perhaps he is principally a poet.

This, however, brings us to the heart of his novels.
All these solitaries are waiting for Godot, for someone
who will take responsibility for them. Molloy feels that
someone is coming to save him. Jacques Moran is ordered
by Youdi to look for Molloy, and, if the order is harsh,
it corresponds to Moran's own tyrannical conception of the
world - he treats his son as arbitrarily as Youdi treats
him. 'Malone meurt' carries the idea a stage further:
Malone is the creator of Macmann (the son of man?) just as
Mr. Beckett is the creator of Malone. Similarly, Lemuel

can kill people because he is the one responsible for them
- like a god or a novelist. The whole subject of 'L'Innommable,' in fact, is the protest of the creator. The voice
behind Molloy and Watt and Murphy complains of their intrusion: Quand j'y pense, au temps que j'ai perdu avec ces
paquets de sciure...(4) Yet, it cannot be rid of its inventions: Mahood or Worm always return. 'L'Innommable' is
one of the profoundest studies of the relation between a
writer and his characters, though it may give too much away
for the comfort of anyone concerned with literature.

Mr. Beckett's characters create and are created. That
is their singularity. Just as the author imposes a pattern
on them by means of his imagination, so they impose a
pattern on the world by means of theirs. Molloy's lack of
knowledge of or real interest in the world around him is
the consequence of his constant creation of a fantasy world
within himself. Moreover, this fantasy world brings with
it entire liberty and entire responsibility. Molloy really
is free, whereas it is Murphy's inability to achieve this
freedom that destroys him. The world is too much with him
- the material world. At the last, Mr. Beckett's characters renounce all action. They busy themselves with creating myths in the darkness of their own minds. It is that
that makes them tick.

With this mythomania or desire to create as one of his
main themes Mr. Beckett comes to rely more and more on the
stream of consciousness technique in the presentation of
his novels. There is a development in this sense from
'Murphy' onwards. Two criticisms might be made of it in
action. First, it is sometimes a bit of a bore: the lack
of rationally connected narrative imposes a considerable
strain on the reader. Secondly, by raising the question of
the relation between the consciousness of the author and
the figures he creates, Mr. Beckett is undermining his
own literary method. A book like 'L'Innommable' goes far
to destroy the convention on which the earlier works were
based. It is only explicable as a stage in a pilgrimage
to silence. And this for a writer is despair.

Yet there is hope in this universe. Though Mr. Beckett
must certainly be connected with the examination of the
human situation which has gone on in France since the war,
he leaves more ways out than Sartre or even Camus. The
diagnosis is more extreme than theirs, but for that very
reason the hints of remedies are more convincing. His
taut, poetic style, purged of the Irishry and conceited wit
of the first novels, can convey appeasement or beauty as
well as abjection. 'Life isn't such a bad old b——' says
Mr. Gorman towards the end of 'Watt.' The human spark that
makes Malone tell himself stories is the compensating

factor. Who knows? Godot may come after all. Meanwhile
there are worse people to wait with than Mr. Beckett.

Notes

1   'never anything ... there ... any more.' (Eds)
2   'Where I am, I don't know, I'll never know, in the
    silence you don't know, you must go on, I can't go on,
    I'll go on.' (Eds)
3   'And I would never do my bees the wrong I had done my
    God, to whom I had been taught to ascribe my angers,
    fears, desires, and even my body.' (Eds)
4   'When I think of the time I've wasted with these bran-
    dips.' (Eds)

29.   RAYMOND JEAN IN 'MONDE'

February 1969, 1

Raymond Jean (b. 1921), Professor of Literature at the
University of Aix-en-Provence, critic, has written on
Surrealism and the 'nouveau roman' in France.

There is a bench at the beginning of the book.(1) Like at
the beginning of 'Bouvard et Pécuchet.' And the things
said by the passers-by who sit on it are hardly more coherent than what Flaubert's heroes said. Their names are
Hackett, Goff, Tetty and, curiously, Nixon. They talk
about everything and nothing in 'the Irish way,' the way
of 'Dubliners.' Their attention is suddenly drawn by a
character called Watt who appears in the novel in this
way: 'Tetty was not sure whether it was a man or a woman.
Mr. Hackett was not sure that it was not a parcel, a
carpet for example, or a roll of tarpaulin, wrapped up in
dark paper and tied about the middle with a cord....' A
little further the face becomes clearer:

    Watt had watched people smile and thought he understood
    how it was done. And it was true that Watt's smile,
    when he smiled, resembled more a smile than a sneer,
    for example, or a yawn. But there was something

wanting to Watt's smile, some little thing was lacking
and people who saw it for the first time, and most
people who saw it saw it for the first time, were sometimes in doubt as to what expression exactly was
intended. To many it seemed a simple sucking of the
teeth.

Such is the odd figure at the center of this novel. It
would be pointless to discuss the title at great length.
It may be that Watt is in fact 'What': Who? What?
Nobody. And Knott, his elusive partner, may be 'Not,'
'Nothing.' It does not matter. One thing is certain: at
the time he appears, Watt is going to the station and
climbs into the train to go to Knott's house.

And then everything starts. Because Knott's household
which he enters as a servant is really the closed world of
lack of meaning and senselessness. The owner is invisible
and meeting him is basically an improbable occurrence:

> This is not to say that Watt never saw Mr. Knott at
> this period, for he did, to be sure. He saw him from
> time to time, passing through the ground floor on his
> way to the garden from his quarters, and he saw him
> also in the garden itself. But these rare appearances
> of Mr. Knott, and the strange impression they made on
> Watt, will be described please God at greater length,
> at another time.

That's all. The rest is made of the dullest, the most
neutral, the most derisory daily occurrences. Things
happen. Which things? They are so insignificant, so
unnecessary, that it is difficult to answer the question.
Watt settles in this universe and manages to make his
own hole in it, with Erskine, the other servant. Knott's
house becomes something of a refuge to him: it is the
'locus' of absurdity itself, but an absurdity so well
organized as to be reassuring. He comes, goes, acts, does
not act, looks around him, questions everything, in a
style reminiscent all at the same time of Sterne, Swift
and Joyce. The doorbell rings? It is Gall, father and
son, the piano tuners: they make their way to the music-
room and perform a series of gestures which gradually lose
their meaning and their reality. Here is a pot. What is
a pot? 'For it was not a pot, the more he looked, the
more he reflected, the more he felt sure of that, that it
was not a pot at all. It resembled a pot, it was almost a
pot, but it was not a pot of which one could say Pot, pot,
and be comforted.' It is in this pot however that is prepared the odd and invigorating mixture which is daily

offered to Knott at a given time and which constitutes his
sole menu. If he does not finish it, it is given to the
dogs. And every day, quite regularly, there is a dog to
empty the bowl.

It is a really incomprehensible mystery about which
Watt's mind sets to work, making all sorts of guesses.
And he goes into calculations, by series, of probabilities
and hypotheses which lead him to explore the whole field
of the possible, according to a logic which in this instance derives from Rabelais or Lewis Carroll. He finally,
in a rather moving way, reduces all that (the possible relations between series, the series of dogs, the series of
men!) to the comparative table of the frogs' song which he
used to hear in his own country, when young 'and well
lying all alone stone sober in the ditch, wondering if it
was not the time and the place and the loved one already,
and the three frogs croaking Krak! Krek! and Krik!...'

In the third part, everything changes. Watt leaves
Knott's house and settles in a distant little bungalow.
New surroundings, new life. This is suddenly told us in
the first person by a narrator called Sam who comes to
share sadly, affectionately, pitifully, woefully, Watt's
loneliness, forming with him the typical 'Beckettian'
couple of mutual help and deprivation: Vladimir and Estragon, Hamm and Clov, Winnie and Willie. It is a long chapter which the hero goes through so bitterly that 'his face
was bloody, his hands also and thorns were in his scalp,'
and 'his resemblance, at that moment, to the Christ
believed by Bosch, then hanging in Trafalgar Square, was
so striking that I remarked it.'

Then Sam disappears, and in the last part Watt finds
himself alone. He will in the end go back toward the
station, will lose himself in useless chats and will finally take a ticket 'to the end of the line.' These last
pages are increasingly jerky, irregular, syncopated. The
book does not end, trampling, drivelling, getting wrapped
up in itself. Words catch themselves in their own traps,
get repeated, bump into each other, stop, as if the
language was gradually seized with total paralysis. At
the end, there are only bits, notes, given in 'addenda'
by Ludovic Janvier, where one can read things like 'Never
Been Properly Born' or 'Sempiternal Penumbra.' The book
closed, one remains for a long time ensnared in this long
flow of words to which translation has given a kind of
biting ingenuousness and a brand new humor.

[Translated by Françoise Longhurst]

Note

1   Jean is reviewing the French translation of 'Watt.'
    (Eds)

30.   BERNARD PINGAUD IN 'QUINZAINE LITTÉRAIRE'

16 and 28 February 1969, 4-6

Contrary to a widely held belief, the great writer is not
the one who continually rewrites the same book.   Rather
it is he for whom each book cancels out the preceding one
because it goes further along the same path.   A definite
choice was made at the beginning, and we can say, in this
sense, that all the works were already contained in the
opening pages.   But we only notice this afterwards, when
the distance covered permits us retrospectively to locate
the point of departure.
      The works of certain authors develop by successive
conquest, annexing new domains one after the other.
Others proceed by reduction: like an ever-tightening
spiral, they go from appearances to essentials, 'from the
periphery to the kernel.'   So it is, as Ludovic Janvier
has shown, with Beckett's works.   The 'kernel' is made up
of the latest brief and suffocating texts of 'Têtes-
Mortes' ('No's Knife' in English) (1967) where rareified
language attains an unsurpassable density.   'Watt,' like
'Murphy,' still belongs to the 'periphery.'   Finished (or
rather abandoned) in 1945, the novel was published in its
original English version in 1953.   But in contrast to
'Murphy,' which he translated himself, Beckett, for reasons unknown, has not, until now, authorized a translation
of 'Watt.'   Thus this text comes to us twenty-three years
late.   We can wonder how the critics would have reacted if
it had appeared on time.   The effect would probably have
been no less striking, but no doubt misled by the masks
behind which Beckett still hid (humorist, story-teller),
we would have neglected certain key passages, and missed
what seems obvious to us now: namely that Beckett's work
is a reflection on language, that it exhausts itself in
saying (in living) the question of speech.   The first and
best critics of 'Molloy' saw it above all as a novel of
non-sense, neglecting (what seem today to be) very clear
remarks ('Saying is inventing') which indicate the limits

of this epic of the absurd.

What then is 'Watt'? Apparently it is first of all a story.

The story of a man named Watt who takes the train one evening to go to the house of a man named Knott. There someone is waiting for him, someone he is to succeed. Mister Knott lives in the middle of a large park. He has two servants: one works on the first floor of the house, the other on the second. When one finishes with the first floor, one goes on to the second. Until the day when, finding a new-comer in the kitchen, the second floor servant realizes that there is nothing for him to do but go. Thus Watt, at the end of the book, is back at the railway station where he had disembarked several months, several years earlier (we don't know how long he worked), asking for a ticket 'to the end of the line.' In the meantime (but is it really in the meantime? Chronology isn't clear either) a curious episode takes place, which stands apart from the rest of the text. Watt is 'transferred to another pavilion' where he completes his stay alone. In the neighboring pavilion, there lives a man named Sam, whose name we have not heard mentioned up to this point, and who turns out to be the narrator. Separated by a barbed-wire fence, meeting only by chance, Sam and Watt establish a ridiculous and ephemeral friendship which ends with Watt's departure. A final explanation concerning Mister Knott is not given.

Interpretation of this passage causes problems. Why do we suddenly leave Knott's house? Why does the park suddenly turn into a kind of camp or asylum, where numerous loners are condemned to live side by side? Are we to believe that Watt, before being finally sent away, has been relieved of his duties. What then is Sam's function, and why don't we see him earlier? It seems that Beckett is not content to fill his story with enigmas, improbabilities, comic digressions and absurd reasonings. He wants to emphasize this story even more by suddenly changing its setting, its perspective, even its action, and by introducing a fictitious narrator to discredit it. But the moment of discreditation is also the most tender moment, when the text swings from drollness to pity, and then the reader, at first amused (we laugh continually while reading 'Watt'), is suddenly *moved*. The narrator's Christian name is clearly identical to that of the author; we can assume that Sam is Beckett himself, or one of Beckett's doubles, his voice in the text. We can also assume that the scene between Sam and Watt (which heralds the other *dédoublements* found throughout the work), located on the brilliant 'periphery' of the narrative, somehow provides us with an opening glance at the 'kernel.'

Before going any further, let us note that the theme of *dédoublement* is not the only theme used here to depict a universe that his later novels and plays have made familiar to us. We should mention, as well, infirmity and metamorphosis (cf. 'The Unnamable'), and odyssey and fall (cf. 'Molloy'). We would also have to analyze the diverse techniques of a perfectly-mastered rhetoric of narrative (a rhetoric of discreditation): interruptions, repetitions, contradictions, about-faces, changes in rhythm and tone, hypertrophic clauses, brutal ellipses, etc. The most characteristic are those dealing with combinations and permutations ('I always loved arithmetic it has paid me back in full,' we read in 'How It Is'); falsely exhaustive enumerations, repetitions in the same or inverse order, meticulous syllogisms, delirious hypotheses, and above all the use (we are tempted to say abuse) of the 'series,' which consists of presenting all the possible combinations of several items: for example the famous scene of the 'sucking'stones' in 'Molloy.'

But these themes, these techniques still belong to the 'periphery.' The appearance of the narrator in the third part of 'Watt' leads us to ponder their real meaning, and at the same time, to consider afresh the pages preceding his arrival. Ludovic Janvier, in analyzing Beckett's narrative works, has shown that they can be roughly divided into three periods: the first, in which the narrator keeps his story at a distance, inventing a character to represent him in it ('Murphy,' 'Watt'); the second, in which character and narrator coincide ('Molloy,' 'Malone Dies,' 'The Unnamable'); the third, in which the narrator, trapped by language, surpassed by his own voice, becomes merely the interpreter or the medium of speech which comes from elsewhere and passes through him ('How It Is'). These three periods remind us of the three 'regions' which Murphy had discerned: namely the 'light,' the 'half-light,' and the 'dark.' The 'light' is the universe of the mirror-narrative, 'radiant abstract of the dog's life.' In the 'half-light,' an esthetic world begins to form, which is no longer 'affligé d'un homologue réel': we can say that this constitutes the world of the work, of the text. Finally, the 'dark' is the world of nothingness, 'a flux of forms, a perpetual coming together and falling asunder of forms,' a universe of decomposition, which is also the universe of the *end* (we know the magical importance of this word for Beckett); in other words, the universe of peace, where speech becomes a murmur, and the murmur becomes silence.

Such a classification brings out the common element of

the three periods, of the three regions: the question of
language. This question, while not yet the 'subject' of
'Watt,' is already raised at several points in the novel.
First it comes up in the passage where Watt sees the meaning of a scene he has just been present at (the visit of
the piano tuners) vanish. This disappearance of meaning
leaves language in suspense, and at the same time gives
it a creative function because one can no longer speak of
nothing and because 'The only way one can speak of nothing
is to speak of it as though it were something.' A little
later, Watt evokes the first week of his stay when his
'words had not yet begun to fail him, or Watt's world to
become unspeakable' which is another way of presenting the
same problem. Finally when Watt wonders about the role of
Erskine, the servant on the second floor, we can't help
but be struck by the linguistic connotations of certain
terms he uses. Everyone present in Knott's house 'signifies' something, even if we don't know what it is; Watt's
life is 'a long languishing hypothesis'; the arrivals and
departures of successive servants form 'a long chain of
interdependencies...'; as for the fundamental presence
(the one which signifies), it doesn't 'vary'; only the
'externals' can vary. Are we forcing our interpretation
if we see in this pattern the classic play between code
and message, between language and speech, and confer upon
the mysterious Mr. Knott the role (here, figurative and
externalized) of the guardian of language, the role played
fifteen years later (at the end of the reductive process)
by the anonymous voice, the 'quaqua voice,' of which the
narrator's broken speech is only the ever-failing instrument?

Except that a key inversion takes place in the middle
of the process. In the first period ('light') as in the
third ('dark') there is distance and submission. But
while in the beginning the master of language - who is, we
suspect, also the narrator, in some way, the supreme narrator - protects and governs all speech (all narrative);
in the end, it is the narrator (or what is left of him)
who obeys the law of language, of 'voice.' In the beginning it was still a question of telling stories; in the
end merely a question of letting oneself be told 'only to
speak, that is to say only to listen. In the beginning
the story was 'without' and could vary infinitely, as we
see by Watt's absurd anecdotes; in the end it is the voice
which is 'without' ('voice first without qua qua on all
sides then in me'), condemning the second-hand orator to
the monotony of ever more sterile repetitions. Going from
the periphery to the kernel, Beckett has lost none of his
brilliant inventive skill; the inventiveness has withdrawn

on its own, making room for pure panting; for the 'immensity of speech' of which Maurice Blanchot has spoken.

Beckett's work has not lost any of its ability to signify either: the latest texts, with their condensed austerity, move us no less, indeed move us much more deeply than the early texts. This is because the organization of Beckett's work is never gratuitous, in other words, the signified is always inseparable from the signifier. In this regard, we can compare expressionist interpretations of Beckett's view of man's tragedy and formalist interpretations of the growing challenge to 'literature' of 'writing,' from 'Murphy' to 'How It Is.' They are either both right or both wrong; the paradox is that, here, the more impoverished speech becomes the more it *says*.

Finally we can ask ourselves - and could we ask a more Beckettian question about Beckett - what will be the 'end' of this undertaking which in a way has never stopped *ending*? If it is true, to quote Maurice Blanchot, that 'each work of literature is a firm defense, a high rampart against the immensity of speech which addresses us, while speaking about us,' we can understand that with its defenses finally down, the work collapses, dissolves along with the narrator into a confused murmur, which Molloy already heard - leaving behind only the frozen eddies, the delicate islets, the fragments of an impossible yet interminable work which Beckett has called 'Têtes-Mortes.'

[Translated by Larysa Mykyta and Mark Schumacher]

'Stories and Texts for Nothing' (1955)

[Written in French; published as 'Nouvelles et Textes pour rien' by Éditions de Minuit, Paris. See headnote to 'No's Knife' (1967) for details of English and American publication.]

---

31. RENÉ LALOU IN 'NOUVELLES LITTÉRAIRES'

22 December 1955

René Lalou (b. 1889), formerly Professor of Literature at the Sorbonne, is the author of 'Histoire de la littéraire française' (1922, 1939). He wrote a regular column for 'Les Nouvelles littéraires.'

Although Samuel Beckett published 'Murphy' in 1947, he only conquered the audience of literary critics four years later when 'Molloy' and 'Malone Dies' appeared. However, many of us were quick to say that this Irishman, with his complete mastery of our language, was one of the most original post-war writers. The following year when Samuel Beckett's 'Waiting for Godot' was produced, Jean Anouilh, Robert Kemp and Gabriel Marcel were among the first to proclaim the value of this tragedy of despair not even lit by a glimmer of consciousness. After 'The Unnamable' in 1953, Beckett now offers us a volume entitled 'Stories and Texts for Nothing.' The fact, brought to our attention by an editor's note, that the 'Stories' date from 1945 and the 'Texts' from 1950 is sufficient to emphasize the interest this collection has for us since it allows us to penetrate Beckett's mental laboratory before the definitive elaboration of the works which were to assure his renown.

If I have avoided the overly precise word 'creation,' it is because I believe that the novels 'Molloy' and 'Malone Dies' existed, dormant at least, in Beckett's imagination when he was composing the three short stories of 1945. For there we already find his constant use of monologue as an artistic technique, his implacably pessimistic vision and his insistence on the degrading functions of the human body. Isn't it characteristic that he speaks of the latter with the *saeva indignatio* of Jonathan Swift rather than with the frank gaiety of Rabelais? Here the memory of the Dean of Saint Patrick is not inappropriate. In fact, many details lead us to recognize that the background for these short stories is the city of Dublin - described in more sordid terms than those evoked by James Joyce whom Samuel Beckett served as secretary.

The three short stories have been grouped in chronological order better to portray three stages in the downfall of a human being. In The Expelled the anonymous narrator, obsessed by the idea of falling, narrates how he owes his reprieve from death to the cabman who has him share the shelter of a stable with his horse. 'When I am abroad in the morning (he declares), I go to meet the sun, and in the evening, when I am abroad, I follow it, till I am down among the dead.' It is indeed from beyond the grave that he will recount his story of The Calmative, in the past tense and in the manner of a myth: and there we will see him wandering across a deserted city to the edge of the sea and the upper gallery of the cathedral, to find himself finally 'in the same blinding void.' More tragic still will be The End where, after having described the preparations for his suicide, he will refuse to pursue a 'story in the likeness of my life, I mean without the courage to end or the strength to go on.'

More than one reader of 'The Unnamable' has had to question the meaning of this furious protestation: 'All these Murphys, Molloys and Malones do not fool me. They have made me waste my time, suffer for nothing, speak of them when, in order to stop speaking, I should have spoken of me and of me alone.' Casting all fiction aside, was Samuel Beckett thus addressing himself to us in his own name? As complex as his monologues are, with their brusque affirmations and negations, denied as soon as they are proferred, it seems that the answer is given in a passage of that inexorable crescendo which the thirteen 'Texts for Nothing' constitute, like so many movements of a musical suite. The man who is confessing in these

'Texts' protests against whoever is making him speak without even bestowing upon him the third person singular, as
he does upon 'his other figments,' upon Molloy and Malone.
Isn't this conflict between the author and his characters
merely a novelist's skillful artifice made admirably clear
by the orchestral finale of the 'Texts'? In searching for
the man behind the writer, I would like to ask Samuel
Beckett the following: is he wholeheartedly committed to
the grievances that this beings (whom he poeticizes in the
last 'text' by calling them 'dream and silence,' but who
have only known the baseness of life) seek to bring
against the human condition?

[Translated by Larysa Mykyta and Mark Schumacher]

32. GENEVIÈVE BONNEFOI IN 'LETTRES NOUVELLES'

March 1956, 424-30

Geneviève Bonnefoi, critic, presently Director of the
Center for Contemporary Art at the Abbaye de Beaulieu, has
written several essays on Beckett's fiction.

Though the 'Stories and Texts for Nothing,' just published
in one volume by Éditions de Minuit, may add nothing to
the work of Samuel Beckett, they allow one, nevertheless,
to note a few landmarks in the development of this work
and to discern its essential themes. The 'Stories,' which
the editor tells us date from 1945, appear to lie between
'Molloy' and 'Malone Dies' in so far as form and thought
are concerned, while the 'Texts for Nothing' are very
close to 'The Unnamable.'
    In the very first pages we find once again a character
dear to the author of 'Waiting for Godot,' that somewhat
metaphysical tramp who haunts his entire work. Always the
same character despite his different names and various
disguises, he remains consistent throughout all of Beckett's writings. He has become so close to us, so familiar, that we almost expect to see him appear at the bend
of a road, staggering along in clothes too loose or too
tight for him, huge greenish greatcoat flapping at his
heels, hat tied to the buttonhole with a shoelace, eyes

half-closed and mouth drooling, the caricature of what was
once a man. Out of what far-away past did he loom into
the author's mind, never again to leave it, this eternal
wanderer, this hallucinatory vagabond? Was he born as a
result of some extraordinary encounter, some powerful
psychological shock, or was he rather constructed, little
by little - by what slow work of sedimentation? - finally
to stand before us, such that we will never again be able
to forget him, a tottering statue, eroded by the wind of
anguish and human misery? No cries, no revolts, no re-
criminations; but can anyone imagine an act of accusation
against our condition more terrible than the existence of
this shrunken creature, crippled and half impotent,
gnawed by vermin and undermined by hunger - masterly
physiological transpositions of flaws, complexes and in-
hibitions. Brother of every wretched, infirm, feeble-
minded, disgraced and impotent creature and yet fiercely
alone in his misery, enclosed in the narrow limits of his
ego without any hope of escape other than death - expected,
accepted and at times deliberately sought out as the final
refuge.

For this pariah, this creature *separated* from society,
the important thing is to find shelter, a refuge where he
can bury himself far from humans and peacefully await the
end of his afflictions, with no other concern than to
'think,' or, so it seems, to listen inwardly to someone
who is not himself thinking and speaking in his place.
For within this derisory husk lives the tiny flame of the
spirit, the restless consciousness which, for Christians,
makes man similar to God, a nagging demon that cannot be
still. In the 'Stories,' this stream of words and thoughts
is still restrained, compared to the way it flows in the
'Texts for Nothing,' in which it overtakes everything.

The ideal place is the house, warm and comfortable, at
the heart of which stands the room, in the depths of which
is found the bed. The bed, sole essential piece of furniture, marvellous refuge against the outside world, isle of
idleness, warmth, immobility, port of embarkation for all
voyages. Let the minimal needs of nourishment and clean-
liness be satisfied in the form of a platter someone
brings and a pot someone empties, and behold our derelict
regressing to the fetal condition, folding in upon himself, as quiet as in the original womb. But let the perfect shelter, for one reason or another, be wanting, and
we then see him wandering aimlessly, grieving for paradise
lost. This is the situation of The Expelled, callously
thrown out of a comfortable house and, in the street,
rather rudely coming into contact with the realities of
existence. Although this is a man 'in the prime of life,'

the scene resembles a painful birth.

The hero of 'The End' is also pushed politely but firmly out of the place - asylum, hospital, poorhouse? - that has sheltered him thus far and provided for his needs. With a meager legacy - a little money, the too-tight clothing of a dead man - he will henceforth have to manage by himself if he wants to 'continue.' No one is less prepared than he to face even ordinary difficulties, and he dreams only of burrowing into some hole until his meager possessions are exhausted. A basement full of rats welcomes him for a while, but he is expelled again, and this time his money is stolen from him. Then the wandering begins, from the city to the country, from the country to the city, and the deterioration accelerates. A cave by the seashore shelters him for a time, but the sea tires him with its 'splashing and heaving, its tides and general convulsiveness,' as doubtless the presence of a companion does also. Having learned that the latter has a hut in the mountains, he goes there without telling him. Lacking door and windows, roof fallen in, strewn with filth and excrement, 'nevertheless it was a roof over my head.' He sleeps there a few days, until hunger forces him out on the road again, towards the city, towards men. But the old grimaces of misery become more and more difficult to perform:

> The humble, ingenuous smile would no longer come, nor the expression of candid misery, showing the stars and the distaff. I summoned them, but they would not come. A mask of dirty old hairy leather, with two holes and a slit, it was too far gone for the old trick of please your honour and God reward you and pity upon me. It was disastrous. What would I crawl with in future?

Beggary, filth, vermin; the Beckettian hero endures all this with indifference. He is absent from himself. Detached from the habitual needs of men - he lives on a little milk, sleeps in the bottom of a boat in an abandoned shed - he is nothing but a pure existence, reduced to itself, without goal and without hope, waiting only for the end. 'Normally I didn't see a great deal. I didn't hear a great deal either. I didn't pay attention. Strictly speaking I wasn't there. Strictly speaking I believe I've never been anywhere.' This eternally absent one, this *Stranger* to the nth degree, this man who wonders sometimes 'if [he is] on the right planet,' we know him well. It is he who cries out his anguish and his contempt, who hurls his hatred and disgust in the face of our world through the great obsessive voices of our time.

Artaud: 'There is not yet a world. Things are not yet
made. The *raison d'être* is not yet found....' Kafka:
'Who is it then? Who then is walking away under the trees
on the quai? Who then is entirely abandoned? Who then
can no longer be saved? On whose grave does the grass
grow?' Michaux: 'Sun, or moon, or forests, or even
flocks, crowds and cities, someone does not like his
traveling companions. Has not chosen, does not recognize,
does not enjoy.' For such as these, the flight to Harrar,
suicide, madness, complete solitude.... And sometimes -
in the very depths of despair - pride, the secret enjoyment of misfortune: 'To contrive a little kingdom, in the
midst of the universal muck, then shit on it, ah that was
me all over' sneers the hero of The End, just before pushing his boat toward the river, the boat in whose bottom a
tiny hole will allow the water to rise slowly while he
thinks of the story he might have told, 'a story in the
likeness of my life,' he says, '...without the courage to
end or the strength to go on.'

 And yet the world exists outside the tomb-refuge. The
sky, stars, wind and sea continue on their courses, and
occasionally nostalgia for their presence draws the
living-dead out of his shelter. Thus, in The Calmative,
we see an old man - already dead - too frightened to
'listen to myself rot,' trying to remain calm by telling
himself a story, just as his father did when he was a
child, night after night reading him a story, always the
same one. Right from the first pages, which seem like an
admirable poem, we rediscover all of Beckett's great
themes, his major obsessions: decrepitude, death, solitude, and that sort of time outside of time which is neither past nor present but an intimate mixture of the two,
which gives to his 'Stories,' apparently so restrained
and so enclosed within the limits of a sordid realism, the
dimensions of infinity. Here are the familiar places he
haunts ceaselessly, the suspected presence of the sea, the
little woods of 'Molloy,' the edge of the forest, the
ditch, and beyond the fields, the city - the same city of
childhood days to which the same character at times
returns, in the transparent disguise of his uncertain
identities.

 Does he himself know what he is going to seek there?
Perhaps it is only the need to hear a human voice, to
assure himself that he still belongs to the world of the
living, that drives him to emerge from his burrow - ruin,
cave or hut in the depths of the forest - to confront the
noises and the terrible light of the city, of life. A
vain effort to mingle with others. Hardly has he attemp-
ted this experience - at the price of enormous

difficulties - when he feels ashamed of this weakness, full of regret for the shelter he should never have left, hampered as he is by his irreducible *difference*. Any communication with this world is impossible for him, and the meager booty of words, gestures and faces that he hoped to carry back with him, 'to add to my collection,' escapes him even before it can take shape. 'So I went in the atrocious brightness, buried in my old flesh, strain- ing towards an issue and passing them by to left and right, and my mind panting after this and that and always flung back to where there was nothing.' From such a total solitude, no exit is possible.

With 'Texts for Nothing' we leave the domain of fiction (scanty as it may have been, and even though it cancels itself at every step, it must be labeled thus) to enter into a desperate monologue, without beginning or end, in the indistinct world of thought in its pure state, caught at its very source and transcribed as is, still hesitant and amorphous: feelings, words, images, memories, regrets, doubts, sarcasm, all jumbled together and overlapping in a hellish saraband. Before us a man watches himself think, listens to himself, endures himself thinking without being able to stop this tide rolling through his head. This voice harping away, all too well-known, full of 'the same old stories,' how many times has he not tried to make it stop?

In vain: sometimes he is driven mad by this inner see- thing, sometimes he endures it passively, resigned, and sometimes he uses it 'to lull me and keep me company' with old stories as in the days of childhood.

At times he tries his hand at a realistic, detailed description of places, objects, landscapes - an effort to cling to reality, to construct something solid. 'To try and tell a story' implies first of all that one must come out of oneself, that one must begin to exist again as a man. One week - he allows himself one week to say what he has to say in spite of all the inner oppositions, after that he can return to his nothingness. We see him invent a friend, a sickly, crochety old comrade in war and in poverty, whom he strains to make really live, ready as he is to dissolve though scarcely born. Quick quick, some words to fill in the empty spaces, to prop up the swaying statue: past, present and future all dovetail and blend together in the gallop of this unbridled narrative that dares not interrupt itself at the risk of falling instantly into dust. 'Quick quick before I weep,' before I perceive that all this is only wind and smoke intended to mask reality, real problems, the true story - the one that is not told, that stopped short long ago in front of the red flame of a lamplit window.

Writing would indeed perhaps be a manner of *being*, if writing were possible. But how to find the strength? What to start with, where to finish? Why choose one story, one idea, rather than another, when so many stories, each as good as any other, are possible, when so many ideas struggle with one another on the ravaged field of con- sciousness, in this head 'strewn with arms laid down and corpses fighting fresh.' Everything is old, worn out, everything has been said, everything is known in advance. How to 'get at me in the end,' to make one's own voice heard deprived of the contribution of others, how to coin- cide, even for a moment, with oneself: Perhaps the *other* way of telling things exists, the 'right aggregate'? '...but there are four million possible, nay probable, according to Aristotle, who knew everything.' The author knows that all this is only arbitrary and false. But at the same time that he feels the futility of these descrip- tions, these stories, he is burdened with the necessity of telling them, the impossibility of not telling them. This is the mandate of Kafka, who said in his own time: 'By nature I can only assume a mandate no one has given me.' And the narrator of 'Texts for Nothing' finds himself transformed into a 'scribe,' faithfully noting what takes place in his mind as though it were a spectacle: '...judge and party, witness and advocate, and he, atten- tive, indifferent, who sits and notes.' The image forming itself in him, a scene glimpsed in the wink of an eye, then the eyes close quickly 'to look inside the head, to try and see inside, to look for me there, to look for someone there, in the silence of quite a different jus- tice, in the toils of that obscure assize where to be is to be guilty.' '...the ears straining for a voice not from without, were it only to sound an instant, to tell another lie.'

The impossibility of grasping his own being, the anxi- ous search for a profound reality, desiring it to be tan- gible and having it escape him, is faithfully reflected in the writing. Equally incapable of making his real voice heard and of keeping silent, he can only remain thus, harping away and successively denying this harping, endlessly raising his hopeless protest. This lucidity, this extreme exigency of truth, constitute the honor of Samuel Beckett at a time when literature is all too often an inconsequential game. These are the same qualities the young Antonin Artaud shows in 'Le Pèse-Nerfs,' replying to those who reproached him with being too demanding of him- self, with 'attaching too much importance to words':

You don't see *my thought* ... I know myself because I am
my own spectator, I am Antonin Artaud's spectator ... I
am the one who has most clearly felt the bewildering
confusion of his language in its relations with
thought. I am the one who has best marked the moment
of its most intimate, imperceptible shifts.

A questioning of existence and of writing, Beckett's work
becomes by this very fact the highest justification - if a
justification is possible - of these activities.

[Translated by Jean M. Sommermeyer]

An Interview with Beckett
(1956)

33. ISRAEL SHENKER IN 'NEW YORK TIMES'

5 May 1956, Section II, 1, 3

Israel Shenker (b. 1925), American journalist for the 'New York Times,' published the first important interview with Beckett.

His parents were Irish, his birthplace was Dublin. The year: 1906. Just fifty years later, Samuel Beckett, a gloomy, despairing man of letters, has a play on Broadway. The critics, the audiences, even the actors in 'Waiting for Godot' wonder what Beckett is saying. There is pretty general agreement that he is no charlatan, but hardly more than enlightened puzzlement about his message.
    Beckett is in no mood to offer explanations. He insists he has never been interviewed, and refers those who want his views to the works he has published.
    Seeing Beckett is hardly less difficult than seeing Godot, who never shows up in the play, though everybody waits for him. Beckett's Paris address is a well-kept secret, and no more than a dozen people know the location of his country cottage.
    The playwright is a gaunt, imposing figure who looks like a fiery apostle. But he does not care what he looks like, and if his clothes look slept in (which they do) he does not appear to notice.
    His Paris apartment is on the eighth floor of a middle-class apartment house - not really shabbier than the Paris average. A number of canvases hang on the walls. His

country cottage was purchased with royalties from 'Godot.'
The garden plot was covered with stones, and Beckett toiled
long hours to clear the site and coax a lawn from the
earth. He has planted trees, and still works like an
ambitious, grubby gardener. A friend notes 'He has the
vocation of degradation - to keep himself from thinking,
like a character in his own books.'

Beckett speaks precisely like his characters - with a
pained hesitation, but also with brilliance, afraid to
commit himself to words, aware that talk is just another
way to stir dust. If he would relax his rule on interviews, this is what he would say (he has said it all, in
precisely this phrasing):

'I came to Paris for the first time as a student at
Trinity in 1926. I came back here in 1928 as an exchange
lecturer at the Ecole Normale Supérieure.

'I was appointed the assistant to the Professor of
French in Dublin for a period of three years. I resigned
after four terms. I didn't like teaching. I couldn't
settle down to work. Then I left Ireland.

'I was in Germany, in London, I was back in Dublin.
I was battering around the place. That's a very confused
period in my own mind.

'I had an elder brother, a quantity surveyor - like my
father. My brother had taken over my father's business
when my father died.

'I didn't like living in Ireland. You know the kind of
thing - theocracy, censorship of books - that kind of
thing. I prefer to live abroad. In 1936, I came back to
Paris and lived in a hotel for a time and then decided to
settle down to make my life here.

'While my mother was alive, I went to her for a month
every year. My mother died in 1950.

'I was never Joyce's secretary, but, like all his
friends, I helped him. He was greatly handicapped because
of his eyes. I did odd jobs for him, marking passages for
him, or reading to him. But I never wrote any of his
letters.

'I was in Ireland when the war broke out in 1939 and I
then returned to France. I preferred France in war to
Ireland in peace. I just made it in time. I was here up
to 1942 and then I had to leave, so I went to the Vaucluse
- because of the Germans.

'During the war I wrote my last book in English - which
was 'Watt.' After the war I went back to Ireland in 1945
and came back with the Irish Red Cross as interpreter and
storekeeper. But I didn't stay long with the Irish Red
Cross.

'In spite of having to clear out in 1942, I was able to

keep my flat. I returned to it and began writing again -
in French. Just felt like it. It was a different experience from writing in English. It was more exciting for
me - writing in French.

'I wrote all my work very fast - between 1946 and 1950.
Since then I haven't written anything. Or at least nothing that has seemed to me valid. The French work brought
me to the point where I felt I was saying the same thing
over and over again. For some authors writing gets
easier the more they write. For me it gets more and more
difficult. For me the area of possibilities gets smaller
and smaller.

'I've only read Kafka in German - serious reading -
except for a few things in French and English - only 'The
Castle' in German. I must say it was difficult to get to
the end. The Kafka hero has a coherence of purpose. He's
lost but he's not spiritually precarious, he's not falling
to bits. My people seem to be falling to bits. Another
difference. You notice how Kafka's form is classic, it
goes on like a steamroller - almost serene. *It seems* to
be threatened the whole time - but the consternation is in
the form. In my work there is consternation behind the
form, not in the form.

'At the end of my work there's nothing but dust - the
namable. In the last book - 'L'Innommable' - there's complete disintegration. No 'I,' no 'have,' no 'being.' No
nominative, no accusative, no verb. There's no way to go
on.

'The very last thing I wrote - 'Textes pour rien' - was
an attempt to get out of the attitude of disintegration,
but it failed.

'With Joyce the difference is that Joyce is a superb
manipulator of material - perhaps the greatest. He was
making words do the absolute maximum of work. There isn't
a syllable that's superfluous. The kind of work I do is
one in which I'm not master of my material. The more
Joyce knew the more he could. He's tending toward
omniscience and omnipotence as an artist. I'm working
with impotence, ignorance. I don't think impotence has
been exploited in the past. There seems to be a kind of
esthetic axiom that expression is achievement - must be an
achievement. My little exploration is that whole zone of
being that has always been set aside by artists as something unusable - as something by definition incompatible
with art.

'I think anyone nowadays who pays the slightest attention to his own experience finds it the experience of a
non-knower, a non-can-er [somebody who cannot]. The
other type of artist - the Apollonian - is absolutely

foreign to me.'

Once Beckett was asked if his system was the absence of a system. 'I can't see any trace of any system anywhere.'

Was Beckett uninterested in economics: did he never treat problems such as how his characters earned their livings? 'My characters have nothing,' he said, and let the matter drop.

Why, Beckett was asked, did he choose to write a play after writing novels? 'I didn't choose to write a play,' he replied, 'it just happened like that.'

Critics have said that 'Godot's' structure and message left the author free to lay down his pen at any moment. Beckett disagrees: 'one act would have been too little and three acts would have been too much.' Like a hunted animal, Beckett paced the floor in his Paris apartment. '"L'Innommable,"' he complained, 'landed me in a situation I can't extricate myself from.'

What to do then, when you find nothing to say? Just what others do - go right on trying?

Beckett answered: 'There are others, like Nicolas de Stael, who threw themselves out of a window - after years of struggling.'

'All That Fall'
(1957)

[Written in English; first performed on the BBC Third
Programme, 13 January 1957; published by Grove Press, New
York, and Faber & Faber, London; translated into French by
Beckett and Robert Pinget as 'Tous ceux qui tombent';
published by Éditions de Minuit, Paris, 1957.]

34. UNSIGNED REVIEW IN 'TIMES LITERARY SUPPLEMENT'

6 September 1957, 528

'All That Fall,' after the phenomenal success of 'Waiting
for Godot,' was commissioned by the B.B.C.'s Third Programme. It was Mr. Beckett's first attempt at writing
directly for radio and it was written in English, not,
like most of the author's recent works, in French. Those
who heard the broadcast, very skilfully produced by Mr.
Donald McWhinnie and excellently acted, especially by
Miss Mary O'Farrell and Mr. J.G. Devlin in the leading
parts of Mr. and Mrs. Rooney, found it a most impressive
and original piece of writing for the ear, comparable in
its impact, though not at all in its tone or mood, with
'Under Milk Wood.' On the page, it does not disappoint.
'Waiting for Godot' is impressive on the page to a reader
who has seen that play performed. He recognizes it as a
masterly piece of craftsmanship, a machine for acting without one wasted gesture or one wasted line; but it is
doubtful whether, apart from a few bravura passages like
Lucky's speech and some rhetorical flourishes of Pozzo's,
'Waiting for Godot' has a literary value separable from
its dramatic value. Critics who have read it, but not

seen it, have occasionally asked what all the fuss was
about.

'All That Fall,' on the other hand, is set not among
allegorical dustbins but in a recognizable though stylized
and indeed caricatured rural Ireland of perhaps thirty or
forty years ago. The use of language has a rich local
flavour, there is a rhetorical zest, a rhythmical extravagance, and a melancholy humour, that recall Synge, or Mr.
O'Casey in his earlier days. There is even a certain
earthy homeliness that might recall some humbler Irish
comic writers, like Mr. Lynn Doyle. The play, as a whole,
must be considered as a tragedy, or at least as a variation on Mr. Beckett's favourite theme that new gulfs open
under old gulfs, that the worst is yet to be. Yet there
are elements in the tragedy that, taken in isolation,
might make first-rate music-hall sketches. And because of
the love of language which informs the whole piece its
total effect is distinctly different from the elegantly
arid desolation of 'Fin de Partie.'

'All That Fall' is a short play in which almost nothing
seems to happen, and yet what is found to have happened in
the end is something irreparable. Mrs. Rooney, an old,
unwieldy Irishwoman, is dragging herself towards the railway station on a Saturday at lunch-time to meet her blind
husband on his way back from his office, and guide him
home. She passes the time of day with a man with a dung-
cart and with a man with a bicycle. A third man with a
motor-car offers her a lift. A comic church-struck spin-
ster helps her up the station steps. The train is late.
And Mrs. Rooney's morose blind husband is annoyed because
she has not told him she is meeting him and he will have
to give Jerry, the boy who usually meets him to lead him
home, some money for nothing. She helps the wretched old
grumbling man down the stairs. He talks gloomily about
Jerry: 'Did you ever wish to kill a child? Nip some young
doom in the bud. Many a time at night, in winter, on the
black road home, I nearly attacked the boy. Poor Jerry!'
He talks about his journey. 'I had the compartment to
myself as usual. At least I hope so, for I made no
attempt to restrain myself. My mind - ' The two old
creatures drag along the road, Mr. Rooney, in long solilo-
quies comparing the misery of going into his office, where
at least he has solitude and 'convenient to the one hand
a bottle of light pale ale and to the other a long ice-
cold filet of hake,' and the misery of staying at home,
lying in bed and having no work to do, but being bothered
all day by 'the dusting, sweeping, airing, scrubbing,
waxing, waning, washing.... And the brays, the happy
little healthy, little howling neighbours' brats.'

We know already that one of Mrs. Rooney's sorrows is to
have lost a girl child long ago (the girl, if alive, would
now be middle-aged). Children pelt the two old things
with mud on their way home. Mr. Rooney also is a black
pessimist. The world is the more bearable to him the less
his senses expose him to it. 'No, I cannot be said to be
well. But I am no worse. Indeed, I am better than I was.
The loss of my sight was a great fillip. If I could go
deaf and dumb I think I might pant on to be a hundred.'
Mrs. Rooney's heart has not hardened as his has. When she
speaks of bad dreams that keep her awake, her 'lifelong
preoccupation with horses' buttocks' and on the puzzle of
a neurologist about a little girl, 'The only thing wrong
with her as far as he could see was that she was dying,'
her wretchedness has an absurdity and a tenderness lacking
in her husband's.

They speak about the text that is to be preached on the
next day at the local Church of Ireland church. 'The Lord
upholdeth all that fall down and raiseth up all those that
be bowed down.' Both old creatures screech with eldritch
laughter. But then, on his last page, Mr. Beckett springs
his trap or turns his screw. Jerry comes in with an odd
object, it resembles a rubber ball, which he asserts Mr.
Rooney has dropped in the station. Mr. Rooney accepts it
reluctantly and shamefacedly, explaining, 'It is a thing I
carry about with me!' And Jerry explains that what kept
the train late was a little girl falling out of a carriage,
on to the line, under the wheels. There is no response to
this, either laughter or tears; only the noise of the wind
and the rain.

The shock of Mr. Beckett's last page has been, as it
were, 'planted' by the introductory music on the first
page, from a house in Mrs. Rooney's way, 'Death and the
Maiden.' It has been 'planted' also by the talk about
Mrs. Rooney's child dead long ago, by the children who
pelt the Rooneys with mud, and by Mr. Rooney's wistful
talk about 'nipping a young doom in the bud.' But we are
not meant to suppose that the blind man actually attacked
the young girl and flung her out of the carriage. What
actually must have happened Mr. Beckett leaves, like Henry
James in 'The Turn of the Screw,' to our own sense of evil.
Mr. Rooney thought he 'had the compartment to himself as
usual. At least,' he says, 'I hope so, for 1 made no
attempt to restrain myself. My mind -.' The reader or
the hearer of the play is left to imagine in numb horror
and pity what the blind man, in the obscenity of his fan-
cied solitude, may have said or done to make the little
girl, of whom he was unaware, fling herself in terror out
of the moving train. This is the real black and hollow

gulf that opens out under Mr. Beckett's painted gulf of comic desperation.

Yet the springing of the trap has an odd effect that makes the final effect of 'All That Fall' like the final effect of 'Waiting for Godot,' not one of mere nihilism. To the text about the Lord upholding all that fall Mr. and Mrs. Rooney can respond with a wild laughter that has an effect of comic blasphemy. To the sheer horror of the girl's death and its circumstances, as the reader shudderingly envisages them, and imagines Mr. and Mrs. Rooney envisaging them, Mr. Beckett's hero and heroine can respond with nothing but silence. The wind and the rain speak for them. After all, the 'nipping of a young doom in the bud' is not a macabre joke and the young life, so shockingly lost, must be taken, in a play which seems to mock sardonically at all values, as a symbol of positive value. It is, at last, something that can be seen to *matter*; and, as in 'Waiting for Godot,' Mr. Beckett fails to make the completely rounded statement of absolute nihilism which it may have been his conscious intention to make.

What raises this play, also, above the mere desolating wit of 'Fin de Partie' is the Irish love of extravagant language that runs through it, a love which, indirectly and perhaps unwillingly on Mr. Beckett's part, becomes a love also of the oddities of character which language can express. There is warmth in the incidental humour, though it may be an unintended warmth, and some of the minor characters, notably the daydreaming churchmouse Miss Fitt, are tiny comic masterpieces. This is a play by a man at the end of his tether; but that tether, tying Mr. Beckett, perhaps reluctantly, to sympathy with those who fall and those who are bowed down, has not yet been broken.

35. DONALD DAVIE IN 'SPECTRUM'

Winter 1958, 25-31

Donald Davie (b. 1922), English poet and critic, since 1968 Professor of English Literature at Stanford University. His 'Collected Poems' appeared in 1972. Among his most highly regarded critical works are 'Purity of Diction in English Verse' (1952), 'Articulate Energy' (1957),

'Ezra Pound: Poet as Sculptor' (1964), 'Thomas Hardy and
British Poetry' (1972), and 'Pound' (1975).

Beckett - how absurd to start this way, yet this is never
said - Beckett is a comic writer. He has yet to write a
book that is not a funny book:

> *Mrs. Rooney:* . . . It's like the sparrows, than many of
> of which we are of more value, they weren't sparrows
> at all.
> *Mr. Rooney:* Than many of which . . . You exaggerate,
> Maddy.

What Mrs. Rooney exaggerates isn't in the first place
man's dignity (his price in terms of sparrows), but the
dignity of his language. By the meticulous correctness
of her syntax ('than many of which') she achieves an elegance so conscious of itself that it becomes absurd, a
parody of all stylistic elegance whatever, insinuating
the suspicion that all the elegances of language, which
seem so superbly to articulate experience, in fact articulate nothing but themselves. Mrs. Rooney knows that her
own faith in language is excessive:

> *Mrs. Rooney:* Do you find anything . . . bizarre about
> my way of speaking? (*Pause.*) I do not mean the
> voice. (*Pause.*) No, I mean the words. (*Pause.*
> *More to herself.*) I use none but the simplest words,
> I hope, and yet I sometimes find my way of speaking
> very . . . bizarre.

As Mr. Rooney says, 'Do you know, Maddy, sometimes one
would think you were struggling with a dead language.'

> *Mrs. Rooney:* Yes indeed, Dan, I know full well what
> you mean, I often have that feeling, it is unspeak-
> ably excruciating.
> *Mr. Rooney:* I confess I have it sometimes myself, when
> I happen to overhear what I am saying.
> *Mrs. Rooney:* Well, you know, it will be dead in time,
> just like our own poor dear Gaelic, there is that to
> be said.

'I know full well . . .,' the very expression by which
Mrs. Rooney admits herself at the mercy of clichés, is
itself a cliché. And in this state, the language can
express the speaker only by betraying him, as in 'There is

that to be said,' the hopeful and consolatory cliché here
applied to the chance of death.

One could be forgiven for thinking that Beckett has
been reading Mr. Kenner on Joyce's use of parody. (The
radio-play is a new genre for Beckett, and it's notable
how, by a comic use of sound-effects, he at once exploits
the medium by parodying it.) At all events, every reader
of Mr. Kenner's book on Joyce will know what to make of
the evidence so far presented. Joyce was forced to use
parody as his central literary device because his subject
dictated it. Simon Dedalus speaks involuntary parody of
eighteenth-century Ciceronianism, and acts a parody of
eighteenth-century manners, because these are the only
norms of speech and behavior which his milieu affords, and
those only in an ossified form. Molly Bloom has access to
different norms, those of nineteenth-century Romanticism;
but these are just as dead as Simon's, and serve her no
better - rather worse in fact, since they were less effi-
cient symbols for feeling even when they were alive. Mrs.
Rooney's formulae are from the same stock as Molly's, and
indeed she is a sort of parody of Molly, grieving, as
Molly did for her dead son, over a dead daughter - 'In her
forties now she'd be. I don't know, fifty, girding up her
lovely little loins, getting ready for the change...' But
Mrs. Rooney differs from both Mrs. Bloom and Mr. Dedalus
in knowing that the formulae cannot be trusted, even
though she uses them. In other words she speaks by formula, but she does not live and feel by formula - or she
strives not to, though her language continually traps her
into it. From this point of view there is more hope for
her, and it may be quite true that the hope will indeed be
consummated when her language is as dead as 'our own poor
dear Gaelic,' that is to say, without the sort of zombie
life it now has, which suffices to thwart her feelings
while good for nothing else. 'There is that to be said.'

Here as elsewhere Beckett stakes new ground away from
Joyce by applying Joycean perceptions of parody to a different dimension of language. Like Mrs. Rooney, he uses
'none but the simplest words,' and accordingly his quarry
is not Joyce's, the word, but the sentence, not in the
first place vocabulary but syntax. It is syntax, rather
than the word in isolation, which parodies itself. Though
language may betray the speaker in a Joycean pun. ('Nip
some young doom in the bud'), more often for Beckett it
does so by syntactical over-elegance. This is what happens
to Maddy with her 'than many of which,' as here to her
husband:

> *Mrs. Rooney:* There is nothing to be done for those
> people!

> *Mr. Rooney:* For which is there? (*Pause.*) That does
> not sound right somehow.

Or else there is a thoroughly dramatic and Wildean reversal
of the expected, as in Maddy's 'There is that to be said,'
or in 'I saved his life once. (*Pause.*) I have not forgotten it.'

For Joyce, what began as a perception about the use of
English by Irishmen became a perception about man and his
language everywhere. Beckett's work up to 'All That Fall'
showed a similar very steady movement towards abstraction
and generalization. From Murphy through to Molloy, the
central figures which give their names to his novels are
steadily stripped of particularity, losing first their
ties with other persons, then (symbolically) their limbs,
finally, with 'L'Innommable,' even that badge of residual
individuality, a name. In tune with this, the milieu
became less and less distinguishable, from the London and
Dublin of 'Murphy' to the nowhere and everywhere of 'Waiting for Godot.' Most people who have noticed this have
supposed that it meant an ever bleaker pessimism about the
human person and human destiny, but it could equally well
be explained as an attempt, like Wordsworth's in his progress from articulate men through peasants and children to
idiots and lunatics, to strip from the human being all
attributes save precisely that of being - a common ground
on which (who knows?) Beckett might stand, as Wordsworth
did, to utter a hurrah for the human race. However that
may be, 'All That Fall' represents a disconcerting break
or harking back in the middle of this development. It is
sited so firmly in a particular milieu, that some of the
jokes need for their appreciation a first-hand knowledge
of the Republic of Ireland today. As usual in these
cases, the jokes when disentangled are not very good ones,
not for export. (For instance, 'Our own poor dear Gaelic'
- if it was ever anybody's own, it certainly wasn't the
shabby-genteel Maddy Rooney's; but to get this you need to
know very exactly the significance, to the Catholic majority in present-day Ireland, of Mrs. Rooney's allegiance
to the Church of Ireland.) Similarly, some of the minor
characters are only too clearly just that. The reviewer
in the London 'Daily Telegraph' spoke of 'Shrewd character
sketches reminiscent of "Under Milk Wood."' And while no
author can be held responsible for the vagaries of his reviewers, this was a misapprehension which Beckett could
have avoided; it is in fact hard to see any point to a
figure like his Miss Fitt (note the schoolboy joke) except
something like Dylan Thomas's assumption that 'a broad
humanity' means copiousness of unrelated particulars:

There she goes, they say, there goes the dark Miss Fitt,
alone with her Maker, take no notice of her. And they
step down off the path to avoid my running into them.
(*Pause*.) Ah yes, I am distray, very distray, even on
weekdays. Ask Mother, if you do not believe me. Hetty,
she says, when I start eating my doily instead of the
thin bread and butter, Hetty, how can you be so distray?
(*Sighs*) I suppose the truth is I am not there, Mrs.
Rooney, just not really there at all.

The dark Miss Fitt ... dark lady of the sonnets ... Mary
Fytton ... alone with her Maker (Shakespeare, lament for
the makaris) ... Mary Fytton without meaning for any but
her creator, his language so decayed he can no longer communicate ... Shakespeare and his language dead or half-
dead ... hence, 'not there, Mrs. Rooney, just not really
there at all.' And, 'doily'? D'-Oyley Carte? Perhaps
not. But once started on this, where do we stop? Shall
we say that this is not 'Under Milk Wood,' but a parody of
that? Not derivative slapstick but its parody? This
having it both ways is Joycean indeed - throw the exegete
a red herring to keep him quiet, and then on with the
motley. Common sense demands that we ignore the lure, and
call this derivative slapstick, just that.
   And the play never recovers from the point, less than
halfway through, where Miss Fitt appears. Up to that
point it has been a joy, and its drama has all been in the
language. From this point on, it is only partly in land-
slips of language, syntax yawning suddenly in crevasses
under the speaker's feet. More and more the significance
is pumped into the text in the manner of the dark lady
nonsense, and the piece ends with ambiguities flying off
in all directions, and a tediously insoluble whodunnit
question-mark over whatever it was unspeakable that the
blind Mr. Rooney did to a child in the train. There is
also a fascination with blasphemy, which most non-Irish
readers will find childish and trivial. The thing to
hold on to is the comedy:

Mrs. Rooney: I remember once attending a lecture by one
   of those new mind doctors, I forget what you call
   them. He spoke -
Mr. Rooney: A lunatic specialist?
Mrs. Rooney: No, no, just the troubled mind. I was
   hoping he might shed a little light on my lifelong
   preoccupation with horses' buttocks.
Mr. Rooney: A neurologist.
Mrs. Rooney: No, no, just mental distress, the name
   will come back to me in the night.

The gratuitous zaniness - 'horses' buttocks' - is of all
jokes the last that can afford to fall flat. And when a
comedian so delicate and resourceful as Beckett does something as lame as this, it is a sign that something is
wrong.

The play goes to pieces. But in the light of Beckett's
other achievements, the handsome thing to do is to remember how comic he is, and how serious, when he is really in
control:

> *Mrs. Rooney:* . . . It's like the sparrows, than many of
> which we are of more value, they weren't sparrows at
> all.
> *Mr. Rooney:* Than many of which . . . You exaggerate,
> Maddy.
> *Mrs. Rooney:* (*with emotion*). They weren't sparrows at
> all!
> *Mr. Rooney:* Does that put our price up?

A concern with the dignity or the decrepitude of language
is, after all, a concern for the dignity or decrepitude of
man. To a writer of the twentieth century who, like his
contemporaries the painters and sculptors, disdains to do
with his art anything more questionable than explore the
nature of his own medium, words in arrangements, the question of human dignity cannot present itself in any other
terms than those of the dignity of human language. But in
those terms it cannot *but* present itself. And Beckett,
when he is not stooping to trick-endings and symbolic puns,
is of those modern writers who have withdrawn into a
sheerly verbal universe, not in order to exclude the more
troublous worlds of experience, but precisely to see all
those wider troubles at work in language as in a microcosm.

And in any case what survives is, formidable and affecting, the figure of Mrs. Rooney. In 'All That Fall,' for
the first time in Beckett's career, it is not a man who is
at the centre of attention. And this makes a great difference. The advent of Maddy Rooney was signalled perhaps
in 'Malone Dies,' by the dying Malone, who obviously
speaks more than any of Beckett's other creations, with
his master's voice: 'Unfortunately our concern here is not
with Moll, who after all is only a female, but with
MacMann ...' This refers to the sustained episode of
MacMann's grotesque amour with Moll as told by Malone.
Just as MacMann's name (son of man) is a pun of a different order from the name of Miss Fitt, so this whole episode in 'Malone Dies' is a good example of how delicately
and seriously Beckett can use allegory. What the allegory

shadows forth, in a blasphemous parody of marriage as a
Christian sacrament (and here the blasphemy too has point
and force), is the divorce of body from mind in post-
Cartesian man. (I'm sorry to use this cant phrase, but
there is abundant evidence that these are the terms, and
this is the historical perspective, of Beckett himself.)
Moll - like that other Molly, Mrs. Bloom - 'stands for'
the body, MacMann for the mind; and Moll's only demand is
that she shall die at the same time as her equally decrepit and impotent lover. It is little to ask, for of
course body and mind should die together. But in fact
Moll dies first. And accordingly MacMann, like Malone
himself, becomes a mind without a body as he waits for
death. In Mr. and Mrs. Rooney mind and body live on
together, bound together by mutual needs which, acknowledged, become affections. And in Mrs. Rooney, for the
first time since the Celia of 'Murphy' but here far more
centrally, Beckett presents the wisdom of the body and
its claims.

Similarly, some light is thrown on the still irritating
and gratuitous conundrum of what happened in the train between Dan Rooney and the child, by Malone's maudlin
reverie on his deathbed:

> 'Or I might be able to catch one, a little girl for
> example, and half strangle her, three quarters, until
> she promises to give me my stick, give me soup, empty
> my pots, kiss me, fondle me, smile to me, give me my
> hat, stay with me, follow the hearse weeping into her
> handkerchief, that would be nice. I am such a good man
> at bottom, such a good man, how is it nobody ever
> noticed it? A little girl would be into my barrow, she
> would undress before me, sleep beside me, have nobody
> but me, I would jam the bed against the door to prevent
> her running away, but then she would throw herself out
> of the window....'

This has far more logic and point in 'Malone Dies' than in
'All That Fall,' because in the novel the allegory has
established an historical perspective in which the reader
may naturally recall how a cult of the immature and the
virginal has been a feature of ages which made an absolute
gulf between the physical and the spiritual conceived of
as mental, between the body and the mind. But if Mr.
Rooney, being male, has something in common with Malone,
it is worth recalling what the latter has to say of himself:

The aeroplane ... has just passed over at two hundred

miles an hour perhaps. It is a good speed, for the
present day. I am with it in spirit, naturally. All
the things I was always with in spirit. In body no.
Not such a fool.'

Mrs. Rooney *is* such a fool, who takes all the risks of
being with things in body; that is why we like and admire
her, as surely her author meant that we should. And from
this point of view his comment on her earlier avatar Moll,
that she was 'only a female,' carries plenty of irony.
And when he says in the novel that our concern is not with
Moll but with MacMann 'unfortunately,' *that* word - so most
readers will feel - need carry no irony at all.
    All the same, Beckett avoids the easy dishonesty of
presenting Mrs. Rooney's indomitable carnality as a pana-
cea. The questions which disabled Watt and Molloy and
Malone - how to know the world, how to know the self - are
no nearer being answered after we have seen Mrs. Rooney
contriving not to worry about them. Her husband's refusal
to retire from business into domesticity represents, in
'All That Fall,' Beckett's renewed acknowledgement of the
right of the masculine intellect to ask questions, which,
being unanswerable, may disable the mind and the body
both.
    Beckett's wit has never been in question. But in cal-
ling him a comic writer one credits him with something
else - humor, with whatever that may or must imply of
affirmation, and pleasure in the human spectacle. If it
is hard to believe in the humor beneath the more bleakly
witty pages of 'Molloy' and 'Malone Dies,' 'All That Fall'
is quite plainly humorous, at least in all that immediately
concerns Mrs. Rooney. It would be pleasant to suppose
that in future work by Beckett the humor will continue to
come to the surface in that way, and that the unfortunate
elements in 'All That Fall' only tell of the strains of
transition to this more humorous mode.

'Endgame'
(1957)

[Written in French as 'Fin de partie'; first performed in French at the Royal Court Theatre, London, 3 April 1957; first performed in Paris at Studio des Champs-Élysées, 26 April 1957; published by Éditions de Minuit, February 1957; first performed in New York at Cherry Lane Theatre, 28 January 1958; first performed in London in English at the Royal Court Theatre, 28 October 1958; translated into English by Beckett; published by Grove Press, New York, 1958, and Faber & Faber, London, 1958.]

---

36. HAROLD HOBSON IN 'SUNDAY TIMES'

7 April 1957, 15

The reception of Samuel Beckett's new play has been precisely what the admirers of 'Waiting for Godot' would desire. 'Fin de Partie' has outraged the Philistines, earned the contempt of half-wits and filled those who are capable of telling the difference between a theatre and a bawdy-house with a profound and sombre and paradoxical joy. Its presentation is among the greatest of the services that the English Stage Company has rendered to the British public.

The plot of the play is extremely simple and extremely odd. Those theatregoers who pride themselves on being up to the advanced drama as it was in 1913 had better be warned that it is not for them. Throughout the piece Hamm, red-robed like a cardinal, sits in the centre of the stage, paralysed and blind. He is attended by a servant, Clov, bowed and misshapen, with arms that hang almost to the

floor, and with a face that expresses every possible variation of human anguish.

Life is coming to an end; possibly also the universe.
Like a refrain running through the entire play is the recurrent statement of Clov that, whatever Hamm asks for,
there is no more of it left, anywhere, or ever will be
again. Some of the objects demanded are banal; some are
grotesque. No matter. They exist no longer; soon, existence itself will exist no longer. There are no more bicycles. There are no more biscuits. There are no more
sedatives. There is no more nature.

In two dustbins at the side of the stage are Hamm's
father and mother, incredibly old, shrivelled, and
feeble. From time to time Clov, with a telescope, clam-
bers up some steps, and looks through the windows of the
bare, grey, prison-like room in which he and Hamm live, on
to the world outside. That world is dying, too. The
human race, 'and all the choir of heaven and furniture of
the earth, in a word, all those bodies which compose the
mighty frame of the world,' are coming to the close of
their adventure. Whilst this slow declension takes place,
Clov wishes to leave Hamm, and Hamm wishes him to remain.

That is all. Simplicity itself, you would say. But you
would, of course, be wrong. It is a fallacy to suppose
that absolutely plain, straightforward statements exclude
obscurity. Mr. Beckett is a poet; and the business of a
poet is not to clarify, but to suggest, to imply, to
employ words with auras of association, with a reaching
out towards a vision, a probing down into an emotion,
beyond the compass of explicit definition. And this is
exactly what the so dangerously simple dialogue of 'Fin
de Partie' does.

It seems as though anyone, without effort, can understand phrases like 'Je te quitte,' or 'Je suis de retour,
avec le biscuit,' or 'La nature nous a oubliés.' It might
even seem that they are not worth understanding. Yet in
them Mr. Beckett shows us a mystery outside the grasp of
any other dramatist now writing.

The aesthetic experience which Mr. Beckett evokes in me is
centred on, first, the disquiet with which Hamm, who in
contrast to the constant distress of Clov, is generally
self-possessed and assured says, 'Assez, il est temps que
cela finisse ... Et cependant j'hésite, j'hésite, à ...à
finir'; and second, on the extraordinary anguish with
which Roger Blin, as Hamm, conducts this piece of dialogue: HAMM: Clov! CLOV: Oui. HAMM: Qu'est-ce qui se

passe? CLOV: Quelque chose suit son cours. (Un temps)
HAMM: Clov! CLOV (agacé): Qu'est-ce que c'est? HAMM: On
n'est pas en train de ... de signifier quelque chose?
CLOV: Signifier? Nous, signifier! (Rire bref) Ah elle
est bonne!

It is all very well for Clov to make a wry joke of the
idea that Hamm and he could possibly mean anything. It is
perfectly obvious from M. Blin's superb and eloquent performance that there is one thing, and one thing only,
which terrifies Hamm. Master of himself in everything
else, he is jellied with fear that things are going to
come to an end. Clov, on the other hand, desires this, as
much as, in his beaten, brutish way, he can desire anything. He dreams of a world 'où tout serait silencieux et
immobile et chaque chose à sa place dernière sous la
dernière poussière.' Such a prospect breaks down Hamm,
who at all other moments is in complete control of things,
in successive waves of panic.

His fear, it should be noted, is not fear of his own
death. It is that, when the whole universe is wound up,
its meaning will be revealed. It is this revelation which
appals him. He wants passionately, not to know what the
revelation is. This fear would seem to correspond to
something fundamental in Mr. Beckett's nature. Mr. Beckett is above all the poet of postponement, of avoidance of
action and decision. That is why Clov shuffles, for walking would bring him to his objective quicker. That is why
he drops his telescope before looking through the window.
It delays his action. That is why Mr. Beckett is always
repetitive.

The point is that by inexhaustible repetition he can
almost indefinitely prevent himself from coming to the
point. A day will arrive when we shall know even as we
are known. Mr. Beckett and all his characters are mortal-
ly afraid of the unveiling of the last dark and terrible
secret. He does not believe, he cannot believe, that the
secret may be something of joy and light. The Paris production of 'Waiting for Godot' was far grimmer than the
British, which looked to Godot with hope. But in Paris it
was clear not only that Godot would not, but that Godot
must not come. It was this production that Mr. Beckett
approved.

This feeling which Mr. Beckett expresses on the stage is
a note heard nowhere else in the contemporary drama.
Beside his sorrow all the personal and political anguishes
of an Anouilh, an Osborne, or a Sartre, are less than a
crumpled rose leaf in the bed. He is without hope and

without faith. But not without nobility; not without
poetry; not without the balance and the beauty of rhythm.
For that reason 'Fin de Partie,' so mournful, so dis-
traught, is a magnificent theatrical experience, and it is
exquisitely played. The mordant humour of Georges Adet's
father in the dustbin, the elegiac memory of departed
happiness which Christine Tsingos's shrunken, piping
mother gets from the word 'hier,' are rewards that make up
for a hundred evenings in the theatre wasted at fatuous
musicals and inane farces. There remains Jean Martin's
Clov. This performance is the very soul made articulate
in brute flesh. I was going to say that if there is a
more frightening actor in Europe or America than M. Martin
I should like to see him. But on second thoughts, I
shouldn't. I am quite satisfied with M. Martin, who is
beyond praise.

'Fin de Partie' is followed by a mime. 'Acte sans
paroles.' Acted by Deryk Mendel with blank desperation,
its last thirty seconds are especially fine.

37.   KENNETH TYNAN IN 'OBSERVER'

7 April 1957, 15

You began Catholic, that is to say, you began with a
system of values in stark opposition to reality....
You really believe in chastity, purity and the personal
God, and that is why you are always breaking out into
cries of c---,s--- and hell. As I don't believe in
these things except as quite provisional values, my
mind has never been shocked to outcries by the existence of water closets - and undeserved misfortunes....
Your work is an extraordinary experiment and I would
go out of my way to save it from destruction or res-
trictive interruption. It has its believers and its
following. Let them rejoice in it. To me it is a dead
end.

That is Wells, writing in 1928 to James Joyce. After
seeing 'Fin de Partie,' which closed last night, I offer
it as an admonitory text to Samuel Beckett, formerly
Joyce's friend. I do not wish to press too far the comparison between the two men. Their styles are utterly different: one gorges on Joyce and slims on Beckett. But

they share an Irish gallows-humour, an absorption in psy-
chiatry, and a grudge against God that the godless never
feel. But above all, in Beckett's private world, one
hears the cry that George Orwell attributed to Joyce:
'Here is life without God. Just look at it!'

As produced in London, 'Waiting for Godot' made
Beckett's world valid and persuasive. Though deserted by
God, the tramps survived, and did so with gaiety, dignity,
and a moving interdependence; a human affirmation was
made. I had heard, and discounted, rumours that Beckett
disliked the London production. These rumours I now
believe. The new play, directed by Roger Blin under the
author's supervision, makes it clear that his purpose is
neither to move nor to help us. For him, man is a pygmy
who connives at his own inevitable degradation. There,
says Beckett, stamping on the face of mankind: there, that
is how life is. And when protest is absent, the step from
'how life is' to 'how life should be' is horrifyingly
short.

Before going any further, I ought to explain what I
think the play is about. I take it to be an analysis of
the power-complex. The hero, a sightless old despot robed
in scarlet, has more than a passing affinity with Francis
Bacon's paintings of shrieking cardinals. He lives in a
womb-shaped cell, attended by Clov, his shambling slave,
on whose eyes he is totally dependent. His throne is
flanked by two dust-bins, wombs within the womb, inhabited
by his parents, Nagg and Nell. Eventually Nell dies,
whereupon the tyrant asks Clov to see what Nagg is up to.
'Il pleure,' says Clov. 'Donc,' says the boss, 'il vit.'
The curtain falls on a symbolic stalemate: King (Nagg)
versus King and Knight (Boss and Clov). The boss is imprisoned for ever in the womb. He can never escape from
his father.

Schopenhauer once said: 'The will is the strong blind
man who carries on his shoulders the lame man who can
see.' Beckett reverses the positions. It is the lame
man, Clov - representing perception and imagination - who
is bowed down by the blind bully of naked will. The play
is an allegory about authority, an attempt to dramatise
the neurosis that makes men love power. So far, so good.
I part company with Beckett only when he insists that the
problem is insoluble, that this is a deterministic world.
'Quelque chose suit son cours': and there is nothing we
can do about it. My interpretation may be incomplete, but
it illuminates at least one of the play's facets. The
blind irascible hero, Hamm, is working on an interminable
novel: does this not bring to mind the blind 'cantankerous
Irishman' by whom Beckett was once employed? Hamm stands

for many things: for the Church, the State, and even Godot
himself; for all the forms of capricious authority. One
of them may perhaps be Joyce.

When I read the play, I enjoyed long stretches of it -
laconic exchanges that seemed to satirise despair, vaudeville *non-sequiturs* that savagely parodied logic. Within
the dark framework I even discerned glimmers of hope. I
now see that I was wrong. Last week's production, porten-
tously stylised, piled on the agony until I thought my
skull would split. Little variation, either of pace or
emphasis, was permitted: a cosmic comedy was delivered as
humourlessly as if its author had been Racine. Georges
Adet, peeping gnome-like from his bin, performed with
charming finesse; otherwise, moaning was the rule, to
which Jean Martin (Clov) conformed with especial intensity. I suddenly realised that Beckett wanted his private
fantasy to be accepted as objective truth. And that nothing less would satisfy him. For a short time I am prepared to listen in any theatre to any message, however
antipathetic. But when it is not only disagreeable but
forced down my throat, I demur.

I was influenced, I admit, by 'Acte sans Paroles,' the
solo mime which followed the play. Here Man (Deryk Mendel)
is a shuffling puppet, obedient to the imperious blasts of
a whistle which send him vainly clambering after a flask
of water, lowered from above only to be whisked out of
reach. He is foiled even when he tries to hang himself,
and ends up inert, unresponsive to whistle and carafe
alike. This kind of facile pessimism is dismaying in an
author of Beckett's stature. It is not only the projection of a personal sickness, but a conclusion reached on
inadequate evidence. I am ready to believe that the world
is a stifling, constricting place - but not if my inform-
ant is an Egyptian mummy.

38. MARC BERNARD IN 'NOUVELLES LITTÉRAIRES'

9 May 1957, 10

Marc Bertrand (b. 1929), Professor of French at the University of California, San Diego, has written extensively
on contemporary French literature.

If Samuel Beckett, in writing 'Endgame,' had wanted to make fun of a certain 'black' theater, he wouldn't have gone about it in any other way: whether he planned it or not, his latest play strangely resembles a parody.

'Waiting for Godot' revealed an author with a sharp sense of the plasticity of theater: colors (web of red threads), lines, and characters gave this work its unexpected resonance, particularly in the first act. 'Endgame,' while showing once again certain of these qualities, has neither the same plenitude, nor the same effectiveness. I was not bored, although there are some dull moments, but I constantly had the impression that I was listening to a medieval *fatrasie*. 'Endgame' has a structure similar to the Middle Ages: *danse macabre*, allegorical characters, scholastic amphigory reminiscent of that found in university decadence, with its Aristotelian ratiocinations, where metaphysics suddenly takes on a farcical tone. The same tone which Molière was to use.

In a symbolic tower, which irresistibly reminds us of Kafka, a sort of Shakespearian king (but out of a *carnaval*, out of a flea market) is seated on a dusty throne; he is the intellectual, paralyzed, blind, as talkative as a fourteenth-century doctor. He is waited upon by the Common Man, halfway between man and beast. So that we won't misunderstand, and so that nothing of the symbol is lost, he has been given a simian appearance: long, dangling arms, curved spine. The intellectual's father and mother are stuffed into two ashbins; from time to time, a lid is lifted and one of the parents begins to talk. It goes without saying that they are both old dotards. For good measure, they are also legless cripples. Quietly they complain that their son has replaced their sawdust with sand; besides it isn't changed often enough. Of course, for having committed such a heinous crime: procreation, no punishment is cruel enough, no contempt profound enough.

On this theme, spiced with humor as it should be, Samuel Beckett offers us his metaphysico-lyrical meditations. The intellectual seeks to be in the center, the center of the world: watching from the battlements (through the intermediary of the Man-monkey-tool) he surveys creation, while on the floor below, his old parents grow weak in their sand as they recall the blissful days of their young love. Surrounding these four characters who symbolize, in an abridged fashion (and this is particularly true of the old couple), all mankind, the universe of course continues to turn, aimless, gloomy, absurd, desolate. Like Christopher Columbus, the intellectual asks from time to time if anything can be seen on

the horizon; but God is dead, there is therefore nothing
to hope for. On this level, we can say that Beckett's
play is resolutely reactionary; it gives man no chance, no
hope. It opens out into nothingness. Science, progress,
faith in mankind or in God - the play throws out all of
these. All that is left is the intellectual with his
ridiculous crown and the childish game of his own creation.

Intoxicated with this nothingness, Beckett indulges in
it with a masochistic voluptuousness; from it he draws,
along with the bitterness, its inner sweetness. Negation
is his strong point; he affirms it constantly, frenetic-
ally, finding in negation a kind of strange pleasure;
there is no doubt that Beckett had a great deal of fun
writing 'Endgame.' For the spectator at the Studio des
Champs-Élysées, things turn out less well, for the author's
amusement doesn't always reach the audience.

[Translated by Larysa Mykyta and Mark Schumacher]

39. JACQUES LEMARCHAND IN 'FIGARO LITTÉRAIRE'

11 May 1957, 14

'Endgame' by Samuel Beckett lends a theatrical reality, a
frightening reality, to a certain daydream that I imagine
we have all yielded to at one time or another: some day,
it matters little under what conditions, there will no
longer be any men on Earth; nor will there be any Earth
then either. One short moment, no more, in the entire
universe, when a single man, the very last man, will have
the task of feeling the last emotion, the last sensation,
of speaking the last word - and that word will not be historic. To young people this seems, if I remember
correctly, frightening, dizzying. To those not so young
it can seem more like a pleasant reassurance that one
should not attach a great deal of importance to winning
literary prizes, nor fret too much about honors granted to
imbeciles. This is a rather peaceful daydream, blending
a fair amount of humor into the inevitable terror that the
end of *everything* arouses in man.

And this terror and comedy have never been presented on
stage in a manner so immediately perceptible, and with so
little rhetoric as well as so much persuasive power, as in
this 'Endgame,' playing at the Studio des Champs-Élysées,

to its infinite honor. It is easy, and legitimate, to
seek and to find in 'Endgame' some sort of sequel to, or
echo of, 'Waiting for Godot.' In fact, Beckett's second
play, although it bears the undeniable stamp of its
author - that clown-like naiveté, with which the characters juggle, to all appearances innocently, our most
secret and serious anxieties - is a play entirely different from 'Waiting for Godot.' Godot has absolutely
refused to come, and no one is waiting for him any more;
what they are waiting for is to 'make an exit;' and words
of waiting, hope, and desire have lost all meaning: the
characters of 'Endgame' simply consent to something they
know is inevitable.

These protagonists have been criticized for not being
very attractive young men. It is true that Beckett's play
is lacking in young leads. One could just as well criti-
cize them for having names that are rather uncommon in the
boulevard theaters. They are called Hamm, Clov, Nagg and
Nell, names reeking of the circus and lacking in distinction. But after all, this is the very last day of the
human race, and it is permissible to imagine that the
saints of the calendar have withdrawn. It is no less
true that these characters are in poor health: Hamm is
paralyzed and cannot leave his armchair; Clov, his slave,
has difficulty walking and shakes with palsy; as for Nagg
and his wife Nell, their situation is quite simple: they
are legless cripples, and each lives in an ashbin, com-
fortably, it seems, considering their smaller size; these
four characters are shut in a sort of bunker, in which
they will certainly have to die. The two windows of this
shelter look out upon a leaden sea and empty land,
equally forsaken by humanity. This is hardly a pleasant
situation, I admit, but it can surely be granted that it
is eminently dramatic.

Among these four human beings there is no other solid-
arity than that arising from self-interest. Nagg and Nell,
who are Hamm's parents, depend on him for the last few
mouthfuls of pap that will prolong their mediocre lives;
Hamm depends on his servant-son, Clov, for the attentions
required by his condition; and if Clov refrains from dis-
patching Hamm, it is simply because he does not have the
'combination to the cupboard' where the last few biscuits
are locked up. And yet there is not one of these human
beings who does not have his dream, a dream he tries to
make the others share, to communicate to them: and this
need to communicate is as vital to their lives as is the
diminishing store of biscuits. From one ashbin to the
other, Nagg and Nell allusively exchange their memories:
that of rowing a boat one April afternoon on Lake Como, or

even the evocation of the accident that crippled them,
draws them closer together; from time to time Hamm pursues
the fabrication of a long drawn-out literary story, for
which, like a true man of letters, he requires an audience.
Clov announces his own imminent departure, though he knows
it to be impossible, and does all he can to convince himself that his departure depends on his will alone.

It is the spectacle of a game that is coming to an end,
of an endgame, that is presented to us in Beckett's play.
The fact that this may be the very game we play all the
time, without ever believing it to be as close as it is to
its end, is made constantly apparent by the way relations
among the four characters are stripped down and reduced to
an elemental level. The humor of this grim play - vigor-
ous, savage, never gratuitous, provoking brusque out-
breaks of laughter - arises also from flashes of confrontation between the actual situation of these characters and
the tremendous futility of their malice as well as of
their moments of tenderness. It arises too from the
frenzy we discover in these characters, which they reveal
in their furious acceptance of their fate: the distant
apparition of what they take to be a human figure, the
discovery of a live rat or a live flea horrifies them.
'But humanity might start from there all over again,'
says Hamm. 'Catch him, for the love of God!' Black humor
indeed, but of a kind that arises spontaneously from feli-
citous and unexpected phrases, from a latent tragi-
comicality that suddenly becomes enormously ludicrous. A
humor whose power is in no way increased by one obscene
pun and two or three instances of coarse language.

I have limited myself to describing only the exterior
aspect of 'Endgame': a poem in dialogue, full of surprises and verbal successes, a play that moves and progresses, despite its immobile protagonists and subtle repetitions, towards a poignant and beautiful ending. As for
any metaphysical conclusions it may imply, naturally it is
for each spectator to understand them to his own liking;
the author leaves them complete latitude, and this is not
the least of the reasons for the fascination one experiences at a performance of 'Endgame.'

Jacques Noel's set, that bare bunker in which the human
race is coming to an end, is stifling; assuredly just as
Beckett must have conceived it. Roger Blin (Hamm), who
ensured the meticulous direction of the play, and Jean
Martin (Clov) are its extremely impressive protagonists;
Germaine de France (Nell) and Georges Adet (Nagg), emerging from their Diogenesque ashbins, succeed in being at
once ludicrous and pathetic.

The performance ends with an 'Act Without Words,' by

Beckett - a pantomime for one actor, carried through to
its termination with the sureness of a great artist by
Deryk Mendel - who, amid silence punctuated by blasts
from a whistle, shows the same qualities of humor and
cruelty we enjoyed in 'Endgame.'

[Translated by Jean M. Sommermeyer]

40. BROOKS ATKINSON IN 'NEW YORK TIMES'

29 January 1958, 32

Brooks Atkinson (b. 1894), drama critic for the 'New
York Times', 1925-42 and 1946-60. His writings about the
theatre can be read in 'Broadway Scrapbook' (1947), 'Brief
Chronicles' (1966), 'Broadway' (1970) and 'The Lively
Years' (1973).

Thanks largely to the bitterness of the direction and the
acting, Samuel Beckett's second play turns out to be quite
impressive. Impressive in the macabre intensity of the
mood, that is.

   For 'Endgame,' which opened at the Cherry Lane last
evening, deals in tones and perversities of expression.
Like 'Waiting for Godot,' it never comes precisely to the
point. Mr. Beckett is wise in choosing the form of the
myth in which to sound his tocsin on the condition of
human society. Since his theme is unearthly, the unearthly form becomes it.

   The stage represents a gloomy brick cavern with spectral light, two grotesque windows that can be reached only
by a ladder, scabrous walls, rubble, decay. There are
four characters - an irascible, blind tycoon in a hard hat
and rags, sitting in a battered pulpit chair; his
shuffling, groaning slave who drags himself around the
stage on futile errands; an elderly man and elderly woman
who live in two ashcans. Once or twice during the course
of Mr. Beckett's harangue of disgust they poke their
death-like faces above the rims of the ashcans and act as
a grisly chorus to the main theme.

   Apparently, the place is somewhere between life and
death, and the time is just short of the night of the

earth's last whimper. Don't expect this column to give a
coherent account of what - if anything - happens. Almost
nothing happens in the sense of action.

But Mr. Beckett, destitute of hope, is flinging a
shroud across the earth's last revels. He is painting a
portrait of desolation, lovelessness, boredom, ruthless-
ness, sorrow, nothingness. Looking out of the window
through a telescope, Clov reports what he sees: 'Zero,
zero, and zero.' Mr. Beckett is preparing us for oblivion.

Whether or not his theme is acceptable or rational, his
director, Alan Schneider, has had the grace to take him at
his own evaluation and stage his play seriously. Although
there is not much physical movement in it, it has continuous tension and constant pressure. The words are the
sounds of fluctuations in temper - from scorn and despair
to sardonic humor, from hopelessness to hatred.

In 'Endgame' as in 'Waiting for Godot,' the central
character is a tyrant. Here he is called Hamm. Lester
Rawlins acts the part with astonishing variety and vigor.
Seated on his silly throne, he gives the whole play a
driving harshness that is baleful and mad, and that stings
the nerves of the audience. In view of the elusiveness of
the dialogue, the fierce clarity of the characterization
he draws is a superb stroke of theatre....

What Mr. Beckett has to say is contrary and nihilistic.
But he is a writer. He can create a mood by using words
as incantations. Although the dialogue is often baffling,
there is no doubt about the total impression. We are
through, he says. Nature has forgotten us. The jig is up.

Under Mr. Schneider's bustling and perceptive direction, inside David Hays' stage design of doom, Mr. Beckett
is getting an intelligent hearing. This is how he feels.
The actors have given him the privilege of saying what he
feels with no equivocating. No one on the stage is asking
him to be reasonable.

Working with Beckett
(1958)

41. ALAN SCHNEIDER IN 'CHELSEA REVIEW'

Autumn 1958, 3-20

Alan Schneider (b. 1917) is the leading American director
of Beckett's plays. He has also written on theatrical
subjects for the 'New York Times,' the 'New Leader,'
'Theatre Arts,' 'Saturday Review,' and other journals.

> I take no sides. I am interested in the shape of
> ideas. There is a wonderful sentence in Augustine:
> 'Do not despair; one of the thieves was saved. Do not
> presume; one of the thieves was damned.' That sentence
> has a wonderful shape. It is the shape that matters.
>
> SAMUEL BECKETT.

In the three years that I have come to know him, the shape
of Samuel Beckett as a human being has come to matter as
much to me as do his plays. Perhaps even more. For Beckett is that most uncompromised of men, one who writes -
and lives - as he must, and not as the world - and the
world's critics - want him to. An artist, who works with
no fears of 'failure', which has fed him most of his writing life, or any expectation of 'success,' which has only
lately greeted him. A friend, who has come unannounced
to see me off at the Gare du Nord although I had not informed him which of the numerous trains to London I might

173

be taking. The head of a physics or math professor set
atop the torso and legs of a quarter-miler; a paradoxical
combination of a Frenchman's fundamental 'commitment' to
life and an Irishman's basic good nature. Such is the
shape of the man who has written some of the most terrifying and beautiful prose of the twentieth century.

My first inkling of Beckett's existence came in Zurich,
Switzerland, during the summer of 1954. A friend of mine
at the Zurich *Schauspielhaus* urged me to look up a new
play they had performed the previous season. It was
called 'Warten auf Godot,' and its French author had
become the rage of intellectual Europe - though, of
course, largely unrecognized in his Paris habitat, and
unknown in English. When I arrived in Paris a few weeks
later, I discovered, after much effort and many blank
stares, that 'En attendant Godot' was being presented at
an off-beat Left Bank playhouse, the Théâtre Babylone.
Not quite sure what to expect, my wife and I went the
following evening. The theatre was tiny, the production
extremely simple. There were nine people in the audience
that first evening, a few more when we came again a night
later. My French is just good enough to get me in and out
of the American Express. Yet through the entire performance I sat alternately spellbound and mystified, knowing
something terribly moving was taking place on that stage.
When the highly stylized 'moon' suddenly rose and night
'fell' at the end of that first act, I didn't have to
understand French in order to react. And when, at the
beginning of the second act, the once-bare tree reappeared
with little green ribbons for leaves, that simple representation of rebirth affected me beyond all reason. Without knowing exactly what, I knew that I had experienced
something unique and significant in modern theatre.
'Godot' had me in the beginnings of a grip from which I
have never escaped.

The next morning I tried to locate the author to see if
the American rights were available. He had no phone, and
no one would give me his home address. I left note after
note, contacted everyone I could think of who might know -
to no avail. Finally a friendly play-agent informed me
that the English-language rights had been acquired by a
British director Peter Glenville, who was planning to present the play in London with Alec Guinness as Vladimir and
Ralph Richardson as Estragon. Besides, added the agent,
the play was nothing an American audience would take -
unless it could have a couple of top-flight comedians
like Bob Hope and Jack Benny kidding it, preferably with
Laurel and Hardy in the other two roles. An American production under those circumstances seemed hopeless, and

Mr. Beckett as far removed as Mr. Godot himself. I came
home to New York and went on to other matters.

The next spring (1955) I had occasion to remember once
more. 'Godot' received its English-language premiere in
London, not with Guinness and Richardson at all but with a
non-star cast at London's charming Arts Theatre Club.
Damned without exception by the daily critics, it was
hailed in superlatives by both Harold Hobson and Kenneth
Tynan (the Atkinson and Kerr of London) in their Sunday
pieces, and soon became the top conversation piece of the
English season. At the same time, the English translation
was published by Grove Press in New York, and began to
sell an extraordinary number of copies not only in New
York City but all over the United States. Everyone who
could read was beginning to hear about this mysterious
'Godot.'

I read and re-read the published version. Somehow, on
its closely-spaced printed pages, it seemed cold and
abstract, even harsh, after the remarkable ambience I had
sensed at the Babylone. When a leading Broadway producer
asked me what I thought of its chances, I responded only
half-heartedly. Intrigued as I had been, I could not at
the moment imagine a commercial production in Broadway
terms.

One day in the fall of that same year, I was visiting my
old Alma Mater, the University of Wisconsin, when to my
utter amazement I received a long-distance phone call from
producer Michael Myerberg asking me if I would be interested in directing 'Waiting for Godot' in New York. He
had Bert Lahr and Tom Ewell signed for the two main roles;
and Thornton Wilder, whose 'Skin of our Teeth' I had
directed for the Paris Festival that summer, had recommen-
ded me. It was like Fate knocking at the door. After a
desperate search through practically every bookshop in
Chicago, I finally located a copy, stayed up all night on
the train studying it with new eyes, and arrived back in
New York to breathe a fervent 'yes' to Myerberg.

Followed a series of conferences with Lahr and Ewell,
both of whom confessed their complete bewilderment with
the play; and with Myerberg, who insisted that no one
could possibly be bewildered, least of all himself. He
did think it might be a good idea, however, for me to see
the English production, perhaps stopping off on the way to
have a talk with Beckett himself. To say that I was
pleased and excited would be a pale reflection of the
reality. And my elation was tempered only by the fear
that Beckett would continue to remain aloof - he had
merely reluctantly consented to a brief meeting with 'the
New York director.'

At any rate, a week later I found myself aboard the U.S.S. 'Independence' bound for Paris and London - and, by coincidence, the table companion and fellow conversationalist of Thornton Wilder, who was on his way to Rome and elsewhere. Crossing the Atlantic with Wilder was a stroke of good fortune and an experience I shall never forget. He greatly admired Beckett, considered 'Godot' one of the two greatest modern plays (the other was, I believe, Cocteau's 'Orpheus'), and openly contributed his ideas about an interpretation of the play, which he had seen produced in both French and German. In fact, so detailed and regular were our daily meetings that a rumour circulated that Wilder was rewriting the script, something which later amused both authors considerably. What was true was that I was led to become increasingly familiar with the script, both in French and in translation, and discovered what were the most important questions to ask Beckett in the limited time we were to have together. More specifically, I was now working in the frame of reference of an actual production situation - a three-week rehearsal period, a 'tryout' in a new theatre in Miami, and, of course, Bert and Tommy. It wasn't Bob Hope and Jack Benny, but that Parisian agent of two summers before had been correct so far. Was she also going to prove correct in terms of the audience response?

Beckett at that time had no phone - in fact, the only change I've noticed in him since his 'success' is the acquisition of one - so I sent him a message by pneumatique from the very plush hotel near the Etoile where Myerberg had lodged me. Within an hour, he rang up saying he'd meet me in the lobby - at the same time reminding me that he had only half an hour or so to spare. Armed with a large bottle of Lacrima Christi, as a present from both Wilder and myself, I stationed myself in the rather overdone lobby and waited for the elusive Mr. Beckett to appear. Promptly and very business-like, he strode in, his tall athletic figure ensconced in a worn shortcoat; bespectacled in old-fashioned steel rims; his face as long and sensitive as a greyhound's. Greetings exchanged, the biggest question became where we might drink our Lacrima Christi; we decided to walk a bit and see if we could come up with a solution. Walk we did, as we have done so many times since, and talk as we walked - about a variety of matters including, occasionally, his play. Eventually, we took a taxi to his skylight apartment in the sixth arrondissement and wound up finishing most of the bottle. In between I plied him with all my studiously-arrived-at questions as well as all the ones that came to me at the moment; and he tried to answer as

directly and as honestly as he could. The first one was
'Who or what does Godot mean?' and the answer was immediately forthcoming: 'If I knew, I would have said so in the
play.' Sam was perfectly willing to answer any questions
of specific meaning or reference, but would not - as
always - go into matters of larger or symbolic meanings,
preferring his work to speak for itself and letting the
supposed 'meanings' fall where they may.

As it turned out, he did have an appointment; so we
separated but not before we had made a date for dinner the
next evening. On schedule, we had a leisurely meal at one
of his favorite restaurants in Montparnasse, then I persuaded him to come along with me to a performance of
'Anastasia' at the Théâtre Antoine. I had directed the
New York production and was interested in seeing what it
would be in Paris; it turned out to be very artificial and
old-fashioned, and Sam's suffering was acute. Immediately
after the last curtain we retired to Fouquet's, once the
favorite café of his friend and companion James Joyce, for
solace and nourishment. Shortly before dawn - since I had
a plane to catch for London - we again separated. But not
before Sam had asked me if it would be additionally helpful if he joined me in London at the performances of
'Godot' there? He had not been to London in some years,
had never liked it since his early days of poverty and
struggle there, but he would be willing to come if I
thought it helpful! I could hardly believe what I heard.
Helpful!

Two days later, Sam came into London incognito, though
some of the London newspapers, hearing rumors of his presence, soon began searching for him. (To this day, he
heartily dislikes interviews, cocktail parties, and all
the other public concomitants of the literary life.) That
night, and each night for the next five days, we went to
see the production of 'Godot,' which had been transferred
by this time to the Criterion in Piccadilly Circus. The
production was interesting, though scenically over-
cluttered and missing many of the points which Sam had
just cleared up for me. My fondest memories are of Sam's
clutching my arm from time to time and in a clearly-heard
stage whisper saying: 'It's ahl wrahng! He's doing it ahl
wrahng!' about a particular bit of stage business or the
interpretation of a certain line. Every night after the
performance, we would compare what we had seen to what he
had intended, try to analyse why or how certain points
were being lost, speak with the actors about their difficulties. Every night, also, we would carefully watch the
audience, a portion of which always left during the show.
I always felt that Sam would have been disappointed if at

least a few hadn't.

Through all this, I discovered not only how clear and logical 'Godot' was in its essences, but how human and how easy to know Sam was, how friendly beneath his basic shyness. I had met Sam, wanting primarily to latch on to anything which might help make 'Godot' a success on Broadway. I left him, wanting nothing more than to please him. I came with respect; I left with a greater measure of devotion than I have ever felt for a writer whose work I was engaged in translating to the stage.

Though Sam felt he could not face the trials of the rehearsal and tryout periods, he promised to make his first trip to the United States once we had opened. As it turned out, he didn't - and we didn't. Of trials, however, there were plenty, somewhat above the usual quota. Doing 'Godot' in Miami was, as Bert Lahr himself said, like doing 'Giselle' in Roseland. Even though Bert and Tommy each contributed brilliantly comic and extremely touching performances, even though I felt more or less pleased with the production and felt that Sam would have been equally so, it was - in the words of the trade - a spectacular flop. The opening night audience in Miami, at best not too sophisticated or attuned to this type of material and at worst totally misled by advertising billing the play as 'the laugh sensation of two continents,' walked out in droves. And the so-called reviewers not only could not make heads or tails of the play but accused us of pulling some sort of a hoax on them. Although by the second week we were reaching - and holding - a small but devoted audience, the initial reception in Miami discouraged producer Myerberg, demoralized the cast, and led to the abandonment of the production. Later in the season, Myerberg changed his mind and brought 'Godot' to Broadway, where it had a critical success; but the only member of the original company to go along was Bert Lahr, who gave substantially the same performance he had given in Miami (but this time without Tom Ewell to match him).

The failure in Miami depressed me more than any experience I had had in the theatre, though I had from time to time anticipated its probability and done all in my power to avoid it. It is typical of Sam that his response to Miami was concerned only with my feelings of disappointment, and never stressed or even mentioned his own. Nor did he utter one word of blame for any mistakes I might have made along the way. Instead he began writing me about his progress on a new play, plans for which he had confided in Paris. He was going to rest for a while at his cottage 'in the Marne Mud' but would try to get to it again as soon as possible.

Somehow, somewhere, I knew I had to make up for Miami
- to myself, and more importantly to Sam. I never saw the
New York production of 'Godot' - perhaps I could not bring
myself to - although I have listened over and over again
to the recordings. Ostensibly, I was in Europe on a
Guggenheim Fellowship, as well as doing some directing in
London. By the middle of the summer, I managed to get to
Paris and once more face Sam. He made things as bearable
as he could for me, and indeed seeing him made them more
bearable. We met several times. I told him the story of
Miami as objectively as I could, and he spoke to me of
what he had heard concerning both productions. - Somehow
he made me feel that what I had at least tried to do in
Miami was closer to what he had wanted - though he never
criticised the efforts of anyone else. What he made me
understand most of all was that he appreciated my concern
with his work, that the actual results in Miami didn't
matter, that failure in the popular sense was something he
had breathed in all his life, and that the only thing
which counted was one's own sense of achievement, one's
own need to be honest with oneself. No other playwright
whom I have ever known could have been so simply and so
unselfconsciously unselfish. I would have done anything
for Sam.

My opportunity was not long in coming. That new play
he was working on was taking shape and had been scheduled
for presentation in Paris in the spring of 1957. 'Fin de
partie' it was called, again with only four characters
(two of them popping out of ashcans) and a special world
of its own. The New York press, intrigued by 'Godot,'
began to publish tidbits about the new play, saying that
it was even more 'weird,' that it dealt with two men
buried up to their necks in wet sand, etc. The title
came to be translated as 'The End of the Game' and even
'The Game is Up' instead of its proper 'Endgame,' as in
the last section of a game of chess. Eventually, as it
turned out, the French production lost its theatre because
of a timid management, and had its premiere (in French)
only through the good offices of the Royal Court in London.
Then another management took it over and it ran in Paris
through the fall. The London critics, with the exception
of Harold Hobson, were even more baffled and negative than
they had been with 'Godot'; even Tynan confessed his deep
disappointment with the newer play's special anatomy of
melancholy. While the French critics were, as usual,
fervently and hopelessly divided.

Sam had sent me a copy of the French text which I
tried, without success, to have someone translate for me.
But I didn't have to read every line to know how I felt.

One day, I sent him a cable asking for the rights to present the play off-Broadway, where I felt it would reach
its proper audience.   I had secured the agreement of Noel
Behn, manager of the Cherry Lane, one of the best and most
intimate of off-Broadway theatres, to present 'Endgame'
there as soon as its current occupant, Sean O'Casey's
'Purple Dust,' had concluded its run; that would probably
be around the first of the year.   And the reason I wanted
to option the play myself was in order to maintain what I
felt was a necessary amount of artistic control over all
the elements of production, a condition which I had not
been able to obtain in my previous encounter with a Beckett play.   Fate was knocking at my door for the second
time - but this time I was furnishing some of the elbow-
grease.

All spring and into the summer I corresponded with Sam
and his New York publisher and agent, Barney Rosset of
Grove Press, about the arrangements to be made.   Although,
as Sam said, he felt strange about negotiating for an
English translation which did not yet exist.   Eventually,
after many weeks, it did exist, eventually it came, and
eventually - and with a sense of real anticipation - I sat
down one evening to read 'the ashcan play,' as it had
generally become known by this time.   In fact, it was only
with the greatest of difficulty that we could get the
press to understand that the two chief characters were *not*
in ashcans.

Though I came to 'Endgame' in exactly the opposite manner in which I had been introduced to 'Godot,' via the
text rather than in the theatre, the experience was
equally impressive.   Of course, I had come more prepared
this time: two years of contact with Sam, a reading and
re-reading of all his novels, and of everything I could
find that had been written about his work.   Whatever the
reasons, I found myself literally bowled over by the scope
and intensity of the new play's material.   Not that I
understood everything Sam was driving at; the text was
much more taut and elliptical than Godot's.   But I was
certainly carried away with the theatrical powers and
possibilities of this alternately terrifying and uproari-
ous, horrible and beautiful, tone-poem.   The gentle aged
couple in the ashcans was, of course, a marvelous invention and yet completely organic to the theme.   But equally
fascinating were the two central figures: the blind, maj-
estic, and yet ever-so-human tyrant Hamm, and his shambling automaton attendant Clov.   Frankly, I didn't spend
much time worrying what all this 'meant' or 'was about' -
whether it was the last four people left on earth after
an atomic explosion; or the older generation being tossed

on the ashheap by the younger; or, as someone suggested, Pozzo and Lucky in the third act of 'Godot.' Just as 'Godot' dealt with a promised arrival that never took place, so 'Endgame' dealt with a promised and unfulfilled departure. More than anything else, it seemed to me to be, in a sense, a kind of tragic poem, man's last prayer to a God that might or might not exist. Far from depressing me, it lifted me out of myself, exhilarated me, provided a dramatic experience as strong as the one I had when I first discovered 'Oedipus' or 'Lear.' And what most delighted me was that in 'Endgame' were more of Sam's special gifts for language and rhythm, for making the sublime ridiculous and the ridiculous sublime.

In fact, I wrote to Barney Rosset that the part of Hamm needed a combination Oedipus, Lear, and Hamlet - a neat trick of casting even at Broadway rates, much less off-Broadway. Nevertheless I was determined to try. And, more importantly, Sam was willing to have me try.

With our arrangements for New York production completed, Sam was anxious that I see the Paris version before it closed at the end of October. No more anxious than I. For, once more, I had stored up a fund of questions which could best be answered in person. Luckily, the manager of the Cherry Lane agreed. A trans-Atlantic voyage is a sizeable item in an off-Broadway budget. But in this case a vital one. So in October I was off on my second pilgrimage to Beckett, this time overnight and by air directly to Paris.

As it happened, Sam and I missed each other at the Gare des Invalides on my arrival, but met at the hotel - this time a modest one in Montparnasse (as befitted off-Broadway). For a week, we met every day and for most of the day, taking long walks (one lovely sunny afternoon we polished off a pound of grapes while strolling through the Luxembourg Gardens), having lunch and dinner together, inhabiting various cafés at all hours. The French production of 'Endgame,' after a run of almost 100 performances, was in its last week; I saw it four times, once while following the English translation with an usher's flashlight until the usher politely told me I was bothering the actors. I spoke with the French cast, especially director Roger Blin, who played Hamm so magnificently; and was able to check on all the technical details of the production. The Paris production had been basically as Sam wanted it, although like all practicing playwrights he was gradually discovering that all actors have personalities and get ideas which may seriously affect the intentions of the author. Again Sam tried to answer all my questions, no matter how stupid they seemed to him - or how often I

asked them. 'What were Clov's visions?' 'Who was that
mysterious Mother Pegg that kept cropping up?' 'What did
it mean for Hamm's and Clov's faces to be red, while
Nagg's and Nell's were white?' (As Sam counter-asked, why
was Werther's coat green? Because the author saw it that
way.)

Each time I read the script or saw the play performed I
had a flock of new questions. Sam was always patient and
ever tolerant; he wanted to help all he could. And he
helped me more than I can ever say or even know. When I
left for home, I knew 'Endgame' a hundred times better
than when I had arrived, knew what Hamm should look like
and sound like, knew how best the ashcans should be placed,
knew how carefully and how exactly I'd have to work on its
rhythms and tones. As for its larger meanings, gradually
the mosaic was falling into place, its design still shadowy but perceivable and inevitable.

The main question - contrary to the one I was generally
asked: Which play did I like better, 'Godot' or 'Endgame'?
- was: Who in New York could and would play Hamm? In
Paris, Blin had given a bravura classic performance in the
grand manner, such as only the French theatre could still
offer. George Devine, whom I had seen and admired many
times, was scheduled to play the role in London; he was
excellent casting. What we needed was something of the
calibre of Paul Muni - who was seriously ill - or Charles
Laughton - who was abroad. I left Paris and Sam's last
piece of advice: 'Do it the way you like, Alan, do it any
way you like!' feeling that somewhere there was bound to
be a Hamm - if only we could find him.

Look for him we did! For over two months, the actors
streamed in and out of the Cherry Lane offices, and the
telephones rang all over New York. Our first choices for
the parents were P.J. Kelly and Nydia Westman - and we
were fortunate in interesting both. To this day, I can
scarcely visualise anyone other than P.J. and Nydia in
those ashcans. For Clov, we had several strong choices,
depending for our final selection on what kind of Hamm we
were to find. Hamm himself remained unobtainable. Muni
was indeed not to be had. Laughton wrote us a letter
saying he was fascinated by the play but would rather have
had Ilse Koch make him into a lampshade than play that
part! Others were intrigued but not available, or available but not intrigued; still others interested but somehow not suited. We despaired, postponed, kept looking.

At last, after a brief trial with another actor, we
came up with what turned out to be an extremely fortunate
choice: a young and relatively unknown performer, Lester
Rawlins, with whom I had worked in Washington some years

back and who since coming to New York had had his considerable talents hidden behind a succession of Shakespearean
beards.   For Clov, we took Alvin Epstein, a specialist in
mime and the 'Lucky' of the New York 'Godot.'   (He was
later succeeded by Gerald Hiken, not available at the time
we were opening, who gave an equally fine performance.)
Rawlins had a very low-pitched and flexible voice of great
timbre, an imposing presence and a countenance like gran-
ite; at times, he would remind me physically of Blin, yet
he succeeded in making the role uniquely and powerfully
his own.   Epstein's stage movement was always arresting
and carefully realised.   And Nell and Nagg were adorable.
The first hurdle had been well jumped, now we were on our
way.

The day after New Year's 1958, we went into rehearsal.
First rehearsals of a new play are always a kind of adventure into the unknown, a stepping out into uncharted
space.   This is especially true of a Beckett play, where
so many of the standard conventions are broken or ignored
- the beginning, the middle and end of an organised plot-
line, clear-cut character progression, dramatic mobility
and color - and yet so many new ones laid down - tones,
rhythms, and cross-currents of relationship, which the
author has built into the very fibre of his material.   No
other author I know of writes stage directions which are
so essentially and specifically valid - as we discovered
to our gain on each occasion when we ventured to disregard
or to oppose them.   His pauses are as much a part of the
text as the words themselves.   And I soon found myself not
only getting more and more faithful to his printed demands
but expecting an equal allegiance from the actors when
they tended to go off on their own tangents - as actors
are wont to do.

As well as designers.   Our setting was being designed
by a talented newcomer, David Hays, whose reputation was
largely based on his designs for O'Neill's 'Long Day's
Journey Into Night' and 'The Iceman Cometh.'   I made the
mistake of showing him photographs of the Paris production, whereupon he tried to do everything exactly differently.   After he had submitted several designs, all of
which were rejected, we discovered that the stone-and-
brick walls of the Cherry Lane stage were marvelously
available and suited to represent Hamm and Clov's 'shelter' - even to the extent of having a doorway at exactly
the proper location for Clov's 'kitchen.'   This discovery
provided us with a most useful and authentic interior
whose actual walls and floor produced sound of great effectiveness, and which could be lit well and simply.   How
to manage the windows posed our only problem; eventually -

and with Sam's wholehearted approval - we painted them,
complete with window frames, boldly and theatrically on
the wall at the back. (One part of the frame was made
practical to allow for its opening near the end of the
play.) No one minded in the slightest except those who
looked for additional philosophical overtones from two
painted windows on a bare brick wall.

Not that we shied away from all 'significance' or
meaning. But I have long ago discovered that the director's function is not so much to explain the author's
meaning to his actors - whose problem of expressing that
meaning to the audience is not necessarily helped by in-
tellectually understanding it - but to see that, through
whatever theatrical means, the actors are led to *do* those
things which will *result* in the author's meaning being expressed. No actors can act out the *meaning* of 'Endgame' -
or any other play. They can and did act the roles of the
various characters in the various situations and moments
and relationships which Beckett had provided for them.
They acted them with interest and variety, I hope, and
with a sense of form but always as actual people in an
actual situation. Beckett himself had always stressed
that he was writing about what he termed a 'local situation,' i.e., Hamm and Clov (as well as Nagg and Nell) were
individual personalities operating in a given set of circumstances. They were not to be considered as abstractions or symbols, or as representing anything other than
themselves. After that, if the audience - or the critics
- wanted to look for significance of some kind, let them
do so, at their own initiative - and peril.

I found, for example, that it became convenient for me
to suggest to the actors that the relation of Hamm and
Clov could be likened to that of the mind and the body,
the intellectual and the physical faculties inseparable
and yet always in conflict. But I never meant that I
thought they *were* the mind and the body, or that that was
what Sam intended. It was simply a theatrical means of
leading the actors into certain areas of creativity and
imagination. And definitely more helpful than figuring
out whether the names of Hamm and Clov meant ham and
cloves, or the Biblical Ham and the cloven foot, and a
dozen other secret codes - all of which were obviously
irrelevant.

Fortunately, the actors were most cooperative. Nydia
Westman, for one, though occasionally or often baffled by
what she had to do or say, strove valiantly and with all
good will to carry out what I asked her to do. P.J. Kelly,
who in his seventy-eight years had had many similar experiences, especially, as he confessed, with Irish

playwrights, was equally agreeable. And they both coped
good-naturedly with the numerous practical problems involved in making entrances and exits and spending an entire evening in two non-custom-made ashcans. While Rawlins and Epstein, one of whom never left his armchair and
the other never allowed to rest from the burden of a constantly uncomfortable stance, did all in their power to
carry out their respective jobs as I kept saying - and
feeling - Sam would have wanted them to.

By the time we were well into rehearsals, the Cherry
Lane management - joined by an optimistic trio known as
Rooftop Productions - had no illusions about my initial
responsibility being to the author. A number of times
during this period, one or the other would get worried
that I was making the play 'too serious.' They occasionally urged me to 'gag it up' a bit here and there - which
I refused to do, especially since I felt that the production abounded with legitimate laughter. Once or twice, I
believe they became upset about one or the other of the
performances - or about what I was doing with them. Had I
not retained that much coveted artistic control by the
very terms of my contract, I might have been forced to
make fundamental changes with which I was completely in
disagreement - or risked being fired. As it was, I resis-
ted all attempts to change or distort what Sam had written,
or go against any of the things he had confided in me
during my Paris sojourn and in subsequent letters.

Personally, I felt rehearsals were going extremely
well; the texture of Sam's writing was gradually emerging,
rich in both its serious and comedic elements. Cast
morale was high. Their dedication to the enterprise
really remarkable, especially in view of the nominal sal-
aries they were getting and the general lack of glamour of
off-Broadway. Interest on the part of the public was also
considerable if not tremendous, though we were not getting
as much publicity as we wanted. Throughout, I kept constantly in touch with Sam, letting him know all our ups
and downs, and continuing to question him in detail - his
answers always opening up new vistas and new possibilities.

Three weeks after rehearsals began, we held the first
of a series of five previews with audiences. The reception was more than any of us had dared to expect. They
laughed and cried at all the proper places, were never
bored, though occasionally or even often, puzzled. And
not only did they not mind sitting through the hour-and-a-
half without intermission (I had refused to add one) but
stayed in their seats, clapping wildly at the end. The
other four audiences reacted similarly, two or three of

them even more enthusiastically. And, miracle of miracles, the word-of-mouth was evidently excellent because we were selling out, an unheard-of event at off-Broadway previews. Advance sales began to hum; the general feeling was that we had a great show. We crossed our fingers and hoped for a good performance on opening night.

Opening night came, and the actors gave the best performance they had yet given. But we found troubles of other sorts. The building's steam pipes had been turned off by accident a half-hour before the curtain went up; and for the first ten minutes, the pipes played a grisly staccato accompaniment to the text that nearly drove me mad and, in my opinion, affected the audience badly. (Afterwards, at least a dozen of my more sophisticated theatre friends told me they thought the sound effects of the pipes were a wonderful touch - though a trifle loud.) In addition, perhaps because the 189-seat Cherry Lane Theatre was more than half occupied by members of the press - something like 100 seats - the audience response was nothing like it had been for the five previews or was going to be for every other night in its run. The audience was respectful but cool. Lines that had brought roars produced hardly a smile, those that had brought smiles produced nothing. Instead of the silences we had previously earned in the more emotional moments of the play, we heard seats creaking and programs rattling. And opening night was the only night that I didn't hear that on-stage alarm clock ticking from the back of the theatre. We were appalled. And I despaired that all our efforts had again been in vain.

That interval between the curtain coming down on opening night and the first appearance of the reviews in the early editions of the morning papers is a period of purgatory than which nothing in the various hells of the theatre is worse. Somehow we managed to survive its more than ordinary length this time, downing the bourbon and making conversation as though it mattered. A TV commentator at midnight said he had hated us, but we didn't expect anything else from television. At about 12:30, someone from the Herald-Tribune rang up and read Walter Kerr's notice directly from the galley sheets. Kerr was respectful if not exactly glowing, somewhat provocative - and there were two or three good quotes. Our spirits, imprisoned since those pipes had started clanking, began to stir. At one o'clock, unable to wait any longer, I rang up the Times myself and got a bored voice which after a bit of prodding promised to locate a 'bulldog' edition containing Brooks Atkinson's column. A few interminable moments later, the voice commented 'It's pretty stiff,'

then having thrown the bomb proceeded to read verbatim an
absolutely beautiful notice from Atkinson, one clearly
understanding the author's intention and point of view, as
well as highly appreciating its representation on the
stage. (A few weeks later, Mr. Atkinson came through with
an excellent and perceptive Sunday column which added
further to our laurels - and our run.) The jubilation was
so intense that we couldn't resist letting Sam know.
Though it was just dawn in Paris, we telephoned him and
told his sleepy self that the two chief critics in New
York had liked the production. As usual, Sam's concern
was with the performers and the management - though he expressed his gratitude and relief at the favorable reception. The wonderful thing was that I knew, as always,
that win, lose, or draw in the notices, Sam's opinion of
the entire venture and of me would have been no different.
The important thing for him was not the winning or losing
of the race but the running of it. I went home for the
first time in over two years with the weight of the Miami
'Godot' off my shoulders.

Kerr and Atkinson weren't the whole story. As is very
usual, the afternoon papers were much more baffled and
much less perceptive. But somehow between the word-of-
mouth of those who had seen the show and the natural curiosity of those who hadn't, 'Endgame' ran three months and
more than 100 performances, and was generally regarded as
one of the serious highlights of the season on or off-
Broadway. The weekly press, most of which came the second
night, was for the most part good; although we got a bad
break when the review in 'Time,' an extremely favorable
one, was crowded out for lack of space. Our audiences
grew more receptive and enthusiastic as the run progressed
- hardly anyone ever walked out - the performances got
fuller and more relaxed, even the publicity improved.
But, best of all, we had not failed Sam. Though he would
not come to New York to see the production, news and comment about it reached him regularly. He seemed to like
the production photographs that had been taken - eventually he will hear the recording of the entire text.
Although by then he must have been sure we were able to
succeed - as much as any production can. Meanwhile, we
continued to look forward to and cherish his occasional
'greetings to the players.'

Beckett's plays stay in the bones. They haunt me
sleeping and waking, coming upon me when I am least aware.
Sometimes a stray bit of conversation heard by accident on
a bus or in a restaurant brings home one of Vladimir's and
Estragon's 'little canters.' Sometimes I find myself
actually reacting like Clov or like Hamm or, more often,

like both simultaneously. Sam's characters seem to me
always more alive and more truly lasting than those in the
slice-of-life realistic dramas with which our stages today
abound. (They will be equally alive when most of those
others are as dead as the characters in 'The Great
Divide.') His words strike to the very marrow - the
sudden sharp anguish of a Pozzo or of a Hamm crying out
for understanding in an uncertain universe; Clov's detailed description of the bleak harsh landscape of our existence on earth. While against and in spite of the harshness and the uncertainty, there is the constant assertion
of man's will, and spirit, his sense of humor, as the
only bulwarks against despair; the constant 'glimmers of
hope', even in the dark depths of that abyss in which we
find ourselves.

And now Sam has written a new one, actually just a cur-
tain-raiser. For one character and a tape-recorder.
'Krapp's Last Tape' it's called, about a man listening to
some tapes he has recorded in the past; and as always it
manages to be both touching and comedic. His first original writing in English, except for the BBC radio play
'All That Fall,' since before the war. An augury? A
switch away from French for a while? With Sam one is
never sure. One only hopes that in whatever language, he
will go on writing for the theatre because one knows that
he will go on extending its boundaries and its dimensions.
Not because he plans it that way, but because that is
where his taste and imagination and talent lead him.

I shall be content to follow. In fact, I'm on my way
over again to see him, a copy of 'Krapp's Last Tape'
packed in my briefcase. It's getting to be a habit.
There are some wonderful sentences in those few pages of
'Krapp's Last Tape' as there are in every one of Sam Beckett's plays. I remember especially a group of them near
the end: 'Perhaps my best years are gone. When there was
a chance of happiness. But I wouldn't want them back.
Not with the fire in me now. No, I wouldn't want them
back.' Taken together, those sentences leave a wonderful
shape. But it is not only their shape that matters. It
is the shape of the man who wrote them.

May 1958

'Krapp's Last Tape' (1958)

[Written in English; first performed at the Royal Court Theatre, London, 28 October 1958; first performed in New York at the Provincetown Playhouse, 14 January 1960; translated into French by Beckett and Pierre Leyris as 'La Dernière Bande'; first performed in Paris, at Théâtre Récamier, 22 March 1960; published by Faber & Faber, London, 1959; Grove Press, New York, 1960; and Éditions de Minuit, Paris, 1960.]

---

42. KENNETH TYNAN IN 'OBSERVER'

2 November 1958, 19

'*Slamm's Last Knock*,' a play inspired, if that is the word, by Samuel Beckett's double bill at the Royal Court:
   The den of Slamm, the critic. Very late yesterday. Large desk with throne behind it. Two waste-paper baskets, one black, one white, filled with crumpled pieces of paper, at either side of the stage. Shambling between them - i.e., from one to the other and back again - an old man: Slamm. Bent gait. Thin, barking voice. Motionless, watching Slamm, is Seck. Bright grey face, holding pad and pencil. One crutch. Slamm goes to black basket, takes out piece of white paper, uncrumples it, reads. Short laugh.
   SLAMM (*reading*): '...the validity of an authentic tragic vision, at once personal and by implication cosmic...'
   Short laugh. He recrumples the paper, replaces it in basket, and crosses to other - i.e., white - basket. He takes out piece of black paper, uncrumples it, reads. Short laugh.

SLAMM (*reading*): '...Just another dose of nightmare gibberish from the so-called author of "Waiting for Godot..."'

Short laugh. He recrumples the paper, replaces it in basket, and sits on throne. Pause. Anguished, he extends fingers of right hand and stares at them. Extends fingers of left hand. Same business. Then brings fingers of right hand towards fingers of left hand, and vice versa, so that fingertips of right hand touch fingertips of left hand. Same business. Breaks wind pensively. Seck writes feverishly on pad.

SLAMM: We're getting on. (*He sighs.*) Read that back.

SECK (*produces pince-nez with thick black lenses, places them on bridge of nose, reads*): 'A tragic dose of authentic gibberish from the so-called implication of "Waiting for Godot,"' Shall I go on?

SLAMM (*nodding head*): No. (*Pause.*) A bit of both, then.

SECK (*shaking head*): Or a little of neither.

SLAMM: There's the hell of it. (*Pause. Urgently.*) Is it time for my Roget?

SECK: There are no more Rogets. Use your loaf.

SLAMM: Then wind me up, stink-louse! Stir your stump!

Seck hobbles to Slamm, holding rusty key descending from piece of string round his (Seck's) neck, and inserts it into back of Slamm's head. Loud noise of winding.

SLAMM: Easy now. Can't you see it's hell in there?

SECK: I haven't looked. (*Pause.*) It's hell out here, too. The ceiling is zero and there's grit in my crotch. Roget and over.

He stops winding and watches. Pause.

SLAMM (*glazed stare*): Nothing is always starting to happen.

SECK: It's better than something. You're well out of that.

SLAMM: I'm badly into this. (*He tries to yawn but fails.*) It would be better if I could yawn. Or if you could yawn.

SECK: I don't feel excited enough. (*Pause.*) Anything coming?

SLAMM: Nothing, in spades. (*Pause.*) Perhaps I haven't been kissed enough. Or perhaps they put the wrong ash in my gruel. One or the other.

SECK: Nothing will come of nothing. Come again.

SLAMM (*with violence*): Purulent drudge! *You* try, if you've got so much grit in your crotch! Just one piti-less, pathetic, creatively critical phrase!

SECK: I heard you the first time.

SLAMM: You can't have been listening.

SECK: Your word's good enough for me.

SLAMM: I haven't got a word. There's just the light, going. (*Pause.*) Are you trying?

SECK: Less and less.

SLAMM: Try blowing down it.

SECK: It's coming! (*Screws up his face. Tonelessly.*) Sometimes I wonder why I spend the lonely night.

SLAMM: Too many f's. We're bitched. (*Half a pause.*)

SECK: Hold your pauses. It's coming again. (*In a rac-onteur's voice, dictates to himself.*) Tuesday night, seven-thirty by the paranoid barometer, curtain up at the Court, Sam Beckett unrivalled master of the unravelled revels. Item: 'Krapp's Last Tape,' Krapp being a myopic not to say deaf not to say eremitical eater of one and one-half bananas listening and cackling as he listens to a tape-recording of twenty years' antiquity made on a day, the one far gone day, when he laid his hand on a girl in a boat and it worked, as it worked for Molly Bloom in Gib-raltar in the long ago. Actor: Patrick Magee, bereaved and aghast-looking grunting into his Grundig, probably perfect performance, fine throughout and highly affecting at third curtain-call though not formerly. Unique, oblique, bleak experience, in other words, and would have had same effect if half the words *were* other words. Or any words. (*Pause.*)

SLAMM: Don't stop. You're boring me.

SECK (*normal voice*): Not enough. You're smiling.

SLAM: Well, I'm still in the land of the dying.

SECK: Somehow, in spite of everything, death goes on.

SLAM: Or because of everything. (*Pause.*) Go on.

SECK (*raconteur's voice*): Tuesday night, eight-twenty by the Fahrenheit anonymeter, 'End-Game,' translated from the French with loss by excision of the vernacular word for urination and of certain doubts blasphemously cast on the legitimacy of the Deity. Themes, madam? Nay, it *is*, I know not themes. Foreground figure a blind and lordly cripple with superficial mannerisms of Churchill, W., Connolly, C., and Devine, G., director and in this case impersonator. Sawn-off parents in bins, stage right, and shuffling servant, all over the stage, played by Jack MacGowran, binster of this parish. Purpose: to analyse or rather to dissect or rather to define the nature or rather the quality or rather the intensity of the boredom inher-ent or rather embedded in the twentieth or rather every other century. I am bored, therefore I am. Comment, as above, except it would have the same effect if a quarter of the words were other words and another quarter omitted. Critique ended. Thesaurus and out.

SLAMM: Heavy going. I can't see.

SECK: That's because of the light going.
SLAMM: Is that all the review he's getting?
SECK: That's all the play he's written.

Pause.

SLAMM: But a genius. Could you do as much?
SECK: Not as much. But as little.

Tableau. Pause. Curtain.

43. ROBERT BRUSTEIN IN 'NEW REPUBLIC'

22 February 1960, 21

Robert Brustein (b. 1927) was drama critic for the 'New Republic' and Professor of Dramatic Literature at Columbia University during the early 1960s. Since 1966, he has been Dean of the Yale Drama School. His books include 'The Theatre of Revolt' (1964), 'Seasons of Discontent' (1965), 'The Third Theatre' (1969), and 'Culture Watch' (1975).

'Krapp's Last Tape' is Samuel Beckett's latest, and very possibly his best, dramatic poem about the old age of the world. Still obsessed with the alienation, vacuity, and decay of life upon a planet devoid of God and hope, Beckett is finally able to sound those chords of compassion which have always vibrated quietly in his other work. Yet, what really strikes me as new is the extraordinary economy of the writing, the absolute flawlessness of the form. 'Godot' and 'Endgame,' for all their great poetry and insight, were ultimately marred, I think, by their length. It is one thing to affirm that life is a string of aimless, inconsequential, and monotonous events; it is quite another to produce and reproduce these events upon the stage. Although Beckett's art, like Ionesco's, lends itself most readily to short statements, the burden of his plays - that one day is very much like another - has led him into labyrinths of *longueur* and repetition.

In 'Krapp,' Beckett disposes of this problem with the aid of a simple mechanical device. Today and tomorrow are, through the use of a tape recorder, simultaneously revealed. Set in the future (I suspect all of Beckett's plays are), this brief and beautiful art-work revolves

around a solitary character, the perfect realization of
Beckett's idea of human isolation. Like so many of the
author's creations, Krapp is incredibly ancient. He
putters laboriously around his hermetic cell, myopically
examining his keys, peering dimly into his books, testing
his shrunken vocal organs on words which please him, pouring whiskey noisily down his throat, sucking toothlessly
on a banana with the same relish and resignation that
Estragon eats his carrot and Nagg his soda biscuit.
Reduced to his most elementary appetites, Krapp has no
purpose or occupation except to listen to his organs die
and to feel his functions fail. He is, like Eliot's
Gerontion, 'an old man in a draughty house under a windy
knob,' but he is without even Gerontion's dream of rain.
   Krapp is surrounded, almost buried, by his past - boxes
upon boxes of magnetic tapes, the vocal diary of his
entire life. The action of the play is the replaying of
one spool, a mundane yesterday recorded 30 years before
when Krapp was middle-aged and already rather juiceless.
The droning, slightly pompous voice from the machine
evokes a variety of responses from the aged Krapp; anger,
interest, melancholy, contempt, despair. A memory of
feeling returns to his withered hand during a description
of the texture of a black rubber ball; after the story of
a girl in a tattered dress glimpsed on a railway platform,
he hurriedly plays the section over; he turns the set off
in disgust in the midst of a rabid, excited account of a
eureka insight into the meaning of life; he collapses into
ruins of longing during the indifferently intoned narrative of a sexual experience in a rocking boat. On the
last tape, Krapp intends to record his present day's activities, but there is now nothing left in him, 'not a
squeak,' nothing but memory, loss, and impotent desire,
nothing to do but put on the old tape and eavesdrop on his
past when he could still press the flesh against another
human body. The curtain descends on Krapp stiffening in
his rented room, his head laid miserably on the machine,
his arms around it like a grotesque and wizened lover. It
is a haunting and harrowing work, brilliantly directed by
Alan Schneider and played by Donald Davis with just the
right balance of pathos and absurdity.

'The Trilogy' (1959-60)

['Molloy,' 'Malone Dies' and 'The Unnamable' were published in one volume by Olympia Press in 1959 and by John
Calder in 1960. The following three reviews are important
early statements on Beckett by three major contemporary
critics.]

---

44. V.S. PRITCHETT IN 'NEW STATESMAN'

2 April 1960, 489

V.S. Pritchett (b. 1900), novelist, critic, story writer
and a director of the 'New Statesman.' Among his most
notable works of fiction are: 'Nothing Like Leather'
(1935), 'Mr. Beluncle' (1951) and 'Collected Stories'
(1956); of criticism: 'The Living Novel' (1946), 'Books in
General' (1953), 'The Working Novelist' (1965) and
'George Meredith and English Comedy' (1970); of autobiography: 'A Cab at the Door' (1968) and 'Midnight Oil'
(1971).

There is a terrifying sentence in James Stephens's account
of his meeting with Joyce in Dublin that unfortunately
came to my mind when I was struggling with Samuel Beckett's trilogy - 'I looked at him', says Stephens, 'without
a word in my mouth except vocabulary'. Will someone not
chart the vivid but interminable ocean of Irish garrulity
for us, point out the shallows and the depths, tell us
where the words are vocabulary only and where they connote

ideas or things, where they are propitiatory magic, where
egomania filling in time and place? Where is language
used for language's sake, and where is it used as a gabble-
gabble ritual to make tolerable the meaninglessness of
life? It would be of practical help to know whether a
writer was drowning well within his own depth or out of
it; and when it would be decent to leave him to it - possibly coming back later, after a smoke, to see how he was
getting on.

One does this with 'Tristram Shandy'. Pending other
guidance, the reader of Beckett's trilogy, 'Molloy',
'Malone Dies', and 'The Unnamable', does the same. They
are lawsuits that never end, vexations, litigations
joined with the tedium, the greyness, the grief, the
fear, the rage, the clownishness, the physical miseries of
old age where life is on the ebb, and nature stands by
smiling idiotically. Why was I born, get me out of this,
let me live on less and less, get me to the grave, the
womb, the last door, dragging this ludicrous, feeble,
windy broken old bag of pipes with me. Find me a hole.
Give me deafness and blindness; chop off the gangrened
leg; somewhere on this rubbish dump where I crawl there
must be some final dustbin, where I can dribble, laugh,
cry and maunder on the this and the that of the general
mystery and occasionally give a toothless grin over an
obscene word or a farcical sexual memory.

Flight, old age, and the wrangle about personal identity, these are Samuel Beckett's themes. A man is a ves-
tige left by to hop around in wearying argy-bargy after
his invisible master: punishment, for the old, unremem-
bered sin. Life is the *belle dame* with the mindless
smirk and she hardly troubles to look at the victim who
has been reduced to the total lethargy of compulsive
speech. That is the joke: the mutilated thing can *talk*.
In the first volume the man is Molloy, the tramp with
crutches, a mixture of simplicity, hurt and lunatic
energy. He can still spit with contempt at society:

One of us at last! Green with anguish. A real little
terrestrial! Choking in the chlorophyll. Hugging the
slaughterhouse walls! Paltry priests of the irrepres-
sible ephemeral!

He bashes along on his bicycle, through the town, trying
to get to his mother. He runs over a dog -

an ineptness all the more unpardonable as the dog,
duly leashed, was not out on the road, but in on the
pavement, docile at his mistress's heels. Precautions

are like resolutions, to be taken with precaution.
The lady must have thought she had left nothing to
chance, so far as the safety of her dog was concerned,
whereas in reality she was setting the whole system of
nature at naught, no less surely than I myself with
my insane demands for more light. But instead of
grovelling in my turn, invoking my great age and infirmities, I made things worse by trying to run away. I
was soon overtaken by a bloodthirsty mob of both sexes
and all ages, for I caught a glimpse of white beards
and little angel faces, and they were preparing to tear
me to pieces

- but the lady stopped them, saying she was taking the dog
to the vet to be put down, in any case, and he had saved
her a painful task.

This volume has all Beckett's headlong comic gift.
Molloy is in the clownish state of senility, his disquali-
fied life has the spirit either of a fairy tale or inverted idyll; and in his pestiferous search for 'more light'
on everything and nothing - mostly the latter - there is a
grin half of mockery and half of frenzy on his scabby face.
His sexual memories are funny because they are few, take
him by surprise, and they are a mixture of the grotesque
and touching, the dirty and the modest. He has dragged
his body around all his life, and it follows him like some
ignorant valet. There is far more to compare with 'Tristram Shandy' in the caprices of this volume and its exploits in self-contradiction in order to hold the floor,
than there is with Joyce.

In the second volume, 'Malone Dies', we move from the
freedom of rebellion to loneliness. Malone, by the way,
may be another aspect of Molloy; he doesn't know who he
is. As far as I can make out the scene of the novel is a
madhouse or infirmary for the old, and Beckett becomes
the grammarian of solitude. The senses are dying. How
does Malone know where the veils of air end and the prison
walls begin? The body turns in smaller and smaller
circles; the mind conjugates trifles. Here Beckett inter-
venes with some satirical observation of normal people, a
trite couple and their favourite son, a piece which might
have come out of 'La Nausée', or Nathalie Sarraute, and we
are reminded that Beckett writes his novels first in
French.

But we return to endless hair-splitting, metaphysical
speculation sliding from association to association, and
these convey that as age increases the tedium of life, so
the unwearying little talker in the brain with his law-
suit against life bosses every half minute of it. Grief

and pity hang between his words; but the book unexpectedly ends in wholesale murder, when the feeble-minded inmates of the infirmary are taken out on a picnic.

In the third volume, Molloy, Malone, Mahood, Murphy -
whatever the name now is - is a lump, almost sightless,
stone deaf, always weeping, mutilated, immoveable, the
helpless centre of a world that he can be conscious of
very rarely. He is about to become Worm, all human identity gone. The archaeological kind of critic who can recover a novel from its ruins may be able to make something
of this volume. I find it unreadable, in the sense that I
cannot move from paragraph to paragraph, from page to
page. It is all significance and no content.

The stream of consciousness, so lively and going drama-
tically from image to image in Joyce, is here a stream of
imageless verbosity occasionally broken by a jab of obscene anger, but grey, grey, and it goes monotonously along
in phrases usually about seven words long, like some regularly bumping old tram. This is, of course, not so much
the stream of consciousness as the stream of solitude and
provides the comedy of overhearing a man talking to himself - Bloom, one recalls, rarely talked; things 'came up'
in his mind. He was in the midst of drama - a comedy that
is genuine enough certainly, but not of boundless interest.

Why is Beckett interesting as a writer? As a contemporary phenomenon, he is one more negative protest against
the world going to the slaughterhouse, one more protest on
behalf of privacy, a voice for myopia. He is a modern Ob-
lomov, fretful and apathetic, enclosed in private fantasy,
dropping off into words instead of sleep. They are eloquent, cunning, unremitting words.

He is far from feeble, for there is a devil-like sly-
ness in the half grin on the faces of his old men who can
hit out with their crutches. What tedium! they exclaim -
speaking not only of existence and human solitude - but,
we suspect, of ourselves. His imagination has the Irish
cruelty and self-destructiveness that Yeats once spoke of.
Beckett's anti-novels, like all anti-novels, have to deal
with small areas of experience because their pretension is
to evoke the whole of life, *i.e.* life unfixed by art; the
result is that these verbose books are like long ironical,
stinging footnotes in small print to some theme not formu-
lated. But there is a flash of deep insight in the madness he evokes: it is strange that in a generation which
has put all its stress on youth and achievement, he alone
should have written about old age, loneliness and decrepitude, a subject which arouses perhaps our deepest repres-
sed guilt and fears. He is the product of a civilisation
which has become suddenly old. He is a considerable,

muttering, comic writer, and although he conveys unbearable pain, he also conveys the element of sardonic ten-
acity that lies at the heart of the comic gift.

45.   FRANK KERMODE IN 'ENCOUNTER'

July 1960, 73-6

Frank Kermode (b. 1919) is King Edward Professor of
Literature at Cambridge.   Among his many books are 'Roman-
tic Image' (1957), 'Puzzles and Epiphanies' (1962), 'The
Sense of an Ending' (1967), and 'Continuities' (1968).

To know your own *avant-garde* you must know in what direction you are moving, and since I do not, I find it un-
helpful to think of Beckett in that connection.   In fact
he seems to be a rather old-fashioned writer, and at one
time it was permissible to think of him as a poor one as
well.   The justice of that can be confirmed by anybody
who bothers to consult the files of 'transition' and to read
Beckett's contribution to the volume of 1932 (Anamyths,
Psychographs, and other Prose Texts) entitled Sedendo et
Quiesciendo - a performance in the manner of the Joycean
monologue which makes these later novels seem by comparison lucid and refreshing.   About this time Beckett is
said to have told Peggy Guggenheim that 'he was dead and
had no feelings that were human.'   He was, however,
learned in a Joycean way, and was one of the few young
writers said by the master to have promise.   His inhumanity and his learning and his promise permitted him to subscribe to Jolas' doctrine that one needed to write 'in a
spirit of integral pessimism' and to 'combat all ration-
alist dogmas that stand in the way of a metaphysical universe.'   This task demanded a consistent and progressive
deformation of language and grammar.   Beckett belonged,
certainly, to the primitivist and decadent *avant-garde* of
1932.
     A year earlier than that he published his little essay
on Proust, which I have long regarded as a model of what
such books ought not to be, for it is obscure, pedantic in
manner, and not, as criticism should be, in the service of
the work it undertakes to elucidate.   Nevertheless it is

the product of a strange and well-endowed mind, and its
perversity is of a kind that writers, not charlatans,
occasionally display. And it has now an additional interest; for Beckett has published obviously important work,
and the 'Proust' not only shows his talent at a formative
stage but discusses what the important work is forbidden
to discuss, namely ideas. It is the best introduction to
Beckett, though not to Proust.

Beckett, for example, is more passionate about Time than
the occasion quite seems to require, speaking of its
'poisonous ingenuity ... in the science of affliction,'
seeing men as ordinarily trapped in vulgar intellectual
errors about past and future, and hiding behind 'the haze
of our smug will to live, of our pernicious and incurable
optimism.' The agents of this false Time are Memory
(voluntary memory of course) and Habit. But occasionally
we break away from them; some shock, some involuntary memory, revives our 'atrophied faculties' and produces a
'tense and provisional lucidity in the nervous system.'
These breaches of the ignoble agreement between the organ-
ism and its environment are terrible and isolating, but
they are the source of all meaning, and, presumably, all
pleasure. Unhappily these 'immediate, total, and delicious deflagrations' are not summoned at will. Life, for
the rest, is necessarily evil; 'wisdom consists in oblit-
erating the faculty of suffering.' In ordinary life we
expiate original sin, the sin of having been born. In
death, or in moments of 'inspired perception,' we escape
from this condition and perceive the 'only reality,' 'the
essence of a unique beauty,' 'that damns the life of the
body on earth as a pensum and reveals the meaning of the
word: "defunctus."'
   This is, of course, not entirely irrelevant to Proust;
but Beckett's Bergsonism has its own rapt, pessimistic
quality. His intuitionist aesthetic is exactly as modern
as T.E. Hulme's; but he meditates much more upon the
desert in which we normally dwell than upon the delicious
oases. The later Beckett is much easier to understand if
one recalls these musings on Time and Habit, the inaccessibility of value, the falsity and terror of man's world,
the expiatory nature of human life. We are poor almost
beyond imagining, especially since we must reject the
mythologies or religions which talk of eternity and
redemption. Their promised revelations come to nothing;
the world is a chaos, directionless (Beckett's characters
never know left from right). The Beckett hero is what
Wallace Stevens, another Bergsonian, called 'The prince of
the proverbs of pure poverty.'

The remarkable thing about 'Waiting for Godot' is the
way in which these sad ideas acquire vitality. Enslavement to Time is treated in the play as the consequence of
Original Sin; Vladimir and Estragon attribute their poverty to the freely-chosen Fall:

> We've lost our rights?
> We've waived them.
> (*They remain motionless, arms dangling, heads
> bowed, sagging at the knees.*)

'Godot' is precisely the sort of tragedy Beckett spoke of
in the Proust book, 'the statement of an expiation...not
the miserable expiation of a codified breach of a local
arrangement, organised by the knaves for the fools...but
of the original and eternal sin.' 'Godot' is 'a
something tale of things done long ago and ill-done.' And
Christ did nothing to change the situation; he was merely
one of the luckier poor, in a warm climate where they
'crucified quick.' 'The best thing,' says Estragon,
'would be to kill me like the other.'
   The dominion of Time and Habit is illustrated by
Pozzo's fussy precision in handling his watch, his pipe,
his vaporiser, and the abject Lucky. Lucky, a representative slave, talks nothing but nonsense about 'a personal
God...outside time without extension Who from the heights
of divine apathia divine athambia divine aphasia loves us
dearly with some exceptions.' Pozzo lectures on Time -
the past colours of morning, the horrors of night to come
- like Swann suddenly apprehensive of the future, breaking
away from that optimism which is a mere biological adap-
tation: 'That's how it is on this bitch of an earth.'
His blindness in the second act, when he answers to the
names of both Cain and Abel and is 'all men,' is another
way of representing the enslavement of human perception.
When he falls nobody can help him up. The little cloud
appears, no bigger than a man's hand - but either it means
nothing or is too disturbing to be considered. The *clochards* do not want Godot; they are terrified when he seems
to be coming, relieved when he doesn't. Pozzo's last
speech tells the truth about Time, and Vladimir sees the
point: 'Habit is a great deadener.' But his understanding
fevers him, and is the prelude to an ineffective annuncia-
tion. Godot's messengers are all ineffective, and leave
the poor with only Habit to confirm them in the acceptance
of their due and natural misery.

What has happened to make 'Godot' a major poetic play?
The pessimism that was an intellectual pose in the Proust

book has rotted down into images; the subman in his pure
poetry has acquired the colour of myth, the banalities of
Habit fall into the rhythm of poetry, the absurdities of
habitual behaviour are invested with the machine-like
quality of music-hall routines and get the Bergsonian
laugh. Our only contact with truth is by means of the
ineffectual angels, Godot's boys; and this leaves us free
to feel the poetry of falling, of inertia, of the malefic
vision, as when Pozzo speaks of this bitch of an earth or
Mrs. Rooney in 'All That Fall' exclaims 'Christ, what a
planet!' Men aspire to absolute infirmity, lame, blind,
crawling on the face of the earth. 'I cannot be said to
be well,' says Mr. Rooney, 'but I am no worse. Indeed, I
am better than I was. The loss of my sight was a great
fillip.' Before the messenger tells them of the cosmic
disaster that made the local train run late, the Rooneys
join in wild laughter at the Wayside Pulpit text: 'The
Lord upholdeth all that fall and raiseth up all that be
bowed down.' Beckett's decaying figures, lying on the
ground, sitting in dustbins, groaning along the road to
nowhere, inhabit a world in which there has certainly been
a Fall, but just as certainly no Redemption.

This pessimism was part of the 'transition' programme,
but it is now given a visionary quality:

> I listen and the voice is of a world collapsing end-
> lessly, a frozen world, under a faint untroubled sky,
> enough to see by, yes, and frozen too. And I hear it
> murmur that all wilts and yields, as if loaded down....
> For what possible end to these wastes where true light
> never was, nor any upright thing, nor any true founda-
> tion, but only these leaning things, forever lapsing
> and crumbling away, beneath a sky without memory of
> morning or hope of night.

So speaks the subman Molloy. His crippled odyssey begins
with his observing, in a directionless wilderness, the encounter of two men, A. and C., victim and murderer, the double
type of Beckett's fallen man. With his bicycle, delusive
support of lameness, emblem of falsely directed movement,
he seeks his daft mother, the sole source of sustenance.
Later, rejecting a form of protection that denied his
humanity, he goes on alone, walking on crutches, crawling,
rolling towards his probably dead mother's door, enduring
'a passion without form or stations,' unable to enumerate
his ills, quite unable to tell left from right. Is Molloy
the ultimate subman, the modern God? 'What is needed for
the definition of man is an inexhaustible faculty of negation...as though he were no better than God.' No; Molloy

is not the end. He even makes a positive recommendation:
the wise response to life is ataraxy. We got where we are
by 'preferring the fall to the trouble of having...to
stand fast,' and now wisdom is to stay lying down. Yet
Molloy's life of falling, shambling, confusing, accepting,
illustrates the true nature of all human life, especially
as, totally outcast, he has on occasion the power of vision, is freed from the blinkers of habit. Thus he describes the act of sex quite empirically (this is horribly
funny) and is capable of intense mathematical activity.
But the moral is this:

> to know nothing is nothing, not to want to know any-
> thing likewise, but to be beyond knowing anything, to
> know you are beyond knowing anything, that is when
> peace enters in, to the soul of the incurious seeker.

Then there may be a message: 'Don't fret, Molloy, we're
coming.' 'Well, I suppose you have to try everything
once, succour included, to get a complete picture of the
resources of their planet. I lapsed down to the bottom of
the ditch.' Molloy is, like everybody else, a murderer.
His last image is again of the encounter between A. and
C., Abel and Cain. 'One had a club.' The message came to
nothing.
  The moderately cheerful ataraxy of Molloy in this, the
most lucid part of the trilogy, is supplemented by the
story of Moran, time-bound and self-serving, whose job it
is to find Molloy. His life has the cruel order of habit:
he bullies his servant, torments his son, goes prudent-
ially to Mass, masturbates systematically, and is proud of
his garden. The mad barren precision of his life is one
of Beckett's best things, and so is its collapse. Moran
loses his son and his purpose; he lies on the ground, in
love with paralysis, and acts only in order to kill a man.
The messenger who comes to him is unintelligible, and
seems to say that according to the Boss, a thing of beauty
is a joy for ever. Could he have meant human life? Moran,
less wise than Molloy, crawls homeward and speculates
theologically. One problem, what was God doing before the
creation? is the classic forbidden enquiry, answered by
Augustine with patristic humour: devising hell for people
who ask such questions. We must endure *sedendo et quiesciendo*. Moran's garden is decayed; he falls into the
poverty brought on us in the first place by wicked curiosity.
  'Molloy' is a powerful book, rich in imagery and theological wit. Yet it is an example of the harm that could
come to artists devoted to what Yvor Winters calls

'primitivism and decadence,' to rendering the delinquency of modern humanity by a deliquescence of form and language. The same may be said more forcibly of 'Malone Dies', the second novel of the trilogy. Its fullness of intellect and its poetry are occasionally Joycean, and there is a wonderful development of Molloy's words on lovemaking (Malone's own sexual activity is even more bizarre than Molloy's): 'Ah, how stupid I am, I see what it is, they must be loving each other, that must be how it is done.' Malone or MacMann (son of man) is bedridden and hazily situated in the world. He lives in mortal tedium. The wisest animal in the book is a learned parrot whose attempt to speak the old tag *nihil in intellectu quod non prius in sensu* always fails after the first three words, and so strikes a blow for pessimistic Bergsonism.

But 'Malone Dies' reminds us that the nearer a book be- comes to directionlessness, to absolute quiescence, the more trying it is to read, especially when it has no paragraphs. And the last novel, 'The Unnamable', gets even nearer to the motionless and senseless subman-god, inhabiting the darkness like a Demogorgon of impotence. He represents the hopelessness of fallen man distilled to such purity that no actual man could ever achieve it, and all are happy compared with him; so that, paradoxically, 'I alone am man and all the rest divine.' He speaks the dirty *logos* and suffers all: 'All these Murphys, Molloys, and Malones.... They never suffered my pains, their pains are nothing compared to mine' (no sorrow like unto his sorrow). He is Existence, a 'big talking ball,' life without the other God; the desperate earth, for which God does nothing except to send inaudible or unintelligible messages. Even Mahood (son of God?) has died uselessly. The paragraph of 130 pages ends: 'I can't go on. I'll go on.' This is the only God we are entitled to, our own true image.

   One may as well allow these books to succeed in their determined attempt to defeat comment. They are almost entirely unsuccessful; we ought to be frank about this, because literary people are usually too willing to take the will for the deed. In Beckett's plays the theatrical demand for communicable rhythms and relatively crude satisfactions has had a beneficent effect. But in the novels he yields progressively to the magnetic pull of the primitive, to the desire to achieve, by various forms of decadence and deformation, some Work that eludes the intellect, avoids the spread nets of habitual meaning. Beckett is often allegorical, but he is allegorical in carefully fitful patches, providing illusive toeholds to

any reader scrambling for sense. The formal effect is
almost exactly described by Winters in his comment on
Joyce: 'The procedure leads to indiscriminateness at every
turn.... He is like Whitman trying to express a loose
America by writing loose poetry. This fallacy, the fallacy of expressive, or imitative form, recurs constantly
in modern literature.' There is indeed ample reason to
think that Beckett's atavistic assumptions are still
widely held, and we have recently been finding out just
how unsympathetic they are to people who do not go in for
'mythical thinking' because they possess a scientific
worldview.

And that of course brings us to C.P. Snow, and the new
novel in the Lewis Eliot sequence.(1) Apart from their
both admiring Proust, there are no resemblances, only
interesting differences, between Beckett and Snow. Each
stands for a lot of what the other deplores. Snow, for
all his gifts of pathos, is, like most scientists, a
meliorist at least, and when he speaks of the 'resonance
between what Lewis Eliot sees and what he feels' he is
not thinking of the inner Eliot as a subman. What Eliot
sees is limited by the mode of feeling allowed him by
Snow, and this is free of atavism but determinedly old-
fashioned. I shall have to let the virtues of this book
go without saying, though they are considerable, deriving
partly from the author's power of narrative, partly from
his honesty about the milieux he knows, and partly from an
authentic compassion. What I want to do is sketch some
of the ways in which such a writer is a-typical, not what
we now expect of artists, whereas Beckett is exactly
typical.
    Scientists are as a rule much more confident than 'we'
are about judgments of character and ability; they have an
established optimism about human achievement and a ruth-
lessness about failure which makes them confident of identifying either. You can tell when a scientist is successful; the rungs are clearly marked F.R.S., etc. This is a
calculus they trust. One thing it cannot possibly measure, however, is what Lawrence called 'the last naked him'
- the essential naïve core of innocence which he thought
to be a possession of the 'human individual' but not of
'the social being.'

> It seems to me that when the human being becomes too
> much divided between his subjective and objective con-
> sciousness, at last something splits and he becomes a
> social being...a divided thing hinged together but not
> strictly individual.

Lawrence was talking about the Forsytes, but here, and in his strictures on Galsworthy's treatment of sex, he might be talking of Eliot and his friends. Snow, for all the sophisticated recording of high academic subterfuge in the face of Justice, for all the skill that makes his wronged scientist odious and the slightly absurd Bursar morally ambiguous, is never much interested in, probably doubts the existence of, 'the last naked him,' an expression you could apply to the heroes of Lawrence and Beckett alike. Character is registered with physiognomic simplicity: 'a reckless face...underneath full lids, her eyes were narrow, treacle-brown, disrespectful, and amused.' Or, on the same page, 'He was a secretive man: people, even those nearest him, thought him cautious, calculating, capable of being ruthless.' As to ability, we see how this is judged in college: 'Brown's reputation had kept steady since my time, Crawford's had climbed a bit, Nightingale's had rocketed.' These are social men: we are concerned with 'the shifts, the calculations, the self-seekingness of men making their way.' Women are mostly spectators here, but are often assessed by a different measure, their sexual activity, or what can be inferred of it. I notice that when somebody does something unexpected, out of character, like the smart barrister at the end, Eliot is always more surprised than I am.

All the same, it has to be admitted that this is how, from day to day, we do go about judging and estimating people; we aren't much concerned with their nuclear innocence, nor yet with their basic poverty. On the whole we find life disappointing rather than desperate; and so, in a sense, Snow, who asks us to throw ourselves into no special posture to read him, is more concerned than Beckett with what daily concerns us. It is only by an effort of will that we can cease to be interested in what interests him. *Sub specie temporis* his Combination Rooms say more to us than Beckett's wet and windy plains, his grovelling exiles. (Let's leave Eternity out of it.) And he's also, it must be said, a great deal easier and more pleasant to read.

Note

1   'The Affair.'

46. NORTHROP FRYE IN 'HUDSON REVIEW'

Autumn 1960, 442-9

Northrop Frye (b. 1912), University Professor of English
at the University of Toronto, and author of 'Fearful Symmetry' (1947), 'An Anatomy of Criticism' (1957), 'The
Well-Tempered Critic' (1963), 'T.S. Eliot' (1963), 'The
Modern Century' (1967), and 'The Critical Path' (1971).

In every age the theory of society and the theory of personality have closely approached each other. In Plato the
wise man's mind is a dictatorship of reason over appetite,
with the will acting as a thought police hunting down and
exterminating all lawless impulses. The ideal state, with
its philosopher-kings, guards and artisans, has the corresponding social form. Michael explains to Adam in 'Paradise Lost' that tyranny must exist in society as long as
passion dominates reason in individuals, as they are
called. In our day Marxism finds its psychological
counterpart in the behaviorism and conditioned reflexes
of Pavlov, and the Freudian picture of man is also the
picture of western Europe and America, hoping that its
blocks and tensions and hysterial explosions will settle
into some kind of precarious working agreement. In this
alignment religion has regularly formed a third, its gods
and their enemies deriving their characteristics from
whatever is highest and lowest in the personal-social
picture. A good deal of the best fiction of our time has
employed a kind of myth that might be read as a psychological, a social, or a religious allegory, except that it
cannot be reduced to an allegory, but remains a myth,
moving in all three areas of life at once, and thereby
interconnecting them as well. The powerful appeal of
Kafka for our age is largely due to the way in which such
stories as 'The Trial' or 'The Castle' manage to suggest
at once the atmosphere of an anxiety dream, the theology
of the Book of Job, and the police terrorism and bureau-
cratic anonymity of the society that inspired Freud's term
'censor.' It was the same appeal in the myth of 'Waiting
for Godot' that, so to speak, identified Samuel Beckett as
a contemporary writer.
    As a fiction writer Samuel Beckett derives from Proust
and Joyce, and his essay on Proust is a good place to
start from in examining his own work. This essay puts

Proust in a context that is curiously Oriental in its view of personality. 'Normal' people, we learn, are driven along through time on a current of habit-energy, an energy which, because habitual, is mostly automatic. This energy relates itself to the present by the will, to the past by voluntary or selective memory, to the future by desire and expectation. It is a subjective energy, although it has no consistent or permanent subject, for the ego that de-sires now can at best only possess later, by which time it is a different ego and wants something else. But an illu-sion of continuity is kept up by the speed, like a motion picture, and it generates a corresponding objective illu-sion, where things run along in the expected and habitual form of causality. Some people try to get off this time machine, either because they have more sensitivity or, perhaps, some kind of physical weakness that makes it not an exhilarating joyride but a nightmare of frustration and despair. Among these are artists like Proust, who look behind the surface of the ego, behind voluntary to invol-untary memory, behind will and desire to conscious percep-tion. As soon as the subjective motion-picture disappears, the objective one disappears too, and we have recurring contacts between a particular moment and a particular object, as in the epiphanies of the madeleine and the phrase in Vinteuil's music. Here the object, stripped of the habitual and expected response, appears in all the en-chanted glow of uniqueness, and the relation of the moment to such an object is a relation of identity. Such a rela-tion, achieved between two human beings, would be love, in contrast to the ego's pursuit of the object of desire, like Odette or Albertine, which tantalizes precisely be-cause it is never loved. In the relation of identity con-sciousness has triumphed over time, and destroys the pri-son of habit with its double illusion stretching forever into past and future. At that moment we may enter what Proust and Beckett agree is the only possible type of para-dise, that which has been lost. For the ego only two forms of failure are possible, the failure to possess, which may be tragic, and the failure to communicate, which is normally comic.

In the early story 'Murphy,' the hero is an Irishman with an Irish interest in the occult - several of Beck-ett's characters are readers of AE - and a profound disin-clination to work. We first meet him naked, strapped to a chair, and practising trance. He has however no interest in any genuine mental discipline, and feels an affinity with the easy-going Belacqua of Dante's 'Purgatorio,' also mentioned in 'Molloy,' who was in no hurry to begin his climb up the mountain. What he is really looking for is a

self-contained egocentric consciousness, 'windowless, like
a monad,' that no outward events can injure or distort.
He is prodded by the heroine Celia into looking for a job,
and eventually finds one as a male nurse in a lunatic
asylum. In the asylum he discovers a kinship with the
psychotic patients, who are trying to find the same thing
in their own way, and his sympathy with them not only
gives him a job he can do but makes him something rather
better than a 'seedy solipsist.' To take this job he turns
his back on Celia and other people who are said to need
him, but in the airless microcosm of his mental retreat
there is the one weak spot that makes him human and not
completely selfish, a need for communication. He looks
for this in the eye of Endon, his best friend among the
patients, but sees no recognition in the eye, only his own
image reflected in the pupil. 'The last Mr. Murphy saw of
Mr. Endon was Mr. Murphy unseen by Mr. Endon.' He then
commits suicide. The same image of the unrecognizing eye
occurs in the one-act play 'Embers' and in 'Krapp's Last
Tape,' where Krapp, more completely bound to memory and
desire than Murphy, and so a figure of less dignity if
also of less absurdity, looks into his mistress's eyes and
says 'Let me in.' Another echo in this phrase will meet
us in a moment.

The figure of the pure ego in a closed auto-erotic
circle meets us many times in Beckett's masturbating,
carrot-chewing, stone-sucking characters. A more traditional image of the consciousness goaded by desire or
memory (an actual goad appears in one of Beckett's panto-
mimes), is that of master and servant. Already in
'Murphy' we have, in the characters Neary and Cooper, an
adumbration of the Hamm and Clov of 'Endgame,' a servant
who cannot sit and a master who cannot stand, bound
together in some way and yet longing to be rid of each
other. 'Watt' tells the story of a servant who drifts
into a house owned by a Mr. Knott, one of a long procession of servants absorbed and expelled from it by some
unseen force. Technically the book is a contrast to
'Murphy,' which is written in an epigrammatic wisecracking
style. In 'Watt' there is a shaggy-dog type of deliberately misleading humor, expressing itself in a maddeningly
prolix pseudo-logic. One notes the use of a device more
recently popularized by Lawrence Durrell, of putting some
of the debris of the material collected into an appendix.
'Only fatigue and disgust prevented its incorporation,'
the author demurely informs us. The most trivial actions
of Watt, most of which are very similar to those we perform ourselves every day, are exhaustively catalogued in
an elaborate pretence of obsessive realism, and we can see

how such 'realism' in fiction, pushed to so logical a conclusion, soon gives the effect of living in a kind of
casual and unpunishing hell. Watt finally decides that
'if one of these things was worth doing, all were worth
doing, but that none was worth doing, no, not one, but
that all were unadvisable, without exception.'

In 'Waiting for Godot,' as everyone knows, two dreary
men in bowler hats stand around waiting for the mysterious
Godot, who never appears but only sends a messenger to say
he will not come. It is a favorite device of ironic fiction, from Kafka to Menotti's opera 'The Consul,' to make
the central character someone who not only fails to mani-
fest himself but whose very existence is called in question. The two men wonder whether in some way they are
'tied' to Godot, but decide that they probably are not,
though they are afraid he might punish them if they desert
their post. They also feel tied to one another, though
each feels he would do better on his own. They resemble
criminals in that they feel that they have no rights: 'we
got rid of them,' one says, and is exhorted by a stage
direction to say it distinctly. They stand in front of
a dead tree, speculating, like many of Beckett's characters, about hanging themselves from it, and one of them
feels an uneasy kinship with the thieves crucified with
Christ. Instead of Godot, there appears a diabolical
figure named Pozzo (pool: the overtones extend from Satan
to Narcissus), driving an animal in human shape named
Lucky, with a whip and a rope. Lucky, we are told, thinks
he is entangled in a net: the image of being fished for by
some omnipotent and malignant angler recurs in 'The Unnamable.' In the second act the two turn up again, but
this time Pozzo is blind and helpless, like Hamm in 'Endgame.'

When the double illusion of a continuous ego and a
continuous causality is abolished, what appears in its
place? First of all, the ego is stripped of all individuality and is seen merely as representative of all of its
kind. When asked for their names, one of the two men
waiting for Godot answers 'Adam,' and the other one says:
'At this place, at this moment of time, all mankind is
us.' Similar echoes are awakened by the Biblical title of
the play 'All That Fall,' with its discussion of the falling sparrow in the Gospels and its final image of the
child falling from the train, its death unheeded by the
only character who was on the train. Other characters
have such names as Watt, Knott and Krapp, suggestive of
infantile jokes and of what in 'Molloy' are called 'decaying circus clowns.' The dramatic convention parodied in
'Waiting for Godot' is clearly the act that killed

vaudeville, the weary dialogue of two faceless figures who will say anything to put off leaving the stage. In the 'gallery of moribunds' we are about to examine there is a series of speakers whose names begin with M, one of whom, Macmann, has the most obvious everyman associations. In this trilogy, however, there is a more thoroughgoing examination of the unreality of the ego, and one which seems to owe something to the sequence of three chapters in 'Finnegans Wake' in which Shaun is studied under the names Shaun, Jaun and Yawn, until he disappears into the larger form of HCE. It is the 'Yawn' chapter that Beckett most frequently refers to. In reading the trilogy we should keep in mind the remark in the essay on Proust that 'the heart of the cauliflower or the ideal core of the onion would represent a more appropriate tribute to the labours of poetical excavation than the crown of bay.'

'Molloy' is divided into two parts: the first is Molloy's own narrative; the second is the narrative of Jacques Moran, who receives a message through one Gaber from an undefined Youdi to go and find Molloy. The echoes of Gabriel and Yahweh make it obvious by analogy that the name 'Godot' is intended to sound like 'God.' Youdi, or someone similar to him, is once referred to as 'the Obidil,' which is an anagram of libido. The associations of Molloy are Irish, pagan, and a Caliban-like intelligence rooted in a disillusioned sensitivity. Moran is French, nominally Christian, and a harsher and more aggressive type of sterility. Molloy, like many of Beckett's characters, is so crippled as to resemble the experiments on mutilated and beheaded animals that try to establish how much life is consistent with death. He is also under a wandering curse, like the Wandering Jew, and is trying to find his mother. There are echoes of the wandering figure in Chaucer's 'Pardoner's Tale,' who keeps knocking on the ground with his staff and begging his mother to let him in. But Molloy does not exactly long for death, because for him the universe is also a vast auto-erotic ring, a serpent with its tail in its mouth, and it knows no real difference between life and death. Overtones of Ulysses appear in his sojourn with Lousse (Circe), and the mention of 'moly' suggests an association with his name. He is also, more Biblically, 'in an Egypt without bounds, without infant, without mother,' and a dim memory of Faust appears in his account of various sciences studied and abandoned, of which magic alone remained. Like the contemporary beats (in 'Murphy,' incidentally, the padded cells are called 'pads'), he finds around him a world of confident and adjusted squares, who sometimes take the form of police and bully him. 'They wake up, hale and hearty, their tongues hanging out for order, beauty and justice, baying for their due.' The landscape around him, described in terms similar to Dante's Inferno, changes, but he is unable to go out of his 'region,' and realizes that he is not moving at all. The only real change is a progressive physical deterioration and a growing loss of such social contact as he has. The landscape finally changes to a forest and Molloy, too exhausted to walk and unable, like Beckett's other servants, to sit, crawls on his belly like a serpent until he finally stops. He arrives at his mother's house, but characteristically we learn this not from the last sentence but from the first one, as the narrative goes around in a Viconian circle.

Just before the end of his account, Molloy, who hears voices of 'prompters' in his mind, is told that help is coming. Moran sets off to find Molloy, aware that his real quest is to find Molloy inside himself, as a kind of Hyde to his Jekyll. He starts out with his son, whom he is trying to nag into becoming a faithful replica of himself, and he ties his son to him with a rope, as Pozzo does Lucky. The son breaks away, Moran sees Molloy but does not realize who he is, and gets another order to go back home. He confesses: 'I was not made for the great light that devours, a dim lamp was all I had been given, and patience without end, to shine it on the empty shadows.' This ignominious quest for self-knowledge does not find Molloy as a separate entity, but it does turn Moran into a double of Molloy, in ironic contrast to his attitude to his son. Various details in the imagery, the bicycle that they both start with, the stiffening leg, and others, emphasize the growing identity. Moran's narrative, which starts out in clear prose, soon breaks down into the same associative paragraphless monologue that Molloy uses. The quest is a dismal failure as far as Moran and Molloy are concerned, but how far are they concerned? Moran can still say: 'What I was doing I was doing neither for Molloy, who mattered nothing to me, nor for myself, of whom I despaired, but on behalf of a cause which, while having need of us to be accomplished, was in its essence anonymous, and would subsist, haunting the minds of men, when its miserable artisans should be no more.'

The forest vanishes and we find ourselves in an asylum cell with a figure named Malone, who is waiting to die. Here there is a more definite expectation of the event of death, and an awareness of a specific quantity of time before it occurs. Malone decides to fill in the interval by telling himself stories, and the stories gradually converge on a figure named MacMann, to whom Malone seems

related somewhat as Proust is to the 'Marcel' of his book,
or Joyce to Stephen and Shem. Here an ego is projecting
himself into a more typical figure (I suppose Malone and
MacMann have echoes of 'man alone' and 'son of man,' respectively, as most of the echoes in Beckett's names appear
to be English), and MacMann gradually moves into the cell
and takes over the identity of Malone. Malone dreams of
his own death, which is simultaneously occurring, in a
vision of a group of madmen going for a picnic in a boat
on the Saturday morning between Good Friday and Easter, a
ghastly parody of the beginning of the 'Purgatorio.'
Dante's angelic pilot is replaced by a brutal attendant
named Lemuel, a destroying angel who murders most of the
passengers.

In 'The Unnamable' we come as near to the core of the
onion as it is possible to come, and discover of course
that there is no core, no undividable unit of continuous
personality. It is difficult to say just where or what
the Unnamable is, because, as in the brothel scene of
'Ulysses,' his fluctuating moods create their own surroundings. One hypothesis is that he is sitting in a
crouched posture with tears pouring out of his eyes, like
some of the damned in Dante, or like the Heraclitus who
became the weeping philosopher by contemplating the flowing of all things. Another is that he is in a jar outside
a Paris restaurant opposite a horsemeat shop, suspended
between life and death like the sibyl in Petronius who
presides over 'The Waste Land.'

Ordinarily we are aware of a duality between mind and
body, of the necessity of keeping the body still to let
the mind work. If we sit quietly we become aware of
bodily processes, notably the heartbeat and pulse, carrying on automatically and involuntarily. Some religious
disciplines, such as yoga, go another stage, and try to
keep the mind still to set some higher principle free.
When this happens, the mind can be seen from the outside
as a rushing current of thoughts and associations and
memories and worries and images suggested by desire, pul-
sating automatically and with all the habit-energy of the
ego behind it. Each monologue in the trilogy suggests a
mind half-freed from its own automatism. It is detached
enough to feel imprisoned and enslaved, and to have no
confidence in any of its assertions, but immediately to
deny or contradict or qualify or put forward another hypothesis to whatever it says. But it is particularly the
monologue of 'The Unnamable,' an endless, querulous, compulsive, impersonal babble, much the same in effect
whether read in French or in English, and with no purpose
except to keep going, that most clearly suggests a 'stream

of consciousness' from which real consciousness is somehow
absent. 'The Unnamable' could readily be called a tedious
book, but its use of tedium is exuberant, and in this
respect it resembles 'Watt.'

The Unnamable, who vaguely remembers having been Malone
and Molloy, decides that he will be someone called Mahood,
then that he will be something called Worm, then wonders
whether all his meditations really are put into his mind
by 'them,' that is, by Youdi and the rest, for his sense
of compulsion easily externalizes itself. If he knows
anything, it is that he is not necessarily himself, and
that it was nonsense for Descartes to infer that he was
himself because he was doubting it. All Beckett's speakers are like the parrot in 'Malone Dies,' who could be
taught to say 'Nihil in intellectu,' but refused to learn
the rest of the sentence. All of them, again, especially
Malone, are oppressed by the pervasive lying of the imagination, by the way in which one unconsciously falsifies
the facts to make a fiction more symmetrical. But even
Malone begins to realize that there is no escape from
fiction. There are no facts to be accurately described,
only hypotheses to be set up: no choice of words will express the truth, for one has only a choice of rhetorical
masks. Malone says of his own continuum: 'I slip into
him, I suppose in the hope of learning something. But it
is a stratum, strata, without debris or vestiges. But
before I am done I shall find traces of what was.'

In 'The Unnamable,' as we make our way through 'this
sound that will never stop, monotonous beyond words and
yet not altogether devoid of a certain variety,' the
Unnamable's own desire to escape to the extent that he
ever formulates it as such, communicates itself to us.
The tired, tireless, hypnotic voice, muttering like a disembodied spirit at a seance, or like our own subconscious
if we acquire the trick of listening to it, makes us feel
that we would be ready to try anything to get away from
it, even if we are also its prisoner. There is little use
going to 'them,' to Youdi or Godot, because they are
illusions of personality too. Conventional religion pro-
mises only resurrection, which both in 'Murphy' and in the
Proust essay is described as an impertinence. But
'beyond them is that other who will not give me quittance
until they have abandoned me as inutilizable and restored
me to myself.' That other must exist, if only because it
is not here. And so, in the interminable last sentence,
we reach the core of the onion, the resolve to find in art
the secret of identity, the paradise that has been lost,
the one genuine act of consciousness in the interlocking
gyres (the Dante-Yeats image is explicitly referred to) of
automatism:

...the attempt must be made, in the old stories incom-
prehensibly mine, to find his, it must be there somewhere, it must have been mine, before being his, I'll
recognize it, in the end I'll recognize it, the story
of the silence that he never left, that I should never
have left, that I may never find again, that I may find
again, then it will be he, it will be I, it will be the
place, the silence, the end, the beginning, the beginning again...

Many curiously significant remarks are made about silence in the trilogy. Molloy, for example, says: 'about me
all goes really silent, from time to time, whereas for the
righteous the tumult of the world never stops.' The Unnamable says: 'This voice that speaks, knowing that it
lies, indifferent to what it says, too old perhaps and too
abased ever to succeed in saying the words that would be
its last, knowing itself useless and its uselessness in
vain, not listening to itself but to the silence that it
breaks.' Only when one is sufficiently detached from this
compulsive babble to realize that one is uttering it can
one achieve any genuine serenity, or the silence which is
its habitat. 'To restore silence is the role of objects,'
says Molloy, but this is not Beckett's final paradox. His
final paradox is the conception of the imaginative process
which underlies and informs his remarkable achievement.
In a world given over to obsessive utterance, a world of
television and radio and shouting dictators and tape re-
corders and beeping space ships, to restore silence is the
role of serious writing.

Interviews with Beckett
(1961)

---

47. GABRIEL D'AUBARÈDE IN 'NOUVELLES LITTÉRAIRES'

16 February 1961, 1, 7

I waited for the author of 'Waiting for Godot' in the
Paris office allocated him by his publisher. But I wondered if he was going to show up: through timidity, un-
sociability, or possibly just as part of his system, until
today, he had energetically refused to be interviewed.

This writer, so often described as being fierce, is now
in his fifties. He's an Irishman, like James Joyce, and
it's said that Joyce preferred Beckett to many of his
other translators. Beckett taught English for three years
at our Ecole Normale and later taught French at Dublin's
Trinity College. In London, he published several books of
poems, a study of Proust, and a novel, 'Murphy,' but
before its release a German bomb destroyed the entire
edition.

Never despair. In 1938, Samuel Beckett came to France
to stay, and thenceforth wrote in French; his trilogy,
'Molloy,' 'Malone Dies,' and 'The Unnamable' drew rave
notices from those critics partial to difficult literature. Nevertheless, even the most fervent among them are
disappointed by his latest work, 'Comment c'est' (How
things are). As for his play, 'Waiting for Godot,' more
generally accessible although nothing happens in it, it
was put on two hundred times at the Théâtre de Babylone
and was triumphantly received in several European countries, notably in Germany.

The question remained: Was the disconcerting Samuel
Beckett going to show up? Yes, there he was!

Both of Molloy's legs are paralyzed, Malone is in death
throes, and the Unnamable is a paraplegic living in a
sort of coffin. But the man who infused life into these
monsters is handsome and healthy-looking, tall, blond, and
well-tanned, with regular and noble features. He looks
closely at you from behind thick spectacles; often his
thin lips curl with a touch of irony and wiliness.

He had just arrived from a village in the Département
of Seine-et-Marne, where he has bought a small piece of
property, thanks to a modest inheritance.

Knowing how he can't stomach the farce of a professional literary life, I told him how I envied him for
being able to work in peace there, and he agreed heartily:
'You're quite right. The country's a lovely place to
write in.'

'So you've done a lot of writing lately?'

'Not a thing. A little gardening. Odd jobs. No
writing though.'

'Is that the truth?'

'Only some very short pieces, sort of short stories.'

He glanced at the door. To clear the air, I told him
that in the past I'd been slightly acquainted with the
children of his master James Joyce when the latter had
lived near the Champs-de-Mars.

Beckett scrutinized me amiably: 'Oh, so you knew
George and poor little Lucia?'

'Why "poor"?'

He gestured vaguely.

'Joyce considered you one of his best translators.
Can it be claimed you are also his disciple? Your long
interior monologues...'

'Oh! well you know, I only translated personally - I
mean all by myself - Anna Livia Plurabelle. But here in
Paris, I've done numerous anonymous translations to earn
my living. Do you mind?'

He sat at his desk and began to sign title pages. So,
like everyone else, Samuel Beckett dedicates his books!
I eased down on the edge of his desk.

'Your novels are rather difficult reading. Were they
hard to write?'

'Oh, yes, but they came in one great spurt of enthusiasm.'

'Enthusiasm?'

'"Malone" grew out of "Molloy," "The Unnamable" out
of "Malone," but afterwards - and for a long time - I
wasn't at all sure what I had left to say. I'd hemmed
myself in. To try to break loose, I wrote those short
texts, those little stories if you wish, that I call
"écrits pour rien."' (Translator's note: double sense,

either 'pointless writings' or 'written pointlessly';
he is referring to 'Nouvelles et Textes pour rien.')

'Have contemporary philosophers had any influence on
your thought?'

'I never read philosophers.'

'Why not?'

'I never understand anything they write.'

'All the same, people have wondered if the existential-
ists' problem of being may afford a key to your works.'

'There's no key or problem. I wouldn't have had any
reason to write my novels if I could have expressed their
subject in philosophic terms.'

'What was your reason then?'

'I haven't the slightest idea. I'm no intellectual.
All I am is feeling. "Molloy" and the others came to me
the day I became aware of my own folly. Only then did I
begin to write the things I feel.'

[Translated by Christopher Waters]

48.   TOM DRIVER IN 'COLUMBIA UNIVERSITY FORUM'

Summer 1961, 21-5

Tom Driver (b. 1925), Professor of Literature and Theology
at the Union Theological Seminary, has written widely
about the modern theatre.

Nothing like Godot, he arrived before the hour. His
letter had suggested we meet at my hotel at noon on Sunday,
and I came into the lobby as the clock struck twelve. He
was waiting.

My wish to meet Samuel Beckett had been prompted by
simple curiosity and interest in his work. American newspaper reviewers like to call his plays nihilistic. They
find deep pessimism in them. Even so astute a commentator
as Harold Clurman of 'The Nation' has said that 'Waiting
for Godot' is 'the concentrate...of the contemporary European...mood of despair.' But to me, Beckett's writing had
seemed permeated with love for human beings and with a
kind of humor that I could reconcile neither with despair
nor with nihilism. Could it be that my own eyes and ears

had deceived me? Is his a literature of defeat, irrelevant to the social crises we face? Or is it relevant because it teaches us something useful to know about ourselves?

I knew that a conversation with the author would not
settle such questions, because a man is not the same as
his writing: in the last analysis, the questions had to be
settled by the work itself. Nevertheless I was curious.

My curiosity was sharpened a day or two before the
interview by a conversation I had with a well-informed
teacher of literature, a Jesuit father, at a conference on
religious drama near Paris. When Beckett's name came into
the discussion, the priest grew loud and told me that
Beckett 'hates life.' That, I thought, is at least one
thing I can find out when we meet.

Beckett's appearance is rough-hewn Irish. The features
of his face are distinct, but not fine. They look as if
they had been sculptured with an unsharpened chisel.
Unruly hair goes straight up from his forehead, standing
so high that the top falls gently over, as if to show that
it really is hair and not bristle. One might say it combines the man's own pride and humility. For he has the
pride that comes of self-acceptance and the humility, perhaps of the same genesis, not to impose himself upon
another. His light blue eyes, set deep within the face,
are actively and continually looking. He seems, by some
unconscious division of labor, to have given them that one
function and no other, leaving communication to the rest
of the face. The mouth frequently breaks into a disarming
smile. The voice is light in timbre, with a rough edge
that corresponds to his visage. The Irish accent is, as
one would expect, combined with slight inflections from
the French. His tweed suit was a baggy gray and green.
He wore a brown knit sports shirt with no tie.

We walked down the Rue de L'Arcade, thence along beside
the Madeleine and across to a sidewalk café opposite that
church. The conversation that ensued may have been en-
grossing but it could hardly be called world-shattering.
For one thing, the world that Beckett sees is already
shattered. His talk turns to what he calls 'the mess,' or
sometimes 'this buzzing confusion.' I reconstruct his
sentences from notes made immediately after our conversation. What appears here is shorter than what he actually
said but very close to his own words.

'The confusion is not my invention. We cannot listen
to a conversation for five minutes without being acutely
aware of the confusion. It is all around us and our only
chance now is to let it in. The only chance of renovation is to open our eyes and see the mess. It is not a

mess you can make sense of.'

I suggested that one must let it in because it is the truth, but Beckett did not take to the word truth.

'What is more true than anything else? To swim is true, and to sink is true. One is not more true than the other. One cannot speak anymore of being, one must speak only of the mess. When Heidegger and Sartre speak of a contrast between being and existence, they may be right, I don't know, but their language is too philosophical for me. I am not a philosopher. One can only speak of what is in front of him, and that now is simply the mess.'

Then he began to speak about the tension in art between the mess and form. Until recently, art has withstood the pressure of chaotic things. It has held them at bay. It realized that to admit them was to jeopardize form. 'How could the mess be admitted, because it appears to be the very opposite of form and therefore destructive of the very thing that art holds itself to be?' But now we can keep it out no longer, because we have come into a time when 'it invades our experience at every moment. It is there and it must be allowed in.'

I granted this might be so, but found the result to be even more attention to form than was the case previously. And why not? How, I asked, could chaos be admitted to chaos? Would not that be the end of thinking and the end of art? If we look at recent art we find it preoccupied with form. Beckett's own work is an example. Plays more highly formalized than 'Waiting for Godot,' 'Endgame,' and 'Krapp's Last Tape' would be hard to find.

'What I am saying does not mean that there will henceforth be no form in art. It only means that there will be new form, and that this form will be of such a type that it admits the chaos and does not try to say that the chaos is really something else. The form and the chaos remain separate. The latter is not reduced to the former. That is why the form itself becomes a preoccupation, because it exists as a problem separate from the material it accommodates. To find a form that accommodates the mess, that is the task of the artist now.'

Yet, I responded, could not similar things be said about the art of the past? Is it not characteristic of the greatest art that it confronts us with something we cannot clarify, demanding that the viewer respond to it in his own never-predictable way? What is the history of criticism but the history of men attempting to make sense of the manifold elements in art that will not allow themselves to be reduced to a single philosophy or a single aesthetic theory? Isn't all art ambiguous?

'Not this,' he said, and gestured toward the Madeleine.

The classical lines of the church, which Napoleon thought
of as a Temple of Glory, dominated all the scene where we
sat.   The Boulevard de la Madeleine, the Boulevard Male-
sherbes, and the Rue Royale ran to it with graceful flat-
tery, bearing tidings of the Age of Reason.   'Not this.
This is clear.   This does not allow the mystery to invade
us.   With classical art, all is settled.   But it is different at Chartres.   There is the unexplainable, and there art
raises questions that it does not attempt to answer.'

I asked about the battle between life and death in his
plays.   Didi and Gogo hover on the edge of suicide; Hamm's
world is death and Clov may or may not get out of it to
join the living child outside.   Is this life-death question a part of the chaos?

'Yes.   If life and death did not both present themselves to us, there would be no inscrutability.   If there
were only darkness, all would be clear.   It is because
there is not only darkness but also light that our situation becomes inexplicable.   Take Augustine's doctrine of
grace given and grace withheld: have you pondered the
dramatic qualities in this theology?   Two thieves are
crucified with Christ, one saved and the other damned.
How can we make sense of this division?   In classical
drama, such problems do not arise.   The destiny of Racine's
Phèdre is sealed from the beginning: she will proceed into
the dark.   As she goes, she herself will be illuminated.
At the beginning of the play she has partial illumination
and at the end she has complete illumination, but there
has been no question but that she moves toward the dark.
That is the play.   Within this notion clarity is possible,
but for us who are neither Greek nor Jansenist there is not
such clarity.   The question would also be removed if we
believed in the contrary - total salvation.   But where we
have both dark and light we have also the inexplicable.
The key word in my plays is "perhaps".'

Given a theological lead, I asked what he thinks about those
who find a religious significance to his plays.

'Well, really there is none at all.   I have no religious feeling.   Once I had a religious emotion.   It was at
my first Communion.   No more.   My mother was deeply religious.   So was my brother.   He knelt down at his bed as
long as he could kneel.   My father had none.   The family
was Protestant, but for me it was only irksome and I let
it go.   My brother and mother got no value from their religion when they died.   At the moment of crisis it had no
more depth than an old-school tie.   Irish Catholicism is
not attractive, but it is deeper.   When you pass a church
on an Irish bus, all the hands flurry in the sign of the

cross. One day the dogs of Ireland will do that too and
perhaps also the pigs.'

But do the plays deal with the same facets of experience religion must also deal with?

'Yes, for they deal with distress. Some people object
to this in my writing. At a party an English intellectual
- so-called - asked me why I write always about distress.
As if it were perverse to do so! He wanted to know if my
father had beaten me or my mother had run away from home
to give me an unhappy childhood. I told him no, that I
had had a very happy childhood. Then he thought me more
perverse than ever. I left the party as soon as possible
and got into a taxi. On the glass partition between me
and the driver were three signs: one asked for help for
the blind, another help for orphans, and the third for
relief for the war refugees. One does not have to look
for distress. It is screaming at you even in the taxis of
London.'

Lunch was over, and we walked back to the hotel with
the light and dark of Paris screaming at us.

The personal quality of Samuel Beckett is similar to
qualities I had found in the plays. He says nothing that
compresses experience within a closed pattern. 'Perhaps'
stands in place of commitment. At the same time, he is
plainly sympathetic, clearly friendly. If there were only
the mess, all would be clear; but there is also compassion.

As a Christian, I know I do not stand where Beckett
stands, but I do see much of what he sees. As a writer
on the theater, I have paid close attention to the plays.
Harold Clurman is right to say that 'Waiting for Godot'
is a reflection (he calls it a distorted reflection) 'of
the impasse and disarray of Europe's present politics,
ethic, and common way of life.' Yet it is not only Europe
the play refers to. 'Waiting for Godot' sells even better
in America than in France. The consciousness it mirrors
may have come earlier to Europe than to America, but it
is the consciousness that most 'mature' societies arrive
at when their successes in technological and economic
systematization propel them into a time of examining the
not-strictly-practical ends of culture. America is now
joining Europe in this 'mature' phase of development.
Whether any of us remain in it long will depend on what
happens as a result of the technological and economic
revolutions now going on in the countries of Asia and
Africa, and also of course on how long the cold war remains cold. At present no political party in Western
Europe or America seems possessed of a philosophy of

social change adequate to the pressures of current history.

In the Beckett plays, time does not go forward. We are always at the end, where events repeat themselves ('Waiting for Godot'), or hover at the edge of nothingness ('Endgame'), or turn back to the long-ago moment of genuine life ('Krapp's Last Tape'). This retreat from action may disappoint those of us who believe that the events of the objective world must still be dealt with. Yet it would be wrong to conclude that Beckett's work is 'pessimistic.' To say 'perhaps,' as the plays do, is not to say 'no.' The plays do not say that there is no future but that we do not see it, have no confidence about it, and approach it hopelessly. Apart from messianic Marxism, where is there today a faith asserting the contrary that succeeds in shaping a culture?

The walls that surround the characters of Beckett's plays are not walls that nature and history have built irrespective of the decisions of men. They are the walls of one's own attitude toward his situation. The plays are themselves evidence of a human capacity to see one's situation and by that very fact to transcend it. That is why Beckett can say that letting in 'the mess' may bring with it a 'chance of renovation.' It is also why he is wrong, from philosophy's point of view, to say that there is *only* 'the mess.' If that were all there is, he could not recognize it as such. But the plays and the novels contain more, and that more is transcendence of the self and the situation.

In 'Waiting for Godot' Beckett has a very simple and moving description of human self-transcendence. Vladimir and Estragon (Didi and Gogo) are discussing man, who bears his 'little cross' until he dies and is forgotten. In a beautiful passage that is really a duet composed of short lines from first one pair of lips and then the other, the two tramps speak of their inability to keep silent. As Gogo says, 'It's so we won't hear...all the dead voices.' The voices of the dead make a noise like wings, sand, or leaves, all speaking at once, each one to itself, whispering, rustling, and murmuring.

Vladimir: What do they say?
Estragon: They talk about their lives.
Vladimir: To have lived is not enough for them.
Estragon: They have to talk about it.
Vladimir: To be dead is not enough for them.
Estragon: It is not sufficient.
      Silence
Vladimir: They make a noise like feathers.

Estragon: Like leaves.
Vladimir: Like ashes.
Estragon: Like leaves.

In this passage, Didi and Gogo are like the dead, and
the dead are like the living, because all are incapable
of keeping silent. The description of the dead voices is
also a description of living voices. In either case,
neither to live nor to die is 'enough.' One must talk
about it. The human condition is self-reflection, self-
transcendence. Beckett's plays are the whispering, rustling, and murmuring of man refusing merely to exist.

Is it not true that self-transcendence implies freedom,
and that freedom is either the most glorious or the most
terrifying of facts, depending on the vigor of the spirit
that contemplates it? It is important to notice that the
rebukes to Beckett's 'despair' have mostly come from the
dogmatists of humanist liberalism, who here reveal, as so
often they do, that they desire the reassurance of certainty more than they love freedom. Having recognized
that to live is not enough, they wish to fasten down in
dogma the way that life ought to be lived. Beckett suggests something more free - that life is to be seen, to be
talked about, and that the way it is to be lived cannot be
stated unambiguously but must come as a response to that
which one encounters in 'the mess.' He has devised his
works in such a way that those who comment upon them
actually comment upon themselves. One cannot say, 'Beckett has said so and so,' for Beckett has said, 'Perhaps.'
If the critics and the public see only images of despair,
one can only deduce that they are themselves despairing.

Beckett himself, or so I take it, has repented of the
desire for certainty. There are therefore released in him
qualities of affirmation that his interpreters often miss.
That is why the laughter in his plays is warm, his concern for his characters affectionate. His warm humor and
affection are not the attributes of defeatism but the con-
sequences of what Paul Tillich has called 'the courage to
be.'

'How It Is'
(1961)

[Written in French; published as 'Comment c'est' by
Éditions de Minuit, Paris; translated into English by
Beckett; published by Grove Press, New York, and John
Calder, London, 1964.]

49. MAURICE NADEAU IN 'EXPRESS'

26 January 1961, 25

After 'The Unnamable' I naively imagined that Samuel
Beckett would not be able to push further his quest, to
descend lower into the abyss of nothingness and solitude
that some imperious genius had forced him to explore. 'He
is condemned to silence or to repetition,' I wrote. After
'The Unnamable' there were 'Texts for Nothing,' 'All That
Fall,' 'Embers,' and today the appearance of 'How It Is,'
after which I would be tempted - had I not been taught by
experience - to repeat the same adventurous prophecy.
It's just that each time, by reducing the part played by
fiction, by destroying the habitual supports of the story
(or dramatic play), Samuel Beckett gives the illusion of
having gone to the very end of that strange ascetic exercise, after which, when the last voice has stopped, there
is only silence, death, and nothingness without sentences.
Is it possible to progress in a state of nothingness? We
have to believe it is since, starting from a point lower
than his last starting-point, he ends up in an even more
deserted no-man's-land.
   In 'How It Is,' the part played by the narrative, the
characters, the relations between them, or even the part

played by what is called the progression of the story
(generally made up of events in which the characters are
implicated) is almost non-existent. Almost nothing happens. But this 'almost nothing' possesses such a force of
combustion that we can see in it, as in Beckett's preceding works, the entire and desperate image of our condition.
We remember the character Mahood in 'The Unnamable,' that
man-trunk imprisoned in a jar out of which only his head
protruded, his eyes unmoving and perpetually open, tears
streaming down his face: we thought we had attained the
absolute in derision and suffering. We were mistaken.

The narrator of 'How It Is,' even if he still possesses
his arms and legs, has lost the habit of a vertical position, even through the artifice of a jar. He is stretched
out in the mud, his face half buried, and if he manages to
move by crawling, 'right leg right arm push pull ten yards
fifteen yards half,' he has lost the use of an audible
voice: his 'brief movements of the lower face' give him
the vague consciousness of a murmur that he alone hears,
of an interior voice (he is not sure that it is his) which
forces a way for itself, every ten or fifteen seconds,
through an endless panting, the panting of an endless
agony. This voice, which runs like a mechanism impossible
to stop, is full of gaps, silences, and rest periods
caused by the panting. Beckett gives us its seismographic
track in one long sentence stripped of syntax, of punctuation marks, of relational words, a sentence which coagu-
lates into large or small packets of words separated by
blank spaces: 'I say it my life as it comes natural order
my lips move I can feel them it comes out in the mud my
life what remains ill-said ill-recaptured when the panting
stops ill-murmured to the mud in the present all that
things so ancient natural order the journey the couple the
abandon all that in the present barely audible bits and
scraps.' Without claiming that this single sentence is
easily readable from beginning to end, we need only murmur
it to ourselves in a panting rhythm to notice that all the
elements of communicable language that the author dropped
had, in fact, little importance. On the other hand, what
remains forces us, for the sake of intelligibility, to
adhere to the words in the rhythm desired by the writer;
what remains conquers us and casts a spell. Here the
screen of language that every great artist tries to burst,
through language itself, in order to directly communicate
the reality he wishes to show us, is pulverized.

The story is divided into three parts, repeatedly
evoked and examined, and the voice must succeed in expressing them, not in order to earn sleep, rest, or death,
that would be too easy, but to accomplish an absurd *pensum*.

Malone, in 'Malone Dies,' Mahood and Worm in 'The Unnamable' were similarly condemned but the hope of dying sustained them.   In 'How It Is' this hope disappears.   When
the cycle is completed: Before Pim, With Pim, After Pim,
the narrator has returned to his point of departure and
without transition will have to set out again.

Before Pim is the journey.   Crawling on his belly,
anguished and alone, with the help of his right hand and
foot, the left hand pulling an old coal sack filled with
tins of food as provisions, the narrator progresses for
months, years, centuries perhaps, always toward the east.
He describes gestures, reduced to a minimum and always the
same, and expresses his sensations: 'close my eyes not
the blue the others at the back and see me on my face the
mouth opens the tongue comes out lolls in the mud and no
question of thirst either no question of dying of thirst
either all this time vast stretch of time.'

His mind functions in slow motion; his memory gives him
only bits of his past 'above in the light.'   He passes
from a sensation to a memory in a pell-mell of images.   He
tells himself absurd stories that never get anywhere, re-
lives meaningless 'little scenes'; it is his way of making
time go by.   Are these his own stories, does he invent
them, are they breathed into him by the voice that he
hears, but which he isn't sure is his own?   We don't know.
Time passes, a time which never ends: 'centuries I can see
me quite tiny the same as now more or less only tinier
quite tiny no more objects no more food and I live the air
sustains me the mud I live on.'

Second part: with Pim or the couple.   During his voyage
the narrator meets a being like himself, similarly lying
in the mud, also holding a sack of provisions in his left
hand.   He examines him on his side, takes his measure by
feeling him, lies half on top of him, pushing him a little
more into the mud, their faces one against the other.
Henceforth the murmur comes from one mouth or the other,
following curious gymnastics.

As if training an animal, in order to create conditioned reflexes, the narrator sticks his can-opener into the
right buttock of his fellow creature; the latter speaks.
He taps him on the head; the other stops speaking.   He
punches him in the back; Pim sings.   With his inordinately
long nails, he scratches the other's back, imprinting long
bleeding letters on it.   Pim answers the questions thus
asked.   The narrator tries to make Pim tell stories, to
make him remember scenes that he might have lived 'above
in the light.'   The stories get entangled, the memories
evoke others in the narrator's mind.   We no longer know
which ones belong to whom.   But that's not important.   All

men have the same laughable and desperate stories to tell.
That's the happy part of the narrator's life, his 'good
moments.' Having found his equal, his brother, whom he
can martyrize, treat like an object and manipulate at his
will, he is indeed no longer alone. He is the torturer
who forms an amorous couple with his victim. He hears
him, understands him, shares his provisions, life and
memories. He loves him. Thanks to Pim he feels that he
exists: 'in a word more lively that's what I was getting
at I've got at it I say it as I hear it more how shall I
say more lively there's nothing better.'
Third part: After Pim: abandonment. The tropism which
pulls the narrator towards the east forces him to leave
Pim, 'right leg right arm push pull ten yards fifteen
yards half,' to return to the original state of the journey, with the added nostalgia of having left Pim, before
becoming in turn the victim of another (that is the law),
Bom, whom he awaits and who will make him undergo exactly
the same brutality, according to the same ritual that he
had to perform on Pim.
His thoughts rise a little above his own destiny. He
sees millions of beings crawling like him, lying in the
mud, alone in the state of 'the journey' or 'the abandon,'
coupled as 'torturers' or as 'victims.' It is a vast geo-
metric constellation where mathematical laws are strictly
adhered to, the torturers falling upon the same victims
and becoming in turn victims of the same torturers, so
that, as the narrator adds in a moment of bitter irony,
there is no way of ever knowing more than a limited number
of beings.
If the narrator was sure of his deeds, if he hadn't
imagined everything down to the delirious mathematical
prolongations, if Pim had really existed, we could easily
take refuge in symbols, and try to translate this story
into concepts. It seems that the situation is worse than
that: the narrator is alone, undeniably alone, and he
could have constructed (the ambiguity is knowingly respected by the author) this phantasmagoria to deceive himself
about his solitude and the length of his agony: 'never any
Pim never any Bom never any journey never anything but the
dark the mud the sack perhaps too it seems constant too
and this voice which knows not what it says or I hear
wrong which if I had a voice a little heart a little head
I might take for mine once without quaqua on all sides
then in me when the panting stops faint now scarce a
breath.' Nothing is sure except the scream 'THAT'S MY LIFE
HERE' and that other, colored with an improbably and
doubtlessly impossible hope: 'I MAY DIE screams I SHALL
DIE screams good.' The last state, the most likely, the

most constantly likely state of 'how it is.'

The difficulty lies in treating this work like any
other, in treating Samuel Beckett like any other author.
Are we in the realm of literature? Are we outside of it?
Certain writers who break all the barriers (conventions)
of art, in order to lodge themselves in you, to ravish
your consciousness and to have all things seen through
their eyes, these writers disarm judgment and annihilate
all desire to comment.

Such is the case with Antonin Artaud or Henri Michaux
who went beyond certain frontiers. Such is the case with
Samuel Beckett. There is nothing to do but to read and
re-read, detach ourselves if possible from the visions of
a delirious exactitude that they communicate to us. Nothing is left for us but to profit from the knowledge they
acquired after experiments which only they could undertake, and not without injury and suffering.

Beckett's 'imperious genius' (I use this expression
once again) always leads him closer to silence. Since
'Murphy,' his first story, how much *impedimenta* has he
abandoned along his path! In 'Molloy' he was still having
fun 'telling,' interlacing vague destinies along the
forest roads where Moran and Molloy got lost.

In 'Malone Dies' we were invited to contemplate a man
who was dying. There it was a question of a simple fact.
But, as in 'Waiting for Godot' or 'Endgame,' his beggar
couples (has it been noticed that they always come two by
two, one playing the torturer, the other the victim) are
still driven, be it toward death, by a vital tension that
links them to our species. The Unnamable already doesn't
have much in common with us, except, as Beckett would want
it, his capacity to suffer.

Outside of this voice which, in 'How It Is,' signals
the presence somewhere of a consciousness, there is no
longer, in this vast expanse of mud (Beckett suggests that
it could very well be nothing more than the totality of
human excretions) where human worms crawl, anything which
reminds us of the superb and derisive parades of the world
in which we live. Fallen from a world of 'light' (childhood? a former 'golden age'? some kind of divine world?
all interpretations are possible), the Pims, the Boms, the
Krums and the Krams pass through a gray and deserted hell
which appears more realistic than those of any religion.
Silence, solitude, defeat, suffering, lasting for centuries, for eternity. Does Beckett mean that this is our
human condition, that this is 'how it is' where we live?
Who would doubt it?

We may miss the good clowns of 'Waiting for Godot.' We
may miss the old parents in the ashbins of 'Endgame.' The

excessive derision of the destiny to which they were reduced succeeds in making us laugh. But what a strange
laugh it is! The same is true of the game of the 'sucking-stones' in Molloy and the waltz of the bowler hats!
Or Malone taking an inventory of his ridiculous riches
before dying.

Of course, these are only ways of making the time pass.
But all the same this whole circus put a certain bitter
gaiety into the narrative. I'm afraid Beckett has finished with all these jokes à la Jarry, with this 'somewhat
dry humor' with which Jacques Vaché answered 'the theatrical and joyless uselessness of everything.' Apart from
the fact that he has never looked down on his creatures
from above, giving us to understand that they watch him
from close up, any kind of parody no doubt appears superfluous to him. 'Nose in the mud.' with everything that
follows, there you have 'how it is.' Describing this
state in all its prolongations is doubtless still in the
realm of literature; for Beckett, it's perhaps also a way
of making the time pass by telling himself stories.

[Translated by Larysa Mykyta and Mark Schumacher]

50. RAYMOND FEDERMAN IN 'FRENCH REVIEW'

May 1961, 594-5

Raymond Federman (b. 1928), novelist, poet, critic, translator, Professor of English and Comparative Literature at
the State University of New York at Buffalo, is the
author of 'Journey to Chaos: Samuel Beckett's Early Fiction' (1965), and co-author with Professor John Fletcher
of 'Samuel Beckett: His Works and Critics' (1970), a critical bibliography. He has also published three novels and
two volumes of poems.

It seemed that after 'L'Innommable,' Samuel Beckett had
led the novel into some kind of impasse from which it
could never emerge, unless by a repetition of what had
already been done. And so one could expect a long silence
on Beckett's part. Having reduced the essential elements
of the novel-plot, characters, action, language - to their

bare minimum, how could any writer push the experiment further?   Yet with the recent publication of
'Comment c'est,' Beckett once more manages to carry the
form of the novel into a completely new and original no
man's land.

This time we are in a world completely stripped of all
norms of life.   And yet, somehow, we are able to identify,
if not a place, or characters, or a story, at least the
human anguish, the pathos of a semi-existence.   The novel
is divided into three distinct parts: Before Pim, With
Pim, and After Pim.   A vague notion of a human being is
crawling in the mud towards a certain destination, towards another wretched being: Pim, whom he meets in part
two and with whom he establishes a stange and painful
relationship.   The first person narrator having reached
his victim in part two, after a slow journey in part one:
'jambe droite bras droit pousse tire dix metres quinze
mètres reste là dans le noir la boue tranquille....'(1)
stretches in the mud next to Pim.   Now he covers parts of
Pim's body with his own, stabs him in the posterior with a
can opener, inscribes bloody words on Pim's back by scrat-
ching him with his nails, hits him on the head to make him
sing, to make him talk, or to force him to stop talking.
Then he leaves Pim, or is it Pam, or Krem, or Kram (for
as usual in a Beckett novel, names are constantly shifting) for a new destination.   At this time begins the journey (of part three) towards a certain Bem - or Bim, or
someone else.   It is not quite certain whom the new victim
will be.   For that matter we are not even sure whether it
is the narrator or Pim who now proceeds towards Bem in
part three (they seem interchangeable).   Nothing is certain in this Beckett world.   The only certainty is this
vicious circle within an infinite and yet limited limbo.
This going to and coming from, in an infinite time at an
excruciatingly slow pace, and always face down in the mud.

The remarkable achievement of Beckett in this novel is
the simplicity and economy with which he manages to create
the situation.   The whole book is built on a series of
simple sentences repeated at various stages in a fragmentary rhythm.   The syntax itself within the punctuationless
sentences is broken and distorted.   Only a few identifi-
able objects appear in the novel: a can opener, a bag full
of sardine and tuna fish cans which the characters drag
along on their journey, and a few broken memories of a
world which seems to lie above in the light, a kind of
lost reality.   And yet, in spite of the disconnected
appearance of the language and of the narration, the whole
construction of the novel is mathematically arranged.   The
whole situation is so well thought out, that one feels

caught up within the strange world of the novel. There is
no way out for the reader, nor is there any escape from
the limbo for Pim, Pem, Pam, Bem.... They are all in motion, in rotation, becoming alternately: tormentors or
victims.

Why then three parts to this novel? One, or at most
two would seem to suffice. Or for that matter why not
four, or ten, or twenty? Beckett himself points out this
possibility in the novel, and again as in 'Waiting for
Godot,' where a third act could have easily followed in
the same pattern as the first or the second act, one could
also expect other parts to continue this novel almost to
infinity. But this time Beckett manages, in the last few
pages of the novel, to destroy the whole construction by
having the narrator pretend that everything described was
an illusion, a creation of the mind, a useless mumbling of
the mouth, thus destroying the whole fiction of the novel.

Beckett, once again, places himself in a most unusual
position among the modern novelists. And even though he
may again be attacked for his pessimism and for his nihilistic view on life, still he seems to redeem himself
through the artistic creation. Only silence could reduce
Beckett's vision to complete 'darkness.' Yet, his insistence on creating more novels, on having his characters -
however distorted - express themselves even in the most
clumsy manner, defeats his nihilism and places the artistic creation above dark reality.

Note

1 'right leg right arm push pull ten meters fifteen
meters stay here in the dark in the mud quietly...' (Eds)

51. JEAN-JACQUES MAYOUX IN 'MERCURE DE FRANCE'

June 1961, 293-7

Jean-Jacques Mayoux (b. 1901), French critic, Professor of
Literature at the Sorbonne, author of many books on Did-
erot, Flaubert, Melville, Joyce, and Beckett, is a close
friend of Beckett.

In 'Mardi,' Melville puts the formula of the refusals
which he has already reached (at twenty eight) in the
mouth of his character Babbalanja: 'Yet in this pruning
will I persist; I will not add, I will diminish; I will
train myself down to the standard of what is unchangeably
true. Day by day I drop off my redundancies; ere long I
shall have stripped my ribs; when I die, they will but
bury my spine.'

After this statement Melville will continue to produce
profusely for almost ten years before falling into a
sudden silence; and it is only the clerk Bartleby who
will incarnate his vision of total deprivation: the clerk
who will no longer copy, no longer move, and whose earthly
possessions are a blanket, a few biscuits in a newspaper
and a few dollars in a handkerchief.

Bartleby is the first 'Beckettian' character. But he
corresponds to Beckett's starting-point: to Murphy, to
Molloy, to Malone. With the 'Texts for Nothing,' with
'The Unnamable,' Beckett reached a new stage; with 'How It
Is' he is there. Reading 'The Unnamable' one might have
thought that it was impossible to go gurther in the negation of the story, in the rejection of characters, in the
Catharian harshness of a retreat into the absolute. 'How
It Is,' with an increased inflexibility and an austerity
which this time - but let us not be too sure - seems to
have reached its ultimate conceivable limit, resumes the
vision and themes of 'The Unnamable.'

Beckett's fictions have always been ambiguous internal
monologues: Beckett's voice, more or less inflected to be
occasionally lent to characters who hardly are characters
or masks, who rather are antimasks, emanations of the
self, more meaningful than this self itself. But already
in 'The Unnamable' Beckett was somehow reversing the usual
writer's attempt, since far from trying to objectify his
voice in various suits of flesh, he discovered with horror
that this voice was 'never his' or rather that there was
nobody who was him, one, indivisible, identical, not only
recognizable but internally recognized, and who could
speak.

It is this dissociated voice which we hear again here:
'Voice once ... on all sides then in me ... scraps of an
ancient voice in me not mine.' It is this voice which he
is the first to listen to, which he listens to himself
shaping, both responsible and surprised (as an animal
sometimes seems surprised by the gestures it makes) and
muttering then a remark, a comment, which would be made
obvious by a change of tone if the monologue was spoken
while it is not only written but devoid, from one end to
the other, of any punctuation: 'it ... fastens who knows

one the last prawns these details for the sake of something' ... 'we're talking of my foot' ... 'we're talking
of a thump on the skull' ... 'a watch wristlet to the feel
it's as I thought it will have its part to play' ...
'better a big ordinary watch.'

One can see in the last example the author who, having
become his own copyist, records with a kind of indifference the first motion of spontaneous creation coming out
of himself, and the changing impulse equally foreign to
the I-witness of a wholly serial existence. Each new
evidence at the edge of consciousness of what we usually
call reality, appears like an echo perceived after the
sensation or first idea, and coming back to him, already
foreign. Beckett remains fully intent on surprising this
inchoate feature, these successive, immediate moves of the
spontaneous but already distinct conscience that occur
already, as in a dream.

The 'I' is therefore little else but a spectator who
sees recorded on an inner screen a successive phantasmagoria, and who interprets it, in the same way that some
painters interpret a spot seen on a wall, and some others
work in haste using the first blot of ink off their brush.
A few images, more or less oneirical and yet in some way
or other controlled, constitute the extraordinarily modest
stock of accessories of our author: the tramp's sack, 'six
stone wet jute food inside.' In short a coal sack. The
food is 'the tins,' tins which bring up through evocative
magic the opener which the narrator finds at hand so to
speak and which becomes, organ creating an unexpected
function, a tool of torture, to be stuck in Pim's arse to
teach him how to behave.

There is about this sack both chance and necessity:
'sack old word first to come one syllable k at the end
seek no other ... that will do the word the thing it's a
possible thing ... what more can you ask a possible thing
see it name it ...'

Chance therefore similar to the surprising, obvious,
unavoidable appearances of dreams. But also necessity of
the imaginative development: 'this sack without which no
travelling....'

Pozzo's suitcase, Lucky's halter, Hamm's armchair or
gaff or handkerchief were of the same kind: 'useful,' says
Beckett. Besides those, there are obsessive images, such
as that of the mud in which everything is sunk, in which
all wallow, and which one eats, spits, inhales.

Pim appears, in the same way as the sack or the tin-
opener, as a necessary and ambiguous accessory of life's
pilgrimage. Ambiguous because it does not much matter
after all whether there is an outside Pim or not. What

matters is that image of Pim, alone possessed by the in-
ventor, only butt, object of his play, subject to his authority, his whim, his cruelty; then as a result of this
treatment, although fairly sluggish at first ('Pim is like
that he will be like that he stays whatever way he's put'),
alone capable of being developed in pseudo-conscience -
or who knows, in real conscience, by the imposition of
suffering. In short Pim is the prototype of that which
happens and changes life; he is part of the situations
that life brings up, and of human condition: 'two strangers uniting in the interests of torment.'

The images had a dream quality: they are there absolutely then suddenly they irretrievably disappear: 'I feel
it forsaking me soon there will be no one never been anyone of the noble name of Pim'.... Hence the need to take
advantage of him while he is there, to extract from him
this surplus of life that man can only get from suffering
which he inflicts or receives.

'I dig my nails into his armpit right hand right pit he
cries I withdraw them thump with fist on skull his face
sinks in the mud.'

But he sings, it is won, as Beckett says; and the
dressage continues until 'a brief murmur,' until the word,
this surplus of conscience. It is the executioner and the
victim, Pozzo training Lucky and Lucky into one, conditioned, bewildered, imbecile and docile: 'what is required
of me ... what is not beyond my powers....'

In Michaux, the anguish, the terror give rise to clawed,
hairy, shapeless monsters, and unimaginable tortures.
With Beckett there has always been only slow and obscure
agonies, and here there is no longer the least story-
making ornament, nothing but these monotonous persecu-
tions, thumps on the skull, tin-opener in the arse, face
in the mud, nothing but this alternation of fundamental
loneliness and the amusements it invents for itself:
'...the four phases through which we pass the two kinds of
solitude the two kinds of company through which tormentors
abandoned victims travellers we all pass and pass again
again....'

One could go on for ever with this derisory evocation;
one would then only see 'instead of me sticking the opener
into Pim's arse Bom sticking it into mine....'

But what is the use of pursuing the 'ubuesque' absurdity of the human condition? 'What the fuck does it matter
who suffers who makes to suffer...' 'linked thus bodily
together each one of us is at the same time Bom and Pim
tormentor and tormented pedant and dunce wooer and wooed
speechless and re-afflicted with speech in the dark the
mud.'

'...Nothing to emend there,' adds Beckett, for once totally in agreement with what the voice to which he so often objects is saying: 'Something wrong there.'

Does he vaguely remember Schopenhauer when he imagines 'someone in another world yes whose kind of dream I am'? The very weak throbbing which one still perceives here, the small move, the small effort to build himself a world, collides each time into a sarcastic reminder: 'All that is nonsense ... never any procession no nor any journey no never any Pim no nor any Bom no never anyone no only me ... and what's my name....'

And yet as if in spite of himself, short elements of scene obstinately rise up, coming back from somewhere to appear on the memory screen, this woman with a wounded back on a hospital bed 'iron bed glossy white two foot wide,' who cannot turn her head and to whom he offers at arm's length, so that she sees it, a bunch of marguerites, of this child's hoop and these last jolts it has before it collapses to the ground.

Is there only, receiving these impressions, suffering these images, a passive clerk, 'the witness bending over me name Kram ... the scribe name Krim ... keeping the record...'? No, there is also the persisting need to play with the data, to rearrange them, in short to make a work of art out of one's misery no matter how great. The symbolic diagram of the last tape is here: 'recordings on ebonite or suchlike a whole life generations ... one can imagine it nothing to prevent one mix it all up change the natural order play about with that.'

He thus remains an artist, in spite of himself; and this voice is the gripping and wonderfully modulated voice of a poet who knows how to orchestrate in one word even the abysms of silence: 'One has no idea of these vast tracts of time...' and who from verse to verse of this book really sings in his blank voice:

'I would go to the end of the world on my knees ... my laughter in dry weather raises the dust on my knees up the gangways between decks with the emigrants....'

'there wherewith to beguile a moment of this vast season....'

[Translated by Françoise Longhurst]

52.   HUGH KENNER IN 'SPECTRUM'

Spring 1961, 3-20

Hugh Kenner (b. 1923), American critic and professor at
Johns Hopkins University, has written books about many of
the major figures of the Modernist movement (most notably
Joyce, Eliot, Pound and Wyndham Lewis). 'Samuel Beckett,'
published by Grove Press in 1961, was the first full-
length study to appear in English, and his 'Reader's Guide
to Samuel Beckett' (1973) is a useful primer.

Samuel Beckett's Malone, in bed, near death, records one
evening an astonishing fact: 'I have had a visit.'

> I felt a violent blow on the head. He had perhaps been
> there for some time. One does not care to be kept
> waiting forever, one draws attention to oneself as best
> one can, it's human. I don't doubt he gave me due
> warning, before he hit me. I don't know what he
> wanted. He's gone now. What an idea, all the same, to
> hit me on the head.

The blow on the head did not preface ampler communication.
The visitor registered his presence, no more. 'His mouth
opened, his lips worked, but I heard nothing.' Malone
studied him at leisure, however; 'he remained some time,
seven hours at least.' Later Malone draws up a written
list of 21 questions, to be submitted if the man returns;
but he does not. The list begins, '1. Who are you?
2. What do you do for a living? 3. Are you looking for
something in particular? What else. 4. Why are you so
cross? ...' 'Strange need,' he notes, 'to know who people
are and what they do for a living and what they want with
you.'
    Strange need, precisely; for how is the question, who
are you, to be answered? Perhaps by a name. But let us
say we know the name, Godot for instance. Who is Godot,
what does he do for a living, and what does he want with
Didi and Gogo? These are not really the things we want to
know. Sometimes we know them. This man's name is Gaber,
he makes his living as a courier of Youdi, and what he
wants with Moran is to dispatch him after Molloy. Knowing this, what do we, or what does Moran, know of Gaber?
If we idly assimilate his name to Gabriel's, and Youdi's

to Yahweh, it is because we can think of nothing better to
do, with the data supplied. Or let us have ampler data,
a whole autobiography, such as Mercier and Camier were
sluiced with in a southbound train:

> An only child I believe, I was born at P——. My parents
> were originally from Q——. From them it was that I
> received, along with the spirochete, the majestic nose
> whose ruins you behold. They were severe with me, but
> just. At the least deflection from rectitude my father
> beat me, with his heavy razor strop, until I bled,
> never failing however to notify my mother, so she could
> paint me with tincture of iodine or alcohol. Here
> doubtless is the explanation of my withdrawn and sec-
> retive character....

...and so on for a thousand mortal words as old Madden
rotates himself before our gaze; and from it we learn only
this, that old Madden is a bore not *per accidens* but by
predilection.

Whether cryptic or copious, talk in the Beckett universe is generally a mode of behavior, like Watt's oscil-
latory walk or Molloy's extraordinary performance with the
sixteen stones. Sometimes, as when Pozzo demands undivid-
ed attention and sprays his throat with the vaporizer, it
is highly studied behavior. But no more than the facial
contortions of Malone's visitor ('his mouth opened, his
lips worked, but I heard nothing') does it satisfy the
'strange need.' This is strangely jarring; we expect
spoken words to reach, not merely gesticulate. But it
conforms to the decorums of a writer whose sensibility,
like Wordsworth's, explores the confines of a universe of
objects, in which people are difficult to distinguish from
apparitions, or else statistics. Wordsworth, it will be
remembered, once on his wanderings encountered a Man, whom
in his account of the incident he likened successively to
(a) a huge stone on a mountain-top; (b) a sea-beast
crawled forth to sun itself; (c) a motionless cloud; and
when the Man commenced to speak,

> his voice to me was like a stream
> Scarce heard; nor word from word could I divide;
> And the whole body of the Man did seem
> Like one whom I had met with in a dream.

Not otherwise did Molloy, for whom 'to restore silence is
the role of objects,' observe that when another spoke, the
words he heard, 'and heard distinctly, having quite a
sensitive ear, were heard a first time, then a second, and

often even a third, as pure sounds, free of all meaning, and this is probably one of the reasons why conversation was unspeakably painful to me.' Over his explanation of this phenomenon presides, we may say, Newton, of the prism and silent face: it was, thinks Molloy, 'a defect of the understanding, perhaps, which only began to vibrate on repeated solicitations, or which did vibrate, if you like, but at a lower frequency, or a higher, than that of ratiocination, if such a thing is conceivable, and such a thing is conceivable, since I conceive it.'

For Wordsworth is the optimistic poet, as Beckett is the weeping comedian, of Newton's quiet machine. The statue in the Cambridge antechapel he recognized for what it was, a thing as silent as the face it represented, the marble index of a mind gone elsewhere, and meanwhile the very likeness of the entranced body. We do not fancy it about to speak; Newton is history's first unspeaking sage, his essential posture of operation summed up by a statue. Socrates in the bust is about to say something, or has just finished, but Newton has nothing to say. He engages in no Confucian or Socratic *viva voce* with disciples. His is something more than the normal mathematician's alogia; for we hear of Euclid teaching pupils, and Pythagoras sociably engaged with his brother cultists. He has no talk, he communes with a universe of objects, and makes note of results, each equation formally a tautology, which he is even negligent about publishing. He likened himself to a lone child gathering shells on the shore of the infinite ocean; so Molloy, 'sitting on the shore, before the sea, the sixteen stones spread out before my eyes,' meditates his problem of groups and cycles. And Wordsworth, having penetrated to the heart of Newton's romance as night after night starlight or moonlight drew his mind back to the statue in the antechapel, became in his turn in emulation of the Newtonian sage the Newtonian poet, the first poet to make a habit of wandering lonely as a cloud, among rocks, and stones, and trees, encountering such things as lone thorns, banks of daffodils, mountains, and occasional human apparitions, lost so far as might be in his wise passiveness, indeed perpetually talking to himself 'like a river murmuring' so that he was (he says so) grateful for the little dog that barked beside him when persons came near, and reminded him to restrain his mutterings and assume a social demeanour.(1) Through the social world, with which he feels no kinship, as through the world of objects, he moves as anomalously as an octopus in a forest; it is a universe for a clown. And he was the first to make a program of writing years afterward about his own experiences, and about himself in the

process of writing them, as Molloy and Moran and Malone do
with such unflagging patience.

In such a universe speech has no place; speech constantly threatens it with disruption. Sound, Descartes
and Newton can account for, but speech defeats them. A
voice reaching out of the interiority of a human person,
with the thrust of my utter uniqueness, expressing, press-
ing out, so much as may be, toward some other person that
sense of 'I' which I alone have: what has Newton or Clerk
Maxwell to say about that? So in Beckett's late dramatic
work we find his cosmos dissociating into plays for
voices alone, and 'actes sans paroles.' This dissociation
exactly parallels that between thing and man. The second
Mime summarizes for the eye the physical universe à la
'Molloy': two men, never present to each other because one
of them is always in a sack, alternately carrying one
another ceaselessly to no end from right to left across a
monolinear expanse of space. By contrast, the second
radio play, 'Embers,' summarizes for the ear the internal
world from which reaches the unique voice: 'Stories,
stories, years and years of stories, till the need came
on me, for someone, to be with me, anyone, a stranger, to
talk to, imagine he hears me, years of that, and then,
now, for someone who ... knew me, in the old days, anyone,
to be with me, imagine he hears me, what I am, now.'
Put beside this a paragraph from 'Watt' -

Watt wore no tie, nor any collar. Had he had a collar,
he would no doubt have found a tie, to go with it.
And had he had a tie, he might perhaps have procured a
collar, to carry it. But having neither tie, nor
collar, he had neither collar, nor tie.

- and we see at once how this fine exercise in reciprocal
negation and the anguish of Henry cannot coexist. Watt's
tie and collar belong to the period of 'stories, stories,
years and years of stories.' That is where the Newtonian
universe belongs also: it was a story Europe told itself
for many decades. If Beckett's comedy derives from mathematics and system, from the impingement of system, and
notably systematic forms of discourse, on experiences to
which they seem inappropriate, it is to our quickening
sense of persons imprisoned inside all this system that
his works owe their grip on our attention. Persons stir
because every word is an utterance. Patterns close because all discourse has shape.

The voice brings us to the mystery of the person, owes
its very existence to that mystery, a mystery that, sour
it and defile it as they will, no Beckett personage ever

lays to rest. Krapp, in the most remarkable short dramatic piece in the language, communes with his own voice
canned; what was once spoken in intimate urgent recreation
of experience -

> We drifted in among the flags and stuck. The way they
> went down sighing, before the stem! (*Pause*.) I lay
> down across her with my face in her breasts and my hand
> on her. We lay there without moving. But under us all
> moved, and moved us, gently, up and down, and from side
> to side....

- is thirty years later reproduced exactly, and again, and
yet again, with precise automatic repetition of nuance,
false as three traced signatures: not a voice any more but
a hideously exact simulacrum of a voice, on magnetic tape:
recollection in tranquillity with an automaton's ven-
geance: a last bitter parody of those vases celebrated in
'Proust,' where the lost past is sealed away. We can see
why the author of 'Mercier et Camier' and the trilogy expresses a recurrent interest in parrots.
  Bring, then, persons into juxtaposition, and perhaps by
some miracle the locked selves will flower. The whole
tension of 'Waiting for Godot' depends on this possibility; for Godot being a person and not a physical law, will
introduce into the repetitive universe of Didi and Gogo
some unpredictable disposition of their affairs: 'Let's
wait and see what he says.' And we see why 'Mercier et
Camier' fritters into aimlessness, the object of the quest
being merely a bicycle. Godot is the perpetual possibility of personal impingement on mechanism; without him,
their interrelation, from long habit, has become a shuffling of limited resources, their conversation a game of
catch ('Come on, Didi, return the ball, can't you, once in
a way?'), their choice either submitting to protracted
existence or terminating it. Godot does not come, but his
perpetual possibility animates the weary trickle of pot-
ency into history.
  Bring, then, persons into juxtaposition, and perhaps
... 'Embers' does so bring them, in Henry's fantasy, and
fiction stops dead at a terrible, poignant climax. Bolton,
in the story Henry tells to himself, has summoned Dr.
Holloway in the dead of night, and when Holloway arrives
can only fix his eye and say in anguish, 'Please! PLEASE!'
The scene is intensely vivid. All Henry's dormant human
capacity flows into his evocation of the 'old man in great
trouble,' of Holloway coming to him through a nearly
interplanetary silence ('Outside all still, not a sound,
dog's chain maybe or a bough groaning if you stood there

listening long enough, white world, Holloway with his
little black bag, not a sound, bitter cold, full moon
small and white, crooked trail of Holloway's galoshes,
Vega in the Lyre very green.') They stand in each other's
presence, and all that Henry wanted from the father who
despised him and the wife he despised suddenly animates a
haunting tableau: Bolton asking mutely for what cannot be
specified, for whatever communion looks out of another's
eyes.

> Then he suddenly strikes a match, Bolton does, lights a
> candle, catches it up above his head, walks over and
> looks Holloway full in the eye. _ (*Pause.*) Not a word,
> just a look, the old blue eye, very glassy, lids worn
> thin, lashes gone, whole thing swimming, and the candle
> shaking over his head.... 'We've had this before,
> Bolton, don't ask me to go through it again.' (*Pause.*)
> Bolton: 'Please!' (*Pause.*) 'Please!' (*Pause.*)
> 'Please, Holloway!' (*Pause.*) Candle shaking and gut-
> tering all over the place, lower now, old arm tired.

[with what sympathy Henry's affections invade the old man
of his fantasy!]

> takes it in the other hand and holds it high again,
> that's it, that was always it, night, and the embers
> cold, and the glim shaking in your old fist, saying,
> Please! Please! (*Pause.*) Begging. (*Pause.*) Of the
> poor.

Holloway covers his face: 'Not a sound, white world,
bitter cold, ghastly scene, old men, great trouble, no
good.'
   Their great trouble is that they are each of them
alone; out of all his intimate sense of his own identity,
which no one else can ever share, comes Bolton's 'Please!'
across the bitter gulf: the distillation of the recurrent
Beckett scene in which two men are brought into each
other's presence and merely look at each other.
   Or merely listen to each other - Krapp and the vanished Krapp imprisoned on the tape; or merely badger each
other - Victor and the committee of interrogators in
'Eleutheria', or engage in reciprocal tyranny - Hamm and
Clov. Or else one, awaited, does not come (Godot); or
one, sought, is not there (Murphy, Molloy); or one, there,
cannot cease to be (The Unnamable). The Beckett tension
is between the person and the mathematical zero; hence his
preoccupation with series and permutation, with the unique
tenacities of declarative syntax, which so order and

encase mute agonies, and with silence. The Beckett plot
is simply an encounter between persons: hence the journey-
ings, the waitings, the confrontations. And the resolu-
tion of the Beckett plot? Either an infinite series, or
else an impasse.

A person cannot be silent, even voyaging through
strange seas of thought; there is no interior silence.
Nor alone, since we cannot imagine what it is not to be
with oneself. Not even by retreating so far as may be
within himself can he escape confrontation with the Other,
since his very words shape alternate persons, his very
musings subdivide himself. Not even by resigning himself,
with Molloy, to 'senseless, speechless, issueless misery'
can he evade the symmetries and permutations that torment
the mind.

Oneself, another person, symmetries, tensions: more
than a dozen years after the trilogy, 'Comment C'est,' an
unexpected return to fiction, gave these themes their
strangest, most abstract, and most hauntingly intimate
development. Built phrase by phrase into a beautifully
and tightly wrought structure, a few dozen expressions
permuted with deliberate redundancy accumulate meaning
even as they are emptied of it, and offer themselves as
points of radiation in a strange web of utter illusion.
For this book is founded on nothing recognizable: compared to it even the trilogy is realistic narrative. It
is built out of little more than a basic French vocabulary and a stock of phrases, and built before our eyes,
employing writing as a metaphor for itself much as 'Endgame' employs the stage, calculating the amount of work
still ahead, admitting ill-judged phrases with an abstracted 'quelque-chose là qui ne va pas,' and finishing
with relief ('bon bon fin de la troisième partie et
dernière'). It evades 'The Unnamable's' difficulties with
the sentence by employing none. So thoroughly does syntax give way to rhythm and architecture that we acquiesce
without discomfort to the total absence of punctuation.
In Molly Bloom's monologue the commas and full stops are
merely left out. By contrast it is the mark of Beckett's
fierce purity that he makes all thought of them seem
irrelevant. The three full stops on these 177 pages are
presumably printer's inadvertencies. The book looks like
a draft of itself, as 'Endgame' feels like a rehearsal of
itself; packets of language, set apart by spaces, like
notes for paragraphs never to be composed, jotted as some
eternal voice dictates ('I say it as I hear it'):

voice once without quaqua on all sides then in me when
I stop panting now in me tell me again finish telling
me invocation...

my life last state last version ill said ill heard ill
recaptured when the panting stops ill murmured to the
mud brief movements of the lower face losses everywhere

From the first words we feel as never before the tension of an alien person:

how it was I quote before Pim with Pim after Pim how it
is part one part two part three I say it as I hear it

Part one is animated throughout by the thought of Pim,
whose name occurs in it some fifty times, nearly always as
the object of some preposition. Before Pim, with Pim,
after Pim; toward Pim, near Pim; the words of Pim, the
watch of Pim: these categories sketch a domain of being,
of moving, and of knowing in which Pim, Beckett's generic
other person, is the stable and ordering principle. Pim
confers, it seems, all the meaning that the life before us
can aspire to. In the absence of his name, acrid memories
circulate without point, small mean words buzz, and we are
reduced to such calming expedients as the drawing of the
free hand over the face ('that's a help when all fails
food for thought'). This, we are given to understand, is
'how it was before Pim,' and the substance of Part one is
the journey toward Pim, a dogged chronicle of slogging
through mud: 'one vast stretch of time when I drag myself
and drag myself amazed that I can the cord sawing my neck
the sack jolting at my side a hand outstretched towards
the wall the ditch that never come.' This journey is over
and now being recapitulated; yet as we follow the narrative, which is generally in the present tense ('I shall
never have any past never had'), Pim lies ahead. To these
facts the reader finds himself paying little attention, so
true are they of all fiction. Beckett has paid close
attention, however, and out of the consequent identifica-
tion of Pim past with Pim future he will spin before the
book is finished an infinite series. This possibility the
reader of the first part is unlikely to notice, despite
ample clues; we suppose therefore that our sojourn in this
bleak time will be redeemed by the person so many allusions promise, and that the minimal assets of this bleak
place (mud, a jute sack, tinned fish, a can opener, a
cord) will assume the proper insignificance of all mere
things when Pim is present at last.

It is legitimate meanwhile to wonder where we are.
Though 'la boue' may vaguely recall the place 'in the
Marne mud' where Beckett moved his belongings by wheel-
barrow during the hungry winter of 1947, and where nine

years later he wrote 'Fin de Partie,' this information is
whimsically extraneous to the present book, the uncertain-
ties of which are not of a geographical order. Mud, darkness, and an indefinite sense of distance determine the
ambience. Molloy recalled how 'the road, hard and white,
seared the tender pastures, rose and fell at the whim of
hills and hollows,' but no such order of experience is in
question here. Such precisions belong to a former life,
'up there in the light,' where others, it seems, still
move, doubtless like the folk Malone envisaged, 'their
great balls and sockets rattling and clacking like
knackers, each on his way.' But here there is no light,
nor no speech except soundless 'brief movements of the
lower face,' nor no walking apparently, since all is a
dragging and crawling ('ten yards fifteen yards half on my
left side right foot right hand push all flat on my belly
mute cries half on my right side left foot left hand push
pull flat on my belly mute cries not a syllable to be
changed in this description'). It is a sort of limbo, one
supposes, or a sort of hell. Toward the end of the journey even the sack is lost, with all its contents.

   Will Pim brighten the world? No, the sojourn with Pim
is distressing beyond expectation. Not a total loss,
though:

> happy period in its way part two I speak of part two
> with Pim how it was they were good moments good for me
> I speak of me good for him too I speak of him too happy
> too in his way I shall know it later I shall know the
> way of his happiness I shall have it I have not yet had
> everything

Pim's happiness consists chiefly in this, 'that but for my
coming he would be nothing but a carcass inert and mute
forever flat in the mud.' His existence as Pim, his very
name, depends on my presence. He lies spreadeagled face
down throughout our séance, clutching a sack of his own,
but from the moment of my arrival commences to emit articulate sounds into the mud, though my efforts to speak are
restricted as before to 'brief movements of the lower
face.' Having ascertained by groping which end of him is
which ('the cries tell me which end is his head but I
could be mistaken'), I take up my position 'in the dark
the mud my head against his my side pressed against his
my right arm around his shoulders he cries no more we rest
thus a good while there are good whiles.' And what is
transacted during our 'vie en commun' is first, an incomprehensible song by Pim, in a foreign tongue perhaps, and
then a series of startling cruelties.

For a moment the voice of Pim ('une voix humaine là à quelque centimètres mon rêve'!) seemed to promise more generous intimacies:

> one day we should set forth again together ... help one another walk fall down in unison and await embracing the moment to resume

- but without explanations the will of this place super-venes; they commence the game of tyrant and victim, that familiar Beckett coupling, like Hamm and Clov, Moran and his son, Pozzo and Lucky, even a little Didi and Gogo. Clov, Lucky, Moran *fils*, are well trained, and pedagogical method is now demonstrated. Clawed beneath the right arm Pim repeatedly utters cries which blows on the skull repeatedly stifle in facefuls of mud; until after aeons of time on being clawed he chances to sing instead of cry, and is encouraged by a blow withheld to interpret the clawed armpit as a command to sing ('question of train-ing'). Next the can-opener is jabbed into his rump until he learns ('not stupid merely slow') that this is the signal to speak. These ritual lessons occupy vast tracts of time, and the author does not omit to tabulate the curriculum of stimuli:

> one a song nails in the armpit two speak canopener in the rump three stop fist on the skull four louder handle of canopener in the kidney

> five softer index in the anus six bravo fusillade on the buttocks seven bad same as three eight again same as one or two as needed

All this is executed neither in sorrow nor in anger, but with an analytic fullness of participation on which many pages are expended.

Once trained, Pim can be conversed with. The mute narrator sustains his part with fist, canopener and nails, in a last refinement tracing written questions on Pim's back ('roman capitals from left to right and from top to bottom as in our civilization': two Chinamen would have observed a different convention). And Pim for his part murmurs responses, having to do with his life 'up there in the light.' His life merges with mine, his voice with my muteness; it is unclear to whom the memories belong:

> that life then he would have had invented remembered a little of each how to tell that business up there he gave it me I made it mine what he sang to me skies especially roads especially...

It is the narrator who claims the most vivid and affecting
memories, of a lost wife, Pam Prim, whom he can barely
bring himself to think about. She terminated, for him, an
energetic career ('tried everything building especially it
flourished all branches especially plaster met Pam I believe'). Their intimacy was brief:

> love birth of love waxing waning dead efforts to revive
> it with the genitals vain again vain she fell from the
> window or threw herself spine fractured

Her death in the hospital, forgiving him (for what?), his
visit there, sitting on her bed holding before her face
the flowers she could not turn her head to see; his walk
away from the place, 'winter skim ice black branches grey
with ice she up there at the end dying forgiving all
white' - these memories he retraces as Henry in 'Embers'
does his life with Ada, or causes Pim to recite as Krapp
plays again and again the tape which embalms his gone passion. Pim is by turns a Lucky to keep company with and
abuse, a Krapp's record of one's own past, shifted out of
one's mind into another less painful location, and an intimate self-telling stories as Henry tells himself stories. Like the tape he can be switched on and off by the
application of stimuli two and three; like oneself, he
murmurs with a creative intimacy Krapp's machine cannot
approximate; like Lucky, Moran *fils*, or Clov he is a
person, inalienably other, filling a need, capable even
of evoking present affection ('arm around his poor shoulders rest we've earned it'). He is plied, after these
memories, with a fusillade of questions to which he
answers yes and no without imparting much enlightenment;
and at length is there no more. So much for Pim.
      So much, at present, for Pim. That was how the encoun-
ter turned out. But, we are given to understand, it
always turns out that way, and the narrator neither exults
in his own cruelty nor regrets it. For in Part three he
is awaiting in his turn a certain Bom, who will serve him,
and has served him before, as he served Pim, after which
he will commence the journey to Pim again. Pim, while he
waits, is now journeying through the mud to torment another. Now, as he waits himself to play the Pim, having in
Part two played the Bom ('c'est notre justice') he reflects on the logistics of the operation: first of the
sacks, of which during an infinite number of journeys an
infinite number are found, exchanged, permuted, and lost
according to a rule as elaborate as the one that governed
Molloy's sucking-stones; then of the personnel, of whom
any number are thinkable, exchanging in set of four the

roles of *bourreau* and *victime*, but each having to do with
only two others, the one ahead of him on the route, whom
he catches up to and torments, the one behind him who catches up to him and torments him. At intervals half are
waiting, half are moving; at alternate intervals, the
couples are about their solemn business. For allied reasons, he notes, a three-part book gives an adequate
sample, for the invariable rhythm which obtains in this
place ('notre justice le veut') is journey, torture, wait,
be tortured, but phase four repeats phase two so exactly
that we can dispense with another torture-piece.

Yet it was not wholly a torture-piece, despite the can-
opener: they shared food, memories, and the sensation of
existing: 'plus vivant il n'y a pas mieux.' Deprived of
Pim we calculate and speculate, alone with the implacable
stammering voice, perhaps my own ('I say it as I hear it').
We may guess, indeed, that the risk of this three-part
account being incomplete, omitting 'a thousand things
little visible or not at all in the present version,' is
negligible, so total was the sharing.

the small need of a life of a voice by one who has
neither

the voice extorted a few words life because that cry is
proof one has only to break through profound good a
little cry all is not lost we drink we offer a drink
good night

they were I quote good moments in part good moments
when you think of them

Pim and I part two and Bom and I part four to come

say after that that it was personal knowledge we had
then of one another

glued together making a single body in the dark the
mud

motionless but for the right arm which moved briefly at
great while all that was necessary

say after that that I knew Pim that Pim knew me that
Bom and I will know one another even fleetingly

But sharing, as he pursues his thoughts, ceases to be
one of his terms of reference; he grows preoccupied again
with questions of symmetry, of literary tactics (how comes

this written account out of a place where one lies flat in
the mud? Why, one Kram, not one of us, writes down my
words in his notebook and then mounts back into the
light); and questions, once again, of logistics. For the
sacks are a puzzle. As he tries explanation after explanation he sounds more and more like a writer trying to sal-
vage a considerable quantity of work in which he has found,
too late, a logical flaw. For the whole unimaginable procession moves on a narrow track eastward (as in Mime II
the two men with sacks are steadily goaded from stage left
to stage right), and as each starts a new journey he must
find a sack of provisions. But if all the sacks have been
in place from eternity, then at each place where a sack is
to be found there must be an infinite number to provide
for the infinite number of travellers each of whom will
halt there: whence, total blockage from the outset:

> such a heaping of sacks at the very start of the route
> that all progression impossible and the caravan having
> barely received its unthinkable first impulse would be
> blocked for ever and congealed in injustice

> then from left to right or west to east the atrocious
> spectacle on into the black night of future time of a
> tyrant abandoned who will never be a victim then a
> short space then his brief journey halted flat at the
> foot of a mountain of provisions the victim who will
> never be tyrant then a long space then another aban-
> doned and so on infinitely

In which case, we perceive in this vertigo of ratiocination, every segment of the route would be blocked, and
equally, by the same reasoning, our justice. There seems
nothing for it but to postulate a superior being who sees
to the supply of sacks as they are needed; and he is just
putting the finishing touches to the theology and eschato-
logy of this new hypothesis, when the *peripeteia* of the
book is suddenly sprung.
   For it is simplest to suppose that no component of the
problem which has been occupying him for sixty pages has
any existence, that he has been telling himself a story,
and that the voice whose words he has been repeating ('I
say it as I hear it') has been his own. No Pim then, no
Bom, no journey, no sack. He tries this out catechetic-
ally, and the voice (his own?) agrees:

> all these calculations yes explanations yes the whole
> story from one end to the other yes completely false
> yes

Nothing, in this case, is real but the mud and the blackness. Even the higher being, the source of the voice and
perhaps of the sacks, disappears; even Sam Beckett, for
that matter, disappears:

> but these stories of a voice yes quaqua yes of other
> worlds yes of someone in another world yes of whom I
> am so to speak the dream yes which he dreams continu-
> ally yes his only dream yes his only story yes ...

> and these stories of up there yes the light yes skies
> yes a little blue yes a little white yes the turning
> earth yes clear and less clear yes little scenes yes
> all balls yes the women yes the dog yes the prayers
> the homes yes balls yes

But almost the final words are 'end of quotation': this
solipsism may be a final delusion imparted by the voice,
and to imagine that he is merely telling himself a story
may be (there is no way to tell, unless he can tell
whether the voice is his own) a delusion that comes on
schedule while one waits for Bom. At any rate,

> good good end of the third and last part there it is
> how it was end of quotation after Pim how it is

So the work closes, balanced on a knife-edge; and so
Beckett rounds off in a perfectly insoluble either-or
this fullest and most philosophical summary of 'the dream
yes which he dreams all the time yes tells all the time
yes his only dream yes his only story yes.'
This work contains no ingredient (unless perhaps mud)
which we have not encountered before. What is new is the
absolute sureness of design. We have had sacks in the
second Mime, crawling in 'Molloy,' a horizontal narrator
in 'Malone Dies,' pages of broken tentative utterance in
'Embers,' tyrant and victim repeatedly, stories told to
oneself repeatedly, lost love in 'Krapp's Last Tape,' a
voice quaqua disturbing limbo in 'The Unnamable,' agonies
of non-identity in the 'Textes pour rien'; the blind Hamm
and the blind Mr. Rooney were at rest and in motion respectively in an utter darkness, and the latter is also
enamored of computations ('Not count! One of the few
satisfactions in life?') Even the technique of communi-
cating by a code of blows was adumbrated by Molloy, seeking to impress 'one knock yes, two no, three I don't know,
four money, five good-by' on his mother's 'ruined and
frantic understanding.' Everything, moreover, that Beckett has written from 'Murphy' onward shows us persons who

once were alive in the bright world and have somehow
ceased to be so. Murphy never thinks of doubting that he
has been fortunate to die into the little chaos within,
but no one after him is quite so sure. Paradise in any
case, if there ever was one, has been lost, and the subtle
argument of 'Proust,' that only involuntary memory can
briefly restore it, is exactly borne out when Pim helps us
recall what without him we cannot reach, the vanished days.
It is even true, as we were told it would be in 'Proust,'
that the attempt to communicate where no communication is
possible is 'horribly comic,' exactly the phrase for the
business with fist and can-opener.

No, what is novel is simply the scale on which his
material is organized, the brilliance no longer local but
gone into the bones of a work that tends to stay in the
memory as a whole. Not that it hangs there like a static
pattern fleshed out: it is a process, a history of effort,
the heroic effort to get itself written. The narrator,
unlike even The Unnamable, is doing without pencil and
paper (how would he even see his notes?), and as he
addresses himself to the more intricate calculations of
Part Three we watch him assembling and reassembling, by
dint of repetition, the data in his memory with the awe we
should bring to the spectacle of a Newton born blind. We
do not expect sentences, they would be an irrelevant
elegance.

And that the master of syntax should have chosen to do
without the sentence, even this is not surprising when we
recall his thematic distrust of accomplishment. It was
almost the last thing left for him to discard from his
repertory, and he gained in discarding it a structural
wholeness, as of a cantilever bridge, only to be achieved
by getting rid of all those little beginnings and endings.
Repeatedly similar components intersect at similar angles,
like girders, and it is with relief, not annoyance, that
we encounter repeatedly like an old friend some tried
formulation, 'jambe droite bras droit pousse tire dix
mètres quinze mètres': a relief we share with the narrator,
who for some instants is spared the necessity of invention.

Our author is indomitable, like Pim singing. Wedged in
this crack, where the very names are provisional, and
without so much as a declarative sentence to call his own,
he excogitates a whole grotesque vision of judgment, on
the scale of a lesser Dante, with greater authority than
when he had all the resources of fiction at his disposal
and wrote the tale of Murphy and his friends, 'là-haut
dans la lumière.' He has always told the same story; the
memories of the road outside the hospital where Pam Prim
died reach all the way back to a poem in 'Echo's Bones':

Exeo in a spasm
tired of my darling's red sputum
from the Portobello Private Nursing Home ...

We might even, with all the books and tales before us,
arrange the story into a chronology. A man (first version) is thrown out of the house by his upright family
(L'Expulsé), and slowly loses the capacity for human
intercourse; or (second version) is so shocked by the
gratuitous death of a loved one that he slowly loses the
capacity for human intercourse; wanders for some years on
the continent and in London ('Murphy'), puzzling over the
realities of the Irish world in which he once participated
('Watt'); has for a while a companion ('Mercier et
Camier') with whom, having become a twilight man, he is
never able to achieve a satisfactory intimacy; rediscovers
a need for his mother ('Molloy') but does not prosecute it;
lapses into telling himself endless stories ('Malone
Dies') and so into an inferno of words ('The Unnamable')
in which the last shreds of his identity dissolve; then
stirred at last by a hunger he has never admitted ('Godot,'
'Embers') for the presence and succor of other persons,
some other person, excogitates out of his now irremediable
darkness ('Comment c'est') a myth of his hopeless situation and a fiction of what release into memory another
presence might bring to it. This coheres agreeably and
will very likely some day be the theme of some biographer
or other. We should recall how Moran commenced his narrative:

Then I went back into the house and wrote, It is mid-
    night.
The rain is beating on the windows. It was not mid-
    night.
It was not raining.

- and reflect that there is likely not an atom of truth in
these conjectures from start to finish. We have been
cunningly closed up in a huge fantasy; and if anyone is
tempted to see behind blind Hamm the figure, say, of James
Joyce exacting minute services of a disciple, it is sufficient to note that Malone's tale touches Malone's life
at many points without its eerie abundance of invention
being thereby explained. Fiction is precisely like mathematics in this, that its normal processes handle non-
existent beings (points without magnitude, lines without
breadth, persons without being), and that a knowing extension of its normal processes will generate beings that
cannot be assimilated by the world of experience. The

surds and the imaginary numbers are irrefutable productions
of a system that finds it has no place for them.

Note

1 See Book IV of the 'Prelude.' In the next book he dis-
closes his life-long passion for Geometry, 'an independent
world, created out of pure intelligence.'

53. UNSIGNED REVIEW IN 'TIMES LITERARY SUPPLEMENT'

21 May 1964, 429

Samuel Beckett's open rejection of the conventions of the
drama and the novel is not a matter of 'experimental
form'. The artist does not 'experiment': his form is
determined and shaped by his vision. This is as true of
Beckett as of Joyce; but whereas Joyce's vision, with all
its complexities, required a firm and complicated structure, Mr. Beckett, who seems resolved to strip everything
down to some fundamental simplicity, devises structures
only to demonstrate their progressive and eventually complete inadequacy. What seem at first ways of ordering
the flux of experience becoming uncertain and unreliable,
and finally part of the general incoherence: the real
structure is the gradual collapse of all structures, the
concretion of his vision of 'How It Is'.
     The speaker in this latest novel, in darkness, flat on
his belly in an endless plain of mud, muttering into the
mud words which for most of the time seem not his own,
tells his story, properly enough, in a succession of
words without punctuation or conventional syntax - verbal
gasps interrupted only by pauses for breath. Yet he pro-
mises a system; he will tell his story in the 'natural
order' and in three parts - 'before Pim with Pim after
Pim' - and for some time, despite flashes backwards and
forwards and glimpses of a life 'above in the light said
to have been mine', this tripartite scheme helps the
reader to make his way through the quagmire of words.
     In the first phase, the speaker crawls intermittently,
with a sack of tins tied round his neck, across the mud;
in the second, he comes upon the prone and motionless Pim
and teaches him to answer certain questions in response to

stimuli inflicted by fingernails, fist or tin-opener; in the third, the speaker, abandoned by Pim, awaits the coming of Bom, who will torment him as he has tormented Pim, while Pim crawls away to where he will find, in turn, his victim.

The three-part structure begins to wobble almost as soon as it has been established. The speaker's life-cycle clearly contains four, not three, parts - journeying to Pim, tormenting Pim, abandoned by Pim, and being tortured by Bom. The offered explanation, that this last stage need not be recorded because it would be merely a repetition of the second, shakes the structure even more radically since it suggests that Pim, Bom, and the speaker are all one.

Moreover, the scheme seems to demand at least one other figure - Pim's victim, Pem - and, after examining a number of hypotheses, the speaker conceives of an infinite number in this procession across the mud, since justice demands that no man shall be a victim without having a victim of his own, nor a tormentor without having his own tormentor.

A different kind of scheme begins to shape itself, for the speaker believes his existence is being closely watched by an observer, Kram, and his words and behaviour written down by a recorder, Krim, and this suggests a representation of Mr. Beckett at work - the author-self recording what is seen by an introspecting self of an infinity of other selves pursuing and cross-examining each other in darkness.

But at last we reach 'a solution more simple by far and by far more radical' presented 'in the familiar form of questions I am said to ask myself and answers I am said to give myself however unlikely that may appear':

> all these calculations yes explanations yes the whole story from beginning to end yes completely false yes.

There is no sack, no tins, no tin-opener, no external voice, no Kram, no Krim, no Bom, and no Pim; this is the final disintegration of the apparently simple and reliable structure of the three stages:

> only me in any case yes alone yes in the mud yes the dark yes that holds yes the mud and the dark hold yes ...

> only me yes alone yes with my voice yes my murmur yes when the panting stops yes all that holds yes panting yes worse and worse no answer WORSE AND WORSE yes flat on my belly yes in the mud yes the dark yes nothing to emend there no the arms spread yes like a cross no answer LIKE A CROSS no answer YES OR NO yes

The structure with all its variants and their attendant hypotheses collapses, and both the structure and the collapse are formal representations of man's vain compulsion to impose an order and a significance on his experience. (Yet even this concluding explicitness may be deceiving, for the questions and answers are so reminiscent of the cross-examining of Pim that they may possibly represent the arrival on the scene of Bom.)

In 'How It is' Mr. Beckett has amplified the image of the 'latent consciousness' given in 'The Unnamable' by adding some kind of temporal extension: the image is of a cyclic process rather than of a state, but, since to Mr. Beckett Time is as illusory as Space, 'process' and 'state' refer only to the image, are merely two ways of looking. At the end of 'The Unnamable' the implication remains that somewhere in the darkness and silence some kind of integral self exists, but in 'How It Is' even this becomes uncertain: the self seems now dissipated into an endless procession of selves, pursuing and tormenting each other, and now resolved again into singularity. One is reminded of Mr. Beckett's assertion in the book on Proust that 'the individual is a succession of individuals'.

All hypotheses, and all the structures which reflect them, are bound to collapse because they are built on the fundamental instability of the self, both individual and infinitely divisible. All that Mr. Beckett can bring back from his explorations is a vision of isolated existence in darkness and mud (which, the speaker conjectures, may be the excrement left by the procession of life) gasping out incoherent and inconsistent words, but it is a vision so intense and so charged with poetic energy that it converts the art-forms in which it is expressed to its own purposes and implants itself ineradicably in the mind of the reader.

54.   JOHN UPDIKE IN 'NEW YORKER'

19 December 1964, 165-6

John Updike (b. 1932) is one of the most prolific and highly regarded American novelists and story writers. His essays and literary criticism can be read in 'Assorted Prose' (1965) and 'Picked-Up Pieces' (1975).

How it is I quote and unquote by Samuel Beckett published
by Grove Press translated from the French by the author
Samuel Beckett

in French how it is is comment c'est which is a pun id est
commencez which means begin in English no pun simply how
it is otherwise not much probably lost in translation

begin beginning not so easy book is written how it is I
quote unquote in words like this unpunctuated clumps of
words with spaces white between the I guess you'd call
them paragraphs I write it as I read it

word clumps no punctuation commas no periods colons no
semi colons none of them ampersands and asterisks not
one but now and then in caps I said in ARE YOU LISTENING
capitals to make it quite clear CAPITALS and there it is
how how it is is written technically considered

aesthetically considered

something wrong here

aesthetically considered quote how it is unquote can
hardly be considered as it is deliberately antiaesthetic
like graphic art of Dubuffet like plastic art of Giacom-
etti whose figures cosmic vastness whittles to such a
painful smallness

style if style it is perhaps conveys effect of panting
more or less for hero who is crawling face down in the mud
and dragging sack of jute containing cans of food also
something in incantatory also makes of language something
viscous which images push through with effort awful effort
blue sky there was one blue did you see it sky

plot faceless nameless hero crawling through the mud as
mentioned dragging sack of cans as mentioned can opener
not mentioned there is one nameless hero murmuring in the
mud and dark alone

when something other in the dark and mud called Pim the
name is PIM comes lies beside or under difficult to gather
precisely which and suffers being stabbed in many places
inducing speech or yells when stabbed with the can opener
just mentioned

then departs or fades or sinks or was entirely imagined by
hero faceless nameless who retrospectively divides his

crawl through mud into three stages before Pim with Pim
after Pim and that is plot of how it is

delightfully retold and thank you

welcome surely clearly hero faceless voice is us mankind
you me brother and mud the earth or hell or both and sack
the body dragged along and Pim is Christ name in Greek
begins chi rho iota looks XPI take away X add M which is
Sam SAM Beckett's favorite letter and you have PIM whose
name is also BOM to come the second coming of PIM is BOM
mob spelled backwards also bomb also KRIM a scribe a tribe
of scribes to follow PIM must be the Christian church
apostles popes so that before Pim with Pim after Pim is
human history how it is demarcated Christianly surely not
sure not clear you're welcome

hero everyman not only Christianly but biologically for as
with elementary organisms mouth and cloaca are confused
and tongue and genitalia and mud and merde and words the
same somehow the panting wriggling struggle evokes the
fish who out of water gasped to breathe evolving manwards

incarnation felt as animal encounter analogy a worm encounters a pebble nibbles then must crawl around it

Pim and hero cruelly copulate with graphic inexpertness a
blasphemous analogy with buggery that Beckett LOUDLY
underlines also analogy with any love affair I quote there
wherewith to beguile a moment of this vast season end of
quote

the period after Pim full of numbers analogy with modern
science the empty universe proliferates with the explicit
mathematicism in which the author so boringly delights
OKAY

attempt to take the novel into bowels beneath society and
circumstance COMMENDABLE obstinacy in producing novels
each one of which is smaller than the one before ADMIRABLE
with less furniture VERY WORTHY kind of fierce poetry YOU
BET out of rancid Platonism WHY NOT but BUT

something wrong here

something undergraduate inert a neo-classicism in which
one's early works are taken as the classics a laziness in
which young urgencies become old rhetoric hermetic avantgardism unviolated by the outer world the world beyond

the skin except the customary almost automatic glimpse of
rural maybe Irish bliss which bothers Beckett like a mote
of blue sky in his eye

this proud priest perfecting his forlorn ritual

the plays OKAY very the stage an altar anyway the radio
plays EVEN BETTER the ear rebuilds the actors foist existence on the words I remember videlicet the wonderful lav-
ender sandals of the messenger boy in a certain production
of Godot and his mystical haircut BUT

in how it is where Joyce and Kafka intersect one misses
now the one and now the other compare The Burrow compare
Nighttown compare The Penal Colony and deplore the relative thinness the sterile stridency

question is the novel no longer a fit vessel for Beckett's
noble sorrow and quote comedy of incapacity unquote Hugh
Kenner

unanswered but good the end of review the END of meditat-
ing upon this mud and subprimate sadism NO MORE no more
thinking upon it few books have I read I will not reread
sooner SORRY but that is how it is

'Happy Days' (1961)

[Written in English; first performed at the Cherry Lane Theatre, New York, 17 September 1961; first performed in London at the Royal Court Theatre, 1 November 1962; published by Grove Press, New York, 1961, and by Faber & Faber, London, 1962; translated into French by Beckett as 'Oh les beaux jours'; first performed in Paris at Odéon-Théâtre de France, 15 November 1963; published by Éditions de Minuit, Paris, 1963.]

55. ROBERT BRUSTEIN IN 'NEW REPUBLIC'

2 October 1961, 45-6

'Happy Days' opens, to the accompaniment of a clanging alarm bell and a blinding flash of white light, on a woman buried up to her breasts in a barren mound of earth. 'Another heavenly day,' she murmurs - stretches - and quickly intones a few snatches of half-forgotten prayer. Fumbling in the large handbag which contains all the essentials of her sorry existence, she proceeds to extract and examine, with laborious attention, the various articles of her toilet, as well as a parasol, a revolver, a nail-file, and a bottle of patent medicine. Having momentarily satisfied her pointless curiosity by finally deciphering the maker's guarantee on the handle of her toothbrush, she stops to affirm the wonder of life and the happiness of her days.

The name of this hopeful futilitarian is Winnie, and for the balance of this brief two-act work she chatters incessantly over such trifles, pitiably determined to invest

that penal servitude which is her life with some semblance
of interest - quoting fragments of 'unforgettable lines'
by English poets, peering into the audience to see if anyone is there, reflecting nostalgically on trivial events
of the past, and, above all, trying to communicate with
her uncommunicable husband, Willie, an ancient who passes
the time sleeping in a hole behind her mound when he is
not by her side (but just beyond her vision) mumbling over
the want ads and obituaries in his yellowing newspaper.
Willie and Winnie exist in a totally vacant world without
diurnal distinctions - even to speak of 'the end of the
day' is to speak 'in the old style' - where time seems
both to have stopped and to be rushing madly forward, and
where progress is measured only by the tedious-rapid advance towards dissolution, decay, and death.   Thus, while
Winnie is trying to kill time, time is more successfully
killing her: by the beginning of the second act, the earth
has risen to her neck, rendering her completely paralyzed.
In this condition, she half-cheerfully, half-desperately,
awaits total interment, still attempting to amuse herself
with memories and to bless even her most harrowing perceptions.   Finally, Willie appears from behind the mound,
crawling on all fours and dressed for a funeral, arthriti-
cally groping towards the revolver which lies up the mound
by his wife's right ear.   Failing in his efforts, he slips
painfully down the mound, whimpering Winnie's name, while
she - mistaking this attempt at suicide or murder as an
act of affection - affirms, with a kind of hideous ecs-
tasy, that 'this is a happy day.   This will have been
another happy day.'   They remain immobilized, as the bells
begin to ring with ominous frequency, and the curtain
descends.

'Happy Days' is, of course, Samuel Beckett's latest dramatic comment on the irony, pathos, and chronic hopelessness
of the human condition; and like all his work it is triumphantly _sui generis_.   Yet, it strikes me, despite certain
obvious felicities in the writing, as the least of his
dramatic efforts.   The language, enjoying none of that
poetic intensity which so ennobled 'Krapp' and 'Godot,' is
flat and prosaic; the symbols are almost nude in their
unambiguousness; and those repetitions of which Beckett is
so fond (successfully avoided only in 'Krapp's Last Tape')
have finally become rather boring.   Worst of all, Beckett
has fallen into self-imitation, which is almost as serious
as imitating others.   His dramatic techniques, though they
owe something to Maeterlinck, have always been extraordinarily compelling, but in 'Happy Days,' these same techniques - by which I mean the abandonment of all anecdote,

the manipulation of Bergsonian time, the static dream
atmosphere, the use of two parallel days laid side by
side, and the employment of a visual metaphor to convey a
spiritual feeling - are used almost mechanically, possessing neither variety nor intensity. Even the most striking thing in the play - the image of Winnie claimed by the
earth (signifying how death is constantly claiming us all)
- is only a visualization of that beautiful perception in
'Godot': 'They give birth astride a grave, the light
gleams an instant, then it's night once more.... The
grave digger puts on the forceps.' In short - and this is
admittedly an odd complaint to lodge against a dramatist
once thought to be the apostle of a mystery, murk, and
meaninglessness - 'Happy Days' is too predictable; so
obvious, in fact, that I experienced the uncomfortable
sensation, before the evening was five minutes old, that
I had written the play myself and was none too pleased
with my handiwork.

Alan Schneider's production is a perfectly competent
rendering of the play - no more, no less. His interpretation is based on strict fidelity to Beckett's intention,
but (though we must not underrate the directorial problems
explicit in a play where the central character is literally rooted to the ground) it never transcends the basic
requirements of the text to achieve an imaginative integrity of its own. Ruth White, as Winnie, has the stage
practically to herself, and she never abuses her mono-
poly. She is a splendid actress, with a truly enviable
range; but while she manages to sharpen all the tortuous
twists of Winnie's shifting moods, I found her a little
too much the pleasant Connecticut clubwoman to capture the
timelessness and placelessness of the role. Her cries of
despair ('My arms. My breasts. What arms? What breasts?
Willie. What Willie?') are nevertheless heart-rending,
and so is her Pollyanna cheeriness.

What of Beckett? He is obviously in a dilemma. Like
Ionesco, he has a single- all-encompassing vision of
existence which leads him to seek not new themes but new
metaphors with which to dramatize the same theme. But,
again like Ionesco, he has so successfully persuaded us of
the validity, coherence, and theatrical relevance of this
vision that we are impatient when he repeats the lesson.
Ionesco's recent work has exposed his severe limitations,
and I doubt if he will ever be much more than a stunning
secondary dramatist. But Beckett, with his superior
power, beauty, and intelligence, has the capacity for
greatness; and it is saddening to see him coast along on
what he already knows. It remains to be seen whether
Beckett will remain in the ditch or will develop in an

entirely new direction.   But whatever the future holds,
his place in the drama is secure.   In a world of the tenth-
rate, even the minor work of this man is like an Orient
pearl.

56.   NIGEL DENNIS IN 'ENCOUNTER'

January 1963, 37-9

Nigel Dennis (b. 1912), novelist, playwright and essayist.
His books include 'Cards of Identity' (1955), 'A House in
Order' (1966), 'Dramatic Essays' (1962), and 'An Essay on
Malta' (1971).

The first thing we are happy to say about 'Happy Days' is
that Mr. Beckett has consented at last to allow woman her
fair share of human futility.   There *was*, admittedly, a
woman in 'End Game,' but she was pretty silent in her
trash-can and did little more than suggest the thought-
less folly of motherhood.   In consequence, we had long
since taken for granted that in Mr. Beckett's view life's
intolerable tedium and pointlessness were noticed only by
men and that they alone suffered the grief of being alive
and the chagrin of being unable to die.   This had seemed
unjust to us, because nowadays there is nothing to prevent a normal woman from stepping out into the world and
falling on her face down those long stone stairs.
    'Happy Days' has corrected this imbalance.   Its spokes-
man is a spokeswoman - and what a healthy difference this
makes!   Mr. Beckett's men, much as we admired them, were
in danger of becoming used up: one or two more plays and
they might have started repeating themselves.   But once
relegated to the background and left to follow their
filthy habits unseen, while woman totters into the foreground, what a large new dimension is added to human
emptiness!   For there is surely no longer the slightest
doubt but that women suffer in a special way.   Women are
not men.   It is unkind and illegal to assume that they
are.   If women were men, marriage would not be the same
problem at all.   Marriage is a life-long union between two
opposing sorts of pain.   The husband that fails to understand this can only exacerbate the opposition.

As soon as the curtain rises on 'Happy Days' we see that this very injustice is being performed. The husband has long since abandoned all responsibility for his wife's pain - or happiness, or whatever you care to call it - and has retreated into a quiet tunnel: we are not actually shown this tunnel, because Mr. Beckett knows that he can count on all of us, men and women, to *imagine* a husband in a tunnel. The husband leaves his tunnel only in order to bury himself behind the newspaper - another gesture that any husband or wife in the audience can recognize easily. We would hazard that the husband's main reason for living either in a tunnel or behind a newspaper is the practical, everyday one of not wanting to listen to his wife's voice: any psychologist that cares to come forward with a more profound explanation must be dismissed as a bachelor, or as a man too blinded by the complexities of his bigotry to appreciate the simple but strong relationship between the ties of marriage and the freedom of the Press.

The husband's abnegation leaves the stage free for his wife, whose difficulties are not his difficulties. Where he wishes to be deaf, she wishes him to hear. But she is no perfectionist, this sensible wife. If he hears only an occasional word, she is pleased; if he grants her a grunt in reply, she is enraptured. What a mercy for the unfortunate man that his wife is buried up to the waist in scorched earth! She cannot take steps to *make* him hear, which she would certainly do if Mr. Beckett had not had the wisdom to bury her. Wisdom? Well, not wisdom, perhaps. Just a small prejudice in favour of his own sex. An appreciation of how much deafness matters to a married man. The lengths to which he will go to ensure it.

We must now ask the following question: in what state of mind should we look at a stage that is empty save for a half-buried wife and the back of a husband's bald head? Well, everyone is bound to differ somewhat on this matter. We know many people who would feel depressed - *only* depressed - when confronted suddenly by such a human spectacle. We know others who would settle back sternly in their seats and prepare themselves for a most useful lecture on the human situation. And both these attitudes seem almost inexplicable. For is it possible, *really*, to half-bury a *diseuse* and en-tunnel her hubby and still demand that the spectacle inspire the sadness of a train-accident in the Simplon Tunnel, or the gravity of a sociological conference? Surely the situation before us is entirely ludicrous and demands an entirely humorous response?

To argue these points is to get very close to Mr.

Beckett's particular kind of power. He has the magic of
impressing people to whom he does not seem funny. These
people realise that he is not a satirist - that he has no
quarrel with any persons or institutions, that he holds
nothing and nobody up to ridicule. They know that he is
a considerable preacher - a sort of unfrocked parson who
no longer believes in a Christian salvation, but only
feels that much worse in consequence. They know he is a
pessimist and that all his plays, no matter in what terms
he couches them, are emphatic in regard to the sadness and
regrettableness of human affairs. They feel these things
so strongly that even if Mr. Beckett sent up his curtain
on two copulating cats, they would only sigh sadly: 'How
true! Oh, the grief of it!'

Certainly, this shows a remarkable sort of power in a
dramatist - is there any *other* dramatist who could present the ludicrous so frankly and get back such a heart-
rending groan? Moreover it *is* in large part the true
nature of Mr. Beckett's power: he does in truth sorrow
with the humourless and mourn with the sad. It is the
humorist who suffers most at Mr. Beckett's hands, because the humorist is always seeing in a Beckett play
whole jokes that are only really half-jokes, and funny
situations that may have been intended otherwise. The
humorist, indeed, tries to strike a bargain with Mr.
Beckett, saying: 'Sad underneath, by all means. But
funny in expression, no?' But the bargain is refused.
Mr. Beckett denies the working agreement that Chekhov
accepted. Laughter, he seems to say, is the most obvious
sort of misery.

Mr. Beckett's intransigence has grieved us very much. We
have danced before him nearly nude, shaking bells in his
ear and calling him 'Uncle.' We have urged him to embrace a madcap image, and we have pointed out with matchless gravity that objects such as bald heads, old boots,
newspapers, and artificial dogs with leaking penises were
brought into the world purely for fun and can never find
inclusion in any solemn category. He has merely dropped
a tear, and passed on - one of those people, probably,
who think that wise advice is one of the few *really funny*
elements in the catastrophe of life.

This has put us in a most embarrassing position. We
spend most of our time pouring measures of bile over
directors and actors who pervert authors' meanings to
their own uses and think that the theatre is just a place
where one obtains the maximum of self-expression with the
minimum of honesty. And now, here we are, ourselves a
member of this low, degraded, filthy tribe, longing to see

Mr. Beckett played without regard for Mr. Beckett. For we
have read and studied the text of 'Happy Days.' We have
spent a *happy day* doing so. We began to smile at the very
first line and went on smiling to the bitter end. Then,
still smiling, we went to the Royal Court and saw it acted.
Our smile fled like a chalk mark, leaving only a black-
board behind.

How can such a thing be possible? Is the human mind,
or voice, such that *any* line and *any* words can be spoken
in an infinite variety of ways, so that the most ridiculous remark can sound tragic and the most tragic cry ridiculous? We know, in fact, that this *is* so, but is there
not a limit somewhere?

'Happy Days' is the tightest and best-managed of Mr.
Beckett's plays. It has double-meanings and perplexing
points, but it moves in a straight line. Two extra and
undesirable characters *threaten* to spoil it by appearing
in person, as they did in 'Godot'; but by admitting them
only to the wife's memory, Mr. Beckett adds magically to
their significance while magnifying his heroine's solit-
ariness. She must make the present tolerable by bringing
her past to bear on it - by remembering to clean her teeth
and say her prayers like a good girl; by extracting moral
lessons of self-help from dreamy recollections. She must
do this on the stage for nearly one and a half hours, with
nothing in the way of material assistance but the contents
of her hand-bag, and nothing in the way of human support
but an occasional remark from her sunken husband.

To make this huge task possible, Mr. Beckett has given
his actress two strong instruments. First, he has made
her lines very ladylike and old-fashioned, so that the
memories which the lady digs up from her Edwardian past
can be recounted with *style*. Second, he has taken good
care that this unfortunate creature, bereft of all mobility, shall have a means of *holding* her audience. This
means is pure-and-simple comedy.

'Another heavenly day' are the rapturous words with
which the play begins. Given the circumstances before our
eyes, could any words be better chosen to start an audience laughing? And as we pass on through the text, we
find that once the lady has started the laughter at the
very beginning, there is no excuse for its failing to continue. No woman, cut off in her prime, can recall a few
stumbling lines of verse and then remark with *no* intent to
amuse: 'A part remains of one's classics to help one
through the day.' No woman can recall *gravely* that her
first kiss took place 'Within a toolshed, though whose
I cannot conceive. We had no toolshed and he most certainly had no toolshed....' If she *can* say this gravely,

what, then, is bawdy *for*? Or is Mr. Beckett regarded with
such horrible awe that even his vulgar innuendoes (and
'Happy Days' is rich in them) must on no account be shared
with the audience?

If the play is not expressed humorously, can it be expressed in any other way? Well, there is a faint possibility that an actress with extraordinary vocal qualities
might persuade her audience to regard her misery with
tears. But in whatever manner we regard the text, we
must have those vocal qualities. It is impossible to read
the play without seeing that it calls for an infinite
variety of vocal modulations - that it is a play of speech
punctuated by pauses.

Mr. Beckett describes his heroine as 'About fifty, well-
preserved, blonde for preference, plump, arms and shoulders bare, low bodice, big bosom....' Miss Brenda Bruce
fits this description perfectly. Her bare arms and shoulders are the very pink of perfection. No bottled fruit
could challenge the excellence of her preservation. Her
bosom is such that were we to be weighed in the balance
with it, we should be found wanting. But beneath this
glorious rebuff to pessimism, what? A voice without a
trace of sonorousness and as flat, hard, and inflexible
as a steel girder. An entirely neutral personality.
A face from which all trace of character and command seem
to have been erased deliberately, as if vitality was an
impropriety. As a philosopher, expounding to students
the dry conclusions of Mr. Beckett's thoughts, Miss Bruce
was conclusively dry. The awful mistake was to suppose
that this was her duty - that she was concerned not with
the lines which the author had written but with the view
of life he was reputed to have. Integrity and fidelity
could hardly have gone farther in the wrong direction:
here was a rare case where even burlesquing and over-
playing would have succeeded much better than misplaced
honesty.

This is a great pity because Mr. Beckett has written a
part which must be regarded as a very great part indeed -
a part so extraordinarily difficult that the actress who
could command it would be the wonder of her profession.
For, think, among other things, of the magnificent sacri-
fices she would have to make. Rooted to one spot, she
would have neither entries nor exits with which to draw
attention away from the play and fix it upon her well-
known hip-action. All those unnecessary and circuitous
glides from one part of the stage to another would be
ruled out; no long rehearsal hours could be wasted on the
chalking of lines and the measuring of frontage. In a

desert of scorched earth, all the theatre's most-prized
professional nonsense would be impossible - none could
hurry forward to apply flame to Abdullah by courtesy of
Ronson, and the interminable pourings of whiskies would
cease. Bereft of all stage traffic, the actress would be
left with nothing but her part; deprived of all action,
she would be forced to think and even to act. In fact,
were it not obvious that Mr. Beckett is a benevolent man,
we should not hesitate to applaud him as a cruel and pitiless instrument of reformation.

It may, of course, be impossible to find an actress
who is prepared to sacrifice all the superfluous things on
which her reputation depends. In that case, there will be
nothing to do but clap a wig and falsies on one of our
talented homosexual actors. We can think of two or three
who could not only catch the tone of 'Happy Days' to perfection but might not be averse to exploiting the gaiety
of buried womanhood. If the outcome was a little hilarious, no objection would be heard from us. For we would
much rather see Mr. Beckett dancing to jig-time than being
bled piously to death at his own altar. There *is* a shrine
at Canterbury, but it is not his.

57. ALFRED SIMON IN 'ESPRIT'

December 1963, 905-9

Alfred Simon (b. 1930), drama critic, a regular contributor to 'Esprit,' has written extensively on modern drama.

Tragedy degree zero. 'It must be disinterred,' he says;
'as it is, it has no meaning.' Samuel Beckett turns his
anthropomorphic ghosts loose right in the middle of
nature, a nature full of emptiness, with no cities, mountains, or trees, the frightful preserve of matter: unbro-
ken by any landmark, flowing away to infinity beneath
one's eyes, or crushing one's shoulders, this is the Un-
limited of Anaximander that still terrifies the descendants of Pascal. A consciousness grows aware of the
horror of its own condition and becomes reduced to this
consciousness of itself; and, as the whole thing takes
place at sunny midday, 'within itself thinks and suffices

unto itself' amid the horror.

Two tramps immobile in a nameless landscape, waiting for a certain Godot. Two old people dying in their ash-bins on the forestage. The chatty torso of an old co-quette 'stuck up to her diddies in the bleeding ground' - 'What does it mean? What's it meant to mean?'

Jean-Jacques Gautier, Jean Dutourd and François Mauriac are determined to understand (and to understand without having seen, the dear men of faith!). What is Beckett's positive contribution to the worldly dossier of mankind? Whether God exists, or not? Whether man has meaning, or not? And what does he make of the 'little child Hope,' of 'man is what he makes himself to be,' of 'I am master of myself as well as of the universe,' and of 'Deliverance for captive souls'?

Beckett replies, 'Forget the classics!' The case of Beckett continues to grow worse, good people! In 'End-game,' the character speaking the final monologue is still able to recall a beautiful line from Baudelaire and stake his last search for one last meaning on it. But here, all this work, this endless plunge, to fish up a few lines of doggerel from a Viennese operetta, after which the play finally consents to cease speaking!

Beckett is very good at the art of making you believe the sun rises in the east, which is the height of mystifi-cation and his own kind of tragedy. He uses a lewd style, çonventions and clichés as traps. Shakespeare is a little like that. But Shakespeare's stories quiver with sound and fury. Beckett's characters have a lot of trouble just moving, and even though they speak abundantly, even though they are really indefatigable, they are unable to cry out, either to complain or to protest, because they are unable to suffer. Occasionally, however, a monosyllable, an ono-matope, even a stomach rumble is sufficient to let all the distress accumulated in centuries of the human condition burst forth from the senseless heap of words with the power of the Aeschylean 'Woe is me.'

Gripping abbreviations whose parodic charge explodes under the noses of the orthodox. Derisory supplications, heart-rending blasphemies. The whole thing begins with a Magnificat. The handmaiden of the Lord salutes the Sun of God, bombarding her point-blank: 'Another heavenly day.' She folds her hands, closes her eyes, moves her lips: mutterings, '...For Jesus Christ sake Amen.' She starts again: mutterings, '...World without end Amen.' The mock-ery of God made man and divine eternity overwhelms the dawning of this false first day. 'Holy light ... blaze of hellish light....'

Places and characters without identity. Everything is

unnamable. Except time. Time abandoning itself to its
pure state - a kind of neutral force, implacable like the
light, that will never end, since it never began. Man,
who is like a tumor on time, can no more live than die.
He is always present at the uncertain beginning of an
interminable endgame: 'Finished, it's finished, nearly
finished, it must be nearly finished.' Death, at the
same time ineluctable and impossible. Because he is
already dead, man will never die. Rationally speaking,
he cannot die. Things deteriorate, winding down toward
immobility, toward silence, death, Nothingness. But it is
impossible for them to get there. And Reason is condemned
to flounder in this impossibility. From the peat-bog where
the two tramps wait for Godot to the ashbins of 'Endgame,'
and from the latter to this woman buried alive, there is a
progression. From one play to the next, from one act to
the next, the evolution is the same. The themes, acts and
plays are repeated. But something changes! 'Something is
taking its course,' going in one direction, always the
same: toward absolute non-sense, toward nothingness. As
Richard Coe has noted, there is a bit of Zeno in Beckett.
The little heap of millet grains is progressively increased by half the quantity that would have to be added to
obtain the total. Thus it will never reach its end. This
is the 'impossible heap' of days in 'Endgame.' In like
manner, Winnie sinks into time rising around her without
reaching the end of her story, because she has no story.
When the play ends, the actors freeze, remain suspended,
as though the film had suddenly jammed. And it is this
fixed image, mechanically fixed, that we carry away with
us from each of the performances to which Samuel Beckett
invites us.

Beckett's characters have nothing to do with realism,
either psychological or social. Nor do they come out of
the cabinet of dreams, like those of Ionesco. They are
neither machines for shouting and gesticulating (theater
of cruelty), nor sacks full of ideas (Sartrean theater).
The matrix of their origin is neither the natural nor the
supernatural, but mythic memory. Ghost-like and clown-
like, they are there. Mankind fallen back into infancy,
back amid primordial terrors, having salvaged from its
passage through adult consciousness only irony and sarcasm. These pithecanthropes of thought, the last survivors, or rather the last victims, of a slow cataclysm,
live out the death of the earth as the gods of the Theo-
gony lived through its birth. And they are as monstrously
comic as the latter. Earth returns to the cosmos, cosmos
returns to chaos. And the last form of man is the cosmo-
pithecoid. The fascination with nothingness that provides

those traumatized by neo-marxism with certain stylistic effects and complaisant games is the source of a new kind of tragedy, a tragedy that starts over from zero (the tragedy of the impossibility of tragedy), whose titles to nobility have been established by Samuel Beckett.

No, they are not sacks full of ideas, the characters in 'Happy Days.' They are immediate and primitive (indeed primordial) and their metaphysical realism is conveyed by extremely concrete language. Winnie tries to decipher an inscription on the handle of her toothbrush. Finally the inscription is complete: 'Fully guaranteed genuine pure hog's setae,' and Winnie asks herself, like a Poussin shepherdess, 'What exactly is a hog?' A half an hour later, the invisible spouse she interrogates answers her furiously: 'Castrated male swine. Reared for slaughter.' Winnie had felt, in the 'Et in Arcadia Ego' of the tooth-brush, the presentiment of an awful truth.

In the first act, Winnie is still able to play with both objects and words; in the second, only words are left to her. At the same time that the theater of Beckett pro-claims the ridiculousness of language, it repeats tire-lessly that man's last resource is language. *A day will come when words themselves will fail*. The downfall of language is linked to the treachery of objects, and it is the collapse of reason that is implied in the treachery of words. It is also the impossibility of both living and dying: the terror of surviving the collapse of reason. As early as 'Waiting for Godot': 'Thinking is not the worst.... What is terrible is to *have* thought.' Becket-tian tragedy is a tragedy of tortured reason. Dedicated to the torment of knowing the unknowable, of comprehend-ing the irrational, of naming the 'unnamable,' man cannot withstand vertigo. This theme, spoken and acted, spoken in gesture and acted in speech, animates the most secret message of 'Happy Days.' Here we must point out Beckett's artistry, great and cruel, yet completely modest and dis-creet. Jacques Lemarchand is right in remarking that it is rather because of her good upbringing than because of cowardice (unless both are acting at the same time, cour-age consisting then in the dignified acceptance of the fundamental cowardice of man) that Winnie conceals from herself the horror of her condition. This discreet un-veiling of horror is related particularly to the collapse of reason. If tragedy is, above all, knowledge, the sudden awareness of truth, then I know of few tragic moments, even among the greatest dramatists, that can compare with the one in which Winnie ceases little by little to pretend to believe in a game she no longer believed in from the beginning. At that moment horror

tightens around her, around this *self*, the last bastion of
reason and dignity. Winnie: 'If the mind were to go.
(Pause.) It won't of course. (Pause.) Not quite.
(Pause.) Not mine. (Smile.)'

Now a few minutes later, the vise tightens on her own
reason. Winnie: 'Reason. (Pause.) I have not lost my
reason. (Pause.) Not yet. (Pause.) Not all. (Pause.)'

And here I permit myself to address François Mauriac
and the subordinates who went to see the performance for
him in the name of threatened values and a papal encyclical
turned to ridicule. No, Samuel Beckett does not calumniate
life. It calumniates itself. I mean, finally, that life
calumniates itself in the person of François Mauriac when
it condemns a great Christian thinker to join the ranks of
the cosmopithecoids without being aware of his role. The
new fact of our epoch is that a believer can no longer believe as though the death of God had not taken place. The
believer also lives in his own way, in his very faith, the
death of God. The pessimistic vision of Beckett has nothing partial, systematic, or arbitrary about it. It is
merely untenable. And here is the tragic paradox of Beckett: he affirms the untenable. And he forces us to affirm
it. Sartre said that life begins on the other side of
despair. For the believer in our time, faith begins after
the death of God. Through Beckett we perceive our own
tortured reason. With Nebel, with Paul Ricoeur, we must
return to the very foundation of tragedy, as it was perceived by the Greeks: the confrontation between an evil
God and human Freedom in revolt: the wickedness of God and
the revolt of man each being implied by the other. What
is the meaning of Winnie on her bare mound? What is the
meaning of Job on his heap of ashes, and of Prometheus on
his rock? The tragedy of the modern period is that man
knows more about God than Job did, and more than Prometheus did about man. But that his knowledge destroys
itself in destroying him. The old myths go on speaking to
us, but no longer have anything to tell us.

The evil God weighs heavy upon Beckett's universe. It
is the dead God. God has killed himself out of wickedness, out of hatred of man. And if he made man in his own
image, then God has killed himself out of self-hatred.
The sado-masochism of God constitutes the very bedrock of
modern tragedy.

Another idea developed by Paul Ricoeur is that there is
morally no escape from tragedy. More precisely, one is
not delivered *from* the tragic, but *in* the tragic. Such
was the power of Attic tragedy. It is not certain, finally, that 'Prometheus Bound' will end in 'Prometheus
Reconciled,' nor that the Furies will change into

Eumenides.   In the tragic horror itself man experiences a
satisfaction produced by the beauty of song and of words.
The sublimity of the word sublimates the tragic.

This is exactly what I feel at the end of the admirable
performance directed by Roger Blin at the theater of Jean-
Louis Barrault.   Nothing unhealthy, not the least hint of
neurosis in the extraordinary performance of Madeleine
Renaud.   Through the overwhelming simplicity of her
acting, dereliction becomes deprivation, and finally renunciation.   But we must not yield to the facile temptation to turn Beckett into an unconscious believer.

Madeleine Renaud plunges us into the sane horror of
'Si le grain ne meurt....' which has meaning only if one
considers its tragic aspect.   But one can concentrate on
that so deeply that the mind will be unable to recover
from it.   Beckett teaches us to take that risk.   At the
level he occupies, the horror of living disqualifies
neither Hemingway's old man, nor Péguy's simple man, nor
the wisdom of Montaigne, nor Franciscan joy.   It disqualifies only the monkey tricks of the cosmopithecoids.
Samuel Beckett has steeped himself in the death of God.
Let those who had no hand in the matter cast at him the
first stone.

[Translated by Jean M. Sommermeyer]

'Poems in English'
(1961)

[Published by John Calder, London, 1961, and by Grove Press, New York, 1963.]

---

58. DONALD DAVIE IN 'NEW STATESMAN'

5 January 1962, 21

Here is Samuel Beckett, bold and seminal intelligence that has convulsed the novel and the drama, offering in verse a mish-mash of Joyce and Eliot out of English, and from French moody abstractions and nonce words to baffle translators; making a lucky strike now and again (mostly with images from Dublin), and yet in the end merely unprofessional, too much at the mercy of whim, risking everything between one line and the next, and over it all the stale whiff of yesterday's avant-garde:

> Ah the banner
> the banner of meat bleeding
> on the silk of the seas and the arctic flowers
> that do not exist.

(The answer is: a sunset).
   This stale pretentiousness is the price that boldness pays, when it is not backed up by professionalism.

'Play'
(1964)

[Written in English; first performed in German translation
at Ulmer Theater, Ulm-Donau, 14 June 1963; first New York
performance at Cherry Lane Theatre, 4 January 1964; first
London performance, National Theatre, 7 April 1964;
translated into French by Beckett as 'Comédie'; first
French performance at Pavillon de Marsan, Paris, 11 June
1964; published by Faber & Faber, London, and Éditions de
Minuit, Paris, 1964; by 'Evergreen Review,' New York,
1965.]

59.   ROBERT BRUSTEIN IN 'NEW REPUBLIC'

1 February 1964, 30

Beckett's new work, 'Play,' is subtitled 'An Act' - it is
more like a spasm, since it comes and goes in an instant.
Still, for all its brevity, it is a strangely moving
experience; and although Beckett is again using a rather
familiar stage image, the piece is something of a new departure. Immobilized in three gigantic urns, above which
only their tilted heads are visible, a man and two women
stare blankly into the middle distance, unable to budge,
unconscious of each other's presence. They represent a
wife, her husband, and his sometime mistress, and now they
seem to be imprisoned in one of the lower circles of hell,
damned to ruminate eternally on their petty lives and
vices. What they recite, in abrupt and discontinuous
phrases, it a litany of adultery, punctuated by the man's
dyspepsia, the woman's screams, the wife's laughter, and
conducted by a cold finger of light which picks at their

273

heads with cruel indifference to pain. Guided by a malicious unseen will, this diabolical beam sets the rhythm and the tone of their damnation - regular and irregular, swift and lazy, stern and humorous. When the spotlight is switched off for a moment, the trio is left mumbling together in a ghastly mummified glow, a hellish triptych in a bourgeois inferno. Mr. Beckett takes about twelve minutes to complete this eerie tableau, thus proving what a deft poet he is; and he is deftly served by Alan Schneider's precise direction, and the flat, droning performances of Frances Sternhagen, Marian Reardon, and Michael Lipton.

'Film'
(1964)

[Written in English in May 1963, produced in 1964 by
Evergreen Theatre, Inc., directed by Alan Schneider; first
shown at Venice Film Festival, 4 September 1965. Pub-
lished in 'Eh Joe and Other Writings,' Faber & Faber,
London, 1967, and in 'Cascando and Other Short Dramatic
Pieces,' Grove Press, New York, 1968.]

60. RAYMOND FEDERMAN IN 'FILM QUARTERLY'

Winter 1966-7, 46-51

Having led the novel form into an inextricable impasse
whereby language itself is totally disrupted, having
stripped the theater of its most essential elements to the
point of literally burying the characters in the ground or
in giant urns, having even experimented with the obsolete
form of the radio play in an effort to silence sound, it
was inevitable that Samuel Beckett should turn to the
cinema, and eventually, as he did more recently, to television.

If Beckett's last novel, 'How It Is,' can be read as an
ultimate indictment of fiction in its failure to communicate reality with words, and his most recent play (approp-
riately entitled 'Play,' and just made into a film under
the direction of Rumanian-born Mariu Karmitz) can be
interpreted as a statement of the theater's failure to
create illusion through gestures and speech, then Beckett's first scenario, 'Film,' consistent with the Beckettian aesthetic system of destruction and purification,
represents an attempt to expose one of the cinema's most

275

flagrant failings today: the exploitation of sound, action, plot, and message to the detriment of the visual image.

Though Beckett may stand here in opposition to the avant-garde cinema whose main tendency is, in fact, to achieve a confusion of the multiple elements of the film, his attempt, as with his theater and fiction, is to return to the essence of the medium. This in itself represents an avant-garde effort. For as Beckett himself has expressed it in one of the few striking statements he has made about the creative process: 'A step forward is, by definition, a step backward.' Therefore, in this first cinematographic venture, Beckett incorporates all the themes and devices he has been exploiting over and over again for more than thirty years, and by simply transposing these to a new medium arrives at a critical judgment of the cinema.

'Film,' a 24-minute piece, featuring 'the funnyman who never smiled,' Buster Keaton, is a dialogueless experiment whose main theme is the picture itself, that is to say, vision within vision. Expertly directed by Alan Schneider, who is responsible for some of the best Beckett productions staged in this country, the film was the first production of Evergreen Theater, a subsidiary of Grove Press, whose entry into the motion picture field is, according to Barney Rosset (chief editor of Grove Press and head of Evergreen Theater) 'a logical extension of our activity as publisher of many of the leading contemporary playwrights and novelists.' It coincides with two important developments in the world of literature and film which tend to bring the two closer together: the growing interest among many important writers in the film as a means of artistic expression, and a growing world-wide audience for creative films which emphasizes the shift of the creative role toward the writer. 'Film' will eventually form part of a trilogy, with the other scenarios by Eugene Ionesco and Harold Pinter.

Though eagerly awaited by Beckett's admirers, 'Film' received a rather cold and negative reception at the Third New York Film Festival both from audience and reviewers. In general, it was found 'vacuous and pretentious,' too simple, too obvious in its symbolism. One critic went so far as to say that it was 'a miserable and morbid exercise' - though the film received several awards at European film festivals. Nevertheless, it is true that anyone even vaguely familiar with Beckett's work in the novel or in the drama might expect a deeper, less naïve, and above all less *obvious* piece of work, simply because Samuel Beckett has acquired the false reputation of being a complex writer; but it is also true that by demanding depth, sophistication, obscure meaning, and intellectual complexity from him we are failing to recognize the basic purpose of his art. For what most people still refuse to accept in all of Beckett's work, and perhaps failed to grasp in this film, is the fact that his entire artistic production is based on the exploitation of the commonplace, the banal, the cliché, in other words, the obvious, or in Beckett's own terms: 'The nothing new.'

In 1949, in a series of dialogues on painting with art critic Georges Duthuit (published in 'Transition'), Beckett made some revealing statements about the dilemma of the artist and art in modern society. Emphasizing that there is nothing new to paint or to say, he defends in a subtle dialectical argument the position of the artist who, even though aware that there is 'nothing to express, nothing with which to express, nothing from which to express, no power to express, no desire to express, together with the obligation to express,' nonetheless continues to create an art '... weary of its puny exploits, weary of pretending to be able, of doing a little better the same old thing, of going a little further along the same dreary road.'

Only if one accepts this paradoxical condition can one understand Beckett's aesthetic position, and more particularly the purpose of the present film. It is by returning to the most basic forms of expression, to the primary sources of any artistic medium (in the case of the cinema to the moving image itself and its silent origin), Beckett seems to suggest, that art can be renewed. Thus, in reference to his own work, to the futility of his own creative efforts, he stated in a recent interview: 'I am working with *impotence* and *ignorance*.' This agony of artistic expression is the theme Beckett has reiterated throughout his work. Why then should we expect from his first film more than what has enabled him to achieve greatness and originality in his novels and plays - basically, the stubborn exploitation of impotence and ignorance, and consequently of artistic failure?

We the quasi-sophisticated theater-going audience, the faithfuls of art films, too often expect from writers such as Beckett messages of deep philosophic meaning, even if we must ourselves impose these values on the work. We are no longer satisfied with the obvious, and yet what seemed so 'obvious' in this film is, in fact, its main theme: the simple reaffirmation of the essence of cinema, that is to say, visual expression of life and movement through photographic manipulation. If we accept this as the basic theme, we can then accept 'Film' as a work of art which exploits its own substance so as to reveal its

own limitation and failure.   Therein lies the originality
and meaning of Beckett's scenario.

Essentially, all of Beckett's work, in the novel as
well as in the drama, exploits its own medium, its own
creative elements, as its central subject.   The novels of
Beckett are all stories of a writer (narrator-hero) who
struggles helplessly with the process of putting words
together in order to fabricate a fraudulent reality, that
of his own fictitious existence within a make-believe
world.   The theater of Beckett, almost always in the form
of a play within a play, reveals in tragicomic terms the
play-ful and futile process of improvising with words and
gestures a theatrical illusion.   It is, therefore, logical
that Beckett's first film should use as its subject its
own essence: visual perception.   In other words, if Beckett's concern in the novel is to expose the agony of linguistic expression, and in the theater to reveal the agony
of verbal and gestic expression, then, turning to motion
pictures, the message he wants to impart is what he himself defines in the screenplay as 'the agony of perceivedness.'

The theme of 'Film,' visual perception, is explicitly
sustained throughout by three striking devices: the
absence of sound, the obsessive presence of eyes (human,
animal, and symbolic), and a limited viewing-angle for the
camera-eye which cannot exceed a 45° angle of vision - and
for the greater part of the film sees the protagonist
strictly from the back.   This perceptual limitation is
exploited even further by the use of different degrees of
luminosity in some images, as well as an increasing blur-
riness intended to reveal the gradual blindness of the
protagonist.   Thus Beckett emphasizes that the cinema
should primarily appeal to the sense of sight, and only
secondarily to the sense of hearing or even to the intellect.   For this reason, not only does he eliminate sound
in favor of visual images, but he renders the meaning of
his script so simple, so apparent that the story itself
becomes trivial, almost irrelevant.

This over-simplification of the plot's meaning was
obvious to everyone who saw the film, and was summed up
by 'Time' in these words: 'It is a stark, black-and-white
portrait of an old man who awaits death in a small, lonely
room.   Seeking absolute solitude, he turns out his cat and
dog, closes the curtains, covers the parrot cage and goldfish bowl with his coat, and blacks out the room's only
mirror.   Finally, he destroys the last reference to the
world in which he has lived, a packet of old photographs.
But he cannot escape himself, and as he lifts his eyes to

the barren wall before him, he comes face to face with the
image of his own deadpan likeness, with a patch over one
blind eye.' Indeed, a very banal, commonplace story whose
symbolic meaning is self-evident, a story which Beckett
has been telling and retelling with comic stubbornness in
his novels, in his plays, and now in this film. In fact,
'Film' is so reminiscent of 'Krapp's Last Tape' that one
cannot fail to relate the two works. But the interest
here does not lie in the story, nor does it lie in the
obvious symbolism or the pathetic condition of the protagonist. It rests essentially on what the 'Time' reviewer seems to have failed to *see*, even though inadvertently
he stresses it in his summary: Beckett's obsessive use of
the eye as the symbol of perception.

This emphasis on visual perception is clearly established at the beginning of the film by a close-up of a
withered human eye which stares grotesquely toward the
audience. This enormous eye announces the theme. As it
picks up the action, it functions both as the perception
of the camera-spectator in pursuit of the protagonist,
and as the perception of the protagonist in pursuit of
himself. This eye follows the main character, Buster
Keaton, as he moves clumsily with his back to the camera
through three different settings: a street scene, a
staircase, and a room. Only at the end of the last sequence does his face come in full view of the camera, in
that moment of revelation when he encounters his own self
- that tortured image against the wall, with a patch over
one blind eye.

From the start of the film, then, an angle of vision
('angle of immunity' Beckett calls it in the script) is
established which does not permit the audience a full view
of the protagonist. Consequently, he cannot become the
'perceiver' but must remain the 'perceived object' viewed
only from behind at an angle never exceeding 45°. Conven-
tionally, the viewer of a film sees more than the characters in the film. One might say that the spectator has a
total perception of the action whereas the characters have
a partial perception. In 'Film,' however, since the field
of vision of the camera-eye never exceeds that of the protagonist, the viewer is denied total perception. It is
this restricted 'angle of immunity' which creates the
'agony of perceivedness.'

One of the main objections to this film, however, may
result from the fact that the two different perceptions
are not clearly established, or too late in the last sequence. Beckett was aware of the difficulty involved here
when he specified in his script that 'throughout first two
parts all perception is E's. E is the camera. But in

third part there is O's perception (O being the protagonist) of the room and contents and at the same time E's
continued perception of O. This poses a problem of
images which I cannot solve without technical help.'
Alan Schneider and Boris Kaufman tried to resolve this
difficulty by following Beckett's own suggestion that
'this difference of quality might perhaps be sought in
different degrees of development, the passage from the one
to the other being from greater to lesser and lesser to
greater definition of luminosity.' Technically this was
not totally successful because the dual perception was
never clearly drawn at the beginning of the film. Though
the 'agony of perceivedness' as expressed by Buster Keaton
and as felt by the viewer represents two separate entities
which converge toward a unified anguish, it remains somewhat gratuitous. Beckett anticipated this when he stated:
'I feel that any attempt to express them [the two separate
perceptions] in simultaneity (composite images, double
frame, superimposition, etc.) must prove unsatisfactory.'

Unable to gain a total view of the character, the spectator is placed in a strained perspective which he cannot
exceed either visually or mentally. Similarly, the actor
himself is restricted both in his movements and actions as
he is forced to remain within the angle of immunity. The
dual perception contained in the eye viewing the object in
flight, and in the object seeking to affirm its own perception of the self, is a limited and anguished vision
which cannot fully apprehend what it sees and what it
seeks. Though Buster Keaton excels in this performance,
particularly since he can only express his perceptual
anguish through the motions of his half-hidden body, his
attempt (and of course that of the director) to have both
visions coincide remains ambiguous. Beckett understood
the problem when he explained in the script that the protagonist is in flight while the viewer is in pursuit, and
that 'it will not be clear until the end of the film that
the pursuing perceiver is not extraneous but the self.'
For the viewer to grasp this requires on his part an unusual effort of acceptance of the camera-eye with the
vision of the protagonist seen objectively and separately
by the same camera-eye. But this is in fact the main
point of this film, or for that matter of all Beckett's
work: to develop in the reader or spectator an extra sense
of perception.

While the man rushes through the first two sequences of
the film (the street and the staircase that lead to the
room) he encounters three other human beings. In the
street he stumbles into an old couple who, upon viewing
his face, react with a fearful expression toward the

camera. A similar reaction of anguish occurs when an old
flower-seller in the staircase sees the protagonist from
the front. It seems then that what the spectator is not
permitted to view causes visual agony for those facing the
other side.

In the room, the protagonist is no longer subjected to
human sight (except of course for the eye of the camera
which, as suggested by the opening shot, is human). He
now enters the field of vision of animals and symbolic
eyes. He is seen by the eyes of a cat, a dog, a parrot,
a gold fish, and symbolically by the eyes of a deity in a
picture on the wall, by the reflection of a mirror, by the
light of the window, and even by two carved holes in the
back of a rocking-chair, which suggest two eyes. Obviously disturbed by these animal and inanimate perceivers,
he feverishly eliminates them one by one. In a stylized
sequence typical of Beckettian comedy, he puts out the cat
and dog, covers the parrot and goldfish with his coat,
closes the curtains, places a blanket over the mirror,
tears the picture on the wall, and then sits down in the
chair thus covering with his back the two eye-like holes.

All this he performs with his back to the camera. However, there remains one last set of eyes which stare at
him from his past, those of the people and of himself at
various stages of life in the old photographs he now examines. These relics of his past existence represent
another perceptual dimension in the film, a kind of play
within the play, or in this case pictures within the picture. In great distress he destroys the photographs, and
seemingly out of sight now of all extraneous perception,
he leans back in the chair to be confronted with his own
inner self, his own inner vision. Projected on the wall
before him appears his own image, seen for the first time
from the front, thus revealing his half-blindness.

The various perceptions which have been established
throughout the film as distinct perspectives are now
gathered into one and interiorized into the protagonist.
This new and concentrated vision results, however, in a
series of blurred images which contrast sharply with the
clarity of the viewer's perception. While the camera and
the spectator have a clear and distinct view, though limited by its angle, the total inner vision of the protagonist is blurred and unprecise. What Beckett suggests here,
and what Boris Kaufman achieves through his excellent
photography, is a visual ambivalence which stresses and
exposes the tragic limitations of external and internal
vision, or as Beckett explains in the introduction of his
script: 'It is a search of non-being in flight from
extraneous perception breaking down in inescapability of

self-perception.'

By exposing the imperfection of the eye, and by reducing the meaning of his plot to self-evidence, Beckett forces the viewer to concentrate on the images themselves, however restricted these may be. But he also uses another device to reinforce his purpose: the absence of sound. The film is silent except for one startling sound which, paradoxically, accentuates the silence. It is a soft 'sssh' spoken in the first sequence by the woman in the couple as she silences her male companion who was about to speak (or scream) when the half-blind protagonist stumbles into them. Forbidden to express his inner reaction in words he stares agonizingly, mouth gaping, into the camera. The same expression appears on the face of the flower-girl, when, unable to express her terror verbally, she transfers this fear to her eyes. The silent spectator in his seat, involved with the images on the screen, is also made to endure the uneasiness and frustration of the situation as he is repeatedly deprived of a clear and full view of the protagonist.

One can conclude, therefore, that the film's purpose is to show the ambiguity of perception, which is shared both by the perceiver and that which is perceived. The perceiver is first represented by the camera-eye and the audience, shifts momentarily to the other three characters in the film, then to the animals, and so on, to become finally the inner vision of the protagonist. Beckett implies by this technique that the 'agony of perceivedness' results from the fact of being seen and yet not being able to apprehend that vision, and, moreover, from seeing and not being able to communicate what is seen. In other words, as with all his other works, Beckett once again exposes not only the limitations of the art form he uses, but also the human limitations.

The novel cannot truly pass for reality, the theater is unable to create believable illusion, and the cinema, which essentially should communicate with the viewer simply through a series of moving images, must rely on sound or other devices to achieve its primary goal. Though it is true that for more than thirty years the cinema did communicate meaning solely through images, and that it is generally agreed that the most powerful and truly cinematic moments are not reliant upon dialogue or sound, nonetheless, most film-makers today ignore the basic communicative power of the image. Too often, in fact, as is the case in experimental films which emphasize photographic manipulation, the images are gratuitous and irrelevant to the whole film. Visual perception alone (as exemplified in 'Film') results in frustration and

failure. This is indeed a paradoxical process of creation, but a process to which Beckett has remained stub-
bornly faithful in his effort to create works of art which
contain their own critical and analytical judgment. As
one of Beckett's own creator-heroes proclaims: to make of
failure 'a howling success.'

'Imagination Dead Imagine' (1965)

[Written in French; published by Éditions de Minuit, Paris, 1965, as 'Imagination morte imaginez'; translated into English by Beckett; published by Calder & Boyars, London, 1965.]

---

61. UNSIGNED REVIEW IN 'TIMES LITERARY SUPPLEMENT'

30 June 1966, 570

In an unusually - where this author is concerned at least - long and informative note, one indeed about half as long as the text itself, on the cover of Mr. Beckett's new work, it is confidently stated that:

> The present short work was conceived as a novel, started as a novel, and in spite of its brevity, remains a novel, a work of fiction from which the author has removed all but the essentials, having first imagined them and created them. It is possibly the shortest novel ever published. It may well be numbered among the greatest.

The book is in fact about 1,500 words in length, so if it is a novel the penultimate statement is certainly true. Of course length may no more be a necessary characteristic of the novel than many other features once thought essential and now held in many quarters to be dispensable. 'Imagination Dead Imagine' certainly describes two people in an imaginary situation and it is equally certainly a work of large implications and of desolate, cruel beauty.

It might not seem so, however, if it had not been apparent
for some time that Mr. Beckett's prose narratives compose
a single, long saga, a saga of exclusion and heroic relin-
quishment as well as of the desperate, perhaps unavailing,
pursuit of finality. 'Islands, water, azure, verdure, one
glimpse and vanished, endlessly, omit', runs the second
sentence.

'Imagination Dead Imagine' creates an image of a small
white rotunda, three feet in height and in diameter,
rising from a flat white plain, in which two bodies, male
and female, lie back to back in the foetal position.
Light comes and goes, being succeeded by intervals of
freezing cold and absolute darkness. The bodies are
alive, as may be seen by holding a mirror in front of
their lips and from the fact that the left eyes open at
intervals and 'gaze in unblinking exposure long beyond
what is humanly possible'. The key sentences, in terms
of what may be discerned about Mr. Beckett's themes from
the rest of his work, appear to be the ironic first: 'No
trace of life anywhere, you say, pah, no difficulty there,
imagination not dead yet, yes, good, imagination dead
imagine'. And the sombre last two:

Leave them there, sweating and icy, there is better
elsewhere. No, life ends and no, there is nothing
elsewhere, and no question now of ever finding again
that white speck lost in whiteness, to see if they
still lie still in the stress of that storm, or of
a worse storm, or in the black dark for good, or the
great whiteness unchanging, and if not what they are
doing.

The first would seem to be Mr. Beckett's usual ironic comment on the fact that fictions are his medium and the last
would seem to suggest not only a conclusion of his saga
but perhaps even a final conclusion about mortality. If
that is the case 'Imagination Dead Imagine' is certainly
an event of importance.

'No's Knife'
(1967)

[Published by Calder & Boyars and subtitled 'Collected
Shorter Prose 1947-1966,' 'No's Knife' includes twenty
pieces, nineteen of which were originally written in
French. The Expelled, The Calmative, The End and the
thirteen Texts for Nothing were first published as
'Nouvelles et Textes pour rien,' 1955; From an Abandoned
Work was first published in 'Trinity News', 1956; Enough
first appeared as 'Assez,' 1966; Imagination Dead Imagine
as 'Imagination morte imaginez,' 1965; and Ping as 'Bing,'
1966. The translations are by Beckett, occasionally in
collaboration with Richard Seaver.]

---

62. CHRISTOPHER RICKS IN 'LISTENER'

3 August 1967, 148-9

Christopher Ricks (b. 1933), Professor of Literature at
Cambridge, is the author of 'Milton's Grand Style' (1963)
and 'Keats and Embarrassment' (1974), and editor of 'The
Poems of Tennyson' (1969). From 1968 to 1975, he was Professor of English at the University of Bristol. He has
reviewed many books by and about Beckett.

'Thanks I suppose, as the urchin said when I picked up his
marbles.' The urchin's murmur (from 'Molloy') shapes
itself by now as the natural reaction to books about Beckett.(1) John Calder - in his exasperating introduction to
his vacuous Festschrift, 'Beckett at Sixty' - has some

words about 'the present flood of Beckett literature'. On
my own shelves, there are now 18 books about Beckett. But
'Beckett at Sixty' doesn't deserve even the urchin's
grudging gratitude. The only two items in it which matter
are some glittering festivities by Hugh Kenner (half exposition, half Expo), and an impassioned paragraph by Harold
Pinter.

John Fletcher's 'Samuel Beckett's Art' deserves more
stress on 'thanks' than on 'I suppose'. It isn't as important as his earlier book, 'The Novels of Samuel Beckett', which tackled with pertinacity the most difficult
and valuable of Beckett's works. But it is scrupulous
and informative (the debt to Dante and to the philosophers; Beckett's mastery of French; the poems and their
allusions), and at least it is not lickspittle.

The three additions to Beckett's own *oeuvre* span more
than 20 years. 'No's Knife' includes the three superb
stories which he wrote in 1945-6: they are Beckett at his
very best, witty, unpredictable, and desperately poignant.
The End is the best possible introduction to Beckett's
fiction. Then there are the 13 'Texts for Nothing', imprisoned because of a conviction that all communication cannot
but be false. Then four fragments, the three bleak ones
listed as Residua - they bring us to 1966, and so to Beckett's recent pitiless depleting of language and situation.
By now Beckett bites off far less than he eschews.

He can be witty about this very fact - his new play,
'Come and Go', can spare only 121 words of dialogue for
its three women moving through their grim permutation-
game, and so Beckett has the grace to call it 'a Dramaticule'. A *tour de force*, but Beckett used to be a dramatist, not a dramaticulist. There is more, though not
enough more, in 'Eh Joe and Other Writings'. 'Eh Joe' is
a television play, with an accusing voice moving in on Joe
in ever harsher close-ups. 'Film' (played by Buster
Keaton) is about the 'anguish of perceivedness' - Keaton
flees from the camera, and from all eyes, but he can't in
the end get away from the 'inescapability of self-perception'. Authoritative and intelligent, both 'Eh Joe' and
'Film' raise to the level of art (minor art) the tensions
and excitements lurking in a weird version of Grand-
mother's Footsteps. 'E [Eye] resumes his cautious approach ... and halts directly in front of O [Object].'

Beckett is still paring away. He would endorse Pater's
creaking cry: 'No surplusage'. But plenty of nonplusage.
As he said in 1938, 'art has nothing to do with clarity,
does not dabble in the clear and does not make clear.'
The hero of the story The Expelled finds mystery reassuring when he comes to ponder his psychological history:

'Poor juvenile solutions, explaining nothing. No need
then for caution, we may reason on to our heart's content,
the fog won't lift.'

Reason on, and strain your ears in the fog - you can
just about hear the murmur of allusions, just about
glimpse the spectral signposts. Beckett is ceaselessly
allusive. But where the literary exhibitionism of his
first fiction, 'More Pricks than Kicks', insisted that the
reader must stoop and pick up the allusions (Shakespeare
Tennyson, Suckling, Keats...), the stratagem of the later
Beckett has been the even more humiliating one of commanding the reader up a cul-de-sac. Alan Schneider (in 'Beckett at Sixty') is confident that the Biblical Ham is 'obviously irrelevant' to 'Endgame'. But *obvious* irrelevance
is precisely what Beckett is never so kind as to provide.
Hamm the hammer, and Clov, Nagg and Nell, all with names
which mean a nail - if you aren't intended to reach towards these significances, then what price coincidence?
Beckett forces upon you a do-it-yourself Tantalus-kit.
He requires you to seek and not to find - it is another of
the frustrations which he puts upon his reader, frustrations some of which have a point.

In 'Come and Go', the three women mention only one
other person: 'Just sit together as we used to, in the
playground at Miss Wade's.' A tantalising hint at Dickens
(praised by Beckett along with Shakespeare in 1929) and
his Miss Wade? She is the lesbian in 'Little Dorrit', who
looked after children and whose life is 'the history of a
self-tormentor'. There is enough aptness about this Miss
Wade for a reader to make towards her - and then not
enough aptness to do anything with. It is a typically
steely Beckett trap.

Staunch men of action like Mr. Schneider (who directed
'Film') don't get trapped. 'Frankly, I didn't spend much
time worrying what all this "meant" or "was about".' So
it is that the middlebrow revenges itself on the highbrow,
by means of a slick travesty of the highbrow's distrust of
paraphrase. Beckett: 'Joyce's writing is not *about* something; *it is that something* itself.'

Harold Pinter is less complacent. He quotes a letter
of his in 1954, praising Beckett: 'he hasn't got his hand
over his heart.' Beckett would like that - he reserved
his bitter contempt for Rilke: 'He cannot hold his emotion.' But just as there are men with not much emotion to
hold, so there's no praise due to him whose hand isn't on
his heart for the reason that he has no heart. Any reader
of Beckett needs to feel convinced that the icy gravity of
style does in fact mask a Swiftian *saeva indignatio*.

Swift has lately been washed and brushed up, and

offered as a decent cleric who valued compromise. There
is something equally preposterous about the institution-
alising of Beckett, the comfortable assimilation, the
pretence that his work isn't really obscure, isn't ever
boring, isn't on the face of it cold and hard. John
Calder achieves the bizarre and demeaning feat of selling
Beckett as a good read: 'Beckett's plots are good, understandable, interesting plots, his situations are believable, his characters quickly become old friends.' One
knows what Beckett thinks of old friends. 'He was kind.
Unfortunately I did not need kindness.'

The crucial question is still the one which Dr Fletcher
fastens on: some of Beckett's readers 'find the fears that
haunt him phantoms'. Many of us think that his fears are
real, that he does indeed 'vent the pent', and that there
is greatness in his exploration of old age, moribundity,
and the dreadful fear of living for ever (the fear that
was at work in Swift's Struldbrugs and in Dante's 'Inferno'). Yet it won't do to pretend that Beckett never rigs
things, whether by design or by obsession. The puerile
coercion of his mimes ('Act Without Words II' is in with
'Eh Joe') has its counterpart in a revealing slip in his
first critical essay in 1929, when he insisted on the
power of Shakespeare's 'fat greasy words':

> Duller shouldst thou be than the fat weed
> That rots itself in death on Lethe wharf.

Shakespeare wrote 'ease', not 'death' - but Beckett
couldn't have that. There is no ease about the rotting
in Beckett. 'For I'm too frightened this evening to
listen to myself rot.'

Is the anguish Beckett's or everybody's? Dr Fletcher
is an excellent exegete, but he ought to leave the polemi-
cal warfare to others:

> William Empson, led astray by his zeal for the right
> cause, publicly complained, in the columns of the
> 'Times Literary Supplement', of the impertinence of
> this Catholic (sic) Irishman who subjected us to the
> unwholesome howls of his religious anguish: he even
> compared him to a dog run over in the street, disturb-
> ing the peace of a suburban night by his indiscreet
> screams of pain.

Dr Fletcher is the one who's astray.(2) Empson never said
anything about Beckett's being a Catholic - he maintained,
truly, that Beckett (like Joyce) has been affected by the
fact that 'in Ireland the religious training of children

is particularly fierce.' And Empson was right 'even' to
compare the anguish to that of a dog with a broken back
('a passer-by can only wish for it to be put out of its
misery'). At any rate, the hero of 'The Unnamable' is
'dumb and howling to be put out of my misery', and toys
wittily with the phrase: 'It's usually with sticks they
put me out of their agony'.

Beckett's inexorable progression is heroic and dispiri-
ting. Dr Fletcher speaks of the 'Texts for Nothing' in
terms of 'vertigo'. Remember Mr Artesian? He hated to
think how many days they added up to, his daily two minutes in the lift:

> So as a final time-saving device he stepped
>   out of the window of his office, which
>   happened to be on the fiftieth floor,
> And one of his partners asked 'Has he
>   vertigo?' and the other glanced out and
>   down and said 'Oh no, only about ten
>   feet more.'

With drama like 'Come and Go', and fiction like 'Ping',
Beckett has only about ten feet more. But how good he is
at falling in slow motion.

Notes

1 Mr Ricks is also reviewing Beckett's 'Come and Go' and
   'Eh Joe,' John Fletcher's 'Samuel Beckett's Art' and
   John Calder's 'Beckett at Sixty.' (Eds)

2 Mr Empson had written in response to a letter published
   the previous week: 'Mr Bagby was quite right, I think,
   to point out the radical ambiguity of "Waiting for
   Godot," but not all ambiguity is good. Here it expresses the sentiment: "We cannot believe in Christianity
   and yet without that everything we do is hopelessly
   bad." Such an attitude seems to be more frequent in
   Irish than either English or French writers, perhaps
   because in Ireland the religious training of children
   is particularly fierce. A child is brought up to believe that he would be wicked and miserable without
   God; then he stops believing in God; then he behaves
   like a dog with its back broken by a car, screaming and
   thrashing on the public road, so that a passer-by can
   only wish for it to be put out of its misery. Surely
   we need not admire this result; the obvious reflection
   is that it was a very unfairly risky treatment to give
   to a child.

"To be sure, we all ought to feel the mystery of the
world, and there is bound to be a kind of literary
merit in any play which makes us feel it so strongly;
but we need not ourselves feel only exacerbated impotence about the world, and if we did we would be certain
to behave badly. "Oh, how I wish I could go to Hell!
Why can't I go to Hell." In itself this peculiar attitude deserves only a rather disgusted curiosity. But
I would hate to suggest a moral censorship against the
play; it is so well done that it is an enlarging experience, very different for different members of the
audience. It would only be dangerous if it was liable
to suck a member into the entire background to be pre-
sumed for the author, and that it cannot do.'
(Letters to the Editor, 'Times Literary Supplement,'
30 March 1956.)   (Eds)

63. DAVID LODGE IN 'ENCOUNTER'

February 1968, 85-9

David Lodge (b. 1935), novelist, critic, Professor of
Literature at Birmingham University. Among his novels
are 'Ginger, You're Barmý' (1962) and 'The British Museum
is Falling Down' (1965); among his critical books are
'The Language of Fiction' (1966) and 'The Novelist at the
Crossroads' (1971).

The enigma of Samuel Beckett's 'Ping' ('Encounter,'
February 1967) derives a special interest from the context
of debate, initiated in these pages by Frank Kermode
(March-April 1966) and carried on by Ihab Hassan (January
1967) and Bernard Bergonzi (May 1967) concerning the contemporary *avant-garde*. Whether fortuitously or not,
'Ping' seems a timely illustrative or testing 'case' for
such critical speculation.
    The speculation is, I take it, concerned basically with
such questions as: is contemporary *avant-garde* literature,
in common with experimental art in other media, making a
much more radical break with 'tradition' than did the
literature and art of what Kermode calls 'paleo-
modernism'? Is it, in effect, seeking the extinction of

literary culture by denying from within the epistemological function of the literary medium itself (*i.e.*, language)? Is it, not literature at all, but 'anti-
literature'? Is it immune to conventional criticism; and
if so, does this demonstrate criticism's impotence, or its
own?

Of the three critics mentioned above, the one who answers these questions in a spirit most sympathetic to radical discontinuity with tradition is Ihab Hassan. The
essential argument of his article The Literature of Silence is that today, 'Literature, turning against itself,
aspires to silence, leaving us with uneasy intimations of
outrage and apocalypse. If there is an *avant-garde* in our
time, it is probably bent on discovery through suicide.'
Beckett is one of Hassan's chief examples:

> Writing for Beckett is absurd play. In a certain
> sense, all his works may be thought of as a parody of
> Wittgenstein's notion that language is a set of games,
> akin to the arithmetic of primitive tribes. Beckett's
> parodies, which are full of self-spite, designate a
> general tendency in anti-literature. Hugh Kenner
> brilliantly describes this tendency when he states:
> 'The dominant intellectual analogy of the present age
> is drawn not from biology, not from psychology ... but
> from general number theory.' Art in a closed field
> thus becomes an absurd game of permutations, like
> Molloy sucking stones at the beach; and 'the retreat
> from the word' (the phrase is George Steiner's) redu-
> ces language to pure ratio.
> Beckett ... comes close to reducing literature to a
> mathematical tautology. The syllogism of Beckett
> assumes that history has spent itself; we are merely
> playing an end game.... Language has become void;
> therefore words can only demonstrate their empti-
> ness.... Thus literature becomes the inaudible game
> of a solipsist.

Professor Hassan must have been gratified by the appearance of 'Ping' in the very next issue of 'Encounter,' for
one of its key-words is *silence*, and in other ways it
appears to confirm his description of Beckett's art.
'Permutation,' for instance, seems an appropriate description of the way language is used in 'Ping': that is, an
unusually limited number of words are repeated to an unusual extent in various combinations. (By 'unusual' I
mean unusual for a piece of literary prose of this
length.) There are only a few words that occur only once
in 'Ping': *brief, hair, nails, scars, torn, henceforth,*

unlustrous. Other words are used at least twice, and most words are used more than twice. The word *white*, which seems to be the most frequently recurring word, is used more than ninety times. Many phrases or word groups are repeated, but rarely an entire sentence. Thus, if the first sentence is divided up into the following word groups:

All known/all white/bare white body fixed/one yard/
legs joined like sewn.

each word group recurs later in the piece, but never with all the other in the same order in a single sentence - always with some modification or addition. Typical variations are:

Bare white body fixed one yard ping fixed elsewhere.
Bare white body fixed one yard ping fixed elsewhere
white on white invisible heart breath no sound.
Bare white one yard fixed ping fixed elsewhere no sound
legs joined like sewn heels together right angle hands
hanging palms front.

It is this kind of repetition with variation that makes 'Ping' so difficult to read, and the label 'anti-literature' a plausible one. Repetition is often a key to meaning in literary discourse, but repetition on this scale tends to defeat the pursuit of meaning. That is, a familiar critical strategy in dealing with narrative prose is to look for some significant pattern of repetition hidden in the variegated texture of the discourse: the variegated texture, by which solidity of specification' is achieved, is woven in a logical, temporal progression, while the pattern of repetition holds the work together in a kind of spatial order and suggests the nature of the overall theme. But in 'Ping' this relationship is inverted: the repetition is far from hidden - it overwhelms the reader in its profusion and disrupts the sense of specificity and of logical, temporal progression. It is extraordinarily difficult to read through the entire piece, short as it is, with sustained concentration. After about forty or fifty lines the words begin to slide and blur before the eyes, and to echo bewilderingly in the ear. This is caused not merely by the elaborate repetition, but also by the meagreness of explicit syntax, the drastic reduction of such aids to communication as punctuation, finite verbs, conjunctions, articles, prepositions and subordination.

All this, then, goes to confirm Hassan's comments; and as

a general account of what Beckett is up to they are no
doubt fair enough. But I must confess to finding something unsatisfactory about this kind of critical response.
I don't see, for instance, how it could help us to distinguish between one piece by Beckett and another, except as
progressive - or regressive - steps towards silence. If
the sole object of the game is to expose the limitations
of language by a bewildering permutation of words, it
wouldn't matter what particular words were used, or what
their referential content was. But I think that the more
closely acquainted we become with 'Ping' the more certain
we become that it does matter what words are used, and
that they refer to something more specific than the futility of life or the futility of art. Beckett is telling
us 'about' something; and if the telling is extraordinarily difficult to follow this is not simply because all
experience is difficult to communicate (though this is
true) but because this experience is difficult to communicate in *this* particular way.

It would be dishonest to make this assertion without going
on to suggest what 'Ping' is about. What follows doesn't
pretend to be a definitive or exclusive reading, but its
tentativeness differs only in degree from the tentativeness imposed on the critic by any complex literary work.
    I suggest that 'Ping' is the rendering of the con-
sciousness of a person confined in a small, bare, white
room, a person who is evidently under extreme duress, and
probably at the last gasp of life. He has no freedom of
movement: his body is 'fixed,' the legs are joined together, the heels turning at right angles, the hands
hanging palms front; the 'heart breath' make 'no sound'.
'Only the eyes only just...' - can we say, *move*? There
are parts of the room he cannot see, and he evidently
can't move his head to see them, though he thinks there is
'perhaps a way out' there.
    The first words of the piece are 'all known,' and this
phrase recurs. But the 'all' that is 'known' is severely
limited and yields 'no meaning' though the narrator is reluctant to admit this: 'perhaps a meaning'. 'Ping' seems
to record the struggles of an expiring consciousness to
find some meaning in a situation which offers no purchase
to the mind or to sensation. The consciousness makes
repeated, feeble efforts to assert the possibility of
colour, movement, sound, memory, another person's presence, only to fall back hopelessly into the recognition
of colourlessness, paralysis, silence, oblivion, solitude.
This rhythm of tentative assertion and collapse is marked
by the frequently recurring collocation 'only just almost
never'.

By colourlessness I mean the predominance of white,
which is no colour, or at least the 'last colour'. The
shining white planes of walls, floor and ceiling, the
whiteness of his own body, make it difficult for the
person to see more than 'traces, blurs, signs'. The
attempt to assert colour - black, rose, light blue, light
grey - nearly always fades into an admission that it is
really 'almost white,' 'white on white,' is 'invisible,'
has 'no meaning':

Traces blurs light grey almost white on white.
Traces blurs signs no meaning light grey almost white.
Traces alone unover given black light grey almost white
on white.
Traces alone unover given black grey blurs signs no
meaning light grey almost white always the same.

Aural experience is equally meagre. There is 'silence
within'. These words are followed by 'Brief murmurs';
but the murmurs are immediately qualified by 'only just
almost never'. However, the next 'murmur' is associated
with the speculation 'perhaps not alone'. A little later
there is another perhaps-phrase, again associated with
'murmur':

Ping murmur perhaps a nature one second almost never
that much memory almost never.

This is a particularly interesting and tantalising sentence. What does 'a nature' mean? A human nature? His
own, or another's? It seems to be associated with memory,
anyway, and memory with meaning, for a few lines later we
get: 'Ping murmur only just almost never one second
perhaps a meaning that much memory almost never.'

Towards the close of the piece I think there are more
definite indications that the character's search for meaning and grasp on life are connected with some effort of
memory, some effort to recall a human image, and thus
break out of total impotence and solitude:

Ping perhaps not alone one second with image same time
a little less dim eye black and white half closed long
lashes imploring that much memory almost never.

'Long lashes imploring' is the most human touch, the most
emotive phrase, in the entire piece. It deviates sharply
from the linguistic norms which have been set up, and
which project a generally de-humanised version of

experience. It therefore has a strong impact, and this is
reinforced by other features of the sentence. The 'image'
is 'a little less dim.' We have met the phrase 'a little
less' before, but not with 'dim' - it is as if only now
can the consciousness complete the phrase it has been
struggling to formulate. The eye is 'black and white' -
it is not black fading into light grey, into almost white,
into white on white.

This sentence, then, seems to mark the apex of the
character's effort at memory. It is 'Afar flash of time,'
but short-lived: almost immediately it is swamped by the
despairing sequence:

> all white all over all of old ping flash white walls
> shining white no trace eyes holes light blue almost
> white last colour ping white over.

The next two sentences also end with the word *over*, as
does the whole piece. *Over*, which makes its first appearance in line 83, seems to echo the curious nonce-word
unover which presumably means 'not over,' and is invariably preceded by the word *alone*, for example: 'Traces
alone unover given black light grey almost white on white.'
Such sentences, which occur mainly in the first half of
the text, seem to define the very limited sense in which
experience is on-going, 'not over'; but after the vision
or image of the eye with 'long lashes imploring' the emphasis shifts to the idea that experience is finished,
over. The formula 'that much memory almost never' is
changed to 'that much memory *henceforth* never' in line
124. The image of the eye recurs unexpectedly in the last
two lines of the piece, with the addition of the word
unlustrous - a word rather striking in itself, and notable
for occurring only this once in 'Ping,' thus giving a
further specificity to the 'eye black and white half-
closed long lashes imploring.' But this seems to be the
last effort of the consciousness - the sentence continues
and ends, 'ping silence ping over.' The image or vision
is over, consciousness is over, the story is over.

I have implied that the black and white eye (singular)
is not one of the character's own eyes, which are, I
think, the ones referred to throughout the passage (in
the plural) as being light blue or grey, tending to the
overall condition of whiteness. This black eye with the
lashes is, I suggest, someone else's eye, part of some
emotional and human connection which the character is
struggling to recall through memory. The effort to do so
is only successful to a very limited extent, and exhausts
him, perhaps kills him: 'ping silence ping over.'

I can't offer any confident explanation of the word *ping*
itself. On the referential level it might denote the
noise emitted by some piece of apparatus, perhaps marking
the passage of time (there are repeated references to
'one second,' though the *pings* do not occur at regular
intervals). On the level of connotation, *ping* is a feeble,
pathetic, unresonant, irritating, even maddening sound,
making it an appropriate enough title for this piece,
which it punctuates like the striking of a triangle at
intervals in the course of a complicated fugue.

The above commentary is based on some introductory remarks
made by the present writer to a discussion of 'Ping' by
some members of the English Department at Birmingham University.(1) My remarks were followed by the independently
prepared comments of a linguist, whose descriptive analysis of the structure of the piece was in general accord
with my own (though it corrected some rash assertions I
had made). I shall try to do justice to the main points
of this linguistic commentary in a general account of the
discussion as a whole.
     In this discussion there was inevitably a good deal of
conflict, but on the whole the measure of agreement was
more striking. A minority of the participants were inclined to think that 'Ping' was indeed a language game, a
verbal construct cunningly devised to yield an infinite
number of interpretations - and therefore, in effect,
resistant to interpretation. It could be about a man
having a bath or a shower or a man under rifle fire or a
man being tortured; *ping* might be the sound of a bullet
ricochetting, or the sound of water dripping or the sound
of a bell, and the bell might be a bicycle bell or a sanc-
tus bell or a typewriter bell (perhaps the writer's own
typewriter bell). But the majority were disposed to find
'Ping' more specifically meaningful, to see it as the
rendering of a certain kind of experience, and as having
a perceptible design. While it might not be possible to
agree on a formulation of the experience more precise than
the effort of a consciousness to assert its identity in
the teeth of the void, the verbal medium was operating
selectively to induce a much more finely discriminated
range of effects than that formulation suggested. Considered as a whole, in isolation, the piece satisfied the
traditional aesthetic criteria of *integritas, consonantia,*
and *claritas*.(2) At the same time it had an obvious continuity with the rest of Beckett's work, and to consider
it in relation to his whole *oeuvre* would be the next logical step in interpretation.
     The two main points of dispute, and the ones where I

feel my own reading of 'Ping' to have been most inadequate, concerned the possibility of some allusion to Christ, and the significance of the word *ping* itself.

As to the first, it was pointed out that there are a number of words and phrases reminiscent of the passion and death of Christ: 'legs joined like sewn,' 'hands hanging palms front' are vaguely evocative of the Crucifixion; 'seam like sewn invisible' suggests the cloak without a seam. More striking is this passage:

> Given rose only just nails fallen white over. Long hair fallen white invisible over. White scars invisible same white as flesh torn of old given rose only just.

The words *nails, hair, scars, flesh, torn,* belong to that (in 'Ping') rare class that occur only once, and their clustering together here might well be designed to alert us to an interpretative clue. For a dizzy moment we entertained the possibility that the whole piece might be a bleakly anti-metaphysical rendering of the consciousness of the dying Christ - Christ in the tomb rather than Christ on the Cross (hence the cramped, cell-like room) - in short, Beckett's version of 'The Man Who Died.' But this reading seemed not only to leave much unexplained, but to be impoverishing; for the piece doesn't read like a riddle to which there is a single answer. However, the possibility of some allusion to Christ cannot, I think, be discounted.

Discussion about the significance of the word *ping* polarised around those who, like myself, regarded it as a noise external to the discourse, which it punctuated at arbitrary intervals, a noise so meaningless as not to enter into the murmur/silence dichotomy, the most meaningless item, in fact, in the character's field of perception; and on the other hand those who regarded it as part of the discourse, as having some conceptual content or as being an ironic, or movingly pathetic, substitute or code-word for some concept that cannot be fully and openly entertained, such as God (*cf*. 'Godot'). Thus the sentence 'Ping elsewhere always there only known not' becomes almost lucid if you replace *Ping* with *God*; and it is interesting to note that this is one of the rare sentences that recur in exactly the same form.

Strengthening this case that *ping* is part of the discourse, or stream of consciousness, rather than an arbitrary intrusion from outside, is the fact that it is associated with a selective number of other words and phrases.

Thus, going through the piece and noting the words which immediately follow the word *ping*, we get the following pattern:

```
ping fixed elsewhere
ping fixed elsewhere
ping fixed elsewhere
Ping murmur
ping murmur
ping silence
Ping murmur
Ping murmur
ping elsewhere
Ping elsewhere
ping murmur
ping fixed elsewhere
Ping murmurs
Ping perhaps a nature
ping perhaps way out
ping silence
Ping perhaps not alone
ping silence
Ping image
Ping a nature
ping a meaning
ping silence
ping fixed elsewhere
Ping elsewhere
Ping perhaps not alone
ping flash
ping white over
Ping fixed last elsewhere
ping of old
Ping of old
ping last murmur
ping silence
ping over
```

This doesn't look like random occurrence. *Ping* tends to be followed by words or phrases which suggest the possibility of some other presence or place: *fixed elsewhere, murmur, image, perhaps a nature, perhaps a way out, perhaps not alone, etc*. It is natural, I think, to look first at the words and phrases which follow *ping*, for if it has a quasi-grammatical status it would appear to be that of a subject - it is, for instance, often the first word of a sentence. If we look at the words and phrases which immediately precede *ping* we get, in fact, a sequence which is no less patterned, but it is interesting that

these words and phrases are mostly of a quite different
order; they tend to stress the bleak limitations of the
character's situation and field of perception: *bare white
body fixed, invisible, never seen, almost never,* are among
the most frequently recurring. We might suggest that *ping*
marks the intervals between the oscillating movements of
the character's consciousness from dull despair to tentative hope; though this leaves open the question of whether
it is part of the discourse, or an intrusion from outside
which stimulates thought in a mechanical and arbitrary
way.

I should note, finally, the ingenious suggestion that
ping alludes to the parlour game 'Ping Pong' which assumes
that all words and concepts can be placed in one of two
great categories, 'Ping' and 'Pong.' Thus, for example,
white is Ping and *black* is Pong; and Beckett's piece is
the account of a man inhabiting a Ping world, struggling
feebly to reach out to or recover a Pong world.

The above discussion, needless to say, leaves much unexplained or in doubt (a phrase which particularly puzzles
me is 'blue and white in the wind'). But it does not suggest, I think, that 'Ping' is not, as it appears at first
sight, totally impenetrable and meaningless. The important point was made in the course of our discussion that
the piece *has* got a syntax: it is rudimentary, but it does
control the possible range of meaning. It would be perverse, for instance, to read the first sentence grouping
the words in this way:

All/known all white bare/white body fixed one/yard
legs/joined like/sewn.

The piece draws on the principles of a shared language,
especially the principle of word order. ('Ping' itself
is the most ambiguous word in the text precisely because
it is the one least defined by any referential or structural function in ordinary usage.) Though these principles
are drastically modified, they are never abandoned. A
good deal of logical organisation persists, as can be demonstrated by reading the text backwards and measuring the
loss of sense.

If Beckett were really writing anti-literature, it
wouldn't matter whether we read the text backwards or forwards, from left to right or from right to left. Of
course, terms like 'anti-literature' and 'literature of
silence' are rhetorical paradoxes aimed to suggest a radical degree of innovation: they are not to be taken literally. But they can have the effect of deterring us from

engaging closely with a text like 'Ping.' To confirm Professor Hassan's comments on Beckett, it is not necessary to give 'Ping' more than a quick, superficial glance. If the object of the exercise is merely to baffle our intelligences and cheat our conventional expectations, why should we bother to do more? But if we do bother to do more, the rewards are surprisingly great. 'Ping' proves, after all, not to be totally resistant to methods of critical reading derived from conventional literature. Its language is not void; its words do not merely demonstrate their emptiness. It is, like any literary artefact, a marriage of form and meaning.

Notes

1   The other participants were: Miss Vera Adamson, K.M. Green, T.P. Matheson, Mrs. Joan Rees, I.A. Shapiro, T.A. Shippey, G.T. Shepherd, J.M. Sinclair, H.A. Smith, S.W. Wells and M. Wilding. This article is published with their kind permission, but it does not pretend to give a full or faithful record of their contributions to the discussion. It is highly selective and based on imperfect memory, and for this reason I have not attributed opinions to individuals.
2   Using these terms in the senses defined by Graham Hough in his 'An Essay on Criticism' (1966), pp. 17-19.

Beckett awarded the Nobel Prize for Literature

(1969)

64. UNSIGNED ARTICLES IN 'THE TIMES'

24-5 October 1969, 1, 3

Stockholm, Oct. 23. - The Irish-born playwright, Samuel Beckett, acknowledged as one of the greatest living dramatists for his pioneering of new modes of theatrical expression, was today awarded the 1969 Nobel Prize for literature.

A leading candidate for the award for many years, the controversial 63-year-old writer, who has lived in Paris since 1937, will receive 375,000 Swedish crowns (about £30,000).

In its criticism the Swedish Academy said Mr. Beckett was being honoured for writing which, in new forms for the novel and drama, acquired its elevation in the destitution of modern man.

Human degradation, loneliness and despair are current themes in Beckett's sombre works, particularly his plays, of which 'Waiting for Godot,' written in one month in 1952, brought him instant recognition after more than 20 years as a relatively obscure poet and novelist. - Reuters.

Tunis. Oct. 23. - Mr. Beckett was believed cut off from journalists and photographers today by floodwaters isolating southern Tunisia. He was last reported in the Hotel Riadh in the small town of Nabeul, but the hotel manager said in answer to a telephone call today that he had left on an excursion.

Those who know the writer's aversion to the press said it was not impossible he was using a ruse to throw reporters off his trail.

Paris. Oct. 24. - Samuel Beckett will accept his Nobel Prize for literature but will not go to Stockholm to receive it, his literary agent predicted today.

Mr. Jerome Lindon, agent and long-time friend of the Irish playwright, said that Mr. Beckett and his wife were going into hiding to avoid any publicity brought by the award. Mr. Lindon, who had talked to Mrs. Beckett on the telephone, added: 'Both of them were distressed by the announcement that Samuel had won the prize.' Mrs. Beckett had described it as a 'catastrophe.'

65. ANDRÉ MARISSEL IN 'NOUVELLES LITTÉRAIRES'

30 October 1969, 12-14

André Marissel (b. 1928), French poet and critic, wrote the first book on Beckett published in France (1963).

Samuel Beckett's position, which we continue to wonder about, is extremely paradoxical: here is a writer who shuns crowds and who, since the appearance of 'Waiting for Godot,' has attracted and moved millions around the world; here is a man who has never claimed to be 'writing for his time' and whom we feel is none the less very representative of our time; finally here is an ironic adversary of hierarchies, official rites and well-established society, suddenly overwhelmed by honors and punished, so to speak, for his natural modesty and self-effacement by the jury awarding the Nobel Prize. According to the Beckettian outlook, that is just one more calamity to bear and, since precisely 'nothing is funnier than unhappiness, its the funniest thing in the world,' the moment seems well-chosen to let oneself laugh. Today no one can any longer escape the gaze or the intervention of others; even hidden cameras exist. Consequently, Samuel Beckett seems to be torn away from his world of loners, weaklings, and victims, to undergo a punishment he hadn't yet explored or described; so true it is that indeed the spectacular dominates everything in 1969: the arrival of the astronauts on the Moon or the attribution of a prize to an author, the arrest of a suspect or a religious ceremony of Australian aborigines....

But, suspending all stupefaction, can't we infer that, well before a dated event such as the Nobel Prize, Samuel Beckett imprudently exposed himself to the 'hénaurmes' fantasies of his time? Very quickly he was classified among the playwrights and novelists of the absurd, and as far as we know, he hasn't stopped publishing. Stemming from this consent, for that is what it is, it seems he has authorized his contemporaries to recognize themselves and thereby detest themselves in his multiple anti-heroes, in his gnawing and rusty speech; and then to produce systems of explanation *ad infinitum*. To refrain momentarily from falling into this, after all, excusable mania, it is necessary to retain the very first impression felt; a reality is thus revealed: a Kafkaesque work bursting from the silence but without rupturing it; a written anomaly appearing as plays and narratives....

However, and this is the drawback to looking for such links, haven't we risked underestimating (by designating Kafka as his precursor) the originality of the Irishman compared to the immense and devouring originality of the Czech? Samuel of Dublin has not copied the writer from Prague in every detail. More deprived, more desperate, and more contorted than the unforgettable Joseph K., he is, because of this asocial wordiness, nihilist banter personified. He does not rebel, as Céline's Bardamu does; he merely laments the way things are. And distrusting ready-made ideas, he refrains from declaring 'Hell is other people' or 'Man is a useless passion' (Sartre). In other words, 'The glutton castaway, the drunkard in the desert' (including Antoine Roquentin, in spite of his nausea) are 'the happy ones'! Murmuring, talking nonsense, spitting, defecating, 'to hunger, thirst, lust every day afresh and every day in vain, after the old prog, the old booze, the old whores, that's the nearest we'll ever get to felicity, the new porch and the very latest garden.' ('Watt')

What a strange happiness found in the daily justification of the logic of decay and of 'aboulic' coherence. For there can no longer be any doubt that in Samuel Beckett's work repetition, re-examination, and stammering make possible the transformation of fundamental and virulent dissatisfaction into a semblance of satisfaction. This is in no way progress; it is more likely a decoy and a regression. In a comparable way Murphy's, Molloy's, Moran's and Malone's (the famous Ms) quest for the absolute degenerated into wandering, then changed into paralysis (the stomping in place of the characters in 'Godot') as if ideal existence was that of an infant dependent on and prisoner of its mother and not the birth into liberty and

individual responsibility. In any case, the roads taken
by the sub-human Beckettian men lead nowhere.

Emaciated and dehumanized these beings condemned never
to die find themselves the same as they were on the day
of the malediction and expulsion. Half-conscious although
very rational they end up crawling in the mud, shutting
themselves up in ashbins and listening to their unceasing
monotonous voices to the point of being mesmerized. Who
are they? Tapes on a tape-recorder ('Krapp's Last Tape')
unwinding without interruption during some sort of shadow
show. Between the spectre of their bodies and their speech
there is no link; they evolve or doze off separated from
others and from themselves, mortified, dazed like yogis or
drug addicts. Who condemned them to internal delusion, to
senility and to the use of tranquilizers? By what aberra-
tion, as soon as we take an interest in their destiny, do
they flee or throw themselves on the 'aggressor'?

Broken, demolished, weakened, hollowed out, they inevitably send us back to those expressions which, however, do
not help at all to define them: lifelong guilt, impotence,
suffocation, mystical delirium..., their universe is one
of destitution. The survivors of an atomic catastrophe
would have risen against the ills conspiring against them,
whose origin at least they could understand; deportees
would have dreamt of escape or suicide. But 'Beckettians'
are no more informed about the causes of their disintegration than we are about the 'Martians' - and they don't
want to make any effort to understand.

An addition, being neither *homo sapiens* nor *homo faber*,
they refuse to be caught in the play of a finalism that
Beckett as a disillusioned Puritan challenges. On the
contrary they dream of an implacable determinism. However, when they dare to think about the concepts of *pain*
and of *fault*, they wish to undergo a torture as vast as
the sin that they are convinced they must eternally expiate. If necessary they try to invent this monstrous sin.
Beggars, and at best scavengers or guards in insane asy-
lums, they are hardly suited to their work; their true
form and substance is that of galley-worms, wood lice,
vile worms and bedbugs. In other words man with or without a capital 'M' no longer exists since he finally admits
his resemblance to refuse, invading diptera, filterable
viruses, and amoebae:

> you are there somewhere alive somewhere vast stretch
> of time then it's over you are there no more alive
> no more then again you are there again alive again it
> wasn't over an error you begin again all over more or
> less in the same place....

So I went in the atrocious brightness buried in my
old flesh straining towards an issue and ... my mind
panting after this and that and always flung back to
where there was nothing ('How It Is')

Obviously Beckett, who does not spare himself, has more
than ever sunk into fable, quasi-intolerable farce, and
symbolic narrative and monologue. His 'consortium of
tyrants' with scandalous bestiality, his morbid senile
nonentities do not only contrast with normal beings; they
are the very opposite of priests and missionaries, of
nurses, of generous and talkative militants, of devoted
young servants, of wise children to whom he applies the
burning poultice of a humor beyond measure. 'Of all
laughter,' he affirms, '(which strictly speaking does not
exist at all but rather stems from hooting) in my opinion
only three types are worth considering namely, bitter
laughter, forced laughter and joyless laughter.' Now
these three types are in fact only one: a tragic destructive laughter corresponding to a strong feeling of venge-
ful baseness and implying a familiarity of the torturer
toward his victim. Thus 'crucified' Beckett's Malones,
Watts, Estragons, Luckys, Hamms or Clovs await the *coup de
grâce* which, laughing, we will give them. They wait until
the moment when triumphing in turn over us and Beckett
they will become a mockery of our own laughter. The
bursting of our individuality in a sort of 'last squawk.'

Samuel Beckett's humor finally seems to be one of the
keys, as well as the most modern element, of a body of
work whose atemporal character cannot be denied. Anouilh
was right when he said, after having applauded 'Waiting
for Godot,' that it was like a 'sketch of Pascal's "Pensées" played by the Fratellinis.' But strangely, the
intellectual aspect does not push away the topical and
momentary; it includes and surpasses it. Beckett is current reality itself, the sum of the dangers that weigh on
us like the sky weighed upon Asterix our ancestor. There
was no need for the 1969 Nobel Prize winner to mention
electronic machinery or nuclear fission, air pollution or
nervous depression, cancer, infarct, genocide or the disappearance of certain animal species. But reading his
books one thinks of all those things incessantly. Didn't
Murphy, the first known 'Beckettian' cry out: 'For every
symptom that is eased, another is made worse.'

[Translated by Larysa Mykyta and Mark Schumacher]

'Mercier and Camier'
(1970)

[Written in French in 1946; published by Éditions de
Minuit, Paris, 1970; translated into English by Beckett;
published by Calder & Boyars, London, and Grove Press,
New York, 1974.]

---

66.   JACQUELINE PIATER IN 'MONDE'

13 June 1970, 1, book section

Jacquline Piatier is literary editor of 'Le Monde.'   She
also writes a regular column for the weekly literary
pages of 'Le Monde' and has often written about Beckett's works.

Like late-blooming flowers, delayed by some unknown dissatisfaction or indifference of the author, two early
works by Samuel Beckett have just been published, his
first novel (1946) written in French, 'Mercier and
Camier,' and a short story, First Love, which should be
compared, at least as to its date (1945), with those contained in the collection 'Texts for Nothing.'   After the
schematic writings of recent years, in which the image is
contracted to the point of becoming a hard symbolic kernel, we find here the pre-Beckett Beckett, prodigal with
his talents and trusting to the word to depict the same
derisory caricature of man and existence.
  'Mercier and Camier' anticipates 'Godot' in novel form.
Two men, not unmitigated tramps, but worn out with age,

boredom, and physical infirmities, decide to leave the
town they live in and go on a journey that will perhaps
give some meaning to their lives. Encumbered by their
baggage - the heavy paraphernalia that will become the
perfect panoply of the Beckett hero - knapsack, umbrella,
bicycle, and greatcoat, which they lose, attempt to find,
then abandon, they get no further than the nearby suburbs, return to the city and part company. Even this
early book is written entirely in dialogues interrupted
by a few rain-drenched urban and rural landscapes.
Representation of the world, of society, is broken up into
various encounters, and not yet reduced, as in 'Godot,' to
the lone apparition of Lucky and Pozzo. Moving from the
earlier to the later work, everything is gradually pared
away, concentrated, made more rigorous in construction.
But in this first narrative, which ambles and meanders
along at the whim of a less constrained imagination, the
author's vaudevillian talent appears more clearly than
ever, along with that bitter, often scatological humor
which makes a joke, as though for decency's sake, out of
the desperate futility of everything.
     The voice rising from the story is the same one we will
hear later on, telling itself, questioning itself, cor-
recting itself, in 'Molloy' and 'The Unnamable.' It does
not yet stammer and its short steady sentences fall like
acid tears. This simple and banal story, of a liaison
which begins with the death of a father and ends at the
birth of a son, tells of the shabby temptation of love and
its horrifying result in procreation. A parody of romance,
playing upon the macabre, the sordid, the grotesque, and
yet as heart-rending as a lament. This is some of Beckett's most beautiful writing, less laden with tenderness
than 'Happy Days' or 'Enough,' but bitter-sweet, like an
ironic dissonance.

[Translated by Jean M. Sommermeyer]

67. A. ALVAREZ IN 'OBSERVER'

6 October 1974, 30

A. Alvarez (b. 1929) has written a novel, 'Hers' (1974), a
study of suicide, 'The Savage God' (1972), and hundreds of
essays and reviews on contemporary literature, several of

which are collected in 'Beyond All This Fiddle' (1968).
His volume on Beckett appeared in the Modern Masters
series in 1973.

It has always been a puzzle to understand how Beckett,
when he had published so little and in such a mannerist
way, could suddenly have produced, as if out of thin air,
a theatrical masterpiece like 'Waiting for Godot.'

Part of the answer is to be found in 'Mercier and
Camier,' written in 1946 but suppressed by the author
until 1970, when it appeared in Paris, and now translated
by him into English. It was the first novel he produced
after he made his crucial decision to get out from under
the weight of Irish rhetoric by abandoning English and
writing, for the next ten years at least, exclusively in
French. The pity is that he has held it back for so long,
since it is a good deal more accessible than 'Watt,' its
dementedly obsessed predecessor, or the increasingly despairing and obscure trilogy which followed.

Like everything of Beckett's up until that time, the
writing is excessively elegant and high-toned, with a
pausing, almost chanting rhythm to the prose and great
shows of mock pedagogy: every two chapters are followed by
a prim, misleading synopsis. As usual, there is no plot
to speak of. The two heroes meet and, after much hesitation, set off on a vague journey which only twice manages
to get them briefly clear of town. They spend a good deal
of time in bars and with a friendly prostitute called
Helen. They kill a policeman, although the synopsis
omits to mention the fact. They curse God and their
various ailments and indulge in a little metaphysics.

Finally, they drift apart and are brought together again
only at the close by Watt, making a useful guest appearance from his previous incarnation in Becketts' oeuvre.
The three of them chat briefly but knowledgeably about
Murphy, the hero of Beckett's first novel. Every so often,
the author himself butts in with comments on his cast and
his style: -

> They advanced into the sunset (you can't deny yourself
> everything), burning up the sky higher than the highest
> roofs.
> A pity Dumas the Elder cannot see us, said Watt.
> Or one of the Evangelists, said Camier.
> A different class, Mercier and Camier, for all their
> faults.

In short, a comedy of high style, terser and, I think,
funnier than any of his other novels.

No doubt the Beckett industry will feed the book gratefully into its insatiable machines. After all, Mercier
and Camier are the prototypes of the twin heroes of the
next novel, Molloy and Moran: there are phrases later
echoed in the plays and bits and bobs which reappear in
the prose; there are the inevitable physical weariness
and spiritual despair, and chaste, beautiful fragments of
description, also inevitable but always unexpected. And
so on. But the core of the novel, of its sustaining
interest and wit, is the dialogue: -

> Your health, sir. He said.
> Pledge it, pledge it, said Mr. Conaire, none deserves
> it more. And rosebud here, he said, would she deign
> to clink with us?
> She's married, said George, and mother of three.
> Fie upon you! cried Mr. Conaire. How can one say
> such things!
> You're being stood a port, said George
> Teresa moved behind the bar.
> When I think what it means, said Mr. Conaire. The
> torn flesh! The pretty crutch in tatters! The
> screams! The blood! The glair! The afterbirth!
> He put his hand before his eyes. The afterbirth!
> he groaned.
> All the best, said Teresa.

'Godot' was still more than two years away, but in
'Mercier and Camier' the authentic dramatic gifts are
already present; above all, the ability to keep the dialogue two jumps ahead of itself and to sustain a train of
thought over the intervening chasms of chat. He also had
the two characters he needed for his great masterpiece,
and their peculiar mixture of vaudeville and melancholia.
All he had to do then was pare away the inessentials,
freeze the action and reach down into that black core of
boredom and despair that is at the centre of all his work.
It took great genius to do that, but now the novel is at
last available we know where he started from.

68.   CHRISTOPHER RICKS IN 'SUNDAY TIMES'

13 October 1974, 36

Beckett finished 'Mercier et Camier,' his first extended
work in French, in 1946. He cannibalised it for 'Waiting
for Godot,' among other things, and then reluctantly published it in French in 1970. And here now is his witty
vigilant translation of it - or rather, re-creation,
since he has tightened it, given much of it a new tone,
and cut out a great deal. (Including some of the most
Beckettish preoccupations, such as a quotation from Dante
and a reference to Sordello.)

The French text has long been known to scholars and it
figures in most of their books. Mercier and Camier are
what Beckett himself calls a pseudocouple (symbiotic, like
fungoid and algoid in lichen, to use his own example).
'As one man' is the recurrent phrase for their doings,
which are an inversion of 'Waiting for Godot': instead of
a pointless waiting, there is a pointless quest. Two
successive questions which they asked themselves were:

    Did what they were looking for exist?
    What were they looking for?

There are the usual Beckett lost properties: sack, bicycle, permutation-games, the longing to be dead, and
casual murder, as well as interlopers from others of his
novels, such as Watt and Murphy.

Beckett once spoke of it as 'a dreadful book,' and
probably it mostly is. At any rate, it is strictly, if
that is the word, for Beckettomanes. And yet it does have
some of his great jokes.

    Do you feel like singing? said Camier.
    Not to my knowledge, said Mercier.

Pure Irish, in that you can't tell whether it is insanely
maladroit or on to something eerily profound. (To God's
knowledge? Or to a psychiatrist's? Who else might have
such knowledge?)

Beckett's translation, with great ingenuity, variety
and beauty, irishes the whole thing. Not just so that we
now hear of 'the denizens of Dublin's fair city,' but
through these juddering Irish bulls. 'Speak up,' said
Mercier, 'I'm not deaf' (where the French has just 'Parle
plus fort, dit Mercier, je n'entends rien'). 'He had felt

even worse, he was in one of his better days' ('Il ne se
sentait pas trop mal...'). 'I was only going to embrace
you,' said Camier. 'I'll do it some other time, when
you're less yourself, if I think of it' (the French
doesn't have that beautifully gloomy reversal of 'when
you're more yourself,' but just 'quand tu seras mieux').
Or this: 'Seen from outside it was a house like any other.
Seen from inside too. And yet it emitted Camier.' (The
French just has '...Camier en sortit.')

A prodigal demented book, on the whole, and yet it has
so many woebegone felicities of phrasing that we had
better rest lugubriously content with its own words:
'Blow, blow, thou ill wind.'

'The Lost Ones' (1970)

[Written in French; published as 'Le Dépeupleur' by Editions de Minuit, Paris; translated into English by Beckett; published by Grove Press, New York, and Calder & Boyars, London, 1972.]

69.   ANNE FABRE-LUCE IN 'QUINZAINE LITTÉRAIRE'

1 and 15 March 1971

Anne Fabre-Luce (b. 1929), critic and Professor of Literature at the University of Paris, Nanterre, is a regular contributor to the 'Quinzaine littéraire.'

Running counter to the most general trend of contemporary literature - with the exception perhaps of the latest experiments of the German avant-garde - Beckett's writing tends toward a most rigorous concision: instead of starting, as does the school of the *Nouveau Roman,* from a kind of general 'IS-NESS' from which the infinitely varied descriptions of the world can be derived, Beckett heads toward this infinitely general 'IS-NESS,' the reduction of all discourse, which only silence can follow. Against the 'say-more' of all literature, he opposes a systematic 'say-less' which manages to summarize and contain all the other 'proliferating' forms of literary discourse.

'The Lost Ones' presents (in this writing we could call indefinitely 'Penult') the last possible stages of what is 'human,' the last currents of useless passion which agitate man before his last great sleep; before the return to an inorganic state, of a body which man has been dragging, and which in turn has been dragging him, since the expulsion from Eden.

With Beckett, the end is ordered - if that were possible - and the final shipwreck becomes the object of a production conceived only because it is impossible to stage. It is a question of representing the 'unthinkable end,' of detailing its visual representation, of *making visible* the progressively growing dimness which must blind all the 'seers' still tortured by conscience. In the 'hypothesis' that Beckett has chosen, this end takes the form of the crepuscular rites indulged in by some two hundred naked bodies contained in a giant cylinder. This cylinder is 'vast enough for search to be in vain. Narrow enough for flight to be in vain.' These bodies condemned to death - and to life - are, even more so, condemned to an impossible quest for some absent mythic divinity of whom they feel they have been deprived. Whence the incessant maneuvers of the bodies who climb ladders (symbolic of course) to reach inaccessible niches which can lead to 'secret' passages opening out on to 'nature's sanctuaries.'

Such is the human microcosm whose 'activities' Beckett governs as in a ballet of phantoms whose end must remain uncertain - since this end is linked to the 'value' of the working hypothesis thus proposed.

In this theater of the (possible) agony of the world, the beings are indistinguishable one from the other, except for what is left of their useless belief in the 'secret' myths of intelligibility or of 'truth.' Their vague yet eager attempts at mating, in order to perpetuate the anonymous survival of the species, are accompanied by the vain desire to once again attain the inaccessible knowledge locked away in the minds of the blind seers.

What we must admire most in 'The Lost Ones,' this metaphor of finitude, is no doubt the surprising union of the singular and the general. Beckett orchestrates the general through his very precise use of the particular: the laws constraining the movements of the bodies for instance, the interdictions weighing upon certain gestures, constitutes essentially representable, concrete elements, and yet, the details seem to be drawn toward the general, as if under the effect of a mysterious magnetization, that of non-signification. The essence of Beckett's art is found in this fundamental propensity of a punctual, intensely singular discourse, whose most minute detail can be *immediately* generalized and nullified as such the moment it refers to the universality of the human condition. Consequently, each individual element in the description takes on a value on the other levels to which it can be related. This 'perfusion' of the particular by the general is constant in Beckett's writing: it is what gives rhythm to the impulses of the signifier over the mass of the text's signifieds.

One will note, furthermore, that the details of the setting always refer to fundamental signifiers: red and yellow, which are the dominant colors in the cylinder, are 'placental' colors *par excellence*. As for the alternately hot and cold temperatures, the successive ascents and descents of the 'climbers' or the 'seekers,' they correspond to the alternate impulses of life and death, granted to the 'panting' that stirs the entire cylinder. This generalized coupling of actions and respiration represents or copies the fundamental rhythm of beings in their useless agony of survival.

As we follow in detail this vast mimesis of indefinitely perpetrated creation and destruction, we are led to think of Bataille and Freud, or of nature with its 'orgy of life and death.'

As for the 'dehumanizer' itself, never identified in the text, it is simultaneously the anguish and the Utopia which the mere idea of death arouses as long as it remains unrealized. These feelings separate the beings one from the other, but do not 'suppress' them. They continue to bother one another, to be each others' hell. In this world no one is alone, but everyone is hopelessly solitary, and interchangeable for the sake of the useless quest which cannot be abandoned.

The end, if we can conceive of it, will be the entrance into the 'calm deserts' beyond the need for a point of reference. Man, degree zero, will merge with the matter whence he came. Blissfully he will once again be a thing among things at the heart of the world's blind adventure. There, perhaps the illusions which have tortured him will disappear, illusions of duration and of matter, the blinding myths of a zenith or even those of a twilight.

[Translated by Larysa Mykyta and Mark Schumacher]

70.   ALAIN BOSQUET IN 'COMBAT'

29 March 1971, 10

Alain Bosquet (b. 1919), French writer and close friend of
Beckett, has published novels, volumes of poetry, and
critical studies. He has written many articles about
Beckett's books and Beckett has translated several of his
poems into English.

I see it again and again: a face rough-hewn, as though the
sculptor, after chiseling, scoring and hollowing it out a
few times, still intended to come back to it, to give more
definition to forms already laid out in masses and angles.
Gray hair on the alert, as if its role were to protect
him; and indeed he endeavours, with every breath as well
as every glance, to defend himself: not just against
others, but also against the air he breathes and the life
within himself that he knows to be so tenacious, to his
detriment. The eyes, in this harsh landscape, an incredible blue mildness: a contradiction, as in a diamond, to
his flesh and his eternal need for self-restraint.
Glasses in a simple inexpensive frame do not diminish his
charm; occasionally, with a brusque gesture - I would even
say an awkward gesture - his passion checked, he raises
them and claps the lenses to his forehead, or even more
violently takes them off and throws them on the table with
the ashtray and matches.
   He is reluctant to speak. One senses the words rising
in this tall body that accuses itself, privately, of
behaving like some sort of scarecrow. Where do they come
from, these words that refuse to be spoken? From the
knees, perhaps; in any case from some obscure zone where
they take shape hesitantly, if not painfully. They are
brief, curt, cutting, pitiless, nasal; and yet one senses
that they would like so much to be generous or even just
affable. One always feels grateful to him for waiting,
waiting interminably while the word struggles so hard to
detach itself from the flesh: this being, so uneasy within
him, and right beside him, is so admirably confided to his
writing. There is a character Beckett, who ventures out
from Malone or Molloy, and timidly hastens to return into
them as soon as his intimates let him do so; a few rare
friends have the gift of restoring the man Beckett to his
books. May they close again upon him!

He has published three more in the last few months. Is he still writing? He claims he can no longer bring any-thing off and that he has simply drawn from either old or almost forgotten works. 'Mercier and Camier,' 'First Love,' and 'The Lost Ones' are fifteen, sixteen, and five years old respectively. Can he be publishing them with joy? But at any rate, publishing is an ordeal, is it not? Sometimes, when he lets himself go and confides something, he admits that the only paraliterary activity that still gives him a few pleasant moments is stage production. These three works seem as though the author had torn them out of a whole, hardly even realizing it. And of course, Beckett is all there, with his mysteries, his ironies, his way of grasping the absurd and making it into necessity. For too long a time people have been talking about the dis-gusting aspects of his deliquescent universe and the per-petual wandering undertaken by each of his characters within his own self, a land in which he cannot recognize himself. As the years go by and the books - shorter and shorter - accumulate, my perspective regarding Beckett has been changing. Since he, out of all our writers, is the one who most naturally creates parables, one should not even wonder whether one is correct or incorrect in inter-preting him in one way or another, provided one clings - with flesh, word and breath - to whatever there is in him that escapes linear truth. By chance, each of the three texts recently published, is, fortunately, symptomatic, a projection of the same psychological and verbal universe whose many examples have appeared in his masterpieces.

'Mercier and Camier' is, to be brief, the dialogue of two monologues, and presents us with one of those pairs of inseparable friends whose most famous avatars are found in 'Waiting for Godot.' Mercier and Camier exist only to make empty responses to one another: they listen to them-selves speak or answer, each locked within himself. They cannot stand each other, but they can hardly bear the knowledge that they are unbearable together. They are the hell of this infirmity: speech. Which of these two mir-rors is more or less distorting than the other? The un-conscious, and a sort of animal habit, drive Mercier to follow in Camier's footsteps, and vice versa. They live to hate each other to the point of knowing that they really ought to make peace with one another. They pro-nounce words for the sake of having something to contra-dict; they make gestures in hopes of undoing them. They are ready to leave: this is a state of mind, and hardly an act at all. To camouflage their vacuity, they load them-selves down with objects: a charade that can scarcely sat-isfy them. A bicycle and a raincoat make up nearly all their baggage. Why bother to travel?

Thus the horror of existence needs to be peopled.
Sometimes objects simply will not do, and so episodic
creatures appear, among whom Mercier and Camier can bustle
around in an almost normal fashion. Later, Beckett's
characters become invalids; for the moment the only infirmity these two have is the incarnate absence they drag
along from one end of their uselessness and boredom to the
other. They amuse themselves making up tricks to play on
each other, in their gray indifference; from time to time
they allow themselves to be caught in the trap. Their
repeated attempts at departure finally urge them on: they
set out. The landscape they travel through - one would
say, pretend to travel through - is as colorless and void
as they are themselves. Under these conditions, what is
the meaning of this ramble in the suburbs of nowhere? Is
this not an example, on the whole, of lying to oneself
unimaginatively, as Beckett says, of salving the soul? -
although neither Mercier nor Camier has any precise idea
of a soul. They would like to feel the desire for a particular desire, but that is not something granted to
everyone.

Interchangeable as they are, do they even know themselves? They jabber away, dredging up plans that have
sunk even lower than themselves, annoy each other, are
unable to leave one another, take a few steps into Nature
as though to convince themselves that she is not worth the
trouble, go back to their own rain, their own skins, their
own little bit of humanity. They draw things out for
themselves without being sensual: what do they feel, other
than their own banality, which does not sadden them? Nor
are they derelicts: millions of beings resemble these
creatures, who resemble only their own shadows. Beckett
demystifies immediacy, spontaneity - rather sluggish here,
it should be pointed out: the pain of living that is not
even felt as pain. In doing this he demystifies the need
to create real characters: neither Camier nor Mercier have
anything to say, anything to be, anything to inspire.
They are like all of us, census numbers erased by fate,
and they scrape along in a moment that is not aware of
constituting any moment at all. Once in a while a few
words coagulate, lungs breathe a little air. One might as
well be dry grass, or a stone that does not even roll.

This solitude for two - shall I say, for one and a
half - is transformed into solitude for one - shall I say
for one half - in 'First Love,' the story of an 'unnamable' who still has the use of his limbs, but in whom
memory is blocked by a heap of rubbish from the past.
This man does not live in the sewer: that would be too

easy; he *is* the sewer. The narrator of 'First Love'
would like to recapture his past self, except that he is
fleeing from his own memory precisely in order to escape
from everything that formerly made up what was already, in
him, a void. The *I* is an immense *one*, a neuter that
sighs, that groans, that grimaces, that aspires to having
enough strength not to forgive itself for its own null
condition. This *I* - very anti-*I* - thus has regrets; true
or false, try to find out! Beckett's humor consists precisely of presenting a humorous aspect of human nothingness: one deceives oneself in order to pretend that there
is a *self*.

To dress one's dreams in rags is a natural and nauseat-
ing ambition. The narrator knew a certain Lulu; sometimes he is less sure of this and prefers to call her
Anne. She was a prostitute, perhaps; she was pregnant
without a doubt; he was sick and bedridden, probably.
Everything happens in words that reconcile and finally
confuse oblivion and imagination, waking and dreaming;
realities and speculations twining around disoriented
whims. In 'How It Is' we witnessed the same sort of
eddying: the guile and confusion of a soul that does not
want to believe in the existence of the soul. A world of
fleeting sensations takes up all the space in this mental
universe, which does not express itself, but translates
as though from an *other* the torment of expressing itself,
even while it vindicates the itch for independent expression of all thoughts or sensations.

The case for dotage, in its sublime and exasperating
state: is this not one of Beckett's uncontested domains?
In the end one feels divided: these approximations destroy - the word is not too strong - everything noble and
pathetic that the interrogation has managed to invent for
itself; after this kind of literature, not even the notions of unhappiness, accursedness and despair remain
intact. For it was a very beautiful thing, very pure,
very intoxicating - I'm kidding - to know oneself to be
miserable. But no, Beckett seems to say, happiness and
unhappiness are idiotic, and suffering is no more glorious
than the rest of it. He demystifies horror as well as
joy, and poetry as well as poetry's opposite.

From another angle, we come out of this lesson in indifference and egalitarianism, administered by insignificance, for ever soiled, and somewhat cleansed in spite of
it all. Something masochistic in us impels us to feel a
sort of grateful revulsion towards it: if everything is so
flat and gray, it is because we can, perhaps, start things
over again, both this universe and our own little bit of
carnality. We have deceived ourselves; we can all agree

on this. Let's wipe out everything and start over, but without the burden of hope. Whether Beckett likes it or not - Nobel prize-winner in spite of himself - he is changing into a moralist. Our distortion, but he will no longer be able to escape from it.

All that was only yesterday: the period of civilized absurdity in others, and of *absurdity in a fluid state* in Beckett. What was human persisted, if only out of respect for matter having by chance and through error formed man. 'The Lost Ones' is more recent, in conception as well as in composition; dated 1966 and published a few weeks ago, it translates certain anxieties that are singularly in accord with the atomic era. Let us say, in a more general way, that there is here a perspective at the heart of which man - with his flaws - no longer plays the only role: not even that of the straight man. The object - here a ladder - takes on an importance man never suspected. Behavior is organized - or disorganized - as a function of laws and presences unfamiliar to us. We no longer derive our anguish from ourselves alone. We are submissive, and without knowing to what order. It is the end of those habits that allowed us to assimilate various phenomena in the universe! Something reigns over us. Form reduces to insects: the form of what and a form destined for what enigma?

'The Lost Ones' describes, in a sort of post-cubist, or post-human, hallucination - Space Odyssey 2002 - the efforts of our ancestors, transformed into our pitiful descendants, to get out of a cylinder with the help of a ladder. Substituted for the original curse is physical torture - space itself has become our most terrible enemy. It is as though God - whom nobody calls by that name - had condemned us to wear an iron collar. Some object inflicts our own skeleton and weight upon us. We are inside a container, which may be Dante's Inferno on earth, or - with tongue in cheek - the pot in which anthropophagous Baal has tossed us to have some fun with his creatures, whom one would think he knows to be unpardonable. Has the Supreme Geometrician suddenly noticed that we have been too free?

And so he has put us into a diving bell. We had fallen into the bad habit of breathing more or less normally; there must be an end to this license: get moving, you ants! now we have to climb, to get out of the cylinder, and at the top fall down again to the bottom of this mental trap, our iron lungs and our interstellar ship at the same time.

Becketts' parables lend themselves to the wildest flights of fancy, and one can never oppose them with a

formal contradiction. This decade aspires to being the
space age. Here Beckett is no longer attacking man, but
the very myth of man propelling himself out of his natal
habitat. Or rather, he makes of the astronaut and the
cosmonaut the symbols of our enslavement: to weight and
weightlessness, to the infinitely great and the infinitely
small, to paralyzing introspection and to self-transcendence. No mercy for this race! And yet some immense form
of hygiene transforms this accusation into an immense
cleansing - into an immense cathartic as well - at the end
of which we have at least - but nothing more - the desire
to disincarnate ourselves. Our resources are inexhaustible, according to Beckett; what remains to be done is for
us to change our nature. It is within our grasp.

[Translated by Jean M. Sommermeyer]

71. UNSIGNED REVIEW IN 'TIMES LITERARY SUPPLEMENT'

11 August 1972, 935

When bright-eyed undergraduates come to write their theses
on Ladder Symbolism in Samuel Beckett, 'The Lost Ones'
will probably be their key book. Murphy, of course,
pulled up the ladder after him when retreating into his
attic, and the narrator's voice rang out after him: 'Do
not go down the ladder, they have taken it away' - an
instruction repeated in 'Watt' and with as much serio-
comic intent. One probable difficulty for the literary
analyst will be in deciding whether the idiom 'pull up the
ladder, Jack, I'm all right' passed into common usage
before or after Beckett's literary rendition of it.
    The theme of 'The Lost Ones' 'Le Dépeupleur' physically
reverses these earlier notions: roughly expressed perhaps,
it might be 'do not come up the ladder, there is nothing
at the top' - an idea which also has its antecedents in
Beckett's writing. There is an incident in 'Endgame' when
Clov ascends the ladder to describe the bleak scene outside, though there is not the kind of direct confrontation
between the character and his severely limited environment
in the present book, which, in keeping with Beckett's
earlier writings, is an abstract, almost mathematical
text, in which a coolly detached eye - not malicious, but
not impassioned either - describes the pointless but

compulsive rituals of a number of meaningless characters,
leaving the reader to apply the paradigm of the wider
aspect of humane experience.

In one of the dialogues with Georges Duthuit, Beckett
spoke of 'the expression that there is nothing to express,
nothing with which to express, no power to express, no
desire to express, together with the obligation to express', a view of creativity which finds its corollary in
Beckett's obsessive expression that the cruel idiocy of
life is inextricably linked with the obligation to live it
out. The lost ones in their cylinder, 'vast enough for
search to be in vain. Narrow enough for flight to be in
vain', offer a precise analogy. The sedentary in the cylinder 'never stir from the coign they have won ... because
they have decided their best chance is there and if they
seldom or never ascend to the niches and tunnels it is because they have done so too often in vain or come there
too often to grief'. 'The searchers', though, climb the
cylinder's ladders to the niches and tunnels, waiting
their turn in queues because 'the use of the ladder is
regulated by conventions of obscure origin, which in their
precision and the submission they exact from the climbers
resemble laws'; once inside the niche or tunnel a searcher
must wait for a ladder to reappear at the lip of his niche
so that he can get back to the floor of the cylinder.

It seems reasonable to suppose that the ladders represent the means by which we achieve knowledge: that the
searching is for knowledge; and that the ladder symbol relates directly to Wittgenstein's remarks in the 'Tracta-
tus': 'My propositions are elucidatory in this way: he who
understands me finally recognizes them as senseless when
he has climbed through them, on them, over them. (He
must, so to speak, throw away the ladder after he has clim
climbed up on it.)' The link between the ladders of Beckett and Wittgenstein has been made before, of course, but
here the analogy seems much more exact; the point would
seem to be that the assumption of knowledge is a farcical
occupation; and Beckett looks down (the notion of an
observer's eye above and beyond the activity in the cylinder is inescapable) with the cool detachment of a chemist
observing the machinations of organisms under the micro-
scope and writing up his notes in that idiosyncratic, dis-
located style - almost one of controlled logorrhoea -
which characterizes the later prose pieces. In his role
of observer, Beckett writes like a celestial clerk, annotating the insanities of life in the cylinder in a cypher
appropriate to that life. The fluctuating temperature
which figures in 'Imagination Dead Imagine,' the strict
if apparently meaningless rituals, the very environment

itself - 'floor and wall are of solid rubber or such like'
- which precludes any trace of anguish or love, fury or
achievement: these breed that terrifying, unmistakable
situation which characterizes Beckett's severe statements
about our existence: an existence in which all effort is
meaningless and prematurely defeated, although the desire
for effort remains unquenchable.

72.   LAWRENCE GRAVER IN 'PARTISAN REVIEW'

XLI, 4, 1974, 622-5

Lawrence Graver (b. 1931), Professor of English at
Williams College, Massachusetts, is the author of 'Conrad's Short Fiction' (1969) and 'Carson McCullers' (1969),
and editor of 'Mastering the Film' (1977). He has written
about Beckett for the 'New Republic,' 'Partisan Review'
and other magazines.

What does a new reader need from a primer on Beckett?(1)
Most likely, he will want help first with those elusive
narratives abstracted beyond all likelihood, tales of
'formal brilliance and indeterminable purport.' Beckett
himself has consistently forsworn hidden meanings and
claims never to have heard the harmonies perceived by
Joyce. But doubts persist. If Beckett is not an allegorist, his novels and plays move teasingly towards generalizations. Which ones, and how do we know?
   On first acquaintance the disparity between style and
subject matter is another source of trouble: 'a bow tie
about a throat cancer,' Beckett once said. Not even Swift
was more poised in treating cruelty and decomposition; and
Beckett's elegant savagery is devoid of indignation.
Here, for instance, he talks of _his_ Lemuel towards the end
of 'Malone Dies':

   Flayed alive by memory, his mind crawling with cobras,
   not daring to dream or think and powerless not to, his
   cries were of two kinds, those having no other cause
   than moral anguish and those, similar in every respect, by means of which he hoped to forestall same.

Horror, studied enumeration, and the legalistic fussiness
at the close - the mix inspires anxious laughter.
'Flayed alive' seems to echo Swift's observation about the
woman whose appearance was altered for the worse, and of
course there is only one other Lemuel. But it is not easy
here (or elsewhere in Beckett) to know exactly what to
make of the allusiveness.

Then, too, there are the inevitable questions about the
movement of Beckett's entire career. John Updike once
called him 'a proud priest perfecting his forlorn ritual,'
and new readers will want some assessment of this most unlikely divine, his canonical books, and his inexhaustible
faculty of negation. What about the shifts back and forth
from English to French and from fiction to drama? How
does one compare and evaluate different pieces of his
ruthlessly minimal art? When is the art of limited means
governed by the law of diminishing returns, and why?

About many of these issues, A. Alvarez is only inter-
mittently helpful. He is an impatient critic, eager to
make stirring generalizations about extremity and terror,
but often too restless to look attentively at the text in
front of him. About Beckett's world he has trustworthy
things to say, but about Beckett's books he is often evasive and misleading. He doesn't much like the fiction (a
fatal disqualification for a survey writer), and in his
desire to get on to the plays, he is unfair to at least
half of Beckett's achievement. Obsessed with their difficulty and seeming narrowness of range, Alvarez does not
see the extraordinary emotional and intellectual variety
of books like 'Molloy' and 'Malone Dies' (written in Beckett's favorite 'incandescent grey'). Nor is he willing to
allow that even the less successful novels have their
glories. 'Watt,' for instance, has Arsene's inspired
monologue on the nature of desire, and the marvelous descriptions of Mr. Hackett, the Galls, and the Micks' -
those 'heroic figures unique in the annals of cloistered
fornication.'

Alvarez is much better on the plays and on Beckett's
importance for the modern theater, but even here haste and
a certain solemnity result in peculiar distortions. He
sees no humor in 'Godot,' misreads the closing scene of
'Endgame,' and flattens some of Beckett's finest writing
with his own heavy prose. After quoting the brilliant description of suicide from 'Eh Joe,' he remarks: 'Like
many other passages in Beckett, this has the sharpness
and economy of poetry and yet remains narrative, taking
the listener effectively from one point in time to
another.' When Alvarez does face a difficult critical
issue straight on, the result can be bizarre, 'Beckett,'

he tells us, 'is not an allegorist; he simply looks allegorical in lieu of anything else - because, that is, he has never been interested in plots.... Hence those larger apparently allegorical meanings are it would seem haphazard; they are the more or less random effects of Beckett's over-education.'

On this point, and on most others, Hugh Kenner is more helpful. Although he and Alvarez must have written their books at roughly the same time, Kenner's 'Guide' reads uncannily like a corrective to the other man's excess. If Alvarez spends five pages explaining why a comparison of Beckett and Ionesco is pointless, Kenner in a sentence says: 'It is not a useful bracketing.' When Alvarez argues that 'the final irreducible content of all Beckett's work is depression,' Kenner chides those who account for Beckett's writing by the simple 'hypothesis of constitutional gloom.' While Alvarez pursues generalizations about desolation in a post-atomic age, Kenner tries to teach his readers 'relevant habits of attention.'

For a critic customarily given to a fancifulness and strutting, Kenner has surprisingly pared his style for the occasion, and generally moves with quiet discernment through three dozen novels, stories, and plays. (There is some talk about torques, valencies, and Pozzo as a Gestapo officer, but much less than one would expect.) Having written on Beckett before and having taught the books for years, he knows how to anticipate the problems an ordinary reader will face:

> Each time we confront a new Beckett work we are installed in some new world, a world where men wait, a world where women sink into the sand, a world where couples lie barely breathing in symmetrical entombment. We deduce the world's rules of order and adduce pertinent memories of other orders.

In his best chapters, Kenner carefully deduces the new rules of order and helps us to see which memories of old orders are pertinent and suggestive. The new rules are those insinuating rituals invented by Beckett to dramatize basic human processes and states: Murphy desiring, Watt serving, Molloy travelling, Moran searching, Malone writing, the Unnamable talking, Estragon waiting, Hamm acting, Krapp listening, and dozens of others falling, crawling, fleeing, dying. Most relevant among the old orders are works of art: 'The Divine Comedy,' Shakespeare's plays, 'Paradise Lost,' and 'The Bible.' Beckett's acerbic allusiveness always emphasizes the distance between his frantic, disintegrating protagonists and the heroes of old, but it also has the mysterious connecting effect of certain kinds of irony. When Nell is discovered to have died in her garbage can and Hamm says: 'Our revels now are ended,' we laugh, feel pain, and are struck by the bizarre suggestiveness of the link with 'The Tempest': Hamm as Prospero, king of his little room, in a play about playing, but perhaps more like Caliban, the beast and the bloody handkerchief, brave new world that has such people in it....and so on. The links are not systematic, like Joyce's, but local, bitter, going into the skin like hooks.

That Beckett is still inventing new rules and asking us to attend to old orders is evident in his most recent extended work, 'The Lost Ones.' That he remains a difficult writer can be shown by a glance at the commentaries provided by Alvarez and Kenner. Published first in French and then two years ago in Beckett's English translation, 'The Lost Ones' describes life inside a flattened cylinder fifty metres round and eighteen metres high. Two hundred and five naked bodies roam about searching in vain for something lost but indeterminate. Against the walls are fifteen ladders which climbers regularly mount in hope of finding temporary refuge in alcoves or a permanent way out of the top of the enclosure. The arena itself is divided into three zones and the searchers into four groups: those who are always searching; those who sometimes pause in their search; those who used to search but now remain sedentary; and those who no longer search and are vanquished. The temperature, rising and falling from 5° to 25° every eight seconds, greatly pains the skin; the light, a dim, quivering yellow, blurs into a 'fiery flickering murk' that eventually burns out the eyes. During the brief course of the narrative, we learn about the laws of the cylinder, and the habits, prerogatives, and sufferings of this 'little band of searchers.' In the final moments, darkness descends, the temperature rests near freezing, and life comes to a stop.

Although Dante appears once with his 'rare, wan smile,' and mention is made of Milton's pandemonium, the notion of hell in 'The Lost Ones' is all Beckett's - blanched, pitiless, described from an enormous height by a voice with ancient and desperate knowledge. As always, the voice is the thing: at first, clipped, dry, incantatory, but notational; low, dull, faintly humming. Gradually, as we attend to the words cut and then positioned as if each were a precious stone, we hear surprising modulations nor apparent at the start. The voice begins to doubt, qualify, and contradict its earlier observations; and from behind the screen of detachment comes the torment of the searching creatures condemned to ardent life in the press and gloom of the cylinder.

Phantasmagorical, but - as often in Beckett - firmly linked to ordinary life. Time and again, the alien events inside the cylinder (the mysterious law-making, the mechanical questing, the sudden explosions of violence) send chills of recognition out to more familiar spheres. Beckett's hell has always been here and now: a place of precise geography, obscure origins, and uncertain purpose, inhabited by creatures who seek, suffer, fail to find, and cannot stop seeking. The earlier versions ('The Trilogy,' 'Godot,' 'Endgame,' and others) are richer, more various and densely populated than 'The Lost Ones,' but this miniature has its own desolate power.

Little of what is provocative about 'The Lost Ones' comes across from the brief remarks of Alvarez and Kenner. Beckett writes of hell; Alvarez calls it purgatory. Alvarez describes the lost bodies 'each searching restlessly for its mate'; the story says clearly enough: 'whatever it is they are searching for it is not that.' After calling Beckett's unadorned threnody 'rather long-winded' like a 'report of a civil service commission,' Alvarez suggests that 'perhaps one motive for the work was to ask how the oldest of Beckett's heroes [Belacqua] looks forty years later.' Kenner gets the image right: the cylinder is 'some nether hell'; but he too is careless about details (falsely describing the vanquished searchers as immobile); and he soon loses interest entirely, ending with a few random comparisons to other pieces of the Beckett residua. 'The Lost Ones' deserves better, and I wish Kenner had coerced his customary habits of attention. There's unexplored life in those sombre ruins.

Note

1   The early part of the review covers two critical books: 'Samuel Beckett' by A. Alvarez and 'A Reader's Guide to Samuel Beckett' by Hugh Kenner. (Eds)

'Not I'
(1972)

[Written in English; first performed by the Repertory
Theater of Lincoln Center, New York, 22 November 1972;
first performed in London at the Royal Court Theatre, 16
January 1973; published by Faber & Faber, London, 1973,
and Grove Press, New York (in 'First Love and Other
Shorts'), 1974.]

73.   EDITH OLIVER IN 'NEW YORKER'

2 December 1972, 124

Edith Oliver (b. 1913) has reviewed off-Broadway plays for
the 'New Yorker' since 1961.

The nearest I can come to describing 'Not I' is to say
that it is an aural mosaic of words, which come pell-mell
but not always helter-skelter, and that once it is over, a
life, emotions, and a state of mind have been made mani-
fest, with a literally stunning impact upon the audience.
Even then, much of the play remains, and should remain,
mysterious and shadowy. It opens in total darkness. A
woman's voice is heard (but so quietly that it almost
mingles with the rattling of programs out front) whispering
and crying and laughing and then speaking in a brogue, but
so quickly that one can barely distinguish the words.
Then a spotlight picks out a mouth moving; that is all the
lighting there is, from beginning to end. The words never
stop coming, and their speed never slackens; they are, we

finally realize, the pent-up words of a lifetime, and they are more than the woman can control. She refers to her own 'raving' and 'flickering brain,' and to her 'lips, cheeks, jaws, tongue, never still a second.' Yet something of great power and vividness - tatters of incidents and feelings, not a story but something - comes through from a dementia that is compounded of grief and confusion. We hear of a sexual episode that took place on an early April morning long ago, when she was meant to be having pleasure and was having none. There is talk of punishment for her sins, and of being godforsaken, with no love of any kind. She is obsessed with the idea of punishment. There was a trial of some kind, when all that was required of her was to say 'Guilty' or 'Not guilty,' and she stood there, her mouth half open, struck dumb. Since then (or maybe not since then), she has been unable to speak, except for once or twice a year, when she rushes out and talks to strangers - in the market, in public lavatories - only to see their stares and almost die of shame. She has 'lived on and on to be seventy.' The light slowly fades, the gabble slides off to whispers and to silence. All the while, a man in monk's garb has been standing in the shadows, listening and occasionally bowing his head. Miss Tandy gives an accomplished performance in what must be an extremely difficult role. Henderson Forsythe is the listener. This production of 'Not I' (I have no idea what the title means) lasts around fifteen minutes. They are about as densely packed as any fifteen minutes I can remember.

74. BENEDICT NIGHTINGALE IN 'NEW STATESMAN'

26 January 1973, 135-6

Benedict Nightingale (b. 1939) is drama critic for the 'New Statesman.'

When I was a boy, in the 1940s and 1950s, one of the most famous sights of the West Kent countryside was a woman in a rough brown smock with string round her waist, body bent forwards, arms working like pistons as she bustled towards Tunbridge Wells station. There she was planning to meet her husband, who had been killed in the first

world war. In time, her walk lost its fever and became
a sort of doleful trudge, and she disappeared from the
roads. I don't know if she may conceivably still be found
in some geriatric ward, staring out of the window and wondering when the war will end; but I do know that her image
came forcefully back to me when I saw 'Not I'. If the
spot that lit up the speaker's mouth, and that only, had
spread to reveal the whole of her body, I would have expected to see much the same hump and rags: if the old
woman of Kent had spoken, I daresay much the same
anguished gabble would have poured from her. All Beckett's plays may be seen as threnodies to wasted lives;
but 'Not I' is more concrete in its characterisation than
most, and as starkly visual as any in its evocation of the
all-but-invisible piece of human driftwood whose monologue it is. It is also unusually painful - tearing into
you like a grappling iron and dragging you after it, with
or without your leave.

The mouth belongs to Billie Whitelaw; and, for some 15
minutes, she pants and gasps out the tale of the character
to whom it belongs, her broken phrases jostling each other
in their desperation to be expressed. It is a performance
of sustained intensity, all sweat, clenched muscle and
foaming larynx, and one which finds its variety only up-
wards: a frantic cackle at the idea that there might be a
merciful God; a scream of suffering designed to appease
this uncertain deity. But it must be admitted that the
breathless pace combines with the incoherence of the
character's thoughts to make the piece hard to follow:
which is why I'd suggest either that it be played twice a
session (though this might prove too much even for Miss
Whitelaw's athletic throat), or that spectators should
first buy and con the script, which Faber is publishing
this week at 40p. After all, one of the many assumptions
which .Beckett's work challenges is that a play should
necessarily strip and show its all (or even much of itself) at first encounter. Like good music, 'Not I'
demands familiarity, and is, I suspect, capable of giving
growing satisfaction with each hearing. Meanwhile, let
me piece together a crib for those too poor or proud to
get the score proper.

'Mouth', as Beckett calls her, was born a bastard,
deserted by her parents, brought up in a loveless,
heavily religious orphanage. She became a lonely,
frightened, half-moronic adult, forever trudging round the
countryside and avoiding others.

    busy shopping centre ... supermart ... just hand in the
    list ... with the bag ... old black shopping bag ...

then stand there waiting ... any length of time ...
middle of the throng ... motionless ... staring into
space ... mouth half-open as usual ... till it was back
in her hand ... the bag back in her hand ... then pay
and go ... not as much as goodbye.

Once she appeared in court on some unnamed charge, and
couldn't speak; once, and only once, she wept; occasionally, 'always winter for some reason', she was seen standing in the public lavatory, mouthing distorted vowels.
But otherwise 'nothing of note' apparently happened until
a mysterious experience at the age of 70. The morning sky
went dark, a ray of light played in front of her. Her
reaction ('very foolish but so like her') was that she was
about to be punished for her sins, and she tried to
scream. Yet neither did she feel pain, nor could she make
a sound; nor hear anything, except a dull buzzing in the
head. Then, suddenly, her mouth began to pour out words,
so many and fast that her brain couldn't grasp them,
though she sensed that some revelation, some discovery,
was at hand. And 'feeling was coming back ... imagine ...
feeling coming back' - to her mouth, lips and cheeks, if
not yet to her numb heart. It is that feeling, those
words, which we are presumably hearing in the theatre;
that mouth, bulging and writhing in its spotlight like
some blubbery sea-creature on the hook, which is now vir-
tually all that is left alive of the speaker after decades
of dereliction.
    Or could it be, as some suspect, that the mouth is
talking, not of itself, but of someone else? I don't
think so. True, the story is told entirely in the third
person, and the play is baldly called 'Not I'. But Beckett helpfully provides a stage direction which seems to
explain that. At key moments, the speaker repeats with
rising horror, 'What? Who? *No SHE*': which is, we're told,
a vehement refusal to relinquish third person'. In other
words, she can't bring herself to utter the word 'I', and
that, I'd suggest, is because she dare not admit that this
wilderness of a life is hers and hers alone. Whenever she
gets near the admission, we get instead that cry of 'no'
and howl of 'she', as if she was denying any possibility
so awful. Things like that happen to other people: they
cannot happen to 'me'. Again, she seems to show symptoms
of what psychiatrists call 'depersonalisation', the condition in which the sufferer has lost nearly all capacity
for emotion and is left with the sensation, not only of
not being himself, but of scarcely being human at all.
Thus she thinks of herself in the third person and, on two
occasions, talks of her body as a 'machine', disconnected

from sense and speech. But it is, of course, quite inadequate to argue that Beckett is offering a clinical study
of a schizophrenic: her predicament is much more representative. Which of us doesn't shut his eyes to his failures,
and who wouldn't rather say 'he' or 'she' of much of his
own irrecoverable life? Who isn't guilty of both evasion
and waste?

The play's resonance is typical. Beckett commonly
takes a particular character, pares it down to the moral
skeleton, and leaves us with the pattern, the archetype:
he refines individuals into metaphors in which we can all,
if we're honest, see bits of ourselves. What distingui-
shes 'Not I' from most of his work is the extent to which
'mouth' is individualised and the relative straightfor-
wardness of its implications. Once the code is cracked,
the stream of consciousness channelled, it isn't a hard
play, nor is it as stunningly pessimistic as some critics
believe. In 'Endgame', for instance, Hamm's room is Hamm's
room, a dying man's skull, the family hearth, society and
the planet Earth, forcing the spectator to spread his poor,
bewildered wits over four or five levels at once; 'Not I's'
stage is a barrenly furnished human mind, and that only.
Again, I can think of few gloomier plays than 'Happy Days',
which equates happiness with gross stupidity, or the one-
minute 'Breath', which defines life as two faint cries and
the world as a rubbish-heap. Invocations of God notwithstanding, 'Not I' has nothing definite to say about the
society, world or universe in which 'mouth' spins out her
existence. It *could* be that some self-fulfilment is possible there for those who don't evade life by crying 'not
I': that *might* be the revelation that tantalises but
eludes her. Unlikely, knowing Beckett; but conceivable.
We should seize hopefully on the slightest chink in such
a man's determinism, the barest scratch on the dark glasses
through which he surveys us all.

It's an entirely self-sufficient play, but not without
echoes from earlier ones: the omnipresence of irrational
guilt; the idea that love causes only suffering; and a
shape and tone that owes something to 'Krapp's Last Tape'
- which is presumably why that piece is also on the programme, with Albert Finney poised over the recording
machine, spooling his way through yet another null past.
Finney proves a bit cavalier with the stage directions,
but achieves a good deal with a voice that markedly thick-
ens and coarsens over the years, and with a face that
scarcely has to move to suggest fear, bewilderment, a
sudden raddled tenderness. I would recommend the production; but its 'Not I' that lingers in my mind, not because
it's more exquisitely written, but because it is, I think,

even more deeply felt. At any rate, the old woman's predicament strikes me as more moving than the old man's.
Perhaps this is because he is cleverer, and she more fragile and vulnerable, and less responsible for her failures; perhaps not. Whatever the reason, it is hard not
to identify with the bent, cowled figure Beckett calls
the 'auditor', who stands half-invisible in the murk of
the stage watching the mouth and, finally, raising his
arms 'in a gesture of helpless compassion'. Compassion is
indeed and exactly what 'Not I' provokes, and more powerfully than anything I've yet seen by Beckett.

Encounters with Beckett
(1975)

75. E.M. CIORAN IN 'PARTISAN REVIEW'

XLIII, 2, 1976, 280-5

E.M. Cioran (b. 1911), philosopher, critic, essayist, was
born in Rumania, but has lived in Paris since 1937. He is
the author of 'The Temptation to Exist' (1970), 'The Fall
into Time' (1970), 'The New Gods' (1974), and 'The Trouble
with Being Born' (1975). He is a friend of Beckett.

To perceive the sort of *separate* man that Beckett is, one
would have to ponder the expression 'to stand apart' -
his tacit motto of every moment - its implication of
solitude and subterranean obstinance, the essence of a
being on the outside, pursuing an implacable and endless
task. The Buddhists say, of one who tends toward illumination, that he must be as relentless as 'a mouse gnawing
a coffin.' Every true writer puts forth such an effort.
He is a destroyer who *adds* to existence, who enriches it
while undermining it.
   'Our allotted time on earth is not long enough to be
used for anything other than ourselves.' This remark by
a poet is applicable to anyone who refuses the extrinsic,
the accidental, the *other*. Beckett, or the incomparable
art of being oneself. Yet with this, no apparent pride,
none of the stigmata inherent in the awareness of being
unique: if the word amenity did not exist, one would have
to invent it for him. Hardly to be believed, almost un-
natural: he never disparages anyone, he is ignorant of
the hygienic function of spite - its salutary virtues, its

usefulness as an outlet. I have never heard him belittle
friends or enemies. That's one form of superiority for
which I pity him, and which must make him suffer unconsciously. If I were prevented from maligning people, what
agitation and uneasiness, what complications I could
expect!

He does not live in time but parallel to time. That is
why it never occurred to me to ask him what he thought of
such an such an event. He is one of those beings who make
you realize that history is a dimension man could have
dispensed with.

Even if he were like his heroes, even if he had never
known success, he would still have been exactly the same.
He gives the impression of never wanting to assert himself
at all, of being equally estranged from notions of success
and failure. 'How hard it is to figure him out! And what
class he has!' That's what I say to myself every time I
think of him. If, by some impossible chance, he were
hiding no secrets at all, to my eyes he would still
appear inscrutable.

I come from a corner of Europe where effusiveness, lack
of inhibition, immediate unsolicited shameless avowals are
the rule, where one knows everything about everybody,
where living with other people is almost equivalent to a
public confessional, where secrets in fact are inconceivable and where volubility borders on delirium.

This alone would suffice to explain why I was to be
subjected to the fascination of a man who is uncannily
discreet.

Amenity does not exclude exasperation. At dinner with
some friends, while they showered him with futilely erudite questions about himself and his work, he took refuge
in complete silence and finally even turned his back to
us - or almost did. The dinner was not yet over when he
rose and left, preoccupied and gloomy, as one might be
just before surgery, or the torture-chamber.

About five years ago, we met by chance on Rue Guynemer;
as he asked if I were working, I told him that I had lost
my taste for work, that I didn't see the necessity of be-
stirring myself, or 'producing,' that writing was an
ordeal for me.... He seemed astonished by this, and I was
even more astonished when, precisely in reference to writing, he spoke of *joy*. Did he really use that word? Yes,
I am sure of it. At the same moment I recalled that at
our first meeting, some ten years earlier at the Closerie
des Lilas, he had confessed to me his great weariness, the
feeling he had that nothing could be squeezed out of words
any more.

Words - will anyone love them as much as he has? They

are his companions, and his sole support. This man who
takes no certitude for granted - one feels how firm and
secure he is among them. His fits of discouragement undoubtedly coincide with the moments when he ceases to believe in them, when he feels they are failing him, evading
him. Without them, he is left dispossessed, he is nowhere. I regret not having marked and counted all the
passages in his work where he refers to words, where he
reflects upon words - 'drops of silence in silence,' as
they are described in 'The Unnamable.' Symbols of frag-
ility transformed into indestructible foundations.

The French text 'Sans' is called 'Lessness' in English,
a word coined by Beckett, as well as its German equivalent
Losigkeit.

Fascinated by this word lessness (as unfathomable as
Boehme's *Ungrund*), I told Beckett one evening that I would
not go to bed before finding an honorable equivalent for
it in French.... Together we had considered all possible
forms suggested by *sans* and *moindre*. None of them seemed
to us to come near the inexhaustible *lessness*, a blend of
loss and infinitude, an emptiness synonymous with apotheo-
sis. We parted company, somewhat disappointed. Back at
home, I kept on turning that poor *sans* over and over in my
mind. Just as I was about to give up, the idea came to me
that I ought to try some derivation of the Latin *sine*.
The next day I wrote to Beckett that *sinéité* seemed to me
to be the yearned-for word. He replied that he too had
thought of it, perhaps at the same moment. Our lucky
find, however, it must be admitted, was not one. We finally agreed that we ought to give up the search, that
there was no noun in French capable of expressing absence
in itself, pure unadulterated absence, and that we had to
resign ourselves to the metaphysical poverty of a preposition.

With writers who have nothing to say, who do not possess a world of their own, one speaks only of literature.
With him, very rarely, in fact almost never. Any everyday topic (material difficulties, annoyances of all kinds)
interests him more - in a conversation, of course. What
he cannot tolerate, at any rate, are questions like: do
you think this or that work is destined to last? That
this or that one deserves its reputation? Of X and Y,
which one will survive, which is the greatest. All eval-
uations of this sort tax his patience and depress him.
'What's the point of all that?' he said to me after a
particularly unpleasant evening, when the discussion at
dinner had resembled a grotesque version of the Last
Judgment. He himself avoids expressing opinions
about his books and plays: what's important to him
are not obstacles that have been overcome, but obstacles

yet to be faced. He merges totally with whatever he
is working on. If one asks him about a play, he will not
linger over the content or the meaning, but over the interpretation, whose most insignificant details he visual-
izes minute by minute - I was about to say second by
second. I will not soon forget his spirited explanation
of the requirements to be satisfied by an actress wishing
to play 'Not I,' in which a single breathless voice dominates space and substitutes itself for it. How his eyes
gleamed as he *saw* that mouth, insignificant and yet invading, omnipresent! One would have thought he was wit-
nessing the ultimate metamorphosis, the supreme downfall
of Pythia!

Having been fond of cemeteries all my life, and knowing
that Beckett liked them too ('First Love,' one may recall,
begins with the description of a cemetery, which is, by
way of parenthesis, the one in Hamburg), I was telling him
last winter, on the Avenue de l'Observatoire, about a
recent visit to the Père-Lachaise Cemetery, and about my
indignation at not finding Proust on the list of 'celebri-
ties' buried there. (I first discovered Beckett's name,
by the way, thirty years ago in the American library, when
I came across his little book on Proust one day.) I don't
know how we ended up with Swift, though now that I think
about it, there was nothing unusual about the transition,
given the funereal nature of his mockery. Beckett told me
he was re-reading the 'Travels,' and that he had a predilection for the 'Country of the Houyhnhnms,' especially for
the scene in which Gulliver is mad with terror and disgust
at the approach of a Yahoo female. He informed me - and
this was a great surprise to me, above all a great disappointment - that Joyce didn't care for Swift. Moreover,
he added, Joyce, contrary to what people think, had no
inclination whatever for satire. 'He never rebelled, he
was detached, he accepted everything. For him, *there was
absolutely no difference between a bomb falling and a leaf
falling.*'

A remarkable judgment, reminding me in its acuity and
strange density of one by Armand Robin, in response to a
question I asked him once: 'Why, after having translated
so many poets, were you never tempted by Chang-Tsu, whose
writings, among those of all the sages, are the most permeated with poetry?' - 'I have thought about doing it
often,' he replied, 'but how can you translate a work that
can only be compared to the *stark landscape of northern
Scotland*?'

How many times, since I have known Beckett, have I
asked myself (an obsessive and rather stupid interrogation, I admit) what sort of relationship there might be

between him and his characters? What could they have in
common? Can anyone imagine a more radical disparity?
Must one assume that not only their existence, but his
also, is bathed in that 'leaden light' noted in 'Malone
Dies'? More than one passage of his seems to me like a
monologue *after* the end of some cosmic epoch. The sensation of entering a posthumous universe, in some geography
dreamed up by a demon, stripped of everything, even of
his curse!

Beings who do not know whether they are alive or not,
and who are prey to an immense fatigue, to a fatigue that
is not of this world (to use a language that runs counter
to Beckett's taste), all conceived by a man who one senses
is vulnerable, who wears, for decency's sake, a mask of
invulnerability. Not long ago, I had, in a flash, a
vision of the bonds that unite them with their author,
with their accomplice. What I saw, or rather what I felt,
in that instant, cannot be translated into an intelligible
formula. Nevertheless, since then the slightest remark
from a hero of his reminds me of the inflections of a
certain voice.... But I hasten to add that a revelation
can be as fragile and as deceptive as a theory.

Right from our first meeting, I realized that he had
reached the extreme limit, that perhaps he had started
there, at the impossible, the extraordinary, at an
impasse. And what is admirable is that he has *stood fast*.
Having arrived at the outset up against a wall, he perseveres as gallantly as he always has: extremity as a
point of departure, the end as advent! Hence the feeling
that this world of his, this transfixed, dying world,
could go on indefinitely, even if ours were to disappear.

I am not particularly attracted to Wittgenstein's
philosophy, but I have a passion for the man. Everything
I read about him has the power to move me. More than once
I have found common traits in him and in Beckett. Two
mysterious apparitions, two phenomena that please one by
being so baffling, so inscrutable. In both, one and the
other, the same distance from beings and things, the same
inflexibility, the same temptation to silence, to a final
repudiation of words, the same desire to collide with
boundaries never sensed before. In another time, they
would have been drawn to the Desert. We now know that
Wittgenstein had, at one time, considered entering a
monastery. As for Beckett, one can very easily imagine
him, a few centuries back, in a bare cell unsullied by any
decoration, not even a crucifix. You think I am rambling?
Consider, then, the faraway, enigmatic, 'inhuman' look he
has in certain photographs.

Our beginnings count, that goes without saying, but we

only take the decisive step toward ourselves when we no
longer have an *origin,* and when we offer just as little
subject-matter for a biography as God does. It is important, and it is not important at all, that Beckett is
Irish. What is certainly false is to claim that he is
the 'perfect example of an Anglo-Saxon.' At any rate,
nothing displeases him more. Is this because of the unpleasant memories he still has of his pre-war stay in
London? I suspect him of accusing the English of 'common-
ness.' That verdict, which he has not expressed but which
I am expressing in his place like a summary of his reser-
vations, if not of his resentments, I cannot personally
subscribe to, and this all the more so because, doubtless
due to a Balkan illusion, the English seem to me to be
the most devitalized and most menaced, and therefore the
most refined and civilized of peoples.

Beckett, who curiously enough feels completely at home
in France, has actually no affinity whatever with a certain hardness, a trait that is eminently French, Parisian
to be precise. Is it not significant that he has put
Chamfort into verse? Not all of Chamfort, true, but only
a few maxims. The enterprise, remarkable in itself and
moreover almost inconceivable (if one considers the absence
of lyric spirit that characterizes the skeletal prose of
the Moralists), is equivalent to an avowal, I dare not say
a proclamation. It is always in spite of themselves
that restrained minds betray the depth of their natures.
Beckett's is so impregnated with poetry that it becomes
indistinguishable from it.

I believe him to be as deliberate as a fanatic. Even
if the world were to collapse, he would neither abandon
work in progress nor change his subject. As far as essentials are concerned, he certainly cannot be swayed. As
for everything else, as for inessentials, he is defenseless, probably weaker than any of us, weaker even than his
characters. Before writing these few notes, I proposed
to reread what Meister Eckhart and Nietzsche had written,
from different perspectives, about 'the noble man.' I did
not carry out my project, but I have not forgotten for a
moment that I thought of doing it.

[Translated by Raymond Federman and Jean M. Sommermeyer]

'That Time' and 'Footfalls'
(1976)

[Written in English; first performed at the Royal Court
Theatre, May 1976; first performed in the USA at the
Arena Stage, Washington, DC, 8 December 1976; published
by Faber & Faber, London, 1976, and Grove Press, New York
(in 'Ends and Odds'), 1976.]

---

76. IRVING WARDLE IN 'THE TIMES'

21 May 1976, 13

Irving Wardle (b. 1929). Drama critic of 'The Times'
since 1963.

Thirteen years separate 'Play' from the two new pieces
that make up the final programme in the Court's Beckett
season, but time has done nothing to change this author's
statement. His people are suspended in a timeless limbo,
dead stars endlessly revolving their past existence in
time. Beyond them is the void, which they hold at bay
with words; but the void is inside them too, for the
memories that obsess them are usually of the utmost banality.

  Beckett's energy goes not into exploring alternative
possibilities for creatures who have reached their desti-
nations, but in discovering new forms in which they can
more eloquently voice their despair. 'Play,' as I remember, struck its first audiences as pretty austere: three
dimly lit figures encased in stone urns, recounting their

separate roles in an ancient adultery, with a total replay of the text at half time. With memories of George Devine's 1964 production and the grimly breakneck Paris version, it came as a big surprise to hear loud guffaws greeting Donald McWhinnie's revival.

I applaud Mr McWhinnie for inviting this response. Increased reverence for Beckett has dulled recognition that he can be a brilliantly comic writer: and 'Play,' with its merciless cuts from melodrama to bathos and its compressed sexual hypocrisies ('God what vermin women. Thanks to you, angel, I said'), superbly shows off his ironic edge. Getting that over at the required speed and detached delivery is the crucial task, and the production is served by four virtuoso performances; three by actors (Anna Massey, Penelope Wilton, and Ronald Pickup) and one by Duncan M. Scott, who operates light changes to the single syllable or hiccough.

The masterstroke of 'Play' is its repeat. We now understand the relationships, the wretched course of the story, and we have had the comedy. The reprise raises no laughter; instead different phrases take on resonance as we join the characters in their imprisoning memory through to the last line which is at once a cadence and a double bar: 'We were not long together ...'

In 'That Time' and 'Footfalls,' irony disappears and with it the sense of human contact. The voice of an unseen mother is heard in the second play, but essentially the environment has contracted to the size of one human skull. Jocelyn Herbert's stage picture for both plays consists of the void: total blackness in 'That Time,' with the head of Patrick Magee, hair outspread as if seen from above, spotlit to the top left of the stage; and in 'Footfalls,' a narrow strip of light downstage where Billie Whitelaw compulsively paces under a skull-like Moon.

Obsessive memory is again the theme, but handled in two opposite styles. The text of 'That Time' is an unpunctuated set of free-associations mainly centred on a particular place - a broken tower surrounded by rubble and nettles where the speaker spent a day as a child and which later took on erotic associations, like the boat in 'Krapp's Last Tape.' What performance demonstrates is that the details do not matter. Magee's voice, emanating from three separate points, purrs through the lines, taking huge phrases in a single breath, and burying the detail in soft somnolent tone. It is the tone that matters. As soon as the voice stops, Magee the listener opens his eyes and breaks into stifled panting until the soothing voice resumes.

The text, in other words, is there to comfort the
listener, and it is delivered in the second person.
In 'Footfalls' (as in 'Not I') the fact that some intolerable memory is involved appears from the speaker's use
of the third person. Again, one receives a misleading
impression from the text, which contains passages suggesting domestic dialogue and realist detail. All this
is thrust into the far distance by Beckett's production.

Punctuated by a chiming bell, the brief opening exchange of dialogue and two solo speeches take the form of
a three-act play, with a sense of immeasurable distance
between the pacing girl and her uncomprehending mother.
'Will you never have done ... revolving it all?' she asks
from her bed: but in this piece, the nature of the obsessive experience remains undisclosed. Miss Whitelaw,
bowed in rags, clutching herself with talon-like fingers,
her features lit in shadowly profile to emphasize the
sunken eye-sockets, maintains her seven-step walk, inton-
ing the details of a small domestic argument with unearthly precision. I do not understand this play; and
by this time in the evening the consistently dim lighting
has become hard on the eyes. But simply in terms of stage
imagery, and the sense of an indefinable, unassuageable
grief, the impression is as potent as that Miss Whitelaw
made in 'Not I.'

77. ROBERT CUSHMAN IN 'OBSERVER'

23 May 1976, 30

Robert Cushman (b. 1943). . Drama critic.

The last slice of Samuel Beckett's seventieth birthday
cake, as served up at the Royal Court, is a triple-
decker, 'Play and Other Plays.'

'Play' comes first. It is the eldest, 13 years old.
A good sprig. With the years it has grown funnier. It
is the one about the three people - a man and two women -
encased in funeral urns. Once they were husband, wife
and mistress. Now they are dead. (I think. Many
agree.) On each of them in turn, a light plays. When it
shines, they jabber, of their past and one another. The

light is cruel. Not only does it prod them to speak, it
will never let them finish. Bored with one, it constantly
moves on to the next, and back again. Having exhausted
their supply of confessions, it starts again. 'Repeat
play exactly,' says the stage-direction.

This repetition is purgatorial for them, but helpful
for us. On the first hearing, we may grasp the shape of
their affair; on the second, we can begin to take in the
details, which are, in a high-class way, sordid. Love is
not lovelier the second time around, and it gets progressively less so. Here are the remnants of a drawing-room
comedy triangle laid out for us *sub specie aeternitatis*.
Thus displayed, played, replayed, whose passions would
not look ridiculous?

Mr Beckett shields us a bit by placing his characters
outside the social circles to which most of us are accus-
tomed. One of his ladies had a butler, whose fate she
momentarily ponders. I might gawp at her at the Hay-
market, but I will not identify with her at the Royal
Court, I know my place, I was taught at the Court. However, when the poor adulterer expressed his distaste for
the tea drunk by his entanglements ('personally I preferred Lipton's') when, as of course they would, they got
together to discuss him - then I laughed.

'Play' impresses me too as a study in the psychology
of interrogation. The trio complain of the light that
oppresses them, but they fear, as much as anything, its
going out. They have come to depend on it. They call it
a 'hellish half-light,' but they fear that really this is
not hell, not eternal. (Their philosophy seems to be
somewhere between 'confession is good for the soul' and
'better the devil you know.') And maybe their fears are
realised. Perhaps, when the light goes out at the end of
'Play,' it goes out for ever, consigning them to a well-
urned rest.

The first play, then, now looks a masterpiece. But
not the second, 'That Time.' Not this time. Like most of
Mr Beckett's plays it deals with the horror of the past.
(I except 'Waiting for Godot,' which is concerned with the
horror of the future, and 'Happy Days,' which satirises
those who are not horrified by the present.) Here is the
haggard face of Patrick Magee, surmounted by flowing grey
hair (like a monstrous halo) and otherwise surrounded by
darkness. Here is Mr Magee's voice, prerecorded, through
three speakers, sounding less like a circular saw than
usual, softened but no more attractive, and decidedly
soporific.

High on the list of the things which I can live, even
die, without would be, had I ever thought of it, Mr Magee

in three-track stereo. Faber and Faber, in the blurb to
the published version (16 pp., 50p) say of Magee and
Magee and Magee: 'The voices speak of the past; nostal-
gic, regretful, elegiac, poignant, fragmentary.' The
adjectives are not really deniable, and I might have used
a couple of them myself. But the substance is only a
re-run of 'Krapp's Last Tape' without the props: a process
of refinement but not necessarily of enrichment.

The third play, 'Footfalls,' moves in the opposite
direction. Yes, I said moves. This is another piece for
one player (Billie Whitelaw, who is extraordinary) and not
only is she visible - dimly, I admit - from her head to
her foot, but she gets about. This is, in all respects,
the nearest thing to a full-length portrait Mr Beckett has
painted in years. Miss Whitelaw is even given a realistic
situation, a woman in her forties looking after her bed-
ridden mother (unseen but vocal). The relationship
('Would you like me to inject you again?' - 'Yes, but it
is too soon') is terrifyingly and - need I say - sparely
evoked. Mother does not really nag; she worries, over her
daughter's ceaseless padding up and down. She never goes
out, just remembers. And that, we can hear the author
saying, is what motion gets you; don't ask me for it
again.

Miss Whitelaw's memories take up half the play, and
they lack nothing of skill in writing or performance.
What they do lack is inevitability; the play does not have
to tell this particular story to make this particular
effect. Common to all three plays are the compulsive
vomitings of the human voice and brain, and the hypnotic
effect of thin white light. Mr Beckett, who provides
rigorous instructions for them all and directed the last
himself, is a gentleman and a showman.

78.   JOHN ELSOM IN 'LISTENER'

27 May 1976, 681

John Elsom (b. 1934). Drama critic.

As if to prove that you cannot judge the size of plays by
their mere length, the Royal Court are rounding off their

Beckett season with three plays, two of which, being
world premieres, are scoops. It is a remarkable evening,
played almost entirely on a dark stage with pale images
piercing the gloom. Each play is a full experience,
distilled to its concentrated essence, requiring no further development, no expansion or contraction, no other
form than that given to it by Beckett.

'Play' is the one seen before in this country; but
this production, directed by Donald McWhinnie, has the
verve of discovery. What he has found are its rhythms,
very complicated but precise, consisting not only of the
phrase rhythms, but of the switching from face to face,
voice to voice, the blackouts and fades. The 'play' concerns the rituals of marriage and adultery. One man and
two women, whose white faces have been robbed of sex,
stand in three urns facing the audience. You cannot see
that they are urns, merely clay shapes in the place of
bodies. Their deadpan voices, punctuated by giggles and
hiccups, patter through the familiar lies, venom and
bitchery. Then, having reached an apparent end, their
faces vanish, reappear in a babble of sound, disappear
again, before the whole play is repeated, at almost double
the speed.

The timing is partly achieved through the virtuosity of
the lighting operator, Duncan M. Scott, who had to remember
248 cues within 17 minutes. A missed or delayed cue would
have been as glaring as a fumbled line, for the humour of
'Play' - a funny as well as sad experience - lies in the
counterpoint between one spotlit face and the next. Sentences are cut off by them. Pauses are held by them.
Scott was working with three actors, Anna Massey, Penelope
Wilton and Ronald Pickup, whose vocally athletic performances would have been ruined by his slightest slipshodness.
As it was, however, the teamwork was immaculate, the understanding of the play crisp and sharp, and there was a thread
of sheer exhilaration in the technical precision.

'That Time' are memories held by a man under some extremity of death, age or sickness. His white face, with
hair streamed out behind him, is all we can see. All we
can hear from that face are panting breaths, which die
away, then resume, then die away. But his memories
have been recorded, and they beat at him from all sides,
at different levels, trying to provoke a reaction from
those staring eyes, those lips gasped apart. The reaction, when it comes, is caused by a sudden silence. The
memories cease to batter him and the mouth cracks into a
smile.

The last play seems almost to belong to a different
genre. It is eerie and seems to tell a story. In

'Footfalls,' a middle-aged woman (though she grows older),
dressed in a Miss Haversham film of folds, paces up and
down, nine steps to the right, nine to the left. She is
listening to the presence of her mother, reduced to a
patch of ectoplasm, in the deep, dark recesses of her mind.
Guilts, memories of loss and the sheer daily troubles of
the world keep the woman to her treadmill, as she ages,
but becomes less capable of even being born, as a separate person.

The ties of an endless childhood, stretching on to a
premature senility, have never been for me so graphically
and compellingly expressed. Billy Whitelaw as the Woman
and Rose Hill as her Mother responded finally to Samuel
Beckett's exact direction; and the three plays together provide a fine conclusion to the Royal Court's Beckett season.

79.   BENEDICT NIGHTINGALE IN 'NEW STATESMAN'

28 May 1976, 723

Anyone who expects a new serenity from the 70-year-old
Beckett should go and be disabused by the birthday cele-
brations at the Court. His spiritual migraine is worse
than ever. In 'Waiting for Godot' the two main characters had a jaunty resilience about them. They shared a
gallows humour, and even seemed to care for one another.
There was a faint possibility that Godot, God, life-force,
Great White Father, call him what you will, might eventually emerge from his hideaway; and certainly he was real
enough to send a messemger to announce his non-arrival.
But now, 21 years later, there is no laughter, no sharing
or caring, and nothing to hope for from the infinite void
beyond. Nothing, that is, except death, which is to be
desired as an escape from that grief and paranoia, those
slavish obsessions, banal memories and hopeless fantasies
that constitute the everyday furniture of a man's consciousness. Meanwhile, the most he can do in self-
defence is to cultivate impersonality, pretending to himself he's an object, an 'it', or at any rate someone
else. Those who deaden themselves with emotional novo-
caine may at least hope to feel less than the usual quota
of pain.

This was the rough conclusion of 'Not I,' which the
Court presented three years ago, and nothing more

conciliatory emerges from his latest playlets, 'That
Time' and 'Footfalls,' both of which seem as dark and
stark as Beckett's precise, elegant despair can make them.
A lifetime's experience shrinks to a babbling mouth,
a ravaged head, or a haggard figure frantically prowling
to and fro. These beings speak of themselves, to themselves: the stage (it seems) is the inside of their
skulls, the characters their withered brain cells, and
the drama their scrambled thoughts. This is the theatre
of total introversion - and yet, surprisingly, the audience is left with a strong objective sense of the wretched
lives on display. Late Beckett may be austere, but he is
not abstract. You can piece together a life-history, or
at least a case-study, from the hints he shyly feeds us.
If you felt philistine enough, you could even rewrite
'Not I' and 'That Time' as documentaries, and sell them
to one of the more socially-conscious directors on BBC-1.

The subject of 'Not I' is the sort of gaunt, bent woman
you sometimes see tottering along the street, eyes down,
string round her waist, a carrier-bag in her hand.
Though Beckett showed us nothing but her writhing lips,
we could readily visualise the rest of her. Similarly,
all we see in 'That Time' is Patrick Magee's face, eyes
mostly shut, hair flaring backwards as if he were some
unearthly blend of Ibsen in his wild old age and the
Michelangelo God. But here is another tramp, another tale
of disintegration. Magee himself doesn't actually speak,
but his recorded voice comes from all parts of the stage,
variously telling us of childhood truancy, an abortive
attempt to revisit the ruined tower where he used to hide,
a love-affair that turns out to have occurred only in his
imagination, and a latter-day existence spent snoozing in
public libraries, and avoiding contact with his 'fellow
bastards'. The memories sprawl into each other, in a
drowsy, unpunctuated murmur, but the final impression is
very vivid. You can see this stumbling, staring creature
in his 'old green greatcoat', and understand why people
cross the road when he bears down on them.

Is this a man free-associating on his deathbed?
Certainly, the hoarse, painful breathing that intersperses
the monologue suggests this: so does the ending, which
settles Magee's mouth into a hideous, grinning rictus, the
frozen sneer of a stone satyr. Again, is the doleful hag
Billie Whitelaw plays in 'Footfalls' actually a ghost - or
a second Miss Havisham, nursing some ancient trauma? Up
and down she tramps, up and down, head bowed, matted
hair dangling, dress in grey-green tatters, skeletal fingers clawing at her own shoulders, and, on the evidence
offered, either or both of these conclusions could be

correct. But it seems literal-minded to pursue such
questions too far. What matters is that Mr Magee's old
man has hardly had a life, and Miss Whitelaw's madwoman
not had one at all. She has, instead, fallen victim to
some strange and obscure fixation: her mind is dizzy with
memories of a church at evensong, the bizarre notion that
she must hear the sound of her own feet, and the plaint-
ive, uncomprehending demands of her invalid mother. She
can, I suspect, be found in many mental wards, ever-
lastingly worrying away at problems that defy solution:
a living spectre, unable to leave the scene of its suffering.

Though Beckett's most recent creations might have
stumbled out of some searing social exposé by Jeremy
Sandford, they wouldn't interest him unless they had a
wider significance as well; and that may provoke resistance from those members of the audience who haven't been
hauled into hospital to be 'wiped off and straightened
out', like the derelict in 'That Time,' or have yet to
stand open-mouthed and drooling in front of a magistrate,
like the peasant woman in 'Not I'. Isn't there something
presumptuous in identifying the bulk of mankind with this
human driftwood? No more so, I think, than in Francis
Bacon's suggestion, graphically made on canvas after canvas, that the world is an abattoir and men raw meat.
Late Beckett writes with a grim beauty, using sharp, concentrated and resonant images of deprivation and anguish
to draw attention to the human waste we see all around
us, if usually in a less extreme form. What worries me
isn't his insistence on this waste, but his apparent
belief that there's no point doing anything about it - in
a godless universe man might as well withdraw into himself and slowly rot. *That's* the pass to which Beckett's
pessimism has brought him at the age of 70: I don't think
there'll be much blowing of squeakers and dancing round
the cake at his birthday party.

'For To End Yet Again'
(1976)

[Eight prose texts, seven of which were originally written
in French, one in English, between 1960 and 1975.   A
French edition, 'Pour finir encore et autres foirades,'
was published by Éditions de Minuit, Paris, 1976; the
first British edition, 'For to End Yet Again,' was published by John Calder, London, 1976; the first American
edition, 'Fizzles,' was issued by Grove Press, 1976.
Translations are by the author.]

---

80.   VALENTINE CUNNINGHAM IN 'NEW STATESMAN'

29 October 1976, 607

Valentine Cunningham (b. 1944). Critic.

Go, litel bok, one feels like saying, but not for long:
however exiguous, Beckett is worth every inflated penny.
He's so full of surprises, and not just verbal ones (after
all he's always had punny aces stashed up his sleeve): on
this occasion there are doctrinal ones. After that re-
morseless paring away, the steely accumulating of less-
nesses, that pincer movement on the void that must logically end in silence: lo, a resurrection. On stage, an
expansion from a mere cry to a fully visible pair of lips
and then - amplitudes! - a whole face. Will, one wonders,
mirabile visu, whole Beckett bodies re-emerge on the
boards, scrambling back from the darkness and out of the
mounds and dustbins? 'For to End Yet Again' endorses such

a possibility. The end in darkness, silence and immobility that the earlier fiction appeared to promise has
still not come. A couple of monstrous bier-carrying
dwarfs are actually in motion, albeit the familiar
frustrated motion ('can never fare nearer to anywhere nor
from anywhere further away'), in a moment of grey dawn
before darkness 'switches on' again.

Just so, a terribly disfigured narrator starts to come
into the light, begins to get out of bed again; another
traveller refuses to concede that he's reached the end of
his hemmed-in, straitened road and 'squeezes through'; a
light gleams over the arena that encloses the millions in
dark silence. In some ways, of course, this postponing
of apocalypse, the transition from lessness into endless-
ness, the shift from ultimates to penultimates or even
antepenultimates, might seem to adumbrate a greater horror
- the considered request for euthenasia turned down, at
best the coming evil day merely put off for a while.
Still to live, where you were settling for the still-
ness of death? Beckett works with his customary dazzle
on *still*, and not just in his text 'Still'. *Still* is
noiseless, *still* is motionless: and these characters,
moving and hearing again, are being snatched from still-
ness. But they are, thus, made to *be* still: to go on
being. And for all the continued minimality of their
existence, the continuing pointlessness of their stasis,
the air of optimism is extraordinary. Especially in 'Old
Earth' (dated, uniquely in this collection, 'Paris,
August 1974'). In a moving testament to the humanity that
many critics want to deny Beckett, its narrator recalls
past loves and deaths, affectionate for what he can see,
standing still at his window. Alive, and humane - as is,
so to say, tellingly proved by this collection - still.

81. A. ALVAREZ IN 'OBSERVER'

19 December 1976, 22

Beckett's new book contains eight more examples of the
strange terminal prose and terminal vision he has been
refining since his last full-length prose work, 'How It
Is.' According to the publishers, these pieces were
written between 1960 and 1976, which means they overlap
with similar fragments already released, like 'Imagination

Dead Imagine' and 'Lessness.'

Like them, they employ a prose which is perfectly lucid yet curiously beyond grammar. The punctuation is cannily reduced so that repeated phrases shift their meaning from sentence to sentence. It is as though Beckett, who has always been passionately interested in music, were using words like notes to play variations on a recurrent theme. Although he writes what is apparently prose, the effect is like that of the best poetry: concentrated, precise, shifting, compressed and insistently concerned with states of mind rather than with narrative. The blurb, correctly, calls it 'literary chamber music.'

The theme on which he plays his variations is one which he has consistently explored, with increasing single-mindedness, all through his career: deprivation and what goes on at the crippled fag-end of life. The figures, where there are any, are stunted, the landscapes desert, the dominant colour grey. In other words, a perfect Christmas present for the man who has, and wants, nothing.

Yet oddly enough, the effect is altogether less gloomy than it sounds. The purity of Beckett's writing, like his utter lack of self-indulgence, gives each piece a continual energy and tension, so that the process of describing a world purged, or exhausted, of all emotion becomes in itself charged with feeling. He remains, even in these brief, bleak fragments, the most original and creative figure around.

'Ghost Trio' and '....but the clouds...'
(1977)

[Written in English; first performed on television by the BBC, 17 April 1977; 'Ghost Trio' published in 'Ends and Odds,' Grove Press, New York, 1976; 'Ghost Trio' and '...but the clouds...' published in 'Ends and Odds,' Faber & Faber, London, 1977.]

82. MICHAEL RATCLIFFE IN 'THE TIMES'

18 April 1977, 6

Michael Ratcliffe; drama critic for 'The Times' since 1967.

Samuel Beckett has worked at BBC television at least once before in recent years - with Patrick Garland and Jack McGowran - and clearly enjoys it. Declining, as usual, to give an interview, he this time offered 'The Lively Arts' the world premiere of two short television plays, meticulously plotted with diagrams by himself, together with the use of unfamiliar photographs and biographical information, notably that not only was young Sam a brilliant scholar but a commanding sportsman, particularly at cricket. He was born on Good Friday, 13th. He bowled off-breaks round the wicket.

Both new plays share a kinship with 'Godot,' each show a man waiting, hoping, listening for the memory and return of a woman once loved. The first, 'Ghost Trio,' is set in a plain cell ('faintly luminous. Colour, none' and in fact, at Beckett's wish, monochrome). A seated figure hunches over a small radio, from which fragments of

352

Beethoven swell and fade. A woman's voice speaks a commentary, fixing the few certainties - door, window,
mirror and bed - of the scene. The man opens the window
first on to nothing, later on to heavy rain; then the door
on to nothing, finally on to a boy who smiles at him and
goes away. The full trio then plays and the man, too,
smiles, appearing content. That is all.

Relax, Martin Esslin advised us, talking to Melvin
Bragg before each play. Relax and surrender to Beckett's
spell: it will grow in your mind.

There is no doubt that the reductionist scale and
austerity of Beckett's late work is effective on the small
screen, although the dynamics are pitched so low that if
the plays were any longer you might well drop off. The
timing of 'Ghost Trio' was mesmeric and Donald McWhinnie's
direction, in which the camera advanced with tremulous
hesitancy on the actor (Ronald Pickup) like a camera in
the prehistoric days of moving films, created a world out
of time and space.

In the second play '...but the clouds ...' a man in
black walks into a pool of light and out of it the other
side to reemerge in a white robe. He retires to a sanctum
at the back to conjure again the vision of his speaking
love (this time we see her face). These movements are
repeated several times and if you are hooked - it is less
immediately impressive than 'Ghost Trio' - it is partly
because you know what is coming next. Tristram Powell's
programme ended with Billie Whitelaw's spectacular performance of 'Not I' directed as at the Royal Court four
years ago by Anthony Page. After the pauses and the
silence, here was the very power of speech run mad.

'Collected Poems in English and French'
(1977)

[Published by John Calder, London.]

---

83. RICHARD COE IN 'TIMES LITERARY SUPPLEMENT'

15 July 1977

Richard Coe (b. 1923). Critic, professor of French, University of Warwick.

It is a singular fact that the writer who has exercised the most profound influence over the third quarter of our by-and-large unpoetic century should be a poet whose formal 'poems' oscillate between the obscure, the imitative and the awkward, who at one point abandoned his own language for another precisely in order to *avoid* writing poetry, and who has finally fashioned a form of linguistic denudation - words used like a child's set of building-blocks - so utterly opposed to poetry in the Tennysonian sense that it suggests not so much stoicism as suicide.

At a rough estimate, note the editors of 'L'Herne,' the mountain - or slagheap? - of adulatory or critical articles which have accumulated about the head of Samuel Beckett (that now familiar head with its eyes 'like a gull's' which he bestowed on his own 'Murphy') is now some 5,000 items high, with sixty-odd full-length books to give the mass solidity and substance. Why? Our times, in so many ways, are less naive than those which came before us:

certainly in their serious evaluation of their own contemporaries. It is hard to imagine that a Robert Montgomery could today acquire the literary reputation,
requiring all the heavy artillery of a Macaulay to demo-
lish it, when every upstart writer has to endure the test
of furnishing substance for a hundred or a thousand young,
trained and cynical university lecturers to present to
their equally disillusioned students for two hours, six
hours, eight hours, without feeling foolish and without
running out of material. Yet Beckett has not only endured
this test, but has left his critics still almost as much
in the dark as ever about the secrets of his power over
the mind.

The present group of texts (1) and articles do a little
- not much, but a little - to clarify the issues. There
is, for the first time, a reasonably full set of Beckett's
'formal' verse, the 'Collected Poems in English and
French'; and from this working collection, one item, the
long-lost 'Drunken Boat' translation (1932) of Rimbaud's
'Bateau ivre,' is also made available in a splendid col-
lector's edition. At the other end of the time-scale,
there is 'Ends and Odds,' a grouping of short plays for
radio and television, the most significant of which,
beginning with 'Not I,' were written in English between
1973 and 1976; whereas the remainder, originally written
in French, date back to 1960-61, and belong to that momen-
tous period of linguistic and conceptual evolution heralded
by the novel 'How It Is'. And embracing the totality there
is the Beckett number of 'L'Herne' - sumptuous as always,
uneven in quality (again as always), but for once, thanks
to its Anglo-Saxon editors, Tom Bishop and Raymond Federman, informed and up to date in its bibliography. (In all
too many previous issues of 'L'Herne,' one has the impression that the editors have been lamentably ignorant of
anything written in any language other than French.

Few poems have fascinated a young generation of future
poets as much as 'Le Bateau ivre' did in the 1920s and
1930s (in 1937, Jean Genet had to steal his copy before
sending the torn-out pages containing the poem, together
with an *explication de texte*, to a Czech student), and it
is satisfying that, after a series of extraordinary haz-
ards, the typescript of Beckett's 'Drunken Boat' has at
last turned up again. Not because it is a superlative
English version of Rimbaud's vision - it is not. But because its very weaknesses tell us so much about Beckett's
problems with language - and hence with the very essence
of poetry. There are some lovely touches: Rimbaud's

> Et dès lors, je me suis baigné dans le poème
> De la mer infusé d'astres et lactescent ...

becomes

> Thenceforward, fused in the poem, milk of stars
> Of the sea ...

but this is followed immediately by the awful

> When, under the sky's haemorrhage, slowly tossing
> In thuds of fever, arch-alcohol of song,
> Pumping over the blues in sudden stains
> The bitter rednesses of love ferment.

Unhappily, far too much of Beckett's early verse in English is like this. He seems painfully fascinated by certain words: *haemorrhage, haemorrhoidal* ('Home Olga'), *henorrhoids* ('Sanies II'). It was the fashion: one recalls Gide's Armand Vedel, in 'Les Faux-monnayeurs,' defiantly proclaiming '*hémorroïdes* ... le plus beau mot de la langue française'. In another vein, Beckett's translation of Eluard's 'L'Amoureuse':

> She is standing on my lids
> And her hair is in my hair

is as good as Yeats's translation of Ronsard - and owes perhaps more to Yeats than to the original.

The translations from the poets (and to the ones already mentioned one could add the 'Anthology of Mexican Poetry' (1958) and the English version of Apollinaire's 'Zone') reveal one significant feature: that Beckett as a 'poet' is playing about on the surface of language. It is a hit-and-miss business. Sometimes it works, sometimes it does not. Because whatever reality it is he is attuned to, it is not that which lies on the linguistic surface. As Artaud maintained, there is a 'poetry *beneath* the poetry.' There is a substratum of experience, unique as pure individualized sensation, mysterious and inexpressible in the essence of its unquestionable *reality*, which can only be impoverished and de-poeticized by its translation into language. And more particularly, into the forgettable, unaccented non-language of useless words - useless, that is, in terms of the immediacy of the experience itself: 'in', 'the', 'a', 'by', 'with', 'from'...

So, in Beckett's development as a poet, there has been a prolonged conflict, not so much between *ideas* and language, as between experience (facts) and language. It is

this, I think, that explains the paradox that Beckett has
persistently denied to anyone who asked him that he had
any ideas - any coherent *Weltanschauung* - whatsoever,
whereas thousands of intelligent men and women throughout
the civilized world are devoting their intellectual energies and emotions to trying to assimilate these very ideas
which he claims to be non-existent.

In one sense, what he claims is absolutely true: he has
no 'ideas' as such. On the other hand, the basic principle of communication itself - how to translate the
facts, the immediate sensations and material three-
dimensionalities, of existence or experience, into an
alternative structure of language, is among the major
problems of contemporary philosophy and literature, and
thus constitutes an 'idea' in itself. An idea about not
having ideas.

By and large (and always with a disconcerting ingredient of humour added) this has been Beckett's dilemma between alternatives: either to let the words take over
entirely and invite the reader by intuition to apprehend
the reality underneath; or to neutralize language as completely as possible (hence the transition into an alien
language, French), so as to permit experience to incarnate
itself in a structure of basic communication with the least
intrusion of 'ideas' or emotional intuitive overtones.
From this point of view, the selection of Beckettian
Quotations, made by Raymond Federman and Michel Ribalka in
'L'Herne,' leaves one with a curious feeling of frustration. It is set out in the traditional La Bruyère manner,
under 'idea' headings: La Solitude, L'Habitude, La Folie,
Le Temps, etc - and in almost every case, the quotations
somehow miss the point.

Beckett is not a Chamfort, as his deliciously parodic
translations reveal. He is quotable, either in terms of
pure surface-language:

> My squinty doaty!
> I hid and you sook ...

or in terms of evocation:

> ESTRAGON.   All the dead voices.
> VLADIMIR.   They make a noise like wings
> ESTRAGON.   Live leaves.
> VLADIMIR.   Like sand.
> ESTRAGON.   Like leaves.

- evocation *not* to be confused with ideas.
  'Ideas', in fact, are that part of human experience

which Beckett treats with the greatest suspicion. Poetry,
for him, is a process by which a rigidly controlled structure of language conveys a directly apprehended structure
of experience with the minimum of distortion through
either thought or emotion. Hence the extraordinary structure of his more recent narrative, dramatic and televisual
experiments. One could argue that these are repetitive:
there is little variation between 'Theatre II' (1960) and
'But the Clouds' (1976). And in fact, one feels that
Beckett is less at home with television or cinema, or even
with the theatre, than in the domain of pure language.

If one of the distinguishing characteristics of great
poetry in English lies in the handling of rhythmic variation, then Beckett must count among the masters. The
best, but all too brief, analysis of rhythms of Beckett's
prose-poetry is that by John Fletcher in 'L'Herne.' But
the detailed analysis of the rhythms of the latest pieces
still remains to be carried out. What Beckett has done in
texts such as 'Bing' or 'Lessness' is to take an under-
lying rhythm not dissimilar from that of blank verse, to
allow as many as possible of the recurrent ten or eleven
syllables to carry an accent, reducing the unaccented to
no more than two or three per line, and then to vary with
great subtlety the permutations and combinations possible
among the fully stressed.

On the one side, existence, experience, facts. On the
other, language, rhythm, poetry. Which is why, in the two
present collections of essays, the best are those which
give us facts (biographical pieces, notably by Jerome
Lindon, Richard Seaver, A.J. Leventhal and Deirdre Bair,
in 'L'Herne'; or Ruby Cohn's pinpointing of parallels between 'Watt' and Kafka's 'The Castle'; or those which
analyse language and structure - for instance, Ludovic
Janvier's outstanding essay, Lieu dire ('L'Herne'). The
weakest are those which guess at the ideas. In those
sixty-odd books and 5,000 articles, most of the 'ideas'
have been pretty well guessed at already. It is the facts
which have been in short supply. 'One man's fact', said
Armand Gatti recently, 'is another man's fantasy.' And
one man's experience can be a whole generation's poetry.
Provided that not too many 'ideas' intrude to obscure the
issue.

Note

1   The review covers three volumes by Beckett ('Collected
    Poems in English and French,' 'Drunken Boat,' and 'Ends
    and Odds') and the 'L'Herne Samuel Beckett,' edited by
    Raymond Federman and Tom Bishop. (Eds)

Select Bibliography

The following sampling emphasizes works that either helped shape or describe the early critical responses to Beckett's work.

COHN, RUBY, 'Samuel Beckett: The Comic Gamut' (1963), a study of the varieties and implications of Beckett's humor.

ESSLIN, MARTIN, ed., 'Samuel Beckett: A Collection of Essays' (1965), a useful sampling of international criticism.

FEDERMAN, RAYMOND, 'Journey to Chaos' (1965), the first extended study of Beckett's early fiction.

FEDERMAN, RAYMOND, and JOHN FLETCHER, 'Samuel Beckett: His Works and His Critics, an Essay in Bibliography' (1970), the most valuable tool for the study of Beckett's career and early public responses to his writing.

FLETCHER, JOHN, 'The Novels of Samuel Beckett' (1964), one of the first substantial studies of Beckett's fiction.

HARVEY, LAWRENCE E., 'Samuel Beckett: Poet and Critic' (1970), an analysis of the body of Beckett's poetry.

KENNER, HUGH, 'Samuel Beckett' (1961), the first full-length study in English of Beckett's achievement, and one of the most influential.

KENNER, HUGH, 'A Reader's Guide to Samuel Beckett' (1973), a helpful introduction to Beckett's work.

MARISSEL, ANDRÉ, 'Samuel Beckett' (1963), the first book in French on Beckett.

ROBINSON, MICHAEL, 'The Last Sonata of the Dead' (1966), a reliable first book on Beckett for new readers.

Index

THE CRITICAL HERITAGE SERIES

GENERAL EDITOR: B. C. SOUTHAM

Volumes published and forthcoming